AF531828

ENCYCLOPAEDIA OF OPERATING SYSTEM

[Volume—Three]

By

Sudhir Kumar

ANMOL PUBLICATIONS PVT. LTD.
NEW DELHI - 110 002 (INDIA)

ANMOL PUBLICATIONS PVT. LTD.
4374/4B, Ansari Road, Daryaganj
New Delhi - 110 002
Phones: 23261597, 23278000
Visit us at: www.anmolpublications.com

Encyclopaedia of Operating System

First Edition, 2004

ISBN 81-261-1792-3 (Set)

PRINTED IN INDIA

Published by J.L. Kumar for Anmol Publications Pvt. Ltd., New Delhi and Printed at Mehra Offset Press, Delhi.

Contents

Vol. 3

Preface

Virtually, an operating system is a program that manages the computer hardware. The components of a computer system are its hardware, software and data. The operating system provides the means for the proper use of these resources in the operation of the computer system. Thus, Operating system is the heart of any computer or we can say operating system is essential part of the computer system. Similarly a course and text on operating system is an essential part of any computer-science education. This field is changing field at breathtakingly rapid rate, as computers are now prevalent in virtually every application, from games for children to the most sophisticated planning tools for governments and multinational firms. Yet the fundamental concepts remain the same and it is clear in all books of operating system.

This work is designed to meet the requirement of introductory course in operating system at the undergraduate and Postgraduate level. It provides a clear description on various concepts that are required for understanding the proper functioning of any operating system.

The hardware text required for an understanding of operating system are included in this book. For coding examples we use predominantly 'C' as well as Java, but the reader can still understand the algorithms without a thorough knowledge of these languages.

The fundamental concepts and algorithms covered in this book are based on the existing commercial operating system in use. The information gathered herein is substantially based on authoritative sources. Our aim is to present these concepts and algorithms in a general setting that is not tied to any particular operating system.

We present a large number of examples that pertain to the most popular operating systems, including Sun Microsystems, Solaris 2, Linux, MS Dos, Windows NT and Windows 2000.

Apart from these some case studies on Unix, and on windows are also included in this work. The entire information is gathered under twenty-seven chapters.

In bringing this text into a book form, I shall be grateful for Mr. J.L. Kumar, Managing Director, Anmol Publications Pvt. Ltd., New Delhi and Mr. J.K. Dawra for their valuable suggestions. Any suggestions for the improvement of the book are also welcome which will be subsequently appended in the revised edition of the book.

— S.K.

17

Distributed Coordination Techniques

The Happened-Before Relation

Since we are considering only sequential processes, all events executed in a single process are totally ordered. Also, by the law of causality, a message can be received only after it has been sent. Therefore, we can define the *happened-before* relation (denoted by →) on a set of events as follows (assuming that sending and receiving a message constitutes an event):

1. If A and B are events in the same process, and A was executed before B, then $A \to B$.
2. If A is the event of sending a message by one process and B is the event of receiving that message by another process, then $A \to B$.
3. If $A \to B$ and $B \to C$ then $A \to C$.

Since an event cannot happen before itself, the → relation is an irreflexive partial ordering.

If two events, A and B, are not related by the → relation (that is, A did not happen before B, and B did not happen before A), then we say that these two events were executed concurrently. In this case, neither event can causally affect the other. If, however, $A \to B$, then it is possible for event A to affect event B causally.

A space-time diagram, such as that in Figure 17.1, can best illustrate the definitions of concurrency and *happened-before*. The horizontal direction represents space (that is, different processes), and the vertical direction represents time. The labelled vertical lines denote processes (or processors). The labelled dots denote events. A wavy line denotes a message sent from one process to another. From this diagram, events A and B are concurrent if and only if no path exists either from A to B or from B to A.

For example, consider Figure 17.1, some of the events related by the *happened-before* relation are

$$p_1 \to q_2,$$
$$r_0 \to q_4,$$
$$q_3 \to r_4,$$
$$p_1 \to q_4 \text{ (since } p_1 \to q_2 \text{ and } q_2 \to q_4).$$

Some of the concurrent events in the system are

q_0 and p_2,
r_0 and q_3,
r_0 and p_3,
q_3 and p_3.

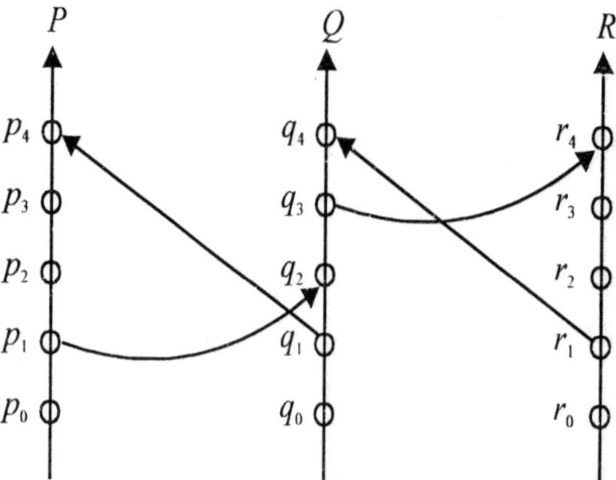

Fig. 17.1. *Relative time for three concurrent processes.*

We cannot know which of two concurrent events, such as q_0 and p_2, happened first. However, since neither event can affect the other (there is no way for one of them to know whether the other has occurred yet), it is not important which happened first. It is important only that any processes that care about the order of two concurrent events agree on some order.

Implementation

To determine that an event A happened before an event B, we need either a common clock or a set of perfectly synchronized clocks. Since neither of these is available in a distributed system, we must define the *happened-before* relation without the use of physical clocks.

We associate with each system event a **timestamp**. We can then define the **global ordering** requirement. For every pair of events A and B, if $A \rightarrow B$, then the timestamp of A is less than the timestamp of B. (Below we will see that the converse does not need to be true.)

How do we enforce the global ordering requirement in a distributed environment? We define within *each* process P_i a **logical clock**, LC_i. The logical clock can be implemented as a simple counter incremented between any two successive events executed within a process. Since the logical clock has a **monotonically** increasing value, it assigns a unique number to every event, and if an event A occurs before event B in process P_i, then $LC_i(A) < LC_i(B)$. The timestamp for an events is the value of the logical clock for that event. This scheme ensures that of any two events in the same process the global ordering requirement is met.

Unfortunately, this scheme does not ensure that the global ordering requirement is met across processes. To illustrate the problem, we consider two processes P_1 and P_2 that communicate with each other. Suppose that P_1 sends a message to P_2 (event A) with $LC_1(A) = 200$, and P_2 receives the message (event B) with $LC_2(B) = 195$ (because the processor for P_2 is slower than the processor for P_1, its logical clock ticks slower). This situation violates our requirement, since $A \rightarrow B$, but the timestamp of A is greater than the timestamp of B.

To resolve this difficulty, we require process to advance its logical clock when it receives a message whose timestamp is greater than the current value of its logical clock. In particular, if process P_i receives a message (event B) with timestamp t and $LC_i(B) \leq t$, then its should advance its clock such that $LC_i(B) = t + 1$. Thus, in our example, when P_2 receives the message from P_1, it will advance its logical clock such that $LC_2(B) = 201$.

Finally, to realize a total ordering, we need only to observe that, with our timestamp-ordering scheme, if the timestamps of two events, A and B, are the same, then the events are concurrent. In this case, we may use process identity numbers to break ties and to create a total ordering.

Mutual Exclusion

In this section, we present a number of different algorithms for implementing mutual exclusion in a distributed environment. We assume that the system consists of n processes, each of which resides at a different processor. To simplify our discussion, we assume that processes are numbered uniquely from 1 to n, and that a one-to-one mapping exists between processes and processors (that is, each process has its own processor).

Centralized Approach

In a centralized approach to providing mutual exclusion, one of the processes in the system is chosen to coordinate the entry to the critical section. Each process that wants to invoke mutual exclusion sends a *request* message to the coordinator. When the process receives a *reply* message from the coordinator, it can proceed to enter its critical section. After exiting its critical section, the process sends a *release* message to the coordinator and proceeds with its execution.

On receiving a *request* message, the coordinator checks to see whether some other process is in its critical section. If no process is in its critical section, the coordinator immediately sends back a *reply* message. Otherwise, the request is queued. When the coordinator receives a *release* message, it removes one of the *request* messages from the queue (in accordance with some scheduling algorithm) and sends a *reply* message to the requesting process.

It should be clear that this algorithm ensures mutual exclusion. In addition, if the scheduling policy within the coordinator is fair [such as first-come, first served (FCFS) scheduling], no starvation can occur. This scheme requires three messages per critical-section entry: a *request*, a *reply*, and a *release*.

If the coordinator process fails, then a new process must take its place. We describe some algorithms for electing a unique new coordinator. Once a new coordinator has been elected, it must poll all the processes in the system, to reconstruct its *request* queue. Once the queue has been constructed, the computation may resume.

Fully Distributed Approach

If we want to distribute the decision making across the entire system, then the solution is far more complicated. We present an algorithm based on the event-ordering scheme.

When a process P_i wants to enter its critical section, it generates a new timestamp, *TS*, and sends the message *request* (P_i, *TS*) to all other processes in the system (including itself). On receiving a *request* message, a process may reply immediately (that is, send a *reply* message back to P_i), or it may defer sending a *reply* back (because it is already in its critical section, for example). A process that has received a *reply* message from all other processes in the system can enter its critical section, queuing incoming requests and deferring them. After exiting its critical section, the process sends reply message to all its deferred requests.

The decision whether process P_i replies immediately to a request (P_i, *TS*) message or defers its reply is based on there factors:

1. If process P_i is in its critical section, then it defers its reply to P_j.
2. If process P_i does not want to enter its critical section, then it sends a reply immediately to P_j.
3. If process P_i wants to enter its critical section but has not yet entered it, then it compares its own *request* timestamp with the timestamp *TS* of the incoming request made by process P_j. If its own *request* timestamp is greater than *TS*, then it sends a reply immediately to P_j (P_j asked first). Otherwise, the reply is deferred.

This algorithm exhibits the following desirable behaviour:

- Mutual exclusion is obtained.
- Freedom from deadlock is ensured.
- Freedom from starvation is ensured, since entry to the critical section is scheduled according to the timestamp ordering. The timestamp ordering ensures that processes are served in a FCFS order.
- The number of messages per critical-section entry is $2 \times (n-1)$. This number is the minimum number of required messages per critical-section entry when processes act independently and concurrently.

To illustrate how the algorithm functions, we consider a system consisting of processes P_1, P_2, and P_3. Suppose that processes P_1 and P_3 want to enter their critical sections. Process P_1 then sends a message *request* (P_1, timestamp = 10) to processes P_2 and P_3, while process P_3 sends a message *request* (P_3, timestamp = 4) to processes P_1 and P_2. The timestamps 4 and 10 were obtained from the logical clocks. When process P_2 receives these *request* messages, it replies immediately. When process P_1 receives the *request* from process P_3 it replies immediately, since the timestamp (10) on its own *request* messagè is greater than the timestamp (4) for process P_3. When process P_3 receives the *request* message from process P_1, it defers its reply, since the timestamp (4) on its *request* message is less than the timestamp (10) for the message from process P_1. On receiving replies from both process P_1 and process P_2, process P_3 can enter its critical section. After exiting its critical section, process P_3 sends a reply to process P_1, which can then enter its critical section.

Because this scheme requires the participation of all the processes in the system, however, it has three undesirable consequences:

1. The processes need to know the identity of all other processes in the system. When a new process joins the group of processes participating in the mutual-exclusion algorithm, the following actions need to be taken:

a. The process must receive the names of all the other processes in the group.
b. The name of the new process must be distributed to all the other processes in the group.

This task is not as trivial as it may seem, since some *request* and *reply* messages may be circulating in the system when the new process joins the group. The interested reader is referred to the Bibliographical Notes for more details.

2. If one process fails, then the entire scheme collapsed. We can resolve this difficulty by continuously monitoring the state of all processes in the system. If one process fails, then all other processes are notified, so that they will no longer send *request* messages to the failed process. When a process recovers, it must initiate the procedure that allows it to rejoin the group.
3. Processes that have not entered their critical section must pause frequently to assure other processes that they intend to enter the critical section. This protocol is therefore suited for small, stable sets of cooperating processes.

Token-Passing Approach

Another method of providing mutual exclusion is to circulate a token among the processes in the system. A token is a special type of message that is passed around the system. Possession of the token entitles the holder to enter the critical section. Since there is only a single token, only one process can be in its critical section at a time.

We assume that the processes in the system are *logically* organized in a **ring structure**. The physical communication network does not need to be a ring. As long as the processes are connected to one another, it is possible to implement a logical ring. To implement mutual exclusion, we pass the token around the ring. When a process receives the token, it may enter its critical section, keeping the token. After the process exits its critical section, the token is passed around again. If the process receiving the token does not want to enter its critical section, it passes the token to its neighbour.

If the ring is unidirectional, freedom from starvation is ensured. The number of messages required to implement mutual exclusion may vary from one message per entry, in the case of high contention (that is, every process wants to enter its critical section), to an infinite number of messages, in the case of low contention (that is, no process wants to enter its critical section).

Two types of failure must be considered. First, if the token is lost, an election must be called to generate a new token. Second, if a process fails, a new logical ring must be established.

Atomicity

We introduced the concept of an atomic transaction, which is a program unit that must be executed **atomically**. That is, either all the operations associated with it are executed to completion, or none are performed. When we are dealing with a distributed system ensuring the atomicity property of a transaction becomes much more complicated than in a centralized system. This difficulty occurs because several sites may be participating in the execution of a single transaction. The failure of one of these sites, or the failure of a communication link connecting these sites, may result in erroneous computations.

The function of the **transaction coordinator** of a distributed system is to ensure that the execution of the transactions in the distributed system preserves atomicity. Each site has its own local transaction coordinator responsible for coordinating the execution of all the transactions initiated at that site. For each such transaction, the coordinator is responsible for the following:

- Starting the execution of the transaction
- Breaking the transaction into a number of subtransactions, and distributing these subtransactions to the appropriate sites for execution
- Coordinating the termination of the transaction, which may result in the transaction being committed at all sites or aborted at all sites

We assume that each local site maintains a log for recovery purposes.

The Two-Phase Commit Protocol

For atomicity to be ensured, all the sites in which a transaction T executed must agree on the final outcome of the execution. T must either commit at all sites or it must abort at all sites. To ensure this property, the transaction coordinator of T must execute a **commit protocol**. Among the simplest and most widely used commit protocol is the **two-phase commit (2PC) protocol**, which we discuss here.

Let T be a transaction initiate at site S_i, and let the transaction coordinator at S_i be C_i. When T completes its execution—that is, when all the sites at which T has executed inform C_i that T has completed—then C_i starts the 2PC protocol.

- **Phase 1:** C_i adds the record <prepare T> to the log and forces the record onto stable storage. It then sends a *prepare* (T) messages to all the sites at which T executed. On receiving such a message, the transaction manager at that site determines whether it is willing to commit its portion of T. If the answer is *no*, it adds a record <no T> to the log, and then it responds by sending an *abort* (T) message to C_i. If the answer is *yes*, it adds a record <ready T> to the log, and forces all the log records corresponding to T onto stable storage. The transaction manager then relies with a *ready* (T) message to C_i.
- **Phase 2:** When C_i receives response to the *prepare* (T) message it sent from all the sites, or when a prespecified interval of time has elapsed since the *prepare* (T) message was sent out, C_i can determine whether the transaction T can be committed or aborted. Transaction T can be committed if C_i received a *ready* (T) message from all the participating sites. Otherwise, transaction T must be aborted. Depending on the verdict, either a record <commit T> or a record <abort T> is added to the log and is forced onto stable storage. At this point, the fate of the transaction has been sealed. Following this, the coordinator sends either *commit* (T) or an *abort* (T) messages to all participating sites. When a site receives that message, it records the message in the log.

A site at which T executed can unconditionally abort T at any time prior to its sending the message *ready* (T) to the coordinator. The *ready* (T) message is, in effect, a promise by a site to follow the coordinator's order to commit T or to abort T. The only situation in which a site can make such a promise is if the needed information is stored in stable storage. Otherwise, if the site crashes after sending ready T, it may be unable to make good on its promise.

Since unanimity is required to commit a transaction, the fate of T is sealed as soon as at least one site responds with *abort* (T). Since the coordinator site S_i is one of the sites at which T

executed, the coordinator can decide unilaterally to abort T. The final verdict regarding T is determined at the time the coordinator writes that verdict (commit or abort) to the log and forces it to stable storage. In some implementations of the 2PC protocol, a site sends an acknowledge T message to the coordinator at the end of the second phase of the protocol. When the coordinator receives the acknowledge T message from all the sites, it adds the record <complete T> to the log.

How to Handle Failure in 2PC

We now examine in detail now 2PC responds to various types of failures. As we shall see, one major disadvantage of the 2PC protocol is that coordinator failure may result in blocking, where a decision either to commit or to abort T may have to be postponed until C_i recovers.

Failure of a Participating Site

When a participating site S_k recovers from a failure, it must examine its log to determine the fate of those transactions that were in the midst of execution when the failure occurred. Let T be one such transaction. We consider each of the possible cases:

- The log contains a <commit T> record. In this case, the site executes redo(T).
- The log contains an <abort T> record. In this case, the site executes undo(T).
- The log contains a <ready T> record. In this case, the site must consult C_i to determine the fate of T. If C_i is up, it notifies S_k regarding whether T committed or aborted. In the former case, it executes redo(T); in the latter case, it executes undo(T). If C_i is down, S_k must try to find the fate of T from other sites. It does so by sending a *query-status* (T) message to all the sites in the system. On receiving such a message, a site must consult its log to determine whether T has executed there, and if so, whether T committed or aborted. It then notifies S_k about this outcome. If no site has the appropriate information (that is, whether T committed or aborted), then S_k can neither abort nor commit T. The decision concerning T is postponed until S_k can obtain the needed information. Thus, S_k must periodically resend the *query status* (T) message to the other sites. It does so until a site recovers that contains the needed information. The site at which C_i resides always has the needed information.
- The log contains no control records (abort, commit ready) concerning T. The absence of control records implies that S_k failed before responding to the prepare T message from C_i. Since the failure of S_k precludes the sending of such a response, by our algorithm C_i must abort T. Hence, S_k must execute undo(T).

Coordinator Failure

If the coordinator fails in the midst of the execution of the commit protocol for transaction T, then the participating sites must decide on the fate of T. We shall see that, in certain cases, the participating sites cannot decide whether to commit or abort T, and therefore these sites must wait for the recovery of the failed coordinator.

- If an active site contains a <commit T> record in its log, then T must be committed.
- If an active site contains an <abort T> record in its log, then T must be aborted
- If some active site does not contain a <ready T> record in its log, then the failed coordinator C_i cannot have decided to commit T. We can draw this conclusion because a site that does

not have a <ready T> record in its log cannot have sent a *ready* (T) message to C_i. However, the coordinator may have decided to abort T, but not to commit T. Rather than wait for C_i to recover, it is preferable to abort T.

- If none of the preceding cases holds, then all the active sites must have a <ready T> record in their logs, but no additional control records (such as <abort T> or <commit T>, Since the coordinator has failed, it is impossible to determine whether a decision has been made, or what that decision is, until the coordinator recovers. Thus, the active sites must wait for C_i to recover. Since the fate of T remains in doubt, T may continue to hold system resources. For example, if locking is used, T may hold locks on data at active sites. Such a situation is undesirable because it may take hours or days before C_i is again active. During this time other transactions may be forced to wait for T. As a result, data are unavailable not only on the failed site (C_i) but on active sites as well. The number of unavailable data increases as the downtime of C_i grows. This situation is called the *blocking* problem because T is blocked pending the recovery of site C_i.

Network Failure

When a link fails, all the messages in the process of being routed through the link of not arrive at their destination intact. From the viewpoint of the sites connected throughout that link, the other sites appears to have failed. Thus, our previous schemes apply here as well.

When a number of links fail, the networks may partition., in this case, two possibilities exist. The coordinator and all its participants may remain in one partition; in this case, the failure has no effect on the commit protocol. Alternatively, the coordinator and its participants may belong to several partitions; in this case, messages between the participant and the coordinator are lost, reducing the case to a link failure, as discussed.

How to Control Concurrency

In this section, we show how certain of the concurrency-control schemes can be modified so that they can be used in a distributed environment.

The transaction manager of a distributed database system manages the execution of those transactions (or subtransactions) that access data stored in a local site. Each such transaction may be either a local transaction (that is, a transaction that executes only at that site) or part of a global transaction (that is, a transaction that executes at several sites). Each transaction manager is responsible for maintaining a log for recovery purposes, and for participating in an appropriate concurrency-control scheme to coordinate the concurrent execution of the transactions executing at that site. As we shall see, the concurrency schemes need to be modified to accommodate the distribution of transactions.

Locking Protocols

The two-phase locking protocols can be used in a distributed environment. The only change needed is in the way the lock manager is implemented. In this section, we present several possible schemes, the first of which deals with the case where no data replication is allowed. The other schemes apply to the more general case where data can be replicated in several sites. We shall assume the existence of the **shared** and **exclusive lock modes**.

Nonreplicated Scheme

If no data are replicated in the system, then the locking schemes can be applied as follows: Each site maintains a local lock manager whose function is to administer the lock and unlock requests for those data items stored in that site. When a transaction wished to lock data item Q at site S_i, it simply sends a message to the lock manager at site S_i requesting a lock (in a particular lock mode). If data item Q is locked in an incompatible mode, then the request is delayed until that request can be granted. Once it has been determined that the lock request can be granted, the lock manager sends a message back to the initiator indicating that the lock request has been granted.

This scheme has the advantage of simple implementation. It requires two message transfers for handling lock requests and one message transfer for handling unlock requests. However, deadlock handling is more complex. Since the lock and unlock requests are no longer made at a single site, the various deadlock-handling algorithms.

Approach of Single Coordinator

Under the single-coordinator approach, the system maintains a *single* lock manager that resides in a *single* chosen site, say S_i. All lock and unlock requests are made at site S_i. When a transaction needs to lock a data item, it sends a lock request to S_i. The lock manager determines whether the lock can be granted immediately. If so, it sends a message to that effect to the site at which the lock request was initiated. Otherwise, the request is delayed until it can be granted, at which time a message is sent to the site at which the lock request was initiated. The transaction can read the data item from *any* one of the sites at which a replica of the data item resides. In the case of a write, all the sites where a replica of the data item resides must be involved in the writing.

The scheme has the following advantages:

- **Simple implementation**: This scheme requires two messages for handling lock requests and one message for handling unlock requests.
- **Simple deadlock handling:** Since all lock and unlock requests are made at one site, the deadlock-handling algorithms can be applied directly to this environment.

The disadvantages of the scheme include the following:

- **Bottleneck:** The site S_i becomes a bottleneck, since all requests must be processes there.
- **Vulnerability:** If the site S_i fails, the concurrency controller is lost. Either processing must stop or a recovery scheme must be used.

A compromise between these advantages and disadvantages can be achieved through a **multiple-coordinator approach**, in which the lock-manager function is distributed over several sites.

Each lock manager administers the lock and unlock requests for a subset of the data items. Each lock manager resides in a different site. This distribution reduces the degree to which the coordinator is a bottleneck, but it complicates deadlock handling, since the lock and unlock requests are not made at a single site.

Majority of Protocol

The majority protocol is a modification of the nonreplicated data scheme that we presented earlier. The system maintains a lock manager at each site. Each manager controls the locks for all the data or replicas of data stored at that site. When a transaction wished to lock a data item Q that is replicated in n different sites, it must send a lock request to more than one-half of the n sites in which Q is stored. Each lock manager determines whether the lock can be granted immediately (as far as it is concerned). As before, the response is delayed until the request can be granted. The transaction does not operate on Q until it has successfully obtained a lock on a majority of the replicas of Q.

This scheme deals with replicated data in a decentralized manner, thus avoiding the drawbacks of central control. However, it suffers from its own disadvantages:

- **Implementation:** The majority protocol is more complicated to implement than the previous schemes. It requires $2(n/2 + 1)$ messages for handling lock requests, and $(n/2 + 1)$ messages for handling unlock requests.
- **Deadlock handling:** Since the lock and unlock requests are not made at one site, the deadlock-handling algorithms must be modified. In addition, a deadlock can occur even if only one data item is being locked. To illustrate, consider a system with four sites and full replication. Suppose that transactions T_1 and T_2 wish to lock data item Q in exclusive mode. Transaction T_1 may succeed in locking Q at sites S_1 and S_3, while transaction T_2 may succeed in locking Q at sites S_2 and S_4. Each then must wait to acquire the third lock, and hence a deadlock has occurred.

Biased Protocol

The biased protocol is based on a model similar to that of the majority protocol. The difference is that requests for shared locks are given more favorable treatment that are requests for exclusive locks. The system maintains a lock manager at each site. Each manager manages the locks for all the data items stored at that site. **Shared** and **exclusive locks** are handled differently.

- **Shared locks:** When a transaction needs to lock data time Q, it simply requests a lock on Q from the lock manager at one site containing a replica of Q.
- **Exclusive locks:** When a transaction needs to lock data item Q, it request a lock on Q from the lock manager at all sites containing a replica of Q.

As before, the response to the request is delayed until the request can be granted.

The scheme has the advantage of imposing less overhead on read operations than does the majority protocol. This advantage is especially significant in common cases in which the frequency of read is much greater than is the frequency of writes. However, the additional overhead on writes is a disadvantage. Furthermore, the biased protocol shares the majority protocol's disadvantage of complexity in handling deadlock.

Primary Copy

In the case of data replication, we may choose one of the replicas as the primary copy. Thus, for each data item Q, the primary copy of Q must reside in precisely one site, which we call the *primary site of Q*.

When a transaction needs to lock a data item Q, it requests a lock at the primary site of Q. As before, the response to the request is delayed until the request can be granted.

Thus, the primary copy enables concurrency control for replicated data to be handled in a manner similar to that for unreplicated data. This method of handling allows for a simple implementation. However, if the primary site of Q fails, Q is inaccessible even though other sites containing a replica may be accessible.

Timestamping

The principal idea behind the timestamping scheme is that each transaction is given a *unique* timestamp used to decide the serialization order. Our first task, then, in generalizing scheme to a distributed scheme is to develop a scheme for generating unique timestamps. Our previous protocols then be applied directly to the nonreplicated environment.

Generation of Unique Timestamps

Two primary methods are used to generate unique timestamps; one is centralized and one is distributed. In the centralized scheme, a single site is chosen for distributing the timestamps. The site can use a logical counter or its own local clock for this purpose.

In the distributed scheme, each site generates a unique local timestamp using either a logical counter or the local clock. The global unique timestamp is obtained by concatenation of the unique local timestamp with the site identifier, which must be unique. The order of concatenation is important! We use the site identifier in the least significant position to ensure that the global timestamps generated in one site are not always greater than those generated in another site.

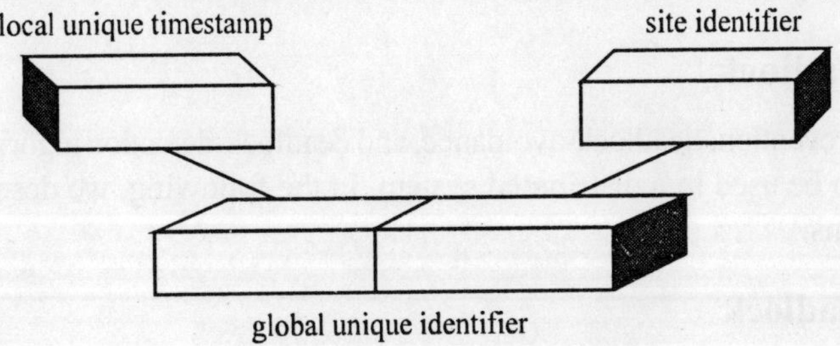

Fig. 17.2. Generation of unique timestamps.

We may still have a problem of one site generates local timestamps at a faster rate than do other sites. In such a case, the fast site's logical counter will be larger than that of other sites. Therefore, all timestamps generated by the fast site will be larger than those generated by other sites. A mechanism is needed to ensure that local timestamps are generated fairly across the system. To accomplish the fair generation of timestamps, we define within each site S_i logical clock (LC_i), which generates the unique local timestamp.

To ensure that the various logical clocks are synchronized, we require that a site S_i advance its logical clock whenever a transaction T_i with timestamp $<x,y>$ visits that site and x is greater than the current value of LC_i. In this case, site S_i advances its logical clock to the value $x + 1$.

If the system clock is used to generate timestamps, then timestamps are assigned fairly, provided that no site has a system clock that runs fast or slow. Since clocks may not be perfectly accurate, a technique similar to that used for logical clocks must be used to ensure that no clock gets far ahead or far behind another clock.

Timestamp-Ordering Scheme

The basic timestamp scheme can be extended in a straightforward manner to a distributed system. As in the centralized case, cascading rollbacks may result if no mechanism is used to prevent a transaction from reading a data item value that is not yet committed. To eliminate cascading rollbacks, we can combine the basic timestamp scheme with the 2PC protocol to obtain a protocol than ensures serializability with no cascading rollbacks. We leave the development of such an algorithm to you.

The basic timestamp scheme just described suffers from the undesirable property that conflicts between transactions are resolved through rollbacks, rather than through waits. To alleviate this problem, we can buffer the various read and write operations (that is, *delay* them) until a time when we are assured that these operations can take place without causing aborts. A read (x) operation by T_i must be delayed if there exists a transaction T_i that will perform a write(x) operation but has not yet done so and $TS(T_j) < TS(T_i)$. Similarly, a write(x) operation by T_i must be delayed if there exists a transaction T_i that will perform either read(x) or write(x) operation and $TS(T_j) < TS(T_i)$. Various methods are available for ensuring this property. One such method, called the **conservative timestamp-ordering scheme**, requires each site to maintain a read and write queue consisting of all the read and write requests, respectively, that are to be executed at the site and that must be delayed to preserve the above property. We shall not present the scheme here. Rather, we leave the development of the algorithm to you.

Handling of Deadlock

The deadlock-prevention, deadlock-avoidance, and deadlock-detection algorithms can be extended so that they can also be used in a distributed system. In the following, we describe several of these distributed algorithms.

Prevention of Deadlock

The deadlock-prevention and deadlock-avoidance algorithms can also be used in a distributed system, provided that appropriate modifications are made. For example, we can use the resource-ordering deadlock-prevention technique by simply defining a global ordering among the system resources. That is, all resources in the entire system are assigned unique numbers, and a process may request a resource (at any processor) with unique number i only if it is not holding a resource with a unique number greater than i. Similarly, we can use the banker's algorithm in a distributed system by designating one of the processes in the system (the *banker*) as the process that maintains the information necessary to carry out the banker's algorithm. Every resource request must be channelled through the banker.

These two schemes can be used in dealing with the deadlock problem in a distributed environment. The global resource-ordering deadlock-prevention scheme is simple to implement and requires little overhead. The banker's algorithm can also be implemented easily, but it may require too much overhead. The banker may become a bottleneck, since the number of messages to and from the banker may be large. Thus, the banker's scheme does not seem to be of practical use in a distributed system.

In this section, we present a new deadlock-prevention scheme based on a timestamp-ordering approach with resource preemption. Although this approach can handle any deadlock situation that may arise in a distributed system, for simplicity we consider only the case of a single instance of each resource type.

To control the preemption, we assign a unique priority number to each process. These numbers are used to decide whether a process P_i should wait for a process P_j. For example, we can let P_i wait for P_j if P_i has a priority higher than that of P_j, otherwise P_i is rolled back. This scheme prevents deadlocks because, for every edge $P_i \rightarrow P_j$ in the wait-for graph, P_i has a higher priority than P_j. Thus, a cycle cannot exist.

One difficulty with this scheme is the possibility of starvation. Some processes with extremely low priority may always be rolled back. This difficulty can be avoided through the use of timestamps. Each process in the system is assigned a unique timestamp when it is created. Two complementary deadlock prevention schemes using timestamps have been proposed:

- **The wait-die scheme:** This approach is based on a nonpreemptive technique. When process P_i requests a resource currently held by P_j, P_i is allowed to wait only if it has a smaller timestamp than does P_j (that is, P_i is older than P_j). Otherwise, P_i so rolled back (dies). For example, suppose that processes P_1, P_2, and P_3 have timestamps 5, 10, and 15, respectively. If P_1 request a resource held by P_2, P_1 will wait. If P_3 requests a resource held by P_2, P_3 will be rolled back.
- **The wound-wait scheme:** This approach is based on a preemptive technique and is a counterpart to the wait-die system. When process P_i requests a resource currently held by P_j, P_i is allowed to wait only if it has a larger timestamp that does P_j (that is, P_i is younger than P_j). Otherwise P_j is rolled back (P_j is *wounded* by P_i). Returning to our previous example, with processes P_1, P_2, and P_3, if P_1 requests a resource held by P_2, then the resource will be preempted from P_2, and P_2 will be rolled back. If P_3 requests a resource hell by P_2, then P_3 will wait.

Both schemes can avoid starvation provided that, when a process is rolled back, it is *not* assigned a new timestamp. Since timestamps always increase, a process that is rolled back will eventually have that smallest timestamp. Thus, it will not be rolled back again. There are, however, significant differences in the way the two schemes operate.

In the wait-die scheme, an older process must wait for a younger one to release its resource. Thus, the older the process gets, the more it tends to wait. By contrast, in the wound-wait scheme, an older process never waits for a younger process.

In the wait-die scheme, if a process P_i dies and is rolled back because it requested a resource held by process P_j, then P_i may reissue the same sequence of requests when it is restarted. If the resource is still held by P_j then P_i will dies again. Thus, P_i may dies several times before acquiring the needed resource. Contrast this series of events with what happens in the wound-wait scheme. Process P_i is wounded and rolled back because P_j requested a resource it holds.

18

Protection

When a process invokes the operation P on an object A, the capability for access to A may be amplified as control passes to the code body of P. This amplification may be necessary to allow P the right to access the storage segment representing A so as to implement the operation that P defines on the abstract data type. The code body of P may be allowed to read or to write to the segment of A directly, even though the calling process cannot. On return from P, the capability for A is restored to its original, unamplified state. This case is a typical one in which the rights held by a process for access to a protected segment must change dynamically, depending on the task to be performed. The dynamic adjustment of rights is performed to guarantee consistency of a programmer-defined abstraction. Amplification of rights can be stated explicitly in the declaration of an abstract type to the Hydra operating system.

When a user passes an object as an arguments to a procedure, we may need to ensure that the procedure cannot modify the object. We can implement this restriction readily by passing an access right that does not have the modification (write) right. However, if amplification may occur, the right to modify may be reinstated. Thus, the user-protection requirement can be circumvented. In general, of course, a user may trust that a procedure indeed performs its task correctly. This assumption, however, is not always correct, because of hardware or software errors. Hydra solves this problem by restricting amplifications.

The procedure call mechanism of Hydra was designed or a direct solution to the *problem of mutually suspicious subsystems.* This problem is defined as follows. Suppose that a program is provided that can be invoked as service by a number of different users (for example, a sort routine, a compiler, a game). When users invoke this service program, they take the risk that the program will malfunction and will either damage the given data, or retain some access right to the data to be used (without authority) later. Similarly, the service program may have some private files (for accounting purposes, for example) that should not be accessed directly by the calling user program. Hydra provides mechanisms for directly dealing with this problem.

A Hydra subsystem is built on top of its protection kernel and may require protection of its own components. A subsystem interacts with the kernel through calls on a set of kernel-defined primitives that defines access rights to resources defined by the subsystem. Policies for use of these resources by user processes can be define by the subsystem designer, but they are enforceable by use of the standard access protection afforded by the capability system.

A programmer can make direct use of the protection system, after acquainting himself with it features in the appropriate reference manual. Hydra provides a large library of system-defined procedures that can be called by user programs. A user of the Hydra system would explicitly incorporate calls on these system procedures into the code of his programs, or would use a program translator that had been interfaced to Hydra.

An Example: Cambridge CAP System

A different approach to capability-based protection has been taken in the design of the Cambridge CAP system. CAP's capability system is simpler and superficially less powerful than that of Hydra. However, closer examination shows that it too can be used to provide secure protection of user-defined objects. CAP, has two kinds of capabilities. The ordinary kind is called a **data capability.** It can be used to provide access to objects, but the only rights provided are the standard read, write, or execute of the individual storages segments associated with the object. Data capabilities are interpreted by microcode in the CAP machine.

The second kind of capability is the so-called **software capability,** which is protected, but not interpreted, by the CAP microcode. It is interpreted by a *protected* (that is, a privileged) procedure, which may be written by an application programmer as part of a subsystem. A particular kind of rights amplification is associated with a protected procedure. When executing the code body of such a procedure, a process temporarily acquires the rights to read or write the contents of a software capability itself. This specific kind of rights amplifications corresponds to an implementation of the seal and unseal primitives on capabilities. Of course, this privilege is still subjects to type verification to ensure that only software capabilities for a specified abstract type are allowed to be passed to any such procedure. Universal trust is not placed in any codes other than the CAP machine's microcode. See Bibliographical Notes for references.

The interpretation of a software capability is left completely to the subsystem, through the protected procedures it contains. The scheme allows a variety of protection policies to be implemented. Although a programmer can define her own protected procedures (any of which might be incorrect), the security of the overall system cannot be compromised. The basic protection system will not allow an unverified, user-defined, protected procedure access to any storage segments (or capabilities) that do not belong to the protection environment in which it resides. The most serious consequences of an insecure protected procedure is a protection breakdown of the subsystem for which that procedure has responsibility.

The designers of the CAP system have noted that the use of software capabilities allowed them to realize considerable economies in formulating and implementing protection policies commensurate with the requirements of abstract resources. However a subsystem designer who wants to make use of this facility cannot simply study a reference manual, as is the case with Hydra. Instead, he must learn the principles and techniques of protection, since the system provides him with no library of procedures.

Protection through Language

To the degree that protection is provided in existing computer systems, it is usually achieved through an operating-system kernel, which acts as a security agent to inspect and validate each attempt to access a protected resource. Since comprehensive access validation is potentially a source of considerable overhead, either we must give it hardware support to reduce the cost of each validation, or we must accept that the system designer may compromise the goals of protection. Satisfying all these goals is difficult if the flexibility to implement protection policies is restricted by the support mechanisms provided or if protection environments are made larger than necessary to secure greater operational efficiency.

As operating systems have become more complex, and particularly as they have attempted to provide higher-level user interfaces, the goals of protection have become much more refined. The designers of protection systems have drawn heavily on ideas that originated in programming languages and especially on the concepts of abstract data types and objects. Protection systems are now concerned not only with the identity of a resource to which access is attempted but also with the functional nature of that access. In the newest protection systems, concern for the function to be invoked extends beyond a set of system-defined functions, such as standard file access methods, to include functions that may be user-defined as well.

Policies for resource use may also vary, depending on the application, and they may be subject to change over time. For these reasons, protection can no longer be considered as a matter of concern to only the designer of an operating system. It should also be available as a tool for use by the application designer, so that resources of an application subsystem can be guarded against tampering or the influences of an error.

Compiler-Based Enforcement

At this point, programming languages enter the picture. Specifying the desired control of access to a shared resource in a system is making a declarative statement about the resource. This kind of statement can be integrated into a language by an extension of its typing facility. When protection is declared along with data typing, the designer of each subsystem can specify it requirements for protection, as well as its need for use of other resources in a system. Such a specification should be given directly as a program is composed, and in the languages in which the program itself is stated. This approach has several significant advantages:

1. Protection needs are simply declared, rather than programmed as a sequence of calls on procedures of an operating system.
2. Protection requirements may be stated independently of the facilities provided by a particular operating system.
3. The means for enforcement do not need to be provided by the designer of a subsystem.
4. A declarative notation is natural because access privileges are closely related to the linguistic concept of data type.

A variety of techniques can be provided by a programming-language implementation to enforce protection, but any of these must depend on some degree of support from an underlying machine and its operating system. For example, suppose a language were used to generate code to run on the Cambridge CAP system. On this system, every storage reference made on the underlying hardware occurs indirectly through a capability. This restriction prevents any process from accessing a resource outside of its protection environment at any time. However, a program may impose arbitrary restrictions on how a resource may be used during execution of a particular code segment by any process. We can implement such restrictions most readily by using the software capabilities provided by CAP. A languages implementation might provide standard protected procedures to interpret software capabilities that would realize the protection policies that could be specified in the language. This schemes puts policy specification at the disposal of the programmers, while freeing them from implementing its enforcement.

Even if a system does not provide a protection kernel as powerful as those of Hydra of CAP, mechanisms are still available for implementing protection specifications given a programming language. The principal distinction is that the *security* of this protection will not be as great as that supported by a protection kernel, because the mechanism must rely on more assumptions about the operational state of the system. A compiler can separate references for which it can certify that no protection violation could occur from those for which a violation might be possible, and it can treat them differently. The security provided by this form of protection rests on the assumption that the code generated by the compiler will not be modified prior to or during its execution.

What, then, are the relatives merits of enforcement based solely on a kernel, as opposed to enforcement provided largely by a compiler?

- **Security:** Enforcement by a kernel provides a greater degree of security of the protection system itself than does the generation of protection-checking code by a compiler. In a compiler-supported scheme, security rests on correctness of the translator, on some underlying mechanism of storage management that protects the segments from which compiled codes is executed, and, ultimately, on the security of files from which a program is loaded. Some of these considerations also apply to a software-supported protection kernel, but to a lesser degree, since the kernel may reside in fixed physical storage segments and may be loaded from only a designated file. With a tagged capability system, in which all address computation is performed either by hardware or by a fixed microprogram, even greater security is possible. Hardware-supported protection is also relatively immune to protection violations that might occur as a result of either hardware or system software malfunction.
- **Flexibility:** There are limits to the flexibility of a protection kernel in implementing a user-defined policy, although it may supply adequate facilities for the system to provide enforcement of its own policies. With a programming language, protection policy can be declared and enforcement provided as needed by an implementation. If a language does not provide sufficient flexibility, it can be extended or replaced, with less perturbation of a system in service than would be caused by the modification of an operation-system kernel.
- **Efficiency:** The greatest efficiency is obtained when enforcement of protection is supported directly by hardware (or microcode). Insofar as software support is required, language-based enforcement has the advantage that static access enforcement can be verified off-line at compile time. Also, since an intelligent compiler can tailor the enforcement mechanism to meet the specified need, the fixed overhead of kernel calls can often be avoided.

In summary, the specification of protection in a programming language allows the high-level description of policies for the allocation and use of resources. A language implementation can provide software for protection enforcement when automatic hardware-supported checking is unavailable. In addition, it can interpret protection specifications to generate calls on whatever protection system is provided by the hardware and the operating system.

One way of making protection available to the application program is through the use of a software capability that could be used as an object of computation. Inherent in this concept is the idea that certain program components might have the privilege of creating or examining these software capabilities. A capability-creating program would be able to execute a primitive operation that would seal a data structure, rendering the latter's contents inaccessible to any program components that did not hold either the seal or the unseal privileges. They might copy the data structure or pass its address to other program components, but they could not gain access to its contents. The reason for introducing such software capabilities is to bring a protection mechanism into the programming language. The only problem with the concept as proposed is that the use of the seal and unseal operations takes a procedural approach to specifying protection. A nonprocedural or declarative notation seems a preferable way to make protection available to the application programmer.

What is needed is a safe, dynamic access-control mechanism for distributing capabilities to system resources among user processes. To contribute to the overall reliability of a system, the access-control mechanism should be safe to use. To be useful in practice, it should also be reasonably efficient. This requirement has led to the development of a number of language constructs that allow the programmer to declare various restrictions on the use of a specific managed resource. These constructs provide mechanisms for three functions:

1. Distributing capabilities safely and efficiently among customer processes: In particular, mechanisms ensure that a user process will use the managed resource only if it was granted a capability to that resource.
2. Specifying the type of operations that a particular process may invoke on an allocated resource (for example, a reader of a file should be allowed only to read the file, whereas a writer should be able both to read and to write): It should not be necessary to grant the same set of rights to every user process, and it should be impossible for a process to enlarge its set of access rights, except with the authorization of the access control mechanism.
3. Specifying the order in which a particular process may invoke the various operations of a resource (for example, a file must be opened before it can be read): It should be possible to give two processes different restrictions on the order in which they can invoke the operations of the allocated resource.

The incorporation of protection concepts into programming languages, as a practical tool for system design, is in its infancy. Protection will likely become a matter of greater concern to the designers of new systems with distributed architectures and increasingly stringent requirements on data security. Then, the importance of suitable language notations in which to express protection requirements will be recognized more widely.

How to Protect Java 2

Java is an object-oriented programming language from Sun Microsystems. Java programs are composed of **classes**, each of which is a collection of data fields and functions (called **methods**) that operate on those fields. The Java virtual machine (JVM) loads a class in response to a request to create instances (or objects) of that class. One of the most novel and useful features of Java is its support for dynamically loading untrusted classes over a network and for executing mutually distrusting classes within the same JVM.

Due to these capabilities of Java, protection is a paramount concern. Class running in the same JVM may be from different sources and may not be equally trusted. As a result, enforcing protection at the granularity of the JVM process is insufficient. Intuitively, whether a request to open a file should be allowed will generally depend on which class requested the open. The operating system lacks this knowledge.

Thus, such protection decisions are handled within the JVM. When the JVM loads a class, it assigns the class to a protection domain that gives the permissions of that class. The protection domain to which the class is assigned depends on the URL from which the class was loaded and any digital signatures on the class file. A configurable policy file determines the permissions granted to the domain (and its classes). For example, classes loaded from a trusted server might be placed in a protection domain that allows them to access files in the user's home directory, whereas classes loaded from an untrusted server might have no file access permissions at all.

It can be complicated for the JVM to determine what class is responsible for a request to access a protected resource. Accesses are often performed indirectly, through system libraries or other classes. For example, consider a class that is not allowed to open network connections. It could call a system library to request the load of the contents of a URL. The JVM must decided whether or not to open a network connection for this request. But which class should be used to determine if the connection should be allowed, the application or the system library?

The philosophy adopted in Java 2 is to require the library class to explicitly permit the network connection to load the requested URL. More generally, in order to access a protected resource, some method in the calling sequence that resulted in the request must explicitly assert the privilege to access the resource. By doing so, this method *takes responsibility* for the request; presumably, it will also perform whatever checks are necessary to ensure the safety of the request. Of course, not any method is allowed to assert a privilege; it can do so only if its class is in a protection domain that is itself allowed to exercise the privilege.

This implementation approach is called **stack inspection.** Every thread in the JVM has an associated stack of its ongoing method invocations. When its caller potentially is not trusted, a method executes an access request within a doPrivileged block to perform the access to a protected resource directly or indirectly. When the doPrivileged block is entered, the stack frame for this method is annotated to indicate this fact. Then, the contents of the block are executed. When an access to a protected resource is subsequently requested, either by this method or a method it calls, a call to check Permissions is used to invoke stack inspection to determine if the request should be allowed. The inspection examines stack frames on the calling thread's stack, starting from the most recently added frame and working toward the oldest. If a stack frame is first found that has the doPrivileged annotation, then checkPremissions returns immediately and silently, allowing the access. If a stack frame is first found for which access is disallowed based on the protection domain of the method's class, then checkPremissions throws an exception. If the stack inspection exhausts the stack without finding either type of frame, then whether access is allowed depends on the implementation (for example, Internet Explorer 4.0 and JDK 1.2 allow access, whereas Netscape 4.0 disallows it).

The gui method of a class in the *untrusted applet* protection domain performs two operations, first a get and then an open. The former is an invocation of the get method of a class in the *URL loader* protection domain, which is permitted to open sessions to sites in the lucent.com domain in particular a proxy server *promy.lucent.com* for retrieving URLs. For this reason, the untrusted applet's get invocation will succeed: the checkPermissions call in the networking library encounters the stack frame of the get method, which performed it open in a doPrivileged block. However, the untrusted applet's open invocation will result in an exception, because the checkPremissions call finds no doPrivileged annotation before encountering the stack frame of the gui method.

Protection domain:	untrusted applet	URL loader	networking
Socket permission:	none	*.lucent.com:80, connect	any

Class:	gui:
	...
	get(url);
	open(addr);
	...
		get(URL u):
		...
		doPrivileged {
		open(*proxy.lucent.com:80');
		}
		<request u from proxy>
		...
			open(Addr a):
			...
			checkPermission(a, connect);
			connect (a);
			...

Fig. 18.1. Stack inspection.

Of course, for stack inspection to work, a program must be unable to modify the annotations on its own stack frame, or to do other manipulations of stack inspection. This is one of the most important differences between Java and many other languages (including C++). A Java program cannot directly access memory. Rather, it can manipulate only an object for which it has a reference. References are unforgeable, and the manipulations are made only through well-defined interfaces. Compliance is enforced through a sophisticated collection of load-time and run-time checks. As a result, an object cannot manipulate its run-time stack, because it cannot get a reference to the stack or other components of the protection system.

More generally, Java's load-time and run-time checks enforce **type safety** Java classes. Type safety ensures that classes cannot treat integers as pointer write past the end of an array, or otherwise access memory in arbitrary ways. Rather, a program can access an object only via the methods defined on that object by its class. This is the foundation of Java protection, since it enables a class to effectively **encapsulate** and project its data and methods from other classes loaded in the same JVM. For example, a variable can be defined as *private* so that only the class that contains it can access it, or *protected* so that it can be accessed only by the class that contains it, subclasses of that class, or classes in the same package. Type safety ensures that these restrictions can be enforced.

Summary

Computer systems contain many objects, and they need to protected from misuse. Objects may be hardware (such as memory, CPU time, or I/O devices) or software (such as files, programs, and abstract data types). An access right is permission to perform an operation on an object. A domain is a set of access rights. Processes execute in domains and may use any of the access rights in the domain to access and manipulate objects. During its lifetime, a process may be either bound to a protection domain or it may be allowed to switch from one domain to another.

The access matrix is a general model of protection. The access matrix provides a mechanism for protection without imposing a particular protection policy on the system or its users. The separation of policy and mechanism is an important design property.

The access matrix is sparse it is normally implemented either as access lists associated with each object, or as capability lists associated with each domain. We can include dynamic protection in the access-matrix model by considering domains and the access matrix itself as objects. Revocation of access rights in a dynamic protection model is typically easier to implement with an access list scheme than with a capability list.

Real systems are much more limited, and tend to provide protection only for files. UNIX is representative, providing read, write, and execution protection separately for the owner, group, and general public for each file. MULTICS uses a ring structure in addition to file access. Hydra, the Cambridge CAP system, and Mach are capability systems that extend protection to user-defined software objects.

Languages-based protection provides finer-grained arbitration of requests and privileges than is possible from the operating system. For example, a singe Java JVM can run several threads, each in a different protection class. It enforces the resource requests through sophisticated stack inspection and via the type safety of the language.

19

Security

Protection, as we discussed in Chapter 18, is strictly an *internal* problem: How do we provide controlled access to programs and data stored in a computer system? **Security**, on the other hand, requires not only an adequate protection system, but also consideration of the *external* environment within which the system operates. Internal protection is not useful if the operator's console is exposed to unauthorized personnel, or if files can simply be removed from the computer system on tapes and disks and taken to an unprotected system. These security problems are management, rather than operating-system, problems.

The infromation stored in the system both data and codes as well as the physical resources of the computer system, need to be protected from unauthorized access, malicious destruction or alteration, and accidental introduction of inconsistency. In this chapter, we examine the ways in which infromation may be misused or intentionally made inconsistent. We then present mechanisms to guard against such occurrences.

Problem of Security

We discussed mechanisms that the operating system can provide (with appropriate aid from the hardware) that allows users to protect their resources (usually program and data). These mechanisms work well only as long as the users confrom to the intended use of and access to these resources. We say that a system is **secure** if its resources are used and accessed as intended under all circumstances. Unfortunately, total security cannot be achieved.Nonetheless, we must have mechanisms to make security breaches a rare occurrence, rather than the norm.

Security violation (or misuse) of the system can be categorized as intentional (malicious) or accidental. It is easier to protect against accidental misuse than against malicious misuse. Among the froms of malicious access are the following:

- Unauthorized reading of data (or theft of infromation)
- Unauthorized modification of data
- Unauthorized destruction of data
- Preventing legitimate use of the system (or denial of service)

Absolute protection of the system from malicious abuse is not possible, but the cost to the perpetrator can be made sufficiently high to deter most, if not all, unauthorized attempts to access the infromation residing in the system.

To protect the system, we must take security measures at four levels:

1. **Physical:** The site or sites containing the computer systems must be physically secured against armed or surreptitious entry by intruders.
2. **Human:** Users must be screened carefully to reduce the chance of authorizing a user who then gives access to an intruder (in exchange for a bribe, for example).
3. **Network:** Much computer data in modern systems travels over private leased lines, shared lines like the Internet, or dial-up lines. The interception of this data could be just as harmful as the break-in of a computer. The interruption of these communications could be a remote **denial-of-service** attack and diminish user's use of and trust of the system.
4. **Operating System:** The system must protect itself from accidental or purposeful security breaches.

Security at the first two levels must be maintained if operating-system security is to be ensured. A weakness at a high level of security (physical or human) allows circumvention of strict low-level (operating-system) security measures.

In many applications, ensuring the security of the computer system is worth considerable effort. Large commercial systems containing payroll or other financial data are inviting targets to thieves. Systems that contain data pertaining to corporate operations may be of interest to unscrupulous competitors. Furthermore, loss of such data, whether via accident or fraud, can seriously impair the ability of the corporation to function.

Now that the hardware has become sufficiently sophisticated to provide protection, the designers of these operating systems are struggling to add security. Unfortunately, adding a feature to a functional system is much more difficult than designing and implementing the feature before the system is built. Later operating systems, such as Windows NT, were designed to provide security features from the beginning.

In the remainder of this chapter, we shall address security at the operating system level. Security at the physical and human levels, although important, is far beyond the scope of this text, security within the operating system and between operating systems is implemented in several ways, ranging from passwords for access to the system to the isolation of concurrent processes running within the system. The file system also provides some degree of protection.

User Authentication

A major security problem for operating system is **authentication**. The protection system depends on an ability to identify the programs and processes currently executing. This ability, in turn, rests on our power to identify each user of the system. A user normally identifies himself. How do we determine whether a user's identity is authentic? Generally, authentication is based on one or more of three items: user possession (a key or card), user knowledge (a user identifier and password), and /or a user attribute (fingerprint, retina pattern, or signature).

Passwords

The most common approach to authenticating a user identity is the use of **passwords.** When the user identifies herself by user ID or account name, she is asked for a password. If the user-supplied password matches the password stored in the system, the system assumes that the user is legitimate.

Passwords are often used to protect objects in the computer system, in the absence of more complete protection schemes. They can be considered a special case of either keys or capabilities. For instance a password could be associated with each resource (such as a file). Whenever a request is made to use the resource, the password must be given. If the password is correct, access is granted. Different passwords may be associated with different access rights. For example, different passwords may be used for each of the following file operations: reading, appending, and updating.

Password Vulnerabilities

Passwords are extremely common because they are easy to understand and use. Unfortunately, passwords can often be guessed, accidentally exposed, sniffed, or illegally transferred from an authorized user to an unauthorized one, as we show next.

There are two common ways to guess a password. One is for the intruder (either human or program) to know the user or to have infromation about the user. All too frequently, people use obvious information (such as the names of their cats or spouses) as their passwords. The other way is to use brute force; trying enumeration, or all possible combinations of letters numbers, and punctuation, until the password is found. Short passwords do not leave enough choices to prevent their being guessed by repeated trials. For example, a four-decimal password provides only 10,000 variations. On the average, guessing 5,000 times would produce a correct hit. A program that could try a password every 1 millisecond would take only about 5 seconds to guess a four-digit password. Enumeration is not as successful at finding passwords in systems that allow longer passwords, that differentiate between uppercase and lowercase letters, and that allows use of numbers and all punctuation characters in passwords. Of course, users must take advantage of the large password space and must not, for example, use only lowercase letters.

The failure of password security due to exposure can result from visual or electronic monitoring. An intruder can look over the shoulder of a user (*shoulder surfing*) when the user is logging in, and can learn the password easily by watching the keyboard. Alternatively, anyone with access to the network on which a computer resides could seamlessly add a network monitor, allowing her to watch all data being transferred on the network (*sniffing*), including user IDs and passwords. Encrypting the data stream containing the password solved this problem.

Exposure is a particularly severe problem if the password is written down where it can be read or lost. As we shall see, some systems force the user to select hard-to-remember of long passwords. Taken to an extreme, this requirement can cause a user to record the password providing much less security than systems that allow easy passwords!

The final method of password compromise, illegal transfer, is the result of human nature. Most computer installations have a rule that forbids users to share accounts. This rule is sometimes implemented for accounting reasons, but often to aid in security. For instance, if one user ID was shared by several users, and a security breach occurred from that user ID, then it is impossible to know who was using that user ID at the time, or even whether the user was an authorized one. With one user per user ID, any user can be questioned directly about use of her account. Sometimes, users break account-sharing rules to help friends or to circumvent accounting, and this behaviour can result in a system being accessed by unauthorized users—possibly harmful ones.

Passwords can be either generated by the system or selected by a user. System-generated passwords may be difficult to remember, and thus users may write them down. User-selected passwords, however, are often easy to guess (the user's name or favourite car, for example). At some sites, administrators occasionally check user passwords and notify the use if his password is too short or otherwise each to guess. Some systems also age passwords, forcing users to change their passwords at regular intervals (every three months, for instance). This method is not foolproof either, because users can easily toggle between two passwords. The solution, as implemented on some systems, is to record a passwords history for each user. For instance, the system could record that last *N* passwords and not allow their reuse.

Several variants on these simple password schemes can be used. For example, the password can be changed frequently. In the extreme, the password is changed for each session. A new password is selected (either by the system or by the user) at the end of each session, and that password must be used for the next session. In such a case, even if a password is misused, it can be used only once. When the legitimate user tires to use a now-invalid password at the next session, he discovers the security violation. Steps can then be taken to repair the breached security.

Encryption of Passwords

One problem with all these approaches is the difficulty of keeping the password secret within the computer. How can the system store a password securely, yet allow its use for authentication when the user presents her password? The UNIX system uses **encryption** to avoid the necessity of keeping its password list secret. Each user has a password. The system contains a function that is extremely difficult—the designers hope impossible—to invert, but is simple to compute. That is, given a value x, it is easy to compute the function value $f(x)$. Given a function value $f(x)$, however, it is impossible to compute x. This function is used to encode all passwords. Only encoded passwords are stored. When a user presents a password, it is encoded and compared against the stored encoded password. Even if the stored encoded password is seen, it cannot be decoded, so the password cannot be determined. Thus, the password file does not need to be kept secret. The function $f(x)$ is tyically an encryption **algorithm** that has been designed and tested rigorously.

The flaw in this method is that the system no longer has control over the passwords. Although the passwords are encrypted, anyone with a copy of the password file can run fast encryption routines against it, encrypting each word in a dictionary, for instance, and comparing the results against the passwords. If the user has selected a password that is also a word in the dictionary, the password is cracked. On sufficiently fast computers, or even on clusters of slow computers, such a comparison may take only a few hours. Because UNIX systems use a well-known encryption algorithm, a hacker might keep a cache of password-cipher pairs to find quickly passwords that have been cracked previously. For this reason, new versions of UNIX store the encrypted password entries in a file readable only by the **superuser**. The programs that compare a presented password to the stored password run setuid to root, so they can read this file but other users cannot.

Another weakness in the UNIX password methods is that many UNIX systems treat only the first eight characters as significant, so it is extremely important for users to take advantage of the available password space. To avoid the dictionary encryption method, some systems disallow the use of dictionary words a passwords. A good technique is to generate your password by using the first letter of each word of an easily remembered phase using both upper and lower characters with a number or punctuation through in for good measure. For example, the phrase "My mother's name is Katherine." Might yield the password "Mmnisk.!". The password is hard to crack, but easy for the user to remember.

One-Time Passwords

To avoid the problems of password sniffing and shoulder surfing, a system could use a set of paired **passwords**. When a session begins, the system randomly selects and presents one part of a password pair; the user must supply the order part. In this system, the user is *challenged* and must *respond* with the correct answer to that challenge.

This approach can be generalized to the use of an algorithm as a password. The algorithm might be an integer function, for example. They system selects a random integer and presents it to the user. The user applies the function and replies with the correct result. The system also applies the function. If the two results match, access is allowed.

Such a method involving the use of algorithmic passwords is not susceptible to exposure; that is, a user can type in a password, and no entity intercepting that password would be able to reuse it. In this variation, the system and user share a secret. The secret is never transmitted over a medium that allows exposure. Rather, the secret is used an input to the function, along with a shared seed. A **seed** is a random number or alphanumeric sequence. The seed is the authentication challenge from the computer. The secret and the seed are used as input to the function *f* (*secret, seed*). The result of this function is transmitted as the password to the computer. Because the computer also knows the secret and the seed, it can perfrom the same computation. If the results match, the user is authenticated. The next time that the user needs to be authenticated, another seed is generated and the same steps ensure. This time, the password is different.

In this **one-time password** system, the password is different in each instance. Anyone capturing the password from one session and trying to reuse it in another session will fail. One-time passwords are among the only ways to prevent improper authentication due to password exposure. Commercial implementations of one-time password systems such as SecurID, for example, use hardware calculators. Most of these are in the shape of a credit card, but have a keypad and display. Some use the current time as the random seed. The user uses the keypad to enter the shared, secret, also knows as a **personal identification number (PIN).** The display shows the one-time password. The use of both a one-time password generator and a PIN is one form of **two-factor authentication**. There are two different types of components needed in this case. Two-factor authentication offers far better authentication protection than single-factor authentication.

Another variation on one-time passwords is the use of a **code book**, or **one-time pad**, which is a list of single-use passwords. In this method, each password on the list is used, in order, once, and then is crossed out or erased. The commonly used S/Key system uses either a software calculator or a code book based on these calculations as a source of one-time passwords.

Biometrics

There are many other variations on the use of passwords for authentication. Palm or hand-readers are common to secure physical access, for example access to a data center. These readers match stored parameters against what is being read from their hand-reader pad. The parameters can include a temperature map, as well as finger length, finger width, and line patterns. These devices are currently too large and expensive to be used for normal computer authentication.

Finger print readers have become accurate and cost-effective, and should become more common in the future. These devices read your finger's ridge patterns and convert them into a sequence of numbers. Over time, they can store a set of sequences to adjust for the location of the finger on the reading pad and other factors. Software can then scan a finger on the pad and compare it to these stored sequences to determine if the finger on the pad is the same as the stored one. Of course, multiple users can have profiles stored, and the scanner can differentiate among them. A very accurate two-factor authentication scheme can result from requiring a password as well as a user name and fingerprint scan. If this infromation is encrypted in transit, the system can be very resistant to spoofing or replay attack.

Program Threats

When a program written by one user may be used by another user, misuse and unexpected behaviour may ensue. Trojan horses, trap doors, and stack and buffer overflow.

Trojan Horse

Many systems have mechanisms for allowing programs written by users to be executed by other users. If these programs are executed in a domain that provides the access rights of the executing user, the other users may misuse these rights. A text-editor program, for example, may include code to search the file to be edited for certain keywords. If any are found, the entire file may be copied to a special area accessible to the creator of the text editor. A code segment that misuses its environment is called a **Trojan horse**. Long search paths, such as are common on UNIX systems, exacerbate the Trojan horse problem. The search path lists the set of directories to search when an ambiguous program name is given. The path is searched for a file of that name and the file is executed. All the directories in the search path must be secure, or a Trojan horse could be slipped into the user's path and executed accidentally.

For instance, consider the use of the "." character in a search path. The "." Tells the shell to include the current directory in the search. Thus, if a user has "." in her search path, has set her current directory to a friend's directory, and enters the name of a normal system command, the command may be executed from the friend's directory instead. The program would run within the user's domain, allowing the program to do anything that the user is allowed to do, including deleting the user's files (which are actually in the friend's directory), for instance.

A variation of the Trojan horse is a program that emulates a login program. An unsuspecting user starts to log in at a terminal and notices that he has apparently mistyped his password. He tries again, and is successful. What has happened is that his authentication key and password have been stolen by the login emulator that was left running on the terminal by the thief. The emulator stored away the password, printed out a login error message, and exited; the user was then provided with a genuine login prompt. This type of attack can be defeated by the operating system printing a usage message at the end of an interactive session or by a nontrappable key sequence, such as the control-alt-delete combination that Windows NT uses.

Trap Door

The designer of a program of system might leave a hole in the software that only she is capable of using. This type of security breach (or **trap door**) was shown in the movie *War Games.* For instance, the code might check for a specific user ID or password, and it might circumvent normal security procedures. Programmers have been arrested for embezzling from banks by including rounding errors in their code, and having the occasional half-cent credited to their accounts. This account crediting can add up to a large amount of money, considering the number of transactions that a large bank executes!

A clever trap door could be included in a compiler. The compiler could generate standard object code as well as a trap door, regardless of the source code being compiled. This activity is particularly nefarious, since a search of the source code of the program will not reveal any problems. Only the source code of the compiler would contain the infromation. Trap doors pose a difficult problem because, to detect them, we have to analyze all the source code for all components of a system. Given that software systems may consist of millions of lines of code, this analysis is not done frequently.

Stack and Buffer Overflow Attack

The stack or buffer-overflows attack is the most common way for an attacker outside of the system, on a network or dial-up connection, to gain unauthorized access to the target system. An authorized user of the system may also use this exploit for **privilege escalation**, to gain privileges beyond those allowed for that user.

Essentially, the attack exploits a bug in a program. The bug can be a simple case of poor programming, in which the programmer neglected to code bounds checking on an input fields. In this case, the attacker sends more data than the program was expecting. Using trial and error, or by examination of the source code of the attacked program if it is available, the attacker determines the vulnerability and writes a program to do the following:

1. Overflow an input field, command-line argument, or input buffer, for example, on a network daemon, until it writes into the stack.
2. Overwrite the current return address on the stack with the address of the exploit code loaded in step 3.
3. Write a simple set of code for the next space in the stack that includes the commands that the attacker wishes to execute, for instance, spawn a shell.

The result of this attack program's execution will be a root shell, or other privileged command execution.

For instance, if a web page form expects a user name to be entered into a field, the attacker could send the user name, plus extra characters to overflow the buffer and reach the stack, plus a new return address to load onto the stack, plus the code the attacker wants to run. When the buffer-reading subroutine returns from execution, the return address is the exploit code, and the code is run.

The buffer-overflow attack is especially pernicious as it can be run within a system and can travel over allowed communications channels. Such an attack can occur within protocols that are expected to be used to communicate with the machine, and therefore can be hard to detect and prevent. They can even bypass the security added by firewalls.

One solution to this problem is for the CPU to have a feature that disallows execution of code in a stack section of memory. Recent versions of Sun's SPARC chip include this setting, and recent versions of Solaris enable it. The return address of the overflowed routine can still be modified, but when the return address is within the stack and the code there attempts to execute, an exception is generated and the program is halted with an error.

System Threats

Most operating systems provide a means for processes to spawn other processes. In such an environment, it is possible to create a situation where operating-system resources and user files are misused. The two most common methods for achieving this misuse are worms and viruses.

Worms

A **worm** is a process that uses the **spawn** mechanism to clobber system perfromance. The worm spawns copies of itself, using up system resources and perhaps locking out system use by all other processes. On computer networks, worms are particularly potent, since they may reproduce themselves among systems and thus shut down the entire network. Such an event occurred in 1998 to UNIX systems on the Internet, causing millions of dollars of lost system and programmer time.

At the close of the workday on November 2, 1998, Robert Tappan Morris, Jr., a first-year Cornell graduate student, unleashed a worm program on one or more hosts connected to the Internet. Targeting Sun Microsystems' Sun 3 workstations and VAX computers running variants of Version 4 BSD UNIX, the worm quickly spread over great distances; within a few hours of its release, it had consumed system resources to the point of bringing down the infected machines.

Although Robert Morris designed the self-replicating program for rapid reproduction and distribution, some of the features of the UNIX networking environment provided the means to propagate the worm throughout the system. It is likely that Morris chose for initial infection an Internet host left open for and accessible to outside users. From there, the worm program exploited flaws in the UNIX operating system's security routines and took advantage of UNIX utilities that simplify resource sharing in local-area networks to gain unauthorized access to thousands of other connected sites. Morris' methods of attack are outlined next.

The worm was made up of two programs, a **grappling hook** (also called a **bootstrap** or **vector**) program and the main program. Named *11.c*, the grappling hook consisted of 99 lines of C code compiled and run on each machine it accessed. Once established on the computer system under attack, the grappling hook connected to the machine where it originated and uploaded a copy of the main worm onto the *hooked* system. The main program proceeded to search for other machines to which the newly infected system could connect easily. In these actions. Morris exploited the UNIX networking utility, **rsh**, for easy remote task execution. By setting up special files that list the host-login name paris, users can omit entering a password each time they access a remote account on the paired list. The worm searched these special files for site names that would allows remote execution without a password. Where remote shells were established, the worm program was uploaded and began executing anew.

The attack via remote access was one of three infection methods built into the worm. The other two methods involved operating-system bugs in the UNIX *finger* and *sendmail* programs. The *finger* utility functions as an electronic telephone directory; the command

```
finger user-name@hostname
```

returns a person's real and login names along with other infromation that the user may have provided, such as office and home address and telephone number, research plan, or clever quotation. *Finger* runs as a background process (or daemon) at each BSD site and responds to queries throughout the Internet. The point vulnerable to malicious entry involved reading input without checking bounds for overflow. The code executed a **buffer-overflow attack.** Morris' program queried *finger* with a 536-byte string crafted to exceed the buffer allocated for input and to overwrite the stack frame. Instead of returning to the *main* routine it was in before Morris' call, the *finger* daemon was routed to a procedure within the invading 536-byte string now residing on the stack. The new procedure executed */bin/sh*, which, if successful, gave the worm a remote shell on the machine under attack.

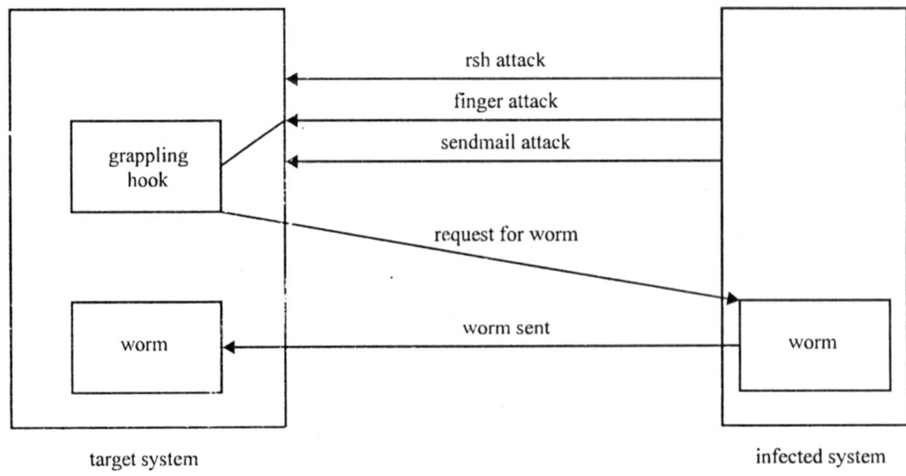

Fig. 19.1. The Morris Internet worm.

The bug exploited in *sendmail* also involved using a daemon process for malicious entry. *Sendmail* routes electronic mail in a network environment. Debugging code in the utility permits testers to verify and display the state of the mail system. The debugging option is useful to system administrators and is often left on as a background process. Morris included in his attack arsenal a call to debug that, instead of specifying a user address, as would be normal in testing, issued a set of commands that mailed and executed a copy of the grappling-hook program.

Once in place, the main worm undertook systematic attempts to discover user passwords. It began by trying simple cases of no password or of passwords constructed of account-user-name combinations, then used comparisons with an internal dictionary of 432 favorite password choice, then went to the final stage of trying each word in the standard UNIX on-line dictionary as a possible password. This elaborate and efficient three-stage password-cracking algorithms enabled the worm to gain further access to other user accounts on the infected system. The worm then searched for *rsh* data files in these newly broken accounts. Any *rsh* entries were tries, and, as described previously, the worm could then gain access to user accounts on remote systems.

With each new access, the worm program searched for already active copies of itself. If it found one, the new copy exited, except for every seventh instance. Had the worm exited on all duplicate sightings, it might have remained undetected. Allowing every seventh duplicate to proceed (possibly to confound efforts to stop its spread by baiting with *fake* worms) created a wholesale infestation of Sun and VAX systems on the Internet.

The very features of the UNIX network environment that assisted the worm's propagation also helped to stop its advance. Ease of electronic communication, mechanisms to copy source and binary files to remote machines, and access to both source code and human expertise allowed cooperative efforts to develop solutions quickly. By the evening of the next day, November 3, methods of halting the invading program were circulated to system administrators via the Internet. Within days, specific software patches for the exploited security flaws were available.

Why did Morris unleash the worm? Action has been characterized as both a harmless prank gone awry and a serious criminal offense. Based on the complexity of starting the attack, it is unlikely that the worm's release or the scope of its spread was unintentional. The worm program took elaborate steps to cover its tracks and to repel efforts to stop its spread. Yet the program contained no code aimed at damaging or destroying the systems on which it ran. The author clearly had the expertise to include such commands; in fact, data structures were present in the bootstrap code that could have been used to transfer Trojan-horse or virus programs. The behaviour of the program may lead to interesting observations, but it does not provide a sound basis for inferring motive. What is not open to speculation, however, is the legal outcome: A federal court convicted Morris and handed down a sentence of three years' probation, 400 hours of community service, and a $10,000 fine. Morris' legal costs were probably in excess of $100,000.

Viruses Attack on Computer

Another form of computer attack is a virus. Like worms, viruses are designed to spread into other programs and can wreak havoc in a system, including modifying or destroying files and causing system crashed and program malfunctions. Whereas a worm is structured as a complete, standalone program, a virus is a fragment of code embedded in a legitimate program. Viruses are a major problem for computer users, especially users of microcomputer systems. Multiuser computers, generally, are not prone to viruses because the executable programs are protected from writing by the operating system. Even if a virus does infect a program, its powers are limited because other aspects of the systems are protected. Single-user systems have no such protections and, as a result, a virus has free run.

Viruses are usually spread by users down loading viral programs from public bulletin boards or exchanging disks containing an infection. In February 1992, for example, two Cornell University students developed three Macintosh game programs with an embedded virus and distributed them to worldwide software archives via the Internet. The virus was discovered when a mathematics professor in Wales downloaded the games, and antivirus programs on his system alerted him to an infection. Some 200 other users had already downloaded the games. Although the virus was not designed to destroy data, it could spread to application files and cause such problems as long delays and program malfunctions. The authors were easy to trace, since the games had been mailed electronically from a Cornell account. New York State authorities arrested the students on misdemeanor charges of computer tampering.

In another incident, a programmer in California being divorced by his wife gave her a disk to load on a disputed computer. The disk contained a virus and erased all the files on the system. The husband was arrested and charged with destruction of property.

In recent years, a common form of virus transmission has been via the exchange of Microsoft Office files, such as Microsoft Word documents. These documents can contain so-called *macros* (or Visual Basic programs) that programs in the Office suite (Word, PowerPoint, or Excel) will execute automatically. Because these programs run under the user's own account, the macros can run largely unconstrained (for example, deleting user files at will).

On occasion, upcoming viral infections are announced in high-profile media events. Such was the case with the *Michelangelo* virus, which was scheduled to erase infected hard disk files on March 6, 1992, the Renaissance artist's 517th birthday. Because of the extensive publicity surrounding the virus, most sit had located and destroyed the virus before it was activated, so it caused little or no damage. Such cases both alert the general public to an alarm it about the virus problem. Antivirus programs are currently excellent sellers. Most commercial packages are effective against only particular, know viruses. They work by searching all the programs on a system for the specific pattern of instructions known to make up the virus. When they find a known pattern, they remove the instructions, *disinfecting* the program. These commercial packages have catalogs of hundreds of viruses for which they search. Viruses and the anti-virus software continue to become more sophisticated. Some viruses modify themselves as they infect other software to avoid the basic pattern-match approach of anti-virus software. The anti-virus software in turn now looks for families of patterns rather than a single pattern to identify a virus.

The best protection against computer viruses is prevention, or the practice of **safe computing**. Purchasing unopened software from vendors and avoiding free or pirated copies from public sources or disk exchange is the safest route to preventing infection. However, even new copies of legitimate software applications are not immune to virus infection: There have been cases where disgruntled employees of a software company have infected the master copies of software programs to do economic harm to the company selling the software. For macro viruses, one defense is to exchange Word documents in an alternative file fromat called rich text **format (RTF).** In contrast to the native Word format, RTF does not include the capability to attach macros.

Another defense is to avoid opening any email attachments from unknown users. Unfortunately, history has shown that vulnerabilities appear as fast as they are fixed. For example, in 2000 the *love bug* virus became very widespread by appearing to be a love note sent by a friend of the receiver. Once invoked by opening the attached Visual Basic script, it propagated by sending itself to the first users in the user's e-mail contact list. Fortunately, except for clogging e-mail systems and user's inboxes, it was relatively harmless. It did, however, effectively negate the defensive suggestion of opening attachments only from people knows to the receiver. A more effective defense method is to avoid opening any attachment that contains executable code. Some companies enforce this as policy by removing all incoming attachments to email messages.

Another safeguard, although it does not prevent infection, does permit early detection. A user must begin by completely reformatting the hard disk, especially the boot sector, which is often targeted for viral attack. Only secure software is uploaded, and a checksum for each file is calculated. The checksum list must then be kept free from unauthorized access. Following any system reboot, a program can recompute the checksums and compare them to the original list; any differences serve as a warning of possible infection.

Because they usually work among systems and not programs, processes, or users, worms and viruses generally pose security, rather than protection, problems.

Denial of Service

The last attack category, denial of service, does not involve gaining information or stealing resources, but rather disabling legitimate use of a system or facility. An intruder could delete all the files on a system, for example. Most denial-of-service attacks involve systems that the attacker has not penetrated. Indeed, launching an attack that prevents legitimate use is frequently easier than breaking into a machines or facility.

These attacks are generally network based. They fall into two categories. The first case is an attack that uses so many facility resources that, in essence, no useful work can be done. For example, a web site click could download a java applet that proceeds to use all available CPU time.

The second case involves disrupting the network of the facility. There have been several successful denial-of-service attacks against major web sites. They result from abuse of some of the fundamental functionality of TCP/IP. For instance, if the attack sends the part of the protocol that says "I want to start a TCP connection," but never follows with the standard "The connection is now complete," there can be several partially started TCP sessions that could eat up all the network resources of the system, disabling any further legitimate TCP connections. These attacks, which can last hours or days, have caused partial or full failure of attempts to use the target facility. These attacks are usually stopped at the network level, until the operating systems can be updated to reduce their vulnerability.

Generally, it is impossible to prevent denial-of service attacks. The attacks use the same mechanisms as normal operation. Frequently, it is difficult to determine if a system slowdown is just a surge in sue, or an attack!

Securing Systems and its Facilities

Securing systems and facilities is intimately linked to intrusion detection.

One method of improving system security is periodically to scan the system for security holes. These scans can be one when the computer has relatively little use, so they will have less effect than logging. Such a scan can check a variety of aspects of the system:

- Short or easy-to-guess passwords
- Unauthorized privileged programs, such as setuid programs
- Unauthorized programs in system directories
- Unexpected long-running processes
- Improper directory protections on both user and system directories
- Improper protections on system data files, such as the password file, device drivers, or even the operating-system kernel itself
- Dangerous entries in the program search path

- Changes to system programs detected with checksum values
- Unexpected or hidden network daemons

Any problems found by a security scan can either be fixed automatically or reported to the managers of the system.

Networked computers are much more susceptible to security attacks than are standalone systems. Rather than attacks from a known set of access points, such as directly connected terminals, we fact attacks from an unknown and large set of access points—a potentially severe security problem. To a lesser extent, systems connected to telephone lines via modems are also more exposed.

In fact, the U.*S*. government considers systems to be only as secure as the system's most far-reaching connection. For instance, a top-secret system may be accessed only from within a building also considered top-secret. The system loses its top-secret rating if any from of communication can occur outside that environment. Some government facilities take extreme security precautions. The connectors into which a terminal plugs to communicate with the secure computer are locked in a safe in the office when the terminal is not in use. A person must know a physical lock combination, as well as authentication infromation for the computer itself, to gain access to the computer.

Unfortunately for systems administrators and computer-security professionals, it is frequently impossible to lock a machine in a room and disallow all remote access. For instance, the Internet network currently connects millions of computers. It is becoming a mission-critical, indispensable resource for many companies and individuals. If you consider the internet a *club*, then as in any club with millions of *members*, there are many good members and some bad members. The bad members have many tools they can use across the Internet to attempt to gain access to the interconnected computers, just as Morris did with his worm.

How can trusted computers be connected safely to an untrustworthy network? One solution is the use of a firewall to separate trusted and untrusted systems. A **firewall** is a computer or router that sits between the trusted and the untrusted. It limits network access between the two **security domains,** and monitors and logs all connections. It can also limit connections based on source or destination address, source or destination port, or direction of the connection. For instance, **web servers** use http to communicate with web browsers. A firewall therefore may allows only http to pass, from all hosts outside the firewall only to the web server within the firewall. The Morris Internet worm used the finger protocol to break into computers, so finger would not be allowed to pass.

In fact, as firewall can separate a network into multiple domains. A common implementation has the Internet as the untrusted domain; a semitrusted and semisecure network, called the **demilitarized zone (DMZ),** as another domain; and a company's computers as a third domain. Connections are allowed from the Internet to the DMZ computers and from the company computers to the Internet, but are not allowed from the Internet or DMZ computers to the company computers. Optionally, controlled communications may be allowed between the DMZ and one or more company computers. For instance, a web server on the DMZ may need to query a database server on the corporate network. With a firewall, all access is contained, and any DMZ systems that are broken into based on the protocols, allowed through the firewall still are unable to access the company computers.

Of course, a firewall itself must be secure and attack-proof, otherwise its ability to secure connections can be compromised. Firewalls do not prevent attacks that **tunnel**, or travel within protocols or connections that the firewall allows. A buffer-overflow attack to a web server will not be stopped by the firewall because the http connection is allowed, it is simply the contents of the http connection that house the attack. Likewise, denial-of-service attacks can affect firewalls as much as any other machines. Another vulnerability of firewalls is **spoofing**, in which an unauthorized host pretends to be an authorized host by meeting some authorization criterion. For example, if a firewall rule allows a connection from a host and identifies that host by its IP address, then another host could send packets using that same address and be allowed through the firewall.

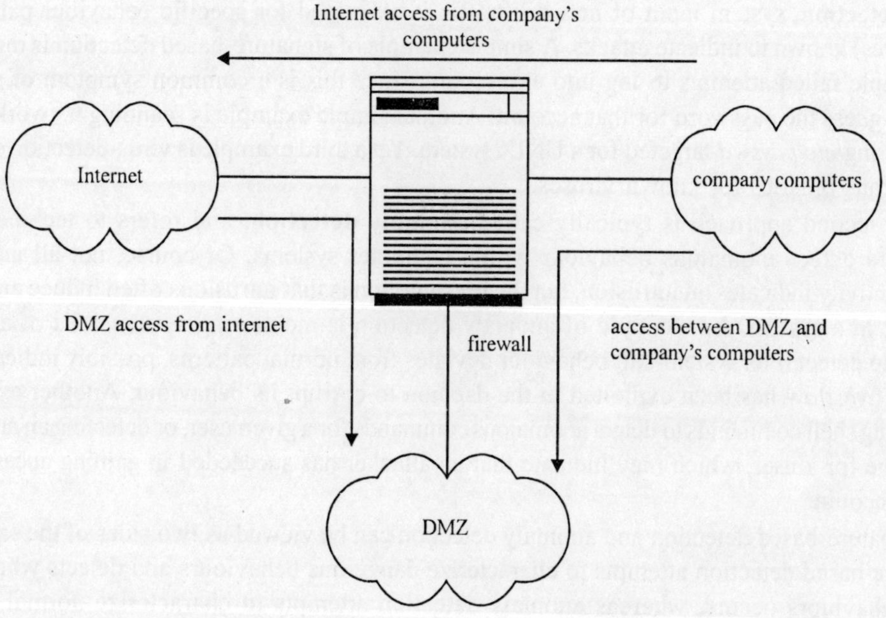

Fig. 19.2. Network security through domain separation via firewall.

Detection of Intrusion

Intrusion detection, as its name suggests, strives to detect attempted or successful intrusions into computer systems and to initiate appropriate responses to the intrusions. Intrusion detection encompasses a wide array of techniques that vary on a number of *axes*. Some of these axes include:

- The time that detection occurs: in real time (while it is occurring) or after the fact only.
- The types of inputs examined to detect intrusive activity. These could include user shell commands, process system calls, and network packet headers or contents. Some forms of intrusions might be detected only by correlating information from multiple such sources.
- The range or response capabilities. Simple forms of response include alerting an administrator of the potential intrusion on somehow halting the potentially intrusive activity, for example, killing a process engaged in apparently intrusive activity. In a sophisticated form of response, a system might transparently divert an intruder's activity to **a trap**—a false resource exposed

to the attacker in order to monitor and gain infromation about the attack; to the attacker, the resource appears real.

These degrees of freedom in the design space for detecting intrusions in systems have yielded a wide range of solutions known as **intrusion-detection systems** (IDS).

Components of an Intrusion

Defining a suitable specification of intrusion turns out to be quite difficult, and thus automatic IDSs today typically settle for one of two less ambitious approaches. In the first, called **signature-based detection,** system input or network traffic is examined for specific behaviour patterns (or **signatures**) known to indicate attacks. A simple example of signature-based detection is monitoring for multiple failed attempts to log into an account, since this is a common symptom of someone trying to guess the password for that account. Another simple example is scanning network packets for the string*/etc/passwd/*targeted for a UNIX system. Yet a third example is virus-detection software, which scans binaries for known viruses.

The second approach is typically called **anomaly detection**, and refers to techniques that attempt to detect anomalous behaviour within computer systems. Of course, not all anomalous system activity indicates an intrusion, but the presumption is that intrusions often induce anomalous behavior in a system. An example of anomaly detection is monitoring system calls of a daemon process to detect if its system-call behaviour deviates from normal patterns, possibly indicating that a buffer overflow has been exploited in the daemon to corrupt its behaviour. Another example is monitoring shell commands to detect anomalous commands for a given user, or detecting an anomalous login time for a user, which may indicate that an attacker has succeeded in gaining access to that user's account.

Signature-based detection and anomaly detection can be viewed as two sides of the same coin: Signature-based detection attempts to characterize dangerous behaviours and detects when one of these behaviuors occurs, whereas anomaly detection attempts to characterize normal (or non-dangerous) behaviours and detects when something other than these behaviours occurs.

These different approaches yield IDSs with very different properties, however. In particular, anomaly detection can detect previously unknown methods of intrusion. Signature-based detection will identify only known attacks that can be codified in a recognizable pattern. As such, new attacks that were not contemplated when the signatures were generated will evade signature-based detection. This problem is well known to vendors of virus-detection software, who must release new signatures with great frequency as new viruses are generated and detected manually.

Anomaly detection is not necessarily superior to signature-based detection, however. Indeed, a significant challenge for systems that attempt anomaly detection is to benchmark "normal" system behaviour accurately. If the system is already penetrated when it is benchmarked, then the intrusive activity may be included in the "normal" benchmark. Even if the system is benchmarked cleanly, without influence from intrusive behaviour, the benchmark must be a fairly complete picture of normal behaviour. Otherwise, the number of false alarms will be excessive.

To illustrate the impact of even a marginally high rate of false alarms, consider an installation consisting of few tens of UNIX workstations from which records of security-relevant events are recorded for purposes of intrusion detection. A small installation such as this could easily generate a million audit records per day. Only one or two might be worthy of an administrator's investigation, however. If we suppose, optimistically, that each such attack is reflected in ten audit records, we can then roughly compute the rate of occurrence of audit records reflecting truly intrusive activity as

$$\frac{2\frac{\text{intrusions}}{\text{day}}\bullet 10\frac{\text{record}}{\text{intrusion}}}{10^6\frac{\text{records}}{\text{day}}}=0.00002$$

Interpreting this as a "probability of occurrence of intrusive records," we denote this as $P(I)$; that is, event I is the occurrence of a record reflecting truly intrusive behaviour. Since $P(I) = 0.00002$, we also know that $P(\neg I) = 1 - P(I) = 0.99998$. Now let A denote the event of the IDS raising an alarm. An accurate IDS should maximize both $P(I|A)$ and $P(\neg I|\neg A)$, that is, the probabilities that an alarm indicates an intrusion and no alarm indicates no intrusion. Focusing on $P(IA)$ for the moment, we can compute this using **Bayes' theorem:**

$$P(I|A)=\frac{P(I)\cdot P(A|I)}{P(I)\cdot P(A|I)+P(\neg I)\cdot P(A|\neg I)}=\frac{0.00002\cdot P(A|I)}{0.00002\cdot P(A|I)+0.99998\cdot P(A|\neg I)}$$

Now consider the impact the fails-alarm rate $P(A\neg I)$ on $P(I|A)$. Even with a very good, true, alarm-rate $P(A|I) = 0.8$, a seemingly good false-alarm rate $P(A\neg I) = 0.0001$ yields $P(I|A) \approx 0.14$ That is, fewer than one in every seven alarms indicates a real intrusion! In systems where a security administrator investigates each alarm, this rate of false alarms is exceedingly wasteful and would quickly teach the administrator to ignore alarms.

This example illustrates a general principle for IDSs: For usability, an IDS must offer an extremely low false-alarm rate. Achieving a sufficiently low false, alarm rate is a serious challenge for anomaly-detection systems, because of the difficulties of adequately benchmarking normal system behaviour. However, research continues to make advances in anomaly detection.

Auditing and Logging (Method of Intrusion Detection)

A common method of instruction detection is **audit-trail processing,** in which security-relevant events are logged to an audit-trail and then matched against attack signatures (in signature-based detection) or analyzed for anomalous behaviour (in anomaly detection). On UNIX systems, a simple pair of programs that can be used to create and analyze audit trails, and initiate responses, are `syslog` and `swatch`. The program syslog creates audit trails and provides a dispatching facility for security-relevant messages. The program swatch applies simple signature-based detection to syslog audit trails as they are created and initiates responses as indications of intrusions are found.

When `syslog` is installed on a UNIX system, a daemon process called `syslogd` is created at system `startup`. Process `syslogd` waits for messages from various possible sources and dispatches them as instructed in the `syslog.conf` configuration file (usually in the */etc/* directory).The process `syslogd` can be set up to accept messages from a range of different sources, by default including the streams log driver */dew/log*, but also from other sources including over a network from other machines. The file `syslogd.conf` consists of pairs, each containing a selector field and an action field. The selector field identifies the messages to which the corresponding action should be applied. The types of actions that can be applies to messages include sending the message to a file, to a list of users, to the `syslogd` daemons on other machines, or a program via a UNIX pipe. As such, `syslogd` provides a centralized facility by which various security-relevant messages can be dispatched.

The `swatch` program, as of April, 2001, is available on the web from http://www.stanford .edu/~atkins/swatch/. It processes messages dispatched to it by the `syslogd` daemon (or other logging programs) and initiates activities when certain patterns are detected. These messages need not be dispatched to `swatch` directly, but may be written to a file that `swatch` reads and analyzes. The `swatch` program matches each audit message against regular expressions listed in a configuration file. With each regular expression, actions to be taken if a match occurs are also listed. Allowable actions include echoing a line to `swatch's` controlling terminal, ringing a bell at `swatch's` controlling terminal, sending a message to a user list via email or the write command, or executing a program with arguments drawn from the audit message.

Each regular expression listed in the `swatch` configuration file can be viewed as a primitive signature for use in signature-based intrusion detection. For example, a useful signature might match any string containing "permission denied" and instruct that a bell signal be directed to `swatch's` controlling terminal. However, the signatures supported by `swatch` are fairly rudimentary, since they are applied to only a single audit message at a time. Attack signatures comprised of multiple actions that would typically be reflected across multiple audit messages will not be detected by this approach commercial audit-trail-processing tolls tend to offer richer processing capabilities.

Tripwire

An example of a simple anomaly detection tool is the **Tripwire file** system integrity-checking tool for UNIX, developed at Purdue University. Tripwire operates on the premise that a large class of intrusions result in anomalous modification of system directories and files. For example, an attacker might modify the */etc/passwd* file of a system to enable the intruder to gain access easily in the future. An intruder might modify system programs, perhaps inserting copies with Trojan horse, or insert new programs into directories commonly found in user shell search paths. Or an intruder might remove system log files to over his tracks. Tripwire is a tool to monitor file systems for added, deleted, or changed files, and to alert system administrators to these modifications.

The operation of Tripwire is controlled by a configuration file `tw.config` that enumerates the directories and files to be monitored for changes, deletions, or additions. Each entry in this configuration file includes a selection mask to specify the file attributes (inode attributes) to monitor for changes. For example, the selection mask might specify that a file's permissions be monitored but its access time be ignored. In addition, the selection mask can instruct that the file contents, or more specifically the result of applying a predefined hash function to the contents, of the file, be monitored for changes. Tripwire offers several different collision-resistant hash functions for this purpose where a hash function f is collision-resistant if, given the result $f(x)$ when applying f to an input file x, it is computationally infeasible to compute a different file x' such that $f(x')$. Thus, monitoring the hash of a file for changes is as good as monitoring the file itself, but string hashes of files requires far less room than copying the files themselves.

When run initially, Tripwire takes as input the tw.config file and computes a signature for each file or directory consisting of its monitored attributes (inode attributes and hash values). These signatures are stored in a database. When run subsequently, Tripwire inputs both tw.config and the previously stored database, recomputes the signature for each file or directory named in tw.config, and compares this signature to the signature (if any) in the previously computed database. Events reported to an administrator include any monitored file or directory whose signature differs from that in the database (a change file), any file or directory in a monitored directory for which a signature does not exist in the database (an added file), and any signature in the database for which the corresponding file or directory no longer exists (a deleted file).

Although effective for a wide class of attacks, Tripwire does have limitations. Perhaps the most obvious is the need to protect the Tripwire program and associated files, in particular the database file, from unauthorized modification. For this reason, Tripwire and its associated files should be stored on some tamper-proof media, such as a write-protected disk or a secure server where logins can be tightly controlled. Unfortunately, this makes it less convenient to update the database after authorized updates to monitored directories and files. A second limitation is that some security-relevant files are *supposed* to change over time, for example, system log files, and Tripwire does not provide a way to distinguish between an authorized and unauthorized change. So, for example, an attack that modifies (without deleting) a system log that would normally change anyway would escape Tripwire's detection capabilities. The best Tripwire can do in this case is to detect certain obvious inconsistencies (for example if the log file shrinks) free and commercial versions of Tripwire are available.

System-Call Monitoring

A more speculative and recent form of anomaly detection is system-call monitoring. This approach monitors process system calls to detect in real time when a process is deviating from its expected system-call behaviour. It leverages the fact that a program implicitly defines the sequences of system calls that it can make, as determined by the set of possible execution paths through the program. For large and complex programs, the set of possible system-call sequences will be enormous and may not be easily determined, much less stored explicitly. Nevertheless, this approach attempts to characterize "usual" system-call behaviour in an abbreviated form so that actual system-call traces can be compared against this characterization to detect anomalous behaviour. A type of intrusion that might be detected this way are attacks that *take over* the process—for example, by exploiting a buffer-overflow vulnerability in the process' program—and then cause the process to execute the attacker's code rather than the original program code. If the attacker's code induces an anomalous system-call sequence, then the intrusion detection system should detect this and take action (for example, kill the process).

One example of this approach, for UNIX processes, was initiated at the University of New Mexico. In this approach, the "usual" system-call sequence for a program is generated by running the program on various inputs, both actual user inputs and inputs designed to elicit a range of behaviours from the program. The system-call sequences thus generated (ignoring parameters) are recorded. For example, one such sequence might be:

```
open, read, mmap, mmap, open, getrlimit, mmap, close
```

This sequence is then used to populate a table indicating, for each system call, which system calls can follow it at a distance of one, two, etc., up to some distance k. For example, suppose we choose $k = 3$. Then, examining the first open, we see that `read` follows at distance one, and `mmap` follows at distances two and three. Similarly, `mmap` follows the `read` at distances one and two, and open follows at distance three. Performing this exercise for each system call,

This table is then stored. During subsequent executions of the program, the system-call sequence is compared to this table to detect discrepancies. For example, if the sequence

```
open, read, mmap, open, open, getrlimit, mmap, close
```

is observed (that is, one mmap is replaced with an open), then the following discrepancies are noted: open follows open at a distance of three; open follows read at a distance of two; open follows open at a distance of one; and `getrlimit` follows open at a distance of two. Whether the IDS determines that this behaviour indicates an intrusion might depend on the number of discrepancies observed—perhaps as a fraction of the total possible number of discrepancies—or on the particular system calls involved.

This approach and others like it have been applies primarily to root processes, such as sendmail, in an attempt to detect intrusions. Root processes are an attractive target for its technique because they typically have a limited set of behaviours and do not change often. In addition, they are common targets for attackers because of their privileged status and because, in the case of network services that accept communication over the network, they can easily be probed by attackers from a distance.

System call	distance = 1	distance = 2	distance = 3
	read getrlimit	mmap	mmap close
read	mmap	mmap	open
mmap	mmap open close	open getrlimit	getrlimit mmap
getrlimit	mmap	close	
close			

Fig. 19.3. Data structure derived from system-call sequence.

Cryptography Technique

In an isolated computer, the operating system can reliably determine the sender and recipient of all interprocess communication, since it controls all communication channels in the computer. In a network of computers, the situation is quite different. A networked computer receives bits *from the wire* with no immediate and reliable way of determining what machine or application sent those bits.Similarly, the computer sends bits onto the network with no way of knowing who might eventually receive them.

Commonly, network addresses are used to infer the potential senders and receivers of network messages. Network packets arrive with a source address, such as an IP address. And when a computer sends a message, it names the intended receiver by specifying a destination address. However, for applications where security matters, we are asking for trouble if we assume that the source on destination address of a packet reliably determines who sent or receives that packet. A rogue computer can send a message with a falsified source address, and numerous computers other than the one specified by the destination address can (and typically do) receive a packet. For example, all of the routers on the way to the destination will *receive* the packet, too. How, then is an operating system to decide whether to grant a request to write a file when it can't trust the named source of the request? And how is it supposed to provide read protection for a file when it cannot determine who will receive the file contents it sends over the network?

It is generally considered infeasible to build a network of any scale in which the source and destination addresses of packets can be *trusted* in this sense. Therefore, the only alternative is somehow to eliminate the need to trust the network. This is the job of cryptography. Abstractly, **cryptography** is used to constrain the potential senders and receivers of a message. Modern **cryptography** is based on secrets called **keys** that are selectively distributed to computers in a network and used to process messages. Cryptography enables a recipient of a message to verify that the message was created by some computer possessing a certain key—the key is the *source* of the message. Similarly, a sender can encode its message so that only a computer with a certain key can decode the message, so that the key becomes the *destination*. Unlike network addresses, however, keys are designed to be computationally infeasible to derive from the messages they were used to generate and from any other public information. Thus, they provide a much more trustworthy means of constraining senders and receivers of messages.

Authentication (Algorithm, Message Authentication Code)

Constraining the set of potential senders of a message is called *authentication*. An authentication algorithm enables the recipient of a message to verify that a message was created by some computer possessing a certain key. More precisely, an authentication algorithm consists of the following components:

- A set K of keys.
- A set M of messages.
- A set of authenticators.
- A function $S: K \rightarrow (M \rightarrow A)$. that is, for each $k \in K$, $S(k)$ is a function for generating authenticators from messages. Both S and $S(k)$ for any k should be efficiently computable functions.
- A function $V: K \rightarrow (M \times A \rightarrow \{\text{true, false}\})$. That is, for each $k \in K$, $V(k)$ is a function for verifying authenticators on messages. Both V and $V(k)$ for any k should be efficiently computable functions.

The critical property that an authentication algorithm must possess is: For a message m, a computer can generate an authenticator $a \in A$ such that $V(k)(m,a)$ = true only if it possesses $S(k)$. Thus, a computer holding $S(k)$ can generate authenticators on messages so that any other computer possessing $V(k)$ can verify them. However, a computer not holding $S(k)$ is unable to generate authenticators on messages that can be verified using $V(k)$. Since authenticators are generally exposed (for example, they are sent on the network with the messages themselves), $S(k)$ must be infeasible to derive from the authenticators.

Authentication algorithms come in two main varieties. In a **message authentication code (MAC),** knowledge of $V(k)$ and knowledge of $S(k)$ are equivalent: one can be derived from the other. For this reason, it is as important to protect $V(k)$ as it is to protect $S(k)$. A simple example of a MAC defines $S(k)(m) = f(k,m)$ where f is a function that is one-way on its first argument (that is, its first argument cannot be derived from its output) and collision-resistant on its second [that is , it is infeasible to find an $m' \neq m$ such that $f(k,m) = f(k,m')$]. A suitable verification algorithm is then $V(k)(m,a) \equiv f(k,m) = a$. Note that k is needed to compute both $S(k)$ and $V(k)$; that is, anyone able to compute one can compute the other.

The second main type of authentication algorithm is a **digital signature** algorithm, and the authenticators thus produced are called *digital signatures*. In a *digital signature* algorithm, it is computationally infeasible to derive $S(k)$ from $V(k)$ and, in particular, V is a one-way function. Thus, $V(k)$ need not be kept secret and can be widely distributed. For this reason, $V(k)$ is called the **public key**, and conversely $S(k)$ (or just k) is the **private key.** Here we will describe one digital signature algorithm known as *RSA* after the names of its inventors. In the RSA scheme, the key k is a pair $\langle d, N\rangle$ where N is the product of two large, randomly chosen prime numbers p and q (for example, p and q are 512 bits each). The signature algorithm is $S(\langle d, N\rangle)(m) = f(m)^d \bmod N$ where f is a collision-resistant function. The verification algorithm is then $V(\langle d, N\rangle)(m,a) \equiv [a^e \bmod N = f(m)]$ where e satisfies $ed \bmod (p-1)(q-1) = 1$.It is widely believed to be computationally infeasible for a computer possessing $V(\langle d, N\rangle)$ (that is, possessing $\langle e, N\rangle$ but not d) to generate $S(\langle d,N\rangle)$ (that is, d).

Encryption (Complementary of Authentication)

Encryption is a means for constraining the possible receivers of a message. Encryption is thus complementary to authentication, and to emphasize this we will provide a parallel treatment of it. An encryption algorithm enables the sender of a message to enforce that only a computer possessing a certain key can read the message. More precisely an encryption algorithm consists of the following components:

- A set K of keys.
- A set M of messages.
- A set C of ciphertexts.
- A function $E: K \rightarrow (M \rightarrow C)$. That is, for each $k \in K$, $E(k)$ is a function for generating ciphertexts from messages. Both E and $E(k)$ for any k should be efficiently computable functions.
- A function $D: K \rightarrow (C \rightarrow M)$. That is, for each $k \in K$, $D(k)$ is a function for generating messages from ciphertexts. Both D and $D(k)$ for any k should be efficiently computable functions.

The essential property that an encryption algorithm must provide is that given a ciphertext $c \in C$, a computer can compute m such that $E(k)(m) = c$ only if it possesses $D(k)$. Thus, a computer holding $D(k)$ can decrypt ciphertexts to the plaintexts used to produce them. However, a computer not holding $D(k)$ is unable to decrypt ciphertexts. Since ciphertexts are generally exposed (for example, they are sent on the network), it is important that it be infeasible to derive $D(k)$ from the ciphertexts.

Just as there are two types of authentication algorithms, there are two main types of encryption algorithms. In the first type, called a **symmetric encryption algorithm,** $E(k)$ can be derived from $D(k)$ and vice versa. therefore, the secrecy of $E(k)$ must be protected to the same extent as $D(k)$. For the past 20 years or so, the most commonly used symmetric encryption algorithm in the U.S. for civilian applications has been the **data encryption standard (DES)** adopted by the National Institute of Standards and Technology (NIST). However, as of April, 2001, DES is considered insecure for many applications because its keys, of 56 bits in length, can be exhaustively searched with moderate computing resources. NIST is thus engaged in adopting a new encryption algorithm, called the **advanced encryption standard (AES),** to replace the DES. The AES algorithm is to be chosen this year.

In an **asymmetric encryption algorithm**, it is computationally infeasible to derive $D(k)$ from $E(k)$, and so $E(k)$ need not be kept secret and can be widely disseminated; $E(k)$ is the public key, and $D(k)$ (or just k) is the private key. Interestingly, the mechanism underlying then RSA signature algorithm can also be used to yield an asymmetric encryption algorithm. Again, the key k is a pair (d, N) where N is the product of two large, randomly chosen prime numbers p and q. The encryption algorithm is $E(\langle d, N\rangle)(m) = m^e \bmod N$ where e, d and N are as before. The decryption algorithm is then $D(\langle d, N\rangle)(c) = c^d \bmod N$.

An Example: SSL

SSL 3.0 is a cryptographic protocol that enables two computers to communicate securely, that is, so that each can limit the sender and receiver of messages to the other. It is perhaps the most commonly used cryptographic protocol on the Internet today, since it is the standard protocol by which web browsers communicate securely with web servers. SSL is a complex protocol with many options. Here we will present only a single variation of it, and even then in a very simplified and abstract form, so as to maintain focus on its use of cryptographic primitives.

The SSK protocol is initiated by a *client* to communicate securely with a *server*. Prior to the protocol, the *server* s is assumed have obtained a **certificate**, denoted cert_s, from another party called a **certification authority** *CA*. This certificate is a structure containing the following:

- Various attributes attrs of the server, such as its unique *distinguished* name and its *common* (DNS) name;
- A public encryption algorithm $E(k_s)$ for the server;
- A validity interval interval during which the certificate should be considered valid;
- A digital signature a on the above information by the *CA*, that is, $a = S(k_{CA})(\langle \text{attrs}, E(k_s), \text{interval}\rangle)$.

Prior to the protocol, the client is presumed to have obtained the public verification algorithm $V(k_{CA})$ for *CA*. In the case of the web, the user's browser is shipped from its vendor containing the verification algorithms of certain certification authorities. The user can add or delete the verification algorithms for certification authorities as she chooses.

When a client c connects to s, it sends a 28-byte random values n_c to the server. s responds with a random value n_s of its own, plus its certificate cert_s. The client verifies that $V(k_{CA})(\langle \text{attrs}, E(k_s), \text{interval}\rangle, a) = \text{true}$ and that the current time is in the validity interval interval. If both of these test are satisfied, then the client generates a random 46-byte **premaster secret** pms and sends cpms =

$E(k_s)$(pms) to the server. The server recovers pms = $D(k_s)$(cpms). Now both in possession of n_c, n_s and pms, the client and server can each compute a shared 48-byte **master secret** ms = $f(n_c, n_s,$ pms), where f is a one-way and collision-resistant function. Only the server and client can compute ms, since only they know pms. Moreover, the dependence of ms on n_c an n_s ensures that ms is a *fresh* values, that is, that it has not been used in a previous protocol run. At this point the client and server both compute the following keys from the master secret ms:

- A symmetric encryption key k_{cs}^{crypt} for encrypting messages from the client to the server
- A symmetric encryption key k_{sc}^{crypt} for encrypting messages from the server to the client
- A MAC generation key k_{cs}^{mac} for generating authenticators on messages from the client to the server
- A MAC generation key k_{sc}^{mac} for generating authenticators on messages from the server to the client

To send a message m to the server, the client sends:

$$c = E(k_{cs}^{crypt})(\langle m, S(k_{cs}^{mac})(m)\rangle).$$

Upon receiving c, the server recovers

$$\langle m, a\rangle = D(k_{cs}^{crypt})(c)$$

and accepts m if $V(k_{cs}^{mac})(m,a)$ = true. Similarly, to send a message m to the client, the server sends.

$$c = E(k_{sc}^{crypt})(\langle m, S(k_{sc}^{mac})(m)\rangle)$$

and the client recovers

$$\langle m, a\rangle = D(k_{sc}^{crypt})(c)$$

and accepts m if $V(k_{sc}^{mac})$ (m,a) = true.

This protocol enables the server to limit the recipients of its messages to the client that generated pms, and the senders of the messages it accepts to that same client. Similarly, the client can limit the recipients of the messages it sends and the sender of the messages it accepts to the party that knows $S(k_s)$ (that is, the party who could decrypt pms). In many applications, such as web transactions, the client needs to verify who the party knowing $S(k_s)$ is. This is one purpose of the certificate cert$_s$, in particular, the attrs field contains information that the client can use to determine the identity—for example, the domain name—of the server with which it is communicating. For applications in which the server also needs information about the client, SSL supports an option by which a client can send a certificate to the server.

Use of Cryptography in Layer Architecture

Network protocols are typically organized in layers, each layer acting as a client to the one below it. That is, which one protocol generates a message to send to its protocol peer on another machine, it hands its message to the protocol below it in the network-protocol stack for delivery to its peer on that machine. For example, in an IP network, TCP (a *transport layer protocol*) acts as a client of IP (a *network layer protocol*): TCP packets are passed down to IP for delivery to the TCP peer at the other end of the TCP connection. IP encapsulates the TCP packet in an IP packet, which it similarly passes down to the *data link layer* to be transmitted across the network to its IP peer on the destination computer. This IP peer then delivers the TCP packet up to the TCP peer on that machine. All in all, the OSI Reference Model, which has been almost universally adopted for data networking, defines seven such protocol layers. Any good networking book will cover this in detail.

Cryptography can be inserted at almost any layer in this model. SSL provides security at the transport layer. Network-layer security that has been standardized (or **IPSec**) defined IP packet formats that allow the insertion of authenticators and the encryption of packet contents. IPSec is becoming widely used as the basis for **virtual private networks.** Numerous protocols also have been developed for applications to use.

In general, there is no definitive answer as to where cryptographic protection is best placed in a protocol stack. On the one hand, more protocols benefit from protections placed lower in the protocol stack. For example, since IP packets encapsulate TCP packets, encryption of IP packets (using IPSec, for example) also hides the contents of the encapsulated TCP packet. Similarly, authenticators on IP packets detect the modification of contained TCP header information.

On the other hand, protection at lower layers in the protocol stack may give insufficient protection to higher-layer protocols. For example, an application server that runs over IPSec might be able to authenticate the client computers from which requests are received. However, in order to authenticate the user at that client computer, an application-level protocol—for example, involving the user typing a password—may need to be used.

Computer-Security Classifications

The U.S. Department of Defense Trusted Computer System Evaluation Criteria specify four divisions of security in systems: A, B, C, and D. The lowest-level classification is division D, or minimal protection. Division D comprises only one class, and is used for systems that failed to meet the requirements of any one of the other security classes. For instance, MS-DOS and Windows 3.1 are in division D.

Division C, the next level of security, provides discretionary protection and accountability of users and their actions through the use of audit capabilities. Division C has two levels: C1 and C2. A C1-class system incorporates some form of controls that allow users to protect private information and to keep other users from accidentally reading or destroying their data. A C1 environment is one in which cooperating users access data at the same levels of sensitivity. Most versions of UNIX are C1 class.

The sum total of all protection systems within a computer system (hardware, software, firmware) that correctly enforce a security policy is known as a **Trusted Computer Base** (TCB). The TCB of a C1 system controls access between users and files by allowing the user to specify and control sharing of objects by named individuals or defined groups. In addition, the TCB requires that the user identify himself before he starts any activities that the TCB is expected to mediate. This identification is accomplished via a protected mechanism or password; the TCB protects the authentication data so that they are inaccessible to unauthorized users.

A C2-class system adds to be requirements of a C1 system via an individual-level access control. For example, access rights of a file can be specified to the level of a single individual. In addition, the system administrator is capable of selectively auditing the actions of any one or more users based on individual identity. The TCB also protects itself from modification of its code or data structures. In addition, no information produced by a prior user is available to another user who accesses a storage object that has been released back to the system. Some special, secure versions of UNIX have been certified at the C2 level.

Division-B mandatory-protection systems have all the properties of a class C2 system, plus they attach sensitivity labels to each object. The B1 class TCB maintains the security label of each object in the system; the label is used for decisions pertaining to mandatory access-control. For example, a user at confidential level could not access a file at the more sensitive secret level. The TCB also denotes the sensitivity level at the top and bottom of each page of any human-readable output. In addition to the normal user name-password authentication information, the TCB also maintains the clearance and authorizations of individual users and will support at least two levels of security. These levels are hierarchical, such that a user may access any objects that carry sensitivity labels equal to or lower than his security clearance. For example, a secret-level user could access a file at the confidential level in the absence of other access controls. Processes are also isolated through the use of distinct address spaces.

A B2-class system extends the sensitivity labels to each system resource such as storage objects. Physical devices are assigned minimum and maximum-security levels that the system uses to enforce constraints imposed by the physical environments in which the devices are located. In addition, a B2 system supports covert channels and the auditing of events that may lead to the exploitation of a covert channel.

A B3-calss system allows the creation of access-control lists that denote users or groups *not* granted access to a given named object. The TCB also contains a mechanism to monitor events that may indicate a violation of security policy. The mechanism notifies the security administrator and, if necessary, terminates the event in the least disruptive manner.

The highest-level classification is division A. A class-A1 system is functionally equivalent to a B3 system architecturally, but uses fromal design specifications and verification techniques, granting a high degree of assurance that the TCB has been implemented correctly. A system beyond class A1 might be designed and developed in a trusted facility by trusted personnel.

The use of a TCB merely ensures that the system can enforce aspects of a security policy; the TCB does not specify what the policy should be. Typically, a given computing environement develops a security policy for certification and has the plan accredited by a security agency, such as the National Computer Security Center. Certain computing environments may require other certification, such as by TEMPEST, which guards against electronic eavesdropping. For example, a TEMPEST-certified system has terminals that are shielded to prevent electromagnetic fields from escaping. This shielding ensures that equipment outside the room or building where the terminal is housed cannot detect what information is being displayed by the terminal.

An Example: Windows NT

Microsoft Windows NT is a relatively new operating system designed to support a variety of security features and levels that range from minimal security to a U.S. government level-C2 security classification. The default security level that NT uses could be described as minimal, but it can be readily configured by the system administrator to the desired level. A utility program, is provided to help the administrator choose the desired security settings. In this section, we examine features that Windows NT uses to perfrom security functions. For more information and background on Windows NT.

The NT security model is based in the notion of **user accounts.** NT allows the creation of any number of user accounts that can be grouped in any manner. Access to system objects can then be permitted or denied as desired. Users are identified to the system by a *unique* Security ID. When a user logs on, NT creates a **security access token** that includes the Security ID for the users, Security IDs for any groups in which the user is a member, and a list of any special privileges that the user has. Examples of special privileges include backing up files and directories, shutting down the computer, logging on interactively, and changing the system clock. Every process that NT runs on behalf of a user will get a copy of the access token. The system uses the Security IDs in the access token to permit or deny access to system objects whenever the user, or a process on behalf of the user, attempts to access the object. Authentication of a user account is typically accomplished via a user name and password, although the modular design of NT allows the development of custom authentication packages. For example, a retinal (or eye) scanner might be used to verify that the user is who she says she is.

NT uses the idea of a subject to ensure that programs that a user runs do not get greater access to the system than the user is authorized to have. A subject is used to track and mange permissions for each program that a user runs, and is composed of the user's access token and the program acting on behalf of the user. Since NT operates with a client-server model, two classes of subjects are used to control access. An example of a **simple subject** is the typical application program that a user executes after he logs on. The simple subject is simply assigned a **security context** based on the security access token of the user. A **server subject** is a process implemented as a protected server that uses the security context of the client when acting on the client's behalf. The technique that allows one process to take on the security attributes of another is called **impersonation.**

Auditing is a useful security technique. NT has auditing built in, and allows many common security threats to be monitored. Examples of auditing that can be used to track threats are failure auditing of logon and logoff events to detect random password break-ins, success auditing for logon and logoff events to detect logon activity at strange hours, success and failure write-access auditing for executable files to track a virus outbreak, and success and failure auditing for file access to detect access to sensitive files.

Security attributes of an object in NT are described by a **security descriptor**. The security descriptor contains the Security ID of the owner of the object (who can change the access permissions), group Security ID used only by the POSIX subsystem, a discretionary access-control list that identifies which users or groups are allowed/not allowed access, and a system access control list that controls which auditing messages the system will generate. For example, the security descriptor of the file *foo.bar* might have owner avi and this discretionary access-control list:

- avi—all access
- group cs—read-write access
- user cliff—no access.

In addition, it might have a system access-control list of audit writes by everyone. An access-control list is composed of access-control entries that contain the Security ID of the individual, and an access mask that defines all possible actions on the object, with a value of AccessAllowed or AccessDenied for each action. Files in NT may have the following access types: `ReadData`, `writeData`, `AppendData`, `Execute`, `ReadExtendedAttribute`, `WriteExtendedAttribute`, `ReadAttributes`, and `WriteAttributes`. We can see how this allows a fine degree of control over access to objects.

NT classifies objects as either container objects or noncontainer objects. **Container objects**, such a directories, can logically contain other objects. By default, when an object is created within a container object, the new object inherits permissions from the parent object. It does so as well if the user copies a file from one directory to a new directory—the file will inherit the permissions of the destination directory. **Noncontainer objects** inherit no other permissions.

However, if a permission is changed on a directory, the new permissions do not automatically apply to existing files and subdirectories; the user may explicitly apply them if she so desires. Also, if the user moves a file into a new directory the current permissions of the file move with it.

In addition, the system administrator can prohibit printing to a printer on the system for all or part of a day and can use the NT Perfromance Monitor to help her spot approaching problems. In general, NT does a good job of providing features to help ensure a secure computing environment. Many of these features are not enables by default, however, to provide an environment close to the one to which the typical personal-computer user is accustomed. For a real Multiuser environment, the system administrator should fromulate a security plan and implement it, using the features that NT provides.

Summary

Protection is an internal problem. Security must consider both the computer system and the environment—people, buildings, businesses, valuable objects, and threats—within which the system is used.

The data stored in the computer system must be protected from unauthorized access, malicious destruction or alteration, and accidental introduction of inconsistency. It is easier to protect against accidental loss of data consistency than to protect against malicious access to the data. Absolute protection of the information stored in a computer system from malicious abuse is not possible, but the cost to the perpetrator can be made sufficiently high to deter most, if not all, attempts to access that information without proper authority.

The various authorization provisions in a computer system may not confer sufficient protection for highly sensitive data. In such cases, data may be encrypted. It is not possible for encrypted data to be read unless the reader knows how to decipher (or decrypt) the encrypted data.

There are several authentication methods beyond standard username and password protection. One-time passwords change the sent data each time to avoid replay attacks. Two-factor authentication requires two forms of authentication, such as a hardware calculator with an activation PIN. Along with biometric devices, these methods greatly decrease the chance of authentication forgery.

There are several types of attacks that can be launched against individual computers or the masses. Viruses and worms are self-perpetuating, sometimes infecting thousands of computers.

Stack and buffer overflow allow a successful attacker to change their level of system access. Denial-of-service attacks prevent legitimate use of target systems.

There are several methods of prevention of detection of security incidents. These include intrusion-detection systems, auditing and logging of system events, monitoring of system software changes, and system-call monitoring. Cryptography can be used both within a system and between systems to prevent interception of information by hackers.

20

Input/Output Principles and Programming

The input/output system is the part of the operating system charged with management of I/O devices. There is a considerable variety of device types attached to computer systems—each with its own encoding, electrical, and timing requirements. Many of them operate asynchronously from the processor, at rates ranging from just a few data transfers per second to millions of data transfers per second. The input/output system is charged with the difficult task of attending to the individual requirements of I/O devices and providing for their efficient and reliable operation, while hiding device-specific details and presenting a uniform abstraction of generic I/O operations to the outer layers of an operating system and, ultimately, to user programs.

The I/O system acts as an interface between programmers and I/O devices. To users, the I/O system provides a device abstraction in which I/O devices, and possibly files, are treated in a uniform manner and are manipulated by means of a set of high-level commands, such as READ_STRING. Higher-level functions of the input/output system, placed at Level 4 in the sample hierarchy. This chapter introduces the low-level functions of the input/output system, including some details of device control and I/O programming.

Since contemporary hardware has the capability to control many facets of I/O operations autonomously and without direct involvement of the main system processor, significant performance benefits may be attained when input/output devices are operated in concurrent fashion. Concurrent I/O operations is accomplished by initiating a number of independent I/O operations before others in progress are completed. On the other hand, concurrent execution of independent tasks requires careful scheduling of many different code sequences and of time-critical events sensed or caused by input/output devices.

The goal of this chapter is to explore the principles of the input/output subsystem, to study the elements of I/O programming, and to introduce the increasing degrees of concurrent execution of I/O operations that the hardware supports. The detailed treatment of management of multiple devices via polling and hierarchical interrupts provides a foundation for the implementation of a kernel. Readers familiar with the intricacies of interrupt structure and I/O programming, or those only marginally interested in implementation details of the multitasking kernel presented in subsequent chapters, may omit this chapter without loss of continuity.

The Input/Output Problem

In this section we focus on the hardware aspects of the input/output subsystem and stress its unique attributes, which both necessitate specialized programming and make concurrent operations possible.

In general, most I/O devices share two important characteristics that largely define the input/output problem:

1. Asynchronous operation
2. The speed gap

The following sections treat each of these characteristics in detail.

Asynchronous Operation

During program execution, the processor engages in numerous transactions with the main memory and I/O devices in order to fetch instructions for executions and to access data operands. For example, READ operations with both memory and devices are typically initiated by the processor, which, some time later, obtains the required items. However, the timing of memory and that of I/O transactions are fundamentally different.

Except possibly when errors occur, memory is always ready to furnish a datum whose address is designated by the processor. It does so within a nearly constant time, the *memory-access time,* which generally lasts at most a few cycles of the processor clock. In that sense, memory may be regarded as operating synchronously with the processor. Another important observation is that the processor waits until the desired item from memory arrives, as the processor has nothing to do until an instruction or datum is fetched.

Given the need to control asynchronous operation, the hardware of the I/O section includes special control signals that enable the processor and device controllers to indicate to each other their status, intentions, and data availability. These are collectively referred to as *handshaking signals.* Before attempting to obtain a datum from a device, the processor normally queries the device for status by using the handshaking protocols. If the I/O datum is actually available, the processor fetches it from the controller; otherwise the processor has to wait. Since that may be a long wait, the operating system may elect to schedule another program for execution in order to prevent the processor from idling while awaiting completion of I/O transactions. When the I/O operation completes, handshaking signals alert the processor to the fact and cause the operating system to resume the related activity.

The Speed Gap: Processor versus Peripherals

As pointer out, there is a difference of several orders of magnitude in the speeds of I/O devices themselves, and of I/O speed in general, relative to the processor-memory bandwidth. When transmitting continuous streams of data, I/O devices may exhibit rates from the order of less than I cps (characters per second) to the order of several million cps—a variation of more than six orders of magnitude. The low end of the spectrum is represented by slow terminals, switches, and displays; the high end belongs to optical communication links and high-performance disk drives. Very high-speed devices are usually interfaced via specialized I/O channels or dedicated processors. They tend to perform data transfers in blocks using *direct memory-access* (DMA) techniques. In contrast, programmed I/O, which is controlled directly by the processor for each individual character, is often limited to the less demanding devices. In this chapter we mostly concentrate on the latter.

In order to appreciate the speed gap, consider a relatively fast CRT terminal with a normal data-transfer rate of 19,200 kbaud (kilobaud). Many terminals use bit-serial data-transfer techniques, so assuming that one character occupies 10 bits (1 start bit, 8 data bits, and 1 stop bit), the data rate is 1920 cps. In other words, when displaying, say, a long file of text, the computer is able to transmit almost 2000 characters per second to the terminal. In practice, the average data rate is likely to be lower since alphanumeric terminals can rarely process and display characters that quickly. This problem is often solved by incorporating hardware buffers into terminals to smooth the speed differences between the input data rate and the display data rate. As a result, peak data rates can be sustained at least for shorter bursts until the buffer is filled.

In any case, 2000 cps is one character transmission every 500 μs (microseconds). Given a processor with instruction execution times in the neighbourhood of 0.1 μs, after transferring a datum to the terminal, the processor has nearly 500 μs to prepare for the next character before the terminal becomes ready to receive it. Assuming that the processor uses just a few cycles to ready a character, then when servicing a relatively fast (non-DMA) peripheral running at its theoretical speed limit, the processor may be idle well over 99% of the time.

One way to improve processor utilization, that is, the proportion of processor cycles spent doing useful work as opposed to waiting for the I/O device to become ready, is to multiplex the processor among a number of I/O devices. The idea is to reduce idling by assigning some other work to the processor while activated I/O operations are in progress. This approach requires hardware assistance in the I/O section in the form of data buffers and handshaking signals, and event synchronization mechanisms such as interrupts. All of those are described in detail in subsequent sections, after a brief exposition of the structure of the I/O interfaces.

Input/Output Interfaces

Hardware controllers (interfaces) act as intermediaries between the computer system and input/output devices. Their purpose is to bridge the speed and signalling-level incompatibilities between the processor and peripherals, and to translate the generic I/O commands issued by the processor into device-specific controls. In this section we explore the basic architecture of the I/O system from the I/O programmer's point of view and stress the hardware issues most pertinent in that context.

I/O hardware is often physically distributed over a number of device interfaces or controllers (we use these terms interchangeably). This is demonstrated in Figure 20.1, which depicts a block diagram of a computer system. This logical structure is readily identifiable in the physical structure of a computer system, and can be observed by removing the protective cover of one. Usually the hub of the system is the backplane, which houses a number of connectors into which various other boards are plugged. The connectors themselves are connected by a number of parallel signal traces, the *system bus,* which serves as a communication medium for interboard exchanges of address, data, and control pulses. The modules above the system bus in Figure 20.1 depict the processor and memory boards. Our present concern is with the input/output controllers (interfaces), three of which are depicted below the system bus in Figure 20.1. The modules, as shown, are divided according to their function. In actual implementations, several different functional units may be physically integrated on a single printed-circuit board.

As their respective labels indicate, the I/O controllers are in charge of the serial, parallel, and DMA devices. Below each of them, a device of the type that would normally be connected to the respective I/O controller is shown. Many terminals, as well as short- and long-haul communication links, use bit-serial line protocols and thus require serial interfaces for connection to a computer system. The majority of printers need parallel interfaces, which are also popular for connecting switches, relays, LEDs, and other line-oriented displays. Finally, DMA-type interfaces are most commonly used by high-performance, block-oriented storage devices, such as disks and tapes, although any other device that exhibits high transfer rates is a candidate for this type of connection. Some examples include local-area networks and sophisticated terminal multiplexers.

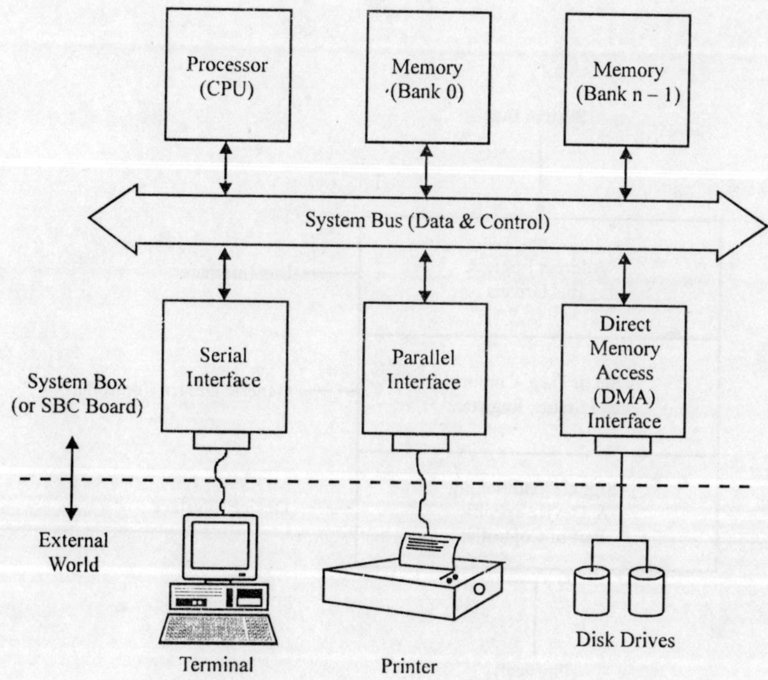

Fig. 20.1. Block structure of a computer system.

An interface board is usually designed to handle one or more devices of the same type or of very similar types. Multiple devices, when supported, are handled either by means of dedicated channels (one per device) or in a daisy-chain fashion. The former method is quite common for terminal controllers, whereas the latter is customary for disk controllers. When the number of similar devices exceeds the capacity of a single controller, more than one controller of the same type may be installed—up to the limit prescribed by the manufacturer. This limit is usually determined by hardware considerations, such as bus loading and the processor's ability to handle the combined throughput at peak loads.

Figure 20.2 represents a very general block diagram of an I/O controller. The controller is divided into three functional layers: (1) bus interface, (2) generic device controller, and (3) device interface. The rationale for the two interface layers is obvious by observing that an I/O controller is positioned between the computer system bus at one end and the I/O device itself at the other. As stated earlier, the I/O section is charged with providing a uniform abstraction of I/O devices to the rest of the system. At the hardware level, this means that, at the system-bus end, each controller must appear as a standard module, capable of participating in all applicable transactions, such as read, write, priority arbitration, interrupt, and DMA cycles. At the device end, the controller must be compatible by providing the specific signals at the required electrical levels. Note that these are device-dependent and typically quite different from the standard computer logic levels. A variety of binary voltage and current levels, and often some analog signals, are required to drive the electromechanical components found in may computer peripheral. This situation normally restricts each individual I/O controller to interface to only a specific collection of functionally similar physical devices.

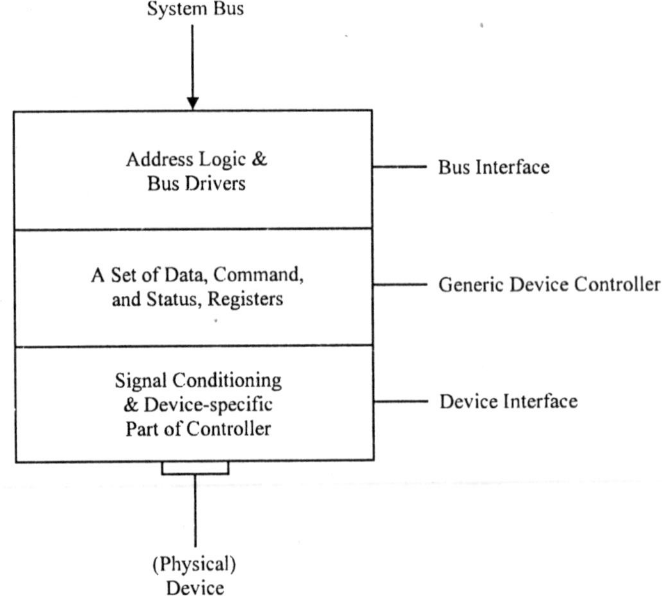

Fig. 20.2. Block structure of an I/O controller.

Although the two described layers are of great concern to hardware designers, the middle layer—the generic device controller—is by far the most important to software designers. It provides a uniform abstraction of I/O devices to systems programmers. In particular, it makes every device appear to be a set of dedicated registers. Status queries, issuing of device-specific I/O commands, and data transfers are all accomplished simply by reading from or writing into these registers. A set of such dedicated registers is usually called an *I/O port.* The more common varieties of I/O ports include parallel ports, serial ports, floppy- and hard-disk controllers, graphic controllers, programmable interval timers, and local-area network controllers. When implemented in LSI or VLSI technology, several I/O ports may be housed in a single integrated circuit.

Figure 20.3 shows the block structure of a typical I/O port. For generality, the port is assumed to be bi-directional, that is, capable of simultaneous data transmission in both input and output directions. A common convention is to interpret the terms *input* and *output* from the processor's point of view. With this convention, *input* refers to data transfers from a device to the processor and *output* denotes communication in the opposite direction. The port in Figure 20.3 is shown as connecting directly to the computer system bus and to the I/O device at its respective ends. Recall from our earlier discussion that some external drivers and receivers may be needed to connect the bus and device to the port. In any event, the most important part of the I/O port's structure is the set of registers that represents the programmer's view of the attached I/O device. The four register types shown in Figure 20.3 represent the major functional categories commonly found in I/O ports:

1. Data registers (input and output buffers)
2. Command registers
3. Status registers

Addresses of I/O ports may be mapped into the memory address space or in a separate address space, called *I/O space.* Consequently, I/O ports are said to be *memory-mapped* or *I/O-mapped*, respectively. I/O-mapped I/O is sometimes referred to as *isolated I/O.* From the programmer's point of view, the primary difference between the two is that memory-mapped I/O ports may be accessed and manipulated like memory, using the full complement of memory-referencing instruction. I/O-mapped ports, on the other hand, must be accessed by means of special hardware instructions, such as IN PORT and OUT PORT, that activate that I/O space address signals.

In general, I/O register manipulation is more efficient in systems where input/output ports are memory-mapped, and the full instruction set—especially bit testing and setting—may use them as source or destination operands. Isolated I/O, due to its separate I/O addressing space, requires copying into the processor registers in order to perform the desired operations, which adds to overhead in I/O processing. Due to its other advantages, such as simplification of address decoders and nonconsumption of the memory address space, isolated I/O is used in some systems. Thus, in addition to knowing the actual physical addresses assigned to I/O ports by hardware in a given system, the programmer must find out into which space they are mapped and use the instructions appropriate to that address space.

Buffer Registers

The primary function of an input buffer is to hold a datum until the processor is ready to accept it. This need arises in multiprogramming systems where a processor is multiplexed among several concurrent activities. As a result, the processor may not always respond instantly to a signal indicating data availability. Because it operates asynchronously, an I/O device may, regardless, produce additional data in the interim. This situation would normally result in lost input characters, as the new data would overwrite the current datum in the buffer before the processor manages to retrieve it. To overcome this problem, I/O controllers contain one or more *buffer* registers that hold a datum in transit until its target destination is ready to accept it.

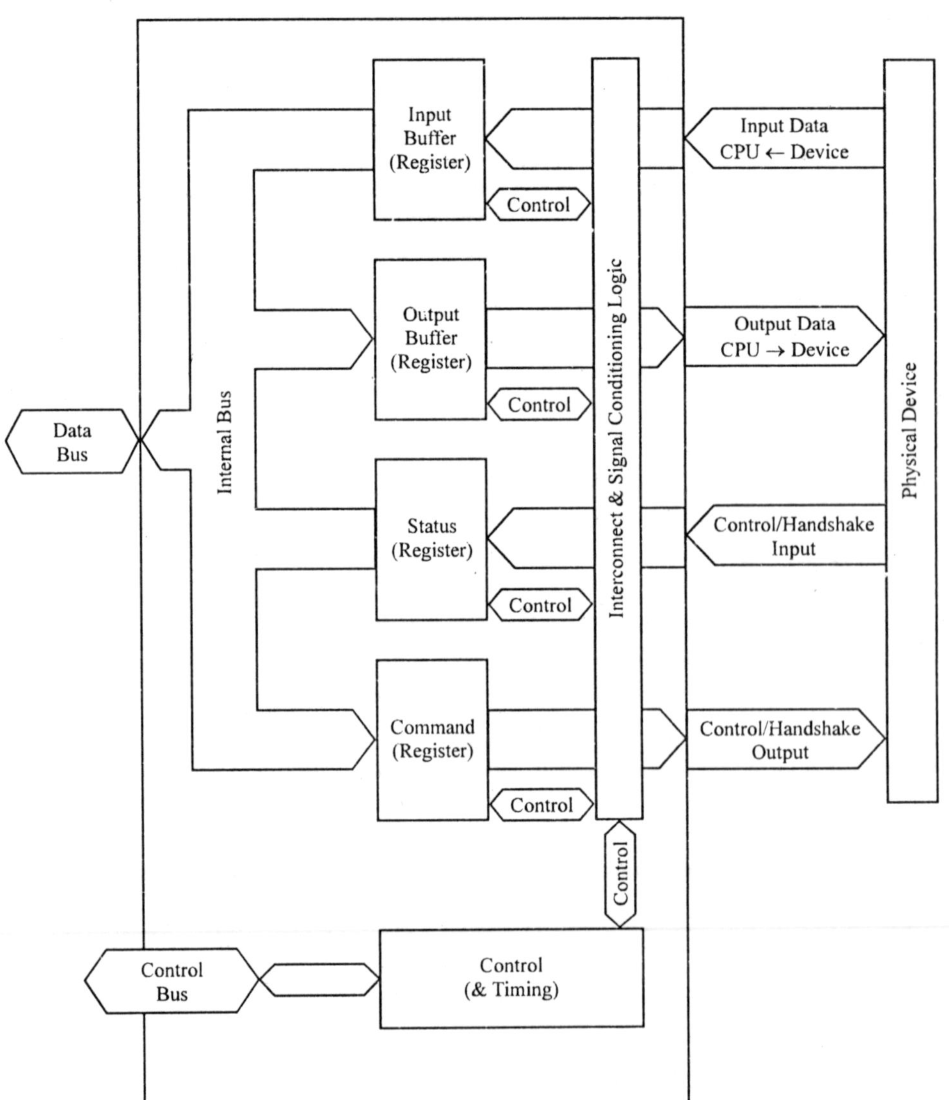

Fig. 20.3. Block structure of an I/O port.

The output buffers primarily serve the purpose of latching the output data written by the processor so that external devices may be provided with steady signals suitable for their timing requirements. Given that the processor is essentially the sender of data, there is usually no notion of lost characters on output as far as it is concerned. In many non-DMA uses, output devices do not require data at a sustained rate. Thus, if the system is not very responsive to an output activity, no characters are lost, and the only potential harm may be to temporarily lower the transfer rate to a specific output device below its maximum acquisition speed. For this reason, multiple buffering is much less frequently used on output than on input. Some I/O ports have provision for output buffering and thus may assist in boosting the output transfer rate if that feature is exploited by the system software. Additional assistance is provided by output devices that contain their own internal buffers in order to boost the peak transfer rate.

Command Registers

Command registers are in charge of transferring I/O commands between a processor and an I/O device. Regardless of the direction of data transfer, the processor usually controls an I/O operation by instructing a device when to perform some action. The processor selects a particular operation from a fixed, device-specific set by writing the corresponding code into the command register. The device usually does not send commands to the processor; it only indicates its current state, which is accessible to the processor via port-status registers.

Commands for a specific device tend to fall into one of two general categories:

1. *Mode-designating commands* select a particular mode of operation, such as input or output, error-checking algorithm, or type of communication protocol. Mode-designating commands are typically issued only once, during the initialization sequence, which is a part of the power-on and reset routines.
2. *Operational I/O commands* govern the timing and mechanics of the actual data transfers. Operational commands cause device-specific control actions, such as enable/disable transmission, seek, read, and write. These commands are issued as often as necessary, which is typically once per data transfer.

A command may occupy a full word, but more often it alters the individual control bits within the command register, leaving other bits unchanged. Serving primarily the processor's need to control devices, command registers are usually write-only registers.

Status Registers

As their name suggests, status registers are used to provide information about the status of the I/O device to the processor. They include such information as device ready or busy, buffer empty or full, and error indications. Status registers are usually implemented as a collection of read-only bits where each bit is associated with some condition, such as READY/NOT_READY. The most common operation on them is testing whether an individual bit is set or not, in order to determine the status of the condition that it represents.

I/O Port Examples

This section describes two representative types of I/O ports—the USART and the interval timer. The intent is to illustrate the use of I/O registers in a realistic setup and to provide a description of I/O operation and hardware from an I/O programmer's point of view.

The Universal Synchronous/Asynchronous Receiver/Transmitter (USART)

The bit-serial mode is used primarily for computer/terminal communication, with or without modems. It is also encountered in numerous varieties of both short- and long-haul communication links and computer networks. The universal synchronous/asynchronous receiver/transmitter (USART) is a LSI/VLSI device that is commonly used to implement serial communication links. A detailed discussion of serial communication and interfacing is beyond the scope of this chapter. Here we just outline the basic notions in order to aid the understanding of the USART's structure as perceived by an I/O programmer.

There are basically two modes of bit-serial data transfer: *asynchronous,* which is used for lower speeds and requires the receiver to synchronize on a character basis using known line speed and start and stop bits appended to each character by the sender, and *synchronous,* where synchronization is performed on a block basis by extracting the timing reference provided by the sender in the data stream itself. Typical USARTs can support either transmission mode; selection is usually made by setting the corresponding bits in the mode register. For the sake of hardware simplicity, in this section we focus on the asynchronous mode of data transmission.

Many USARTs support simultaneous bi-directional data transmission, often called *full duplex.* Depending on the type of connection and the encoding of data, each character consists of 5 to 8 data bits, plus an initial start bit (a 0 bit) and 1 or 2 stop bits (1 bits). The sending USART performs parallel-to-serial conversion and emits data bits on the communication line, one at a time. The duration of each bit on the line is determined by the data rate of the link. The USARTs at both ends must be initialized to run at this rate. The sending USART also appends start and stop bits to each character. They are used for synchronization and error detection by the receiving USART, which subsequently strips them off in order to forward only the data bits to its processor after completion of the serial-to-parallel conversion.

A USART is also capable of verifying the integrity of the received data by means of the parity bit. When the parity control option is activated by setting the corresponding bits in the mode register, a parity bit is appended to each character by the sending USART. Its value is computed on the basis of the number of 1s in the associated data bits, and on the basis of the parity mode selected (odd or even). The receiving USART computes its own value of parity on the basis of the received data bits and the parity mode, if any, in effect. The computed parity bit is then compared to the received parity bit, and any discrepancy is flagged via the status register to indicate a receive error.

Figure 20.4 depicts as asynchronous communication link with *U*(*S*) ARTs at both ends. As shown, system A is transmitting the 7-bit data pattern (1010011 binary) that is the ASCII code for the letter *S*. The corresponding serial bit stream—assuming 7 data bits, even parity, and 1 stop bit -- is shown as it would appear on the line. As indicated, USARTs receive and deliver characters in parallel when interacting with their respective host processors, whereas the values actually transmitted have quite a different format. In particular, start, stop, and parity bits are generated by the sending USART and are inspected and then stripped off by the receiving USART. This is simple example of an I/O interface handling the idiosyncrasies of a specific device and hiding them from the higher levels of hierarchy—the processor and the I/O programmer in particular.

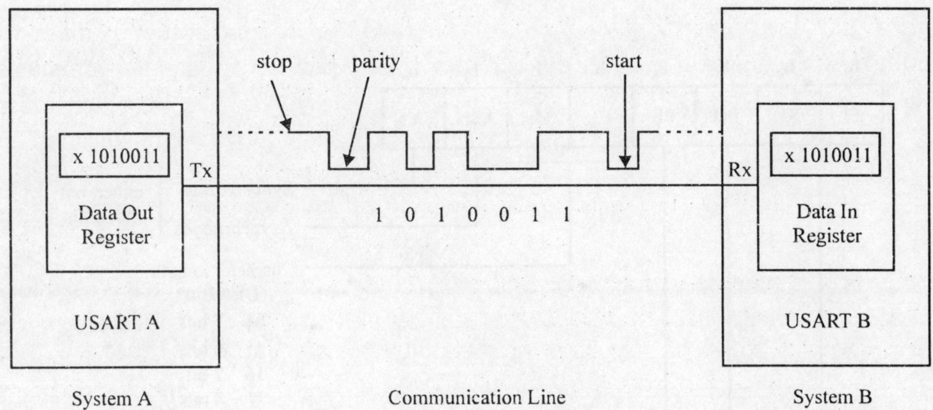

Fig. 20.4. An asynchronous communication link.

From the point of view of the generic I/O controller discussed earlier, a USART consists of input and output buffer registers, command registers, and status registers. Other parts of a USART, which are of lesser importance to a systems programmer, include a fair amount of logic for parallel-to-serial conversions, start- and stop-bit mechanization, parity handling, and character synchronization. The number of input buffers typically varies between two and four, whereas one or two buffers are most common on the output. Command and status registers provide the processor with the means of controlling a USART's operation. Their description is a bit more involved, so let us structure it around the sequence of steps typical for programming a USART.

After a power-up or a software reset, the USART is brought to a known state. The details of this action are product-specific, but the process commonly readies the USART for a mode command that writes into the mode register. As Figure 20.5(a) suggests, communication-line parameters—such as the asynchronous or synchronous operation, number of data bits in a character, even/odd or no parity, and line speed—are selected by setting the mode register. Most of these parameters are characteristics of the communication link and must be set identically in the USARTs at both ends. In general, they must not be changed once the link becomes operational, as any disparity would result in garbled data.

Once initialized, the USART is ready to receive operational commands. These are used to enable or disable reception or transmission of characters, or to enable or disable the interrupt-generating logic that signals character arrivals and output-buffer empty conditions. Now shown in the figure are link-handshaking control bits. They may be used to control a modem, when one is connected, or as a rudimentary line-control protocol in computer-to-computer communication via serial links. In addition, some commands, such as local or remote loopback, may be included for testing purposes. Unlike initialization commands, operational commands may be issued at any time during normal operation.

The status register dynamically indicates the state of input and output buffers, and reception errors. For simplicity, some device-specific features, such as the status of modem-control lines, are not illustrated in Figure 20.5. However, they could be implemented in the unused bits and/or in additional registers.

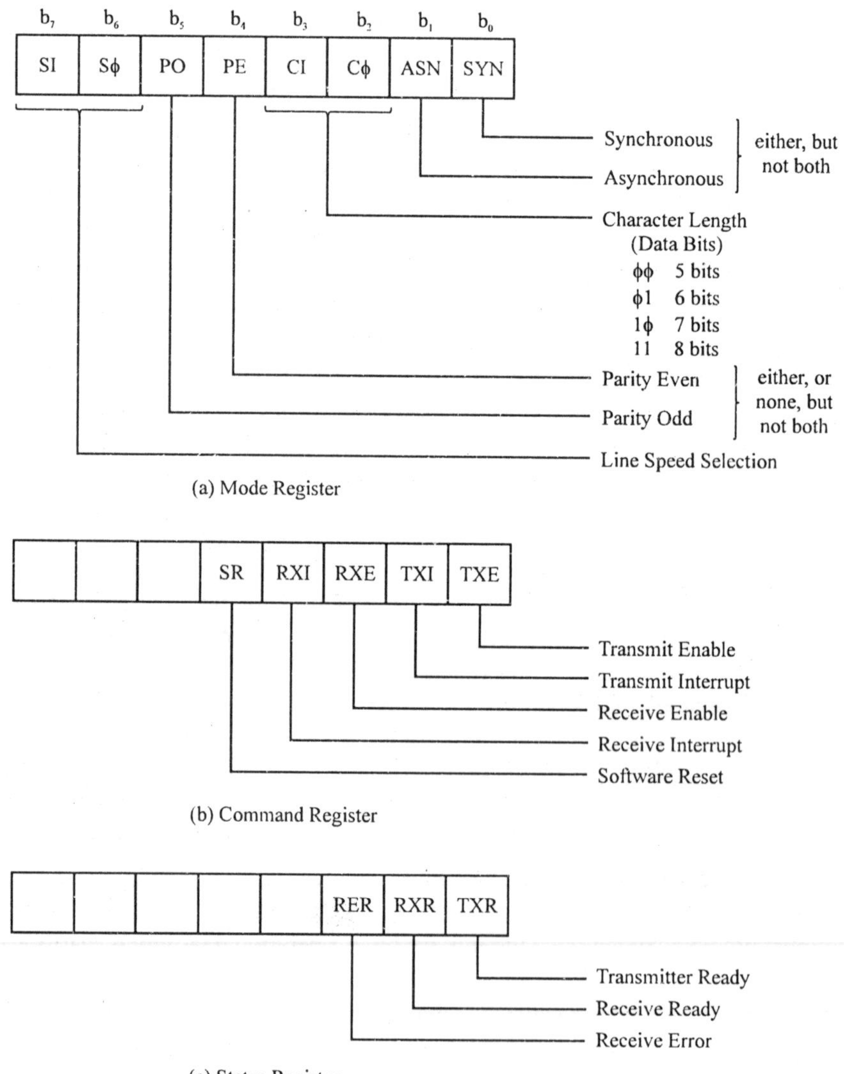

Fig. 20.5. USART registers.

Programmable Interval Timer (PIT)

Programmable interval timers (PITs) contain one or more programmable counters or interval timers. They are capable of counting external pulses and of generating an output signal of programmable shape and duration. These versatile devices may be used as the system time base, a real-time clock (RTC), a baud-rate generator (for USARTs), an event counter, motor control, or a music generator, as well as in numerous other timing and counting applications. In the discussions that follows, we focus on the PIT as a time base and a real-time clock, functions found in virtually all operating systems.

When used for timing purposes, the PIT generates a periodic interrupt that restores control momentarily to an operating system. The PIT does this by counting external pulses provided by a stable clock of known frequency. The PIT's output is usually set for the pulse mode and connected directly to the processor's interrupt-request section. The time period between two successive timer interrupts is programmed by writing a pulse-count constant into the PIT's register. The variables that determine the interrupt interval are the clock period or frequency, and the count constant, according to the formula:

$$\text{Interval} = (\text{Clock period}) \times (\text{Count constant})$$

Most often, the clock frequency and the desired interval are known, leaving the count constant to be calculated. For example, given a 2 MHz clock and a desired timing interval of 20 ms, the count constant is determined as:

$$\text{Clock period} = \frac{1}{2 \times 10^{6}} = \frac{1}{2} \times 10^{-6} = 0.5\mu\text{s}$$

$$\text{Count constant} = \frac{20 \times 10^{-3}}{0.5 \times 10^{-6}} = 40 \times 10^{3}$$

In other words, in order to have a PIT fed by a 2 MHz clock generate a pulse every 20 ms, its respective register should be loaded with the counting constant of 40,000.

From the system programmer's point of view, a PIT is a device that needs initialization and an interrupt service routine. Unlike a USART, no handshaking or extensive status checking is necessary for a PIT. Furthermore, PITs intended for timing applications often include automatic count-register reloading when the register counts down to zero. This reduces the processor's involvement to initialization and mode selection only, and simplifies accurate timekeeping when it is used for the time-of-day application.

A typical PIT contains mode and command registers to which the processor may write in order to control the PIT. Mode commands include selection of the output characteristics. Typically, a count register may produce a single event or may be programmed to produce a periodic event by setting the register for automatic reload. The mode may also select a signal source to count, such as a crystal-clock input, an external input, or the output of another counter register. Operational commands are usually limited to START COUNTING and STOP COUNTING. The processor can also query a PIT for status and read the running count of a specified timer. Given the common presence of several independent counters on a chip, command registers usually include some provision for addressing them individually.

Program-Controlled I/O

This section presents the basic principles of I/O programming. It begins with a simple case of a single I/O device using the program-controlled I/O method. A more realistic situation involving the control of multiple devices is discussed later on.

Controlling a Single Device

A typical program-controlled input transaction is illustrated in Figure 20.6. Output transactions consist of the same basic steps in a slightly permuted order.

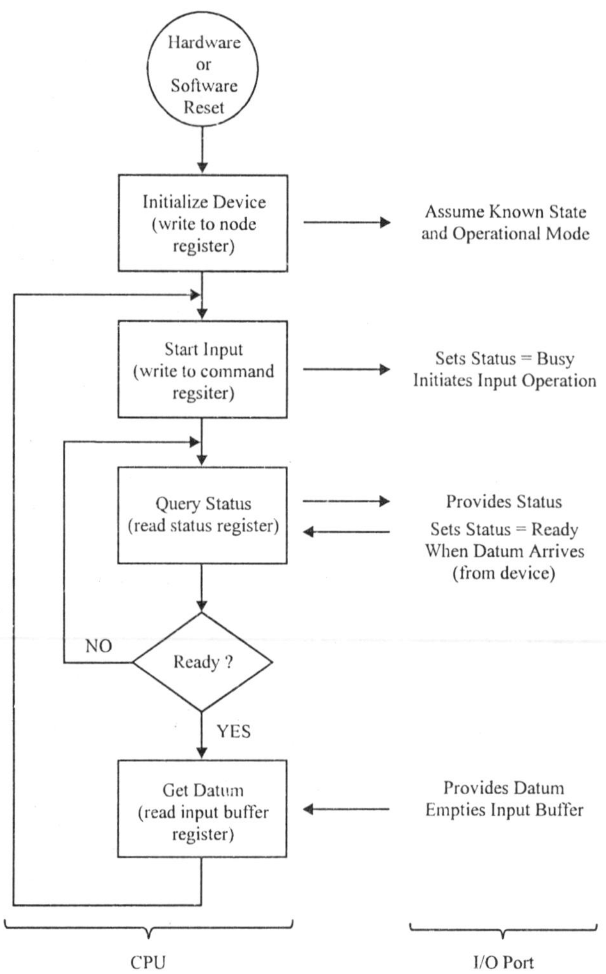

Fig. 20.6. Program-controlled input transaction.

Device initialization is normally performed after the system is powered up, although subsequent reinitialization is possible after software-commanded resetting of individual devices. The primary purpose of initialization is to select the desired mode of operation after the device is brought to a known state by a hardware or a software reset.

In general, prior to each I/O transaction, the processor indicates its desire to transfer or receive data by issuing a START_I/O command. This is accomplished by writing the corresponding bit pattern into the command register of the I/O port in the respective device interface. Upon receipt, the I/O port sets a status bit to *busy,* to indicate that an operation is in progress. When data become available in the input buffer, or an output buffer becomes empty, the I/O port signals the event by setting a corresponding bit in its status register to the *ready* state. The processor may determine the setting of status bits at any time by reading the I/O port's status register. When it discovers that the port is ready, the processor may read the data from the input buffer or place data in the output buffer, depending on the direction of the transfer in question. At this point another I/O transaction may be initiated and the whole cycle is repeated. On input, status flags signify the completeness of a data transfer (input buffer full); on output, they indicate the readiness of the device for new data transfer from the processor (output buffer empty). The I/O command sequences are somewhat automated for many USARTs. In particular, placing a datum in the output buffer and reading a datum from the input buffer also act as implicit START OUTPUT and START INPUT commands, respectively.

The assembly-language coding of the USART initialization and data input and output sequences for a hypothetical machine are given in Program 20.1. Sample constants follow the format of the USART registers given in Figure 20.5 and the initialization is performed for the line characteristics described in Figure 20.4. For simplicity and generality, the only addressing modes used are direct addressing and immediate addressing, which is indicated by a # sign preceding the operand. All instructions have two operands, which are assumed to be in the *destination, source* order. For example,

```
        MOVE        USCMD, #RESET
```

loads the literal (immediate operand) RESET into the USART's command register.

Hardware initialization is markedly product-specific. Only a few of the basic operations are shown in the INITUS section of Program 20.1. First, the RESET command is given to the USART in order to bring it to a known state. This usually implies clearing buffers, status flags, and other registers and preparing the USART to receive the mode command.

Initialization in Program 20.1 continues with selecting the mode of operation and, in the example given, enabling transmission. This particular sequence would be used for system A in Figure 20.4 (sender USART), and system B's initialization would differ only in enabling the reception instead. For bi-directional links, both USARTs should be enabled by writing #RXENAB + #TXENAB into the command register.

```
            USART register addresses
USMODE      EQU     ...     ;mode register
USCMD       EQU     ...     ;command register
USSTAT      EQU     ...     ;status register
```

(contd.)

```
USDIN      EQU   ...        ;input data buffer
USDOUT     EQU   ...        ;output data buffer
;    mode definition constant
MODE       EQU   xx011010B     ; mode=async, even, parity, 7 bits
;    command definition constants
TXENAB     EQU   00000001B     ;transmit enable
RXENAB     EQU   00000100B     ;receive enable
RESET      EQU   00010000B     ;reset USART
;    status definition constants
TXRDY      EQU   00000001B     ;transmitter ready
RXRDY      EQU   00000010B     ;receiver ready
RXERR      EQU   00000100B     ;receive error
;    USART initialization
INITUS:    MOVE  USCMD,#RESET         ;reset USART
           MOVE  USMODE,#MODE         ;set mode of operation
   ...                                ;other device-specific
                                      ;commands and housekeeping
           MOVE  USCMD,#TXENAB        ;enable transmission, interrupts off
     transmit (output) a character—system A
WTOUT:     BITTEST      USSTAT,#TXRDY       ;ready to send a character?
           BNSET WTOUT                      ;no, try again
           MOVE  USDOUT,RC                  ;ready, send from RC
     receive (input) a character—system B
WAITIN:    BITTEST      USSTAT,#RXRDY       ; has a character arrived?
           BNSET        WAITIN              ; no, try again
           BITEST       USSTAT,#RXERR       ; arrived, is it OK?
           BSET         RECERR              ; bad, process error
           MOVE         RA,USDIN            ; OK char, save it in RA

   ...
RECERR:    MOVE         RB,USSTAT           ;receive-error, save status in RB
           MOVE         RA,USDIN            ; and clean-up USART inbuffer
   ...
```

Program 20.1. Program-controlled input/output.

The two remaining sections of code in Program 20.1 illustrate the *program-controlled I/O* method, where the processor busily tests the status of an I/O device until it becomes ready for the next transfer. The input section consists of testing the status register repetitively until a datum arrives, an event that the USART indicates by setting the RXRDY bit in its status register. The instruction used is BITEST, which is assumed to perform an AND operation between its two operands and to set the processor condition-code flags accordingly. BITEST is assumed to affect neither the source nor the destination operand. This type of instruction is often used to test the individual bits of an I/O port's registers. Two types of conditional jumps, BSET and BNSET, are used in Program 20.1 to branch if the bit tested by the BITEST instruction is found to be set or not set, respectively.

Once the character arrives, the program checks for a reception error. If none is detected, the datum is fetched from the input buffer register and placed into the processor register RA. Alternatively, control is passed to the error-handling section. Its rudimentary form is shown in Program 20.1 beginning with the label RECERR.

The output code, like the input, consists of a loop that is executed repetitively until the USART becomes ready to receive a new character. This type of loop is used for both input and output and is called the *busy-wait loop.* It is the basis of the program-controlled I/O method. This is the simplest form of I/O programming and is found only in single-user systems and in some dedicated I/O processors. Its main shortcomings are:

1. Low processor utilization
2. Difficulty in handling multiple I/O devices

A simple timing analysis of the output code, using our earlier assumptions of a 1920 cps transfer rate and a 0.1 μs instruction execution time, indicates that the busy-wait loop is executed approximately 2500 times for each character transferred. In other words, even with the relatively fast peripheral driven at its maximum speed, *2500 unsuccessful status register tests are performed for each successful one* (resulting in the actual output), yielding an affective processor utilization of well below 1%. However, by busy-waiting, the processor is devoting the full 100% of its execution cycles to the output device, although only less than 1% of them represent useful work.

The second **while** statement in PRINT represents a busy-wait loop. The loop tests the status of the IOPORT and keeps looping until the OUTRDY flag is set indicating the I/O port's readiness to accept the next character for transmission. The KEEPTESTING comment is included to make the statement more readable by suggesting the repetitive operation indicated in a form that may not be intuitively obvious at first. Namely, the value of the IOPORT_STATUS variable is not affected by any statements in the program; it is changed only by external events and devices. However, changes of IOPORT_STATUS control the program's execution so that the reader must envision changes to IOPORT_STATUS occurring autonomously and observe how the program behaves in response to them. As suggested by our earlier examples, 99% of a program's execution time may be spent executing this particular statement.

```
program/module computeprint;
const
max = ...;      {max length of output}
outrdy = ...;  {ioport output ready}
type
text = array [1..max] of char;
var
data : text;
```

(contd...)

```
number of: integer;
procedure compute(var comdata: text; var count: integer);
...
procedure print(outdata: text; outcount : integer);
var
outindex : integer;
begin
outindex := 1;
while outcount 0 do
begin
while ioport_status outrdy do [keeptesting];
ioport_dataout := outdata[outindex];
outindex := outindex + 1;
outcount := outcount – 1
end {while}
end; {print}
begin {computeprint}
initialize_hardware;
while true do     {forever}
begin
compute(data, numberof);
print(data, numberof)
end {while}
end {computeprint}
```

Program 20.2. Program-controlled output.

When the flag is set by hardware (IOPORT_STATUS = OUTRDY), control passes to the next statement, which places a new character in the I/O port's output buffer. Figure 20.7 is a timing diagram of the flow of control of Program 20.2. It demonstrates that computation and I/O proceed sequentially and that the processor is not multiplexed between the two activities. Given that the procedure PRINT uses program-controlled I/O, effective processor utilization in the execution of PRINT is very low.

Controlling Multiple Devices: Polling

As described, programmed I/O is not of much practical interest because it can support only systems with a single I/O device. A common approach to handling multiple I/O devices with programmed I/O capitalizes on the low processor utilization of the busy-wait loop. The trick is to expand the loop to test the status of several I/O devices, and to branch to the appropriate I/O service routine of the first one that is found to be ready. This is called *polling,* and its busy-wait loop has the following format:

Test status of device 1
If ready, go to service routine 1
Test status of device 2
If ready, go to service routine 2
.
.
Test status of device *n*
If ready, go to service routine *n*
Repeat polling sequence

The device service routines contain a few instructions to perform the actual I/O and to update buffer pointers and counters. They usually do not test the status of the respective I/O device, since the status test is made just prior to entering the service routine. Each service routine terminates with a branch back to a test in the polling sequence. Relative device priorities can be established by controlling the target of the branch out from a service routine. If the branch is always to the beginning of the polling sequence, priorities are fixed and dependent on the device's position in the polling sequence, with the top position having top priority. Alternatively, branching back to the sequence to the point following the call to the service routine results in rotating priority. Rotating priority provides fairness in the sense that each device has an equal chance of being serviced over a period of time.

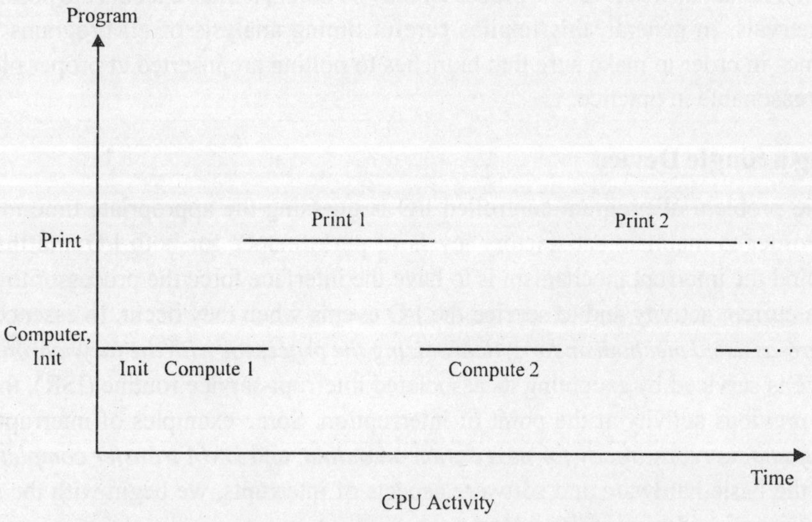

Fig. 20.7. Timing diagram of Program 20.2.

I/O response time is closely related to the polling strategy in effect. We consider two related performance measures: *latency*, the time that elapses from the moment a device becomes ready until it's service routine is entered, and *I/O bandwidth,* the maximum I/O rate that may be sustained without loss of data. Let us, without loss of generality, assume that all device service routines are of equal duration, T. With fixed polling priorities, the highest-priority device, in the worst case, may experience a latency of T and sustain burst I/O rates of up to 1/T. Unfortunately, at maximum rate, high-priority I/O may tie up the processor so that no other device receives service. In practice, because the processor is much faster than typical I/O devices, rarely does one device utilize the entire capacity of the processor in a polled system. If this situation were to occur, it would best be handled by a dedicated processor. However, this extreme example shows how fixed-priority systems can be monopolized by a single device. Consequently, I/O performance can be guaranteed only for the highest-priority device. All other devices must have their expected performance rated relative to the behaviour of the higher-priority devices. With a rotating priority, the worst-case latency is $(n - 1)\ T$, and the I/O bandwidth is no less than $1/(nT)$ for *each device* in the system.

In principle, the notion of polling may be extended to provide multitasking in a general-purpose system without resorting to interrupts. Since polling is essentially a variation of the busy-wait loop, continuous polling would most likely result in many unsuccessful tests and low effective processor utilization. The basic idea here is to perform some background computational activity, and to execute the device-polling sequence only occasionally. However, the question is both how often to poll and how to implement that frequency in a general-purpose system. If polling frequency is high, it degenerates to busy-waiting, with most of its problems. On the other hand, infrequent polling increases processor utilization but may also result in higher latency, thereby reducing performance and possibly causing loss of data. The "right" frequency is also system-and configuration-dependent.

Even if these issues are resolved and the suitable polling frequency chosen, the problem of implementation remains. Whatever the processor may be doing, it must execute the polling sequence at chosen intervals. In general, this implies careful timing analysis of all programs in terms of execution times in order to make sure that branches to polling are inserted at proper places, which is clearly unreasonable in practice.

Controlling a Single Device

The basic problem of program-controlled I/O is guessing the appropriate time to test device readiness in order to maintain satisfactory levels of performance for both I/O and the processor. The idea behind the interrupt mechanism is to have the interface force the processor to temporarily relinquish its current activity and to service the I/O events when they occur. In essence, interrupts are a *hardware-assisted mechanism for synchronizing the processor with the (asynchronous) events.* After a device is serviced by executing its associated interrupt-service routine (ISR), the processor resumes the previous activity at the point of interruption. Some examples of interrupt-generating signals are *input data ready, ready for next datum on output,* and *DMA transfer completed.* In order to introduce the basic hardware and software aspects of interrupts, we begin with the simple case of a single interrupting device in the system.

Context Switch

With interrupt-driven I/O the processor is typically engaged in some other activity until a significant I/O event occurs and raises an interrupt request. This forces transfer of control to a service routine. Since control is given back to the interrupted activity after the interrupt request is serviced, the hardware must save at least the current value of the program counter (PC) before reloading it with the address of the interrupt-service routine.

Given that they are triggered in response to external I/O events, interrupt requests themselves are asynchronous with respect to the processor. This means that the times of their occurrences are unpredictable, and interrupts may suspend other programs at virtually any point in time. When the ISR starts executing, being a sequence of instructions itself, it will inevitably modify the processor registers, status flags, and possibly some memory locations. Upon completion of the ISR, control is returned to the interrupted activity. The interrupted program can continue its execution correctly only if it finds its view of the machine to be in the same state as it was just prior to the interrupt. In other words, the *context* of the interrupted program must be preserved while the ISR is executing, and restored before control is subsequently returned. If no common variables are shared by the interrupted program and the ISR, the *context* may be taken to mean the values of all processor registers and status flags. However, only the part of the context that is actually *modified* by the interrupt-service routine needs to be saved.

The process of changing context from an executing program to an interrupt handler is called the *context switch,* and its control requires a combination of hardware and software. Since the interrupted program knows neither when an interrupt will assume control of the processor nor which part of the machine context will be modified by the interrupt routine, the interrupt-service routine itself is charged with saving and restoring the context of the preempted activity.

It was already indicated that the program counter is saved as a part of the hardware interrupt-recognition sequence. In some computers, the same hardware also saves the rest of the state, that is, flags and all other program-accessible registers, thus relieving the ISR of the burden. Another school of thought suggests that saving more than the minimum is too costly and increases the overhead of each interrupt. This reasoning is based on the observation that some interrupt routines modify only a subset of system registers. Consequently, it is more efficient to save only the affected subset of registers during a context switch. Machines based on this philosophy usually save the minimal state automatically and leave the rest to software, as there is no simple way to instruct the hardware which particular subset of registers to save (although this has been done in the VAX architecture, for example). Because no single approach is acceptable, many different solutions have been implemented. Some processors save only the PC and status flags; others save all registers and flag's and many save selected registers and flags. The recent trend seems to be to provide several options in the instruction set, and let the I/O programmer choose the one best suited for the specific application. In any case, both hardware and software sequences typically use the system stack for temporary storage of program context.

Interrupt-Service Routine (ISR)

Except for context saving and restoring, an ISR is essentially a piece of code that is executed in response to an external event. As such, it usually consists of a few instructions to transfer data, check for errors, and update pointers—a structure very similar to the service-routine part of program-controlled I/O. No testing of device readiness need be performed in the ISR, because an ISR is entered only when an I/O event occurs. Hence, device readiness may be taken for granted.

An interrupt request that invokes an ISR is an electrical signal. That signal must be removed when the corresponding interrupt handler responds to the request. So the ISR code must, at some point, notify the I/O port to the remove its interrupt request signal. Otherwise, the same request would interrupt the processor continuously even after the I/O processing had been completed. In such a case, the processor would be prevented from doing any useful work. The act of a processor notifying an I/O port or an interrupt controller to remove an interrupt request is called an *interrupt acknowledge*. Many I/O ports combine this function with buffer register accessing, so that by simply retrieving or supplying a datum for input or output, respectively, the processor acknowledges the corresponding interrupt. So, for many USARTs, both START_I/O and the interrupt-acknowledge function are side effects of reads and writes to the buffer registers.

A peculiarity of ISR code is that, unlike a procedure, it is called by hardware. Except possibly for initialization procedures that set up interrupt vectors, non-ISR code should contain no references to ISR code. Each ISR should terminate with the return-from-interrupt instruction, if one exists in the given instruction set. Special provisions to that effect must be provided if an ISR is coded in a high-level language.

Program 20.3 illustrates the coding of an interrupt-service routine and demonstrates how computations may be overlapped with I/O in order to improve the system's throughput, even when executing a single program. The program is basically an interrupt version of COMPUTERPRINT with double buffering added for additional I/O overlap. The two new constructs introduced in this example are the statements for manipulating the interrupt mechanism (enable and disable), and the *process* keyword which designates an interrupt-service routine.

The sample ISR process, PRINT, is embedded in the START_OUTPUT procedure. Syntactically, it follows the structure of a procedure in terms of the declaration and scopes of the variables. Since an ISR should never be explicitly invoked by software, an ISR process should be parameterless. Semantically, an ISR process is invoked by hardware via the interrupt linkage mechanism, and its last *end* statement should be compiled as an RTI instruction or its equivalent for a given architecture.

The main section of the program INTERRUPT_CP begins by initializing hardware. The first statement disables interrupts in order to prevent any I/O processing until the I/O port is initialized for the desired mode of operation. Enable interrupts and disable interrupts are simply the HLL representations of the corresponding machine-language instructions, such as EI and DI, or STI (for set interrupts) and CLI (for clear interrupts). The final step of initialization is to place the address of the interrupt-service routine in the fixed memory location, in order to indicate to the hardware interrupt sequence where to transfer control when the I/O port becomes ready. For reasons of compatibility with subsequent programs, this statement uses the term vector.

The purpose of the PRINT process is to output OUTCOUNT characters from the OUTDATA array. One character is transferred in response to each interrupt request. Therefore, it takes OUTCOUNT interrupts for PRINT to complete one full cycle. When the IOPORT becomes ready to output a character, it raises its ready flag, which in turn asserts an interrupt request. When interrupts are enabled, an interrupt request invokes the hardware interrupt-recognition sequence. In our example, this sequence transfers control to the PRINT process. PRINT then saves the context of the interrupted activity, outputs the next character, and tests whether all OUTCOUNT of them have been processed. If not, it restores the saved context and returns from interrupt. The process PRINT is coded assuming that the interrupt is implicitly acknowledged by placing the next character in IOPORT's output buffer; otherwise it should include an explicit interrupt-acknowledge statement.

```
program/module interruptCP;
const
    max = ...;        {max length of output}
type
    text = array [1...max] of char;
var
    data1, data2 : text; {data buffers}
    outdone : boolean; {flag: done printing output}
procedure compute (var comdata: text; var count : integer);
...
procedure start_output (outdata: text; outcount: integer);
    var
     outindex ; integer;
process print;
begin
while true do
begin
{await_printer_interrupt}
save_context;
ioport_dataout := outdata[outindex];
outindex := outindex + 1;
outcount := outcount – 1;
if outcount = 0
then
begin
disable_interrupts;
outdone := true
end;
restore_context
end {while}
end; {print}
begin {start-output}
outindex := 1;
outdone := false;
enable_interrupts
end; {start_output}
begin {interruptCP}
disable_interrupts;
initialize_hardware;
```

(contd...)

```
connect_interrupt_vector(print);
compute(data1, num1);                   {compute1}
start_output(data1, num1);              {start printing1, and}
compute(data2, num2);                   {compute2 concurrently}
while not outdone do {keeptesting};     {wait till 1 printed}
start_output(data2, num2);              {start printing2; and]
compute(data1, num1);                   { compute3 concurrently}
while not outdone do {keeptesting};     {wait till 2 printed}
start_output(data1, num1);              {start printing3, and}
compute(data2, num,1);                  {computer4 concurrently}
...
end {interruptCP}
```

Program 20.3. Interrupt-driven compute-print.

This version of the program relies on software double buffering, global signalling of variables, and interrupt enabling/disabling in order to overlap computations with I/O. The main part of the program, after initialization, performs the first batch of computations and instructs procedure COMPUTE to place results in DATA1 and NUM1—the first buffer and its associated character-count variable. It then invokes START_OUTPUT to output the results. START_OUTPUT sets the OUTDONE synchronization flag to false to indicate that output is in progress, and it enables interrupts. At this point it returns to the main section, since the PRINT process will be servicing the interrupts as they come. While output of DATA1 is taking place at a rate determined by the output device, the second computation is initiated by the main program. This is our first example of interleaved program execution in a computer system.

The main section awaits completion of printing of DATA1 by testing the OUTDONE flag, which is set to true when a run of PRINT is completed. Busy-waiting in the main, during testing of the OUTDONE flag, does not impede progress of the interrupt-driven PRINT. When PRINT completes, buffer DATA1 is freed and becomes available for the next batch of results. The main section then invokes the second output and the third computation. The order of procedure invocation, although arbitrary in principle, must be as indicated in Program 20.3 if overlapped operation is desired.

A careful reader will notice that PRINT actually disables interrupts even while the transmission of the last character in a string may still be in progress. This, on output does no harm because it simply means that no interrupt should be accepted when the I/O port's output buffer becomes empty after processing the last character.

How much have we gained in terms of performance by going from the program-controlled to the interrupt-driven version of this program? In the latter case, with sufficient buffering, at best both processor and I/O utilization of nearly 100% might be achieved. This is contrasted with possibly less than 1% processor utilization in the program-controlled I/O case. Yet the total performance improvement will not be increased by more than a factor of 2! The reason is that, by overlapping two activities, we cannot do better than reduce the resulting execution time to that of the longer routine. Fully sequential execution would take an amount of time equal to the sum of the two routines, and that can be at most twice the overlapped time. Another important observation is that program-controlled I/O is, in general, capable of providing higher I/O bandwidth than interrupt-driven I/O. That is, assuming a single I/O device, the maximum I/O bandwidth for a given computer system is obtained by calculating the time it takes to move data in and out by means of the program-controlled I/O, with all status tests being successful (i.e., with virtually 100% processor utilization). Under the same assumptions, the data throughput for interrupt-driven I/O would have to be lower, due to the overhead of context switching (saving and restoring). For this reason, designers of dedicated I/O systems, for example, communications front-end processors, should seriously consider program-controlled I/O.

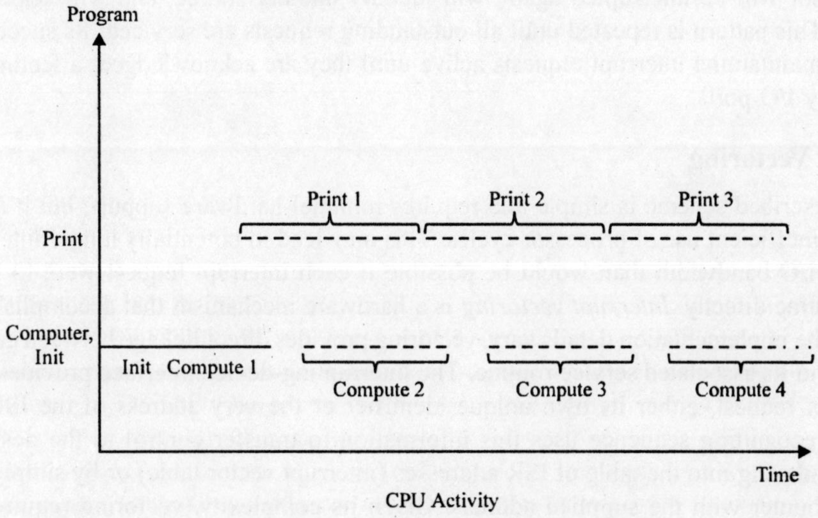

Fig. 20.8. Timing diagram of Program 20.3.

Controlling Multiple Devices

It would appear that we have invested a lot of energy to produce a not-so-spectacular gain. However, truly significant performance improvement may be obtained by overlapping a *multitude* of interrupt-driven I/O processes with a number of processor-bound activities. This mode of operation requires support from the operating system in terms of scheduling, synchronization, and protection.

When multiple I/O interfaces perform their data transfers in the interrupt-driven mode, the means for recognizing a specific source of interrupt and handling a hierarchy of priority levels must be provided by either the hardware or the system software. Since the number of separate interrupt request lines in a computer system is usually smaller than the number of possible sources of interrupt, the processor, in general, cannot deduce which particular device needs service just on the basis of having received an interrupt signal on a given line. Obviously, some extensions to the basic interrupt recognition mechanisms are needed for this purpose. Probably the simplest way is to retain the hardware transfer of control to a fixed memory location, as we have assumed in the single-source case. In other words, every interrupt request in the system, no matter what its cause might be, forces the processor to transfer control to the same place. The essential difference between this method and program-controlled I/O polling is that, with interrupts, the polling routine is entered only when at least one device is *known to be ready;* that is, success is guaranteed, and only a limited number of processor cycles may be lost in testing devices that are not ready but that precede the active one in the sequence.

In particular, when several interrupt requests are pending simultaneously, the one with the highest priority is serviced first. As a part of that process, the interrupt is acknowledged to the specific interface in question, and its request signal is removed from the system bus. The remaining interfaces, however, continue to hold their request lines active, pending acknowledgement. In turn, the processor will be interrupted again, will identify another source, and will acknowledge and service it. This pattern is repeated until all outstanding requests are serviced. Its success hinges on interfaces maintaining interrupt requests active until they are acknowledged, a feature commonly provided by I/O ports.

Interrupt Vectoring

The described scheme is simple and requires minimal hardware support, but it may result in somewhat inefficient use of processor cycles. This may lead to potentially longer interrupt latency and lower I/O bandwidth than would be possible if each interrupt request were to branch to its service routine directly. *Interrupt vectoring* is a hardware mechanism that accomplishes this task. Although the implementation details vary, vectoring provides direct linkage between each source of interrupt and its associated service routine. The interrupting-device interface provides, as a part of its interrupt request, either its own unique identifier or the very address of the ISR itself. The hardware-recognition sequence uses this information to transfer control to the designated ISR, either by indexing into the table of ISR addresses (interrupt vector table) or by simply loading the program counter with the supplied address. Given its complexity, vectoring requires additional hardware in each interface or, more often, a specialized I/O port, the *programmable interrupt controller* (PIC) to assist of vectoring of interrupts. The trend in high-end micro-processors, an active brewery of new architectural definitions, seems to be the use of fairly large interrupt vector tables and a reliance on a cascaded PICs to provide a complex hierarchy of interrupts with support for a number of uniquely identifiable sources. The number of connected physical devices may be enlarged by multiplexing individual levels with the aid of polling. Note that when polling is combined with vectoring, the cycles wasted on polling are significantly reduced, since polling sequences are shorter when interrupt vectors transfer control to the appropriate subgroups of devices.

One approach is to assign a different level of priority to each unique source that can be vectored, or to clusters of devices if the number of distinct levels is more limited. This ordering is normally recognized by hardware priority arbiters (resolvers), which honor requests in the order of their relative priorities. The system integrator, and sometimes the end user, is thus given the freedom to assign relative importance to each peripheral device and to make this decision known to the hardware by programming the PIC and the related I/O port registers. In this way, peripherals may be provided with service tuned to their requirements, and high-performance devices can operate at the best possible rates without interference from the lower-speed devices. In addition, time-critical events may be guaranteed comparatively low interrupt latency, an extremely important requirement in real-time systems.

In our previous discussion, and in Program 20.3, we have made the implicit assumption that an ISR has higher priority than the (background) activity that the processor engages in when there are no interrupts. Whenever an interrupt occurs, the processor suspends the background program and enters the ISR. A simple expansion of this logic suggests that a higher-priority request should likewise preempt the service routine for a lower-priority interrupt. Note that, because each ISR saves and restores the context of the preempted activity, any depth of interrupt nesting may be supported without problems. Conversely, a request of lower priority that the one currently being serviced should be made to wait until it becomes the highest-priority active request. As a practical example, we do not want to service a printer interrupt in the midst of receiving a high-priority network broadcast.

Levels of Interrupt Control

The enforcement of this logic imposes considerable demands on the interrupt-recognition mechanism. In particular, it must be able to permanently weigh priorities of the routines being executed against the incoming requests, and to decide accordingly whether to invoke context switching, vectoring, and updating of the highest active priority or to let an interrupt remain pending without interfering with the execution in progress. Obviously, this is a job to be done by hardware, but this may be too costly to support in architectures not intended exclusively for multiprogramming environments. Many microprocessors rely on sophisticated PICs to provide the full range of these services in hardware. Fortunately, by following some relatively simple rules and utilizing interrupt-related features commonly provided by hardware, this task may also be accomplished by software with relatively little overhead. Before outlining the usual approach to this problem, let us first explore the available tools.

In general, there are three levels of interrupt control, some or all of which may be implemented in any given system:

1. *Global system level:* enable interrupt (EI) and disable interrupt (DI) instructions
2. *Selective control of interrupt levels:* masking
3. *Individual-device level of interrupt control:* I/O port registers

Global interrupt enable/disable is a rather coarse, brute-force method that is found in virtually all computer systems.

The next level is the ability to selectively enable or disable certain interrupt levels or related clusters, which is often called *interrupt masking.* This is usually accomplished by providing an interrupt mask register and some means of altering its contents. Interrupt masking typically consists of a collection of bits that, depending on their settings, enable or disable the corresponding interrupt levels. In addition to handling priority control, the ability to mask interrupts is useful for limiting spurious interrupts, by disabling all levels that are unused in a given configuration. As usual, the implementation details vary; interrupt masks may have dedicated registers within the processor, may be a part of the processor status word, or may require the addition of the PIC to provide them.

The last and finest level of interrupt control is an individual I/O interface. By manipulating the interrupt enable/disable bits within the command registers of I/O ports, even specific devices with in a group sharing a priority level or an interrupt-request line may be selectively allowed or denied the ability to interrupt the processor. Sample interrupt-control bits for a USART are shown in Figure 20.5.

Priority Levels

As discussed earlier, the common practice is to enable higher-priority levels and to disable the lower-priority one immediately upon entering an ISR. An interesting question is whether the interrupt level that the ISR itself is running at should be enabled. Leaving that level enabled usually results in problems. In systems where several devices may share the same priority level, enabling that level within an ISR could result in preemptions between equals and lock up the entire system, as none of the routines may be able to reach the point of acknowledging its own interrupt request.

A more subtle problem, encountered even when interrupt levels are not shared, is the issue of an interrupt-service routine preempting itself. If the interrupt is acknowledged early enough within the ISR, the same device—especially if multiple-buffered—may be ready for another I/O transaction and generate a new interrupt. In general, this is both difficult to handle correctly (the ISR would have to be reentrant) and undesirable, since it could irrecoverably disturb the order of transferred data. For these reasons, it is a common practice to enable all higher levels and disable all lower levels, including a routine's own level, in an interrupt-service routine. Some computer systems have these rules implemented in hardware, and others in software—typically in the operating-system kernel—using the hardware provisions described in this section.

A Summary of Interrupt Processing

The sample sequence presented here refers to a typical input operation, assuming that the I/O port in question has already been initialized for interrupt-driven I/O and that the associated priority level is enabled. Output transactions follow the same logic, with slightly permuted initial steps. Due to many different practical implementations, the exact order of individual steps may vary somewhat in different computer systems.

1. The processor initializes input by issuing a START_INPUT command to the I/O port. The processor may begin and/or continue executing some unrelated sequence of instructions until the activated input is completed by the I/O port.
2. The I/O port sets its input status bit to *busy* and initiates the device-specific input action.
3. When the input datum is assembled in the I/O port's input buffer, the port sets its input-status bit to *ready* and raises its interrupt-request line.
4. When the processor is in an interruptible mode (the instruction in progress is completed and interrupts are enabled) and the I/O port's request becomes the highest-priority pending interrupt request, the hardware interrupt-recognition sequence is initiated on the device's behalf:
   (a) Interrupts are disabled.
   (b) The hardware part of the context is saved.
   (c) The source of interrupt is identified (through polling or vectoring).
   (d) Control is transferred to the ISR.
5. Within the interrupt-service routine, the following actions take place:

(a) Higher-priority levels of interrupt are enabled (lower and equal levels remain off).
(b) The software part of the context is saved.
(c) A datum is obtained from the I/O port's buffer.
(d) The interrupt is acknowledged, and the I/O port responds by removing its interrupt request; possibly, another START_INPUT command is issued.
(e) Other interrupt processing and housekeeping is completed.
(f) The software part of the saved context is restored.
(g) The return-from-interrupt instruction is executed.

6. Whether by means of RTI or some additional instructions, the hardware part of the context is restored, and the interrupt priority levels, up to that of the interrupted program, are enabled.

Concurrent I/O

This section illustrates how multiple interrupts may be employed to improve system performance and component utilization through interleaved operation. Our primary aim is to motivate the potential for concurrent operation normally provided by the I/OI hardware.

Program 20.4 is used as a vehicle for the demonstration and illustration of the main points to be made in this section. Many details of interrupt handling, especially priorities, are hidden or just implied in Program 20.4 because of the HLL coding. This is the level of the I/O programming involvement often encountered by application programmers. In a way, this example demonstrates the importance of understanding the interrupt-handling strategy of the underlying system, even if one does not have to manipulate the interrupts directly. Naturally, operating-system designers and system programmers would have to be intimately involved in its details, and especially observe the interplay and implied interaction among program components resulting from the particular interrupt priority and management scheme at hand. We highlight some details as we proceed with the explanation of Program 20.4.

The program basically consists of three related but not too tightly coupled activities:

1. Interrupt-driven input of a line of text from the terminal
2. Some unspecified processing of these data
3. Interrupt-driven output of the data collected by the input routine

This program is a simplification of some of the functions performed by a terminal I/O driver and by an operating-system routine for handling the human interface, often called the *console-monitor routine.* From the system's point of view, the terminal consists of two independent logical devices: an input device (keyboard) and an output device (CRT display or hard-copy output). As explained in the description of a USART, each of these devices possesses its own set of data registers, as well as dedicated portions of the command and status registers. This is clearly illustrated by the fact that many terminals, when online, do not echo input characters. More specifically, anything typed on the keyboard is sent directly to the system, which, in turn, typically echoes some characters back to the display via a separate output routine, for the user's convenience and verification. The output routine in Program 20.4 has exactly this function; it simply echoes (displays or prints) a line of text to an output device.

Data processing in Program 20.4 is assumed to use the input data for some purpose, but not to modify them in any way before their output is completed. For example, PROCESS_DATA might simply parse the input searching for valid commands to the operating system in order to invoke the appropriate service.

Program 20.4 contains three versions of the main section in order to introduce increasing degrees of concurrency. The first version is strictly sequential, and its primary purpose is to illustrate the required order of events, and the logic of the three procedures. As before, the main program disables interrupts in order to initialize the hardware and to place addresses of the two interrupt-service routines into the appropriate entries of the vector table. In Program 20.4 interrupt enabling and disabling is done at the port level, thus affecting only the individual device. By choosing the specific vectors, relative priorities are, in effect, assigned to the two ISRs. After that, the main section enters its *forever* (while true) part.

The repetitive sequence consists of obtaining a line of input, processing it, and echoing via the output routine. Input-line variables in this example are assumed to be of variable length up to MAX line-length characters. An input sequence is assumed to be terminated by a special character, such as RETURN (carriage return). When the terminator is received, KEYBOARD deactivates itself and sets the INDONE flag to announce the availability of a line of input to the rest of the system. The main program awaits this event by busily testing the flag. This assumes that the main program is running at a lower priority than the KEYBOARD process. No explicit priority is assigned to the main program, following the usual convention that each hardware priority level takes precedence over the default priority for non-I/O-related routines. Alternatively, a level of priority lower than that of either ISR should be assigned to the main routine.

```
program/module concurrentIO;
const
max = 80;           {max length of output}
line_end = return;   {line termination character}
type
text = array [1..max] of char;
var
indata, outdata, save_data : text; {data buffers}
indone, outdone : boolean;      {completion flags}
inindex, incount, outindex, outcount, save_count : integer;
procedure process_data;
procedure start_input;
process keyboard;
begin
while true do
begin
{await_kbd_interrupt}
save_context;
kbd_status :=ioport_status;
kbd_data := ioport_datain;              {interrupt acknowledge}
```

(contd...)

```
if kbd_status = OK
then {error-free reception}
begin
indata[inindex] := kbd_data;
inindex := inindex + 1;
incount := incount + 1;
if kbd_data = line_end
then    {line of input completed}
begin
ioport_command := kbd_interrupts_disable;
indone := true
end {if}
end {if}
else handle_error(kbd_status); {reception errors}
restore_context
end {while}
end; {keyboard}
begin {start_input}
indone := false;
inindex := 1;
incount := 0;
ioport_command := kbd_interrupts-enable
end; {start_input}

procedure start_output;
process display;
begin
while true do
begin
{await_dsp_interrupt }
save_context;
ioport_dataout := outdata[outindex];
outindex := outindex +1;
outcount := outcount – 1;
if outcount = 0
then    {line printed}
begin
ioport_command := dsp_interrupts_disable;
outdone := true
```

(contd...)

```
end; {if}
restore_context
end {while}
end; {display}
begin {start_output}
outdone := false;
outindex := 1;
outcount := save_count;
ioport_command := dsp_interrupts_enable
end; {start_output}
{MAIN – version 1}
begin {concurrentIO}
ioport_command := kbd_and_dsp_interrupts_disable;
initialize_hardware;
connect_interrupt_vectors(kbd, dsp);
while true do          {forever}
begin
start_input;                              {activate input(x)}
while not indone do {keeptesting};    {await completion}
copy(indata, outdata);
save_count :=incount;
process_data;          {process input(x)}
start_output;          {echo input(x)}
while not outdone do {keeptesting}
end {while}
end {concurrentI/O, version 1}
{MAIN –version 2}
begin {concurrentIO}
ioport_command ;= kbd_and_dsp_interrupts_disable;
initialize_hardware;
connect_interrupt_vectors(kbd, dsp);
while true do
begin
start_input;                              {activate input(x)}
while not indone do {keeptesting};    {await completion}
copy(indata, outdata);
save_count := incount;
start_output;          {echo input(x), and}
process_data;          {process it concurrently}
```

(contd…)

```
while not outdone do {keeptesting}
end {while}
end {concurrentIO, version2}
{MAIN –version 3}
begin {concurrentIO}
ioport_command :=kbd_and_dsp_interrupts_disable;
initialize_hardware;
connect_interrupt-vectors(kbd, dsp);
outdone := true;
start_input; {activate input(1)}
while true do
begin
while not indone do {keeptesting);    {await input(x)}
copy(indata, save_data};              (save input(x)}
save_count := incount;
start_input;                          {activate input(x+1)}
while not outdone do {keeptesting}; {await output(x–1)  }
copy(save_data, outdata);             {input(x) to outdata  }
start_output;                         {echo input(x), and}
process_data                          {process it concurrently}
end {while}
end {concurrentIO, version 3}
```

Program 20.4. Concurrent input/output.

The second version of the main program introduces some interleaving, by coactivating the output and processing of a line of data. Since processing is compute-bound and output is interrupt-driven, the two activities may be conveniently interleaved. As indicated by the timing diagram presented in Figure 20.9(b), this strategy is very similar to the one used in Program 20.3.

The third version goes a significant step beyond, by allowing all three activities to progress toward their completion concurrently. This is accomplished by overlapping output and the processing of a batch of input with the assembling of the next line of input. This is sometimes referred to as a *type-ahead* feature, where the user may start entering a line of input even before the previous one is echoed.

In order to make this mode of operation possible, characters collected by a complete cycle of the KEYBOARD process are copied to the SAVE_DATA array for subsequent echoing by the DISPLAY process. This frees the INDATA buffer for the next line of input, allowing immediate activation of the input routine. When output (echoing) of the previous line of text is completed, the line to text saved in SAVE_DATA is copied to the OUTDATA array, and the output routine is activated. Being interrupt-driven, both input and output routines operate concurrently. Possible competition between the two when they simultaneously need activation is resolved by the interrupt priority-arbitration logic. The reader should observe that the two ISRs must run at different levels of priority, but that it does not really matter which one is higher. Naturally, interleaved execution may result in occasional preemption of the lower-priority level, but that should not be a cause for concern in our example. The common practice is to assign higher priority to the input routine and thus minimize the possibility of losing characters. This, as explained before, is not a problem on output.

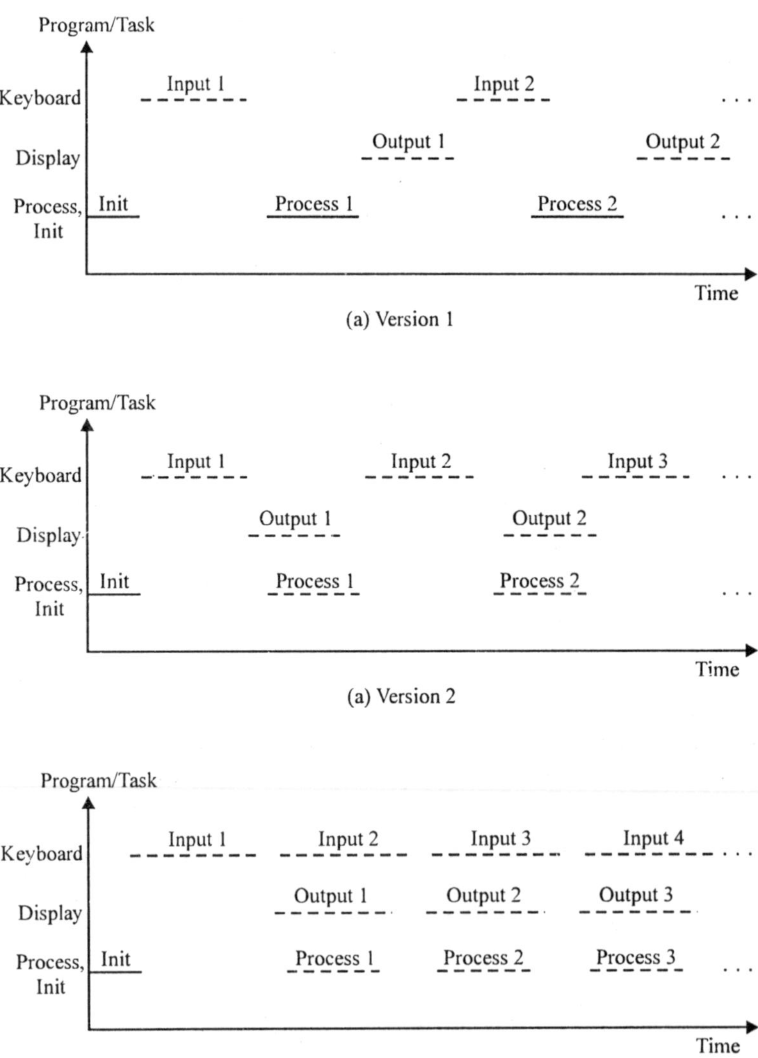

Fig. 20.9. Timing diagram of Program 20.4.

Following the processing of a line of input, the main program awaits completion of the next line of input if it is not already assembled by the KEYBOARD process. Input data are stored in the SAVE_DATA array until their output can be initiated, and the described sequence of events is repeated. This process is illustrated by the timing diagram in Figure 20.9c. Note that, due to limited buffering, input cannot get ahead of output by more than one line at a time. This is enforced in the main program by means of testing the two completion flags.

In general, careful tuning of a program in order to increase the degree of concurrency among its routines may be rendered obsolete by changes in configuration, say, from human input to computer-computer input. For this and other reasons, overlapping within a program should not be carried to extremes. The best way to improve system performance and component utilization is to introduce concurrency at the *system level* and to charge the operating system with multiplexing a system's resource among all active programs. This, obviously, increases the probability of having some useful work assigned to the processor, without the need to indulge in a study of the timing patterns of any single program. Implementation of such a multitasking kernel is described in the two chapters that follow.

Summary

Due to the pronounced speed gap between a processor and I/O devices, the processor may be heavily underutilized if it is dedicated to servicing a single device at a time, as in the program-controlled method of I/O. Having discovered that there is the need, and usually the processing capacity, for handling the I/O devices concurrently, we looked at the available hardware support.

Concurrent operation of I/O devices is supported by input/output ports that provide handshaking signals and buffering of data. Handshaking is necessary to synchronize devices with the processor in order to exchange data. Due to the asynchronous operation of I/O devices and the processor, input buffering is desirable to help prevent the loss of date until the processor can switch attention to the I/O transaction in progress.

Processor utilization, interrupt latency, and compound system I/O bandwidth may all be improved by using vectored interrupts and hardware-assisted enforcement of interrupt priorities. Such elaborate interrupt mechanisms facilitate multiplexing of the processor among a number of devices. In addition, they allow tuning of individual device response times in accordance with the relative importance of the related operations.

Interrupt-driven I/O operations may be interleaved to improve throughput even when executing a single program. But this requires careful timing analysis and tuning of individual programs, which is difficult and impractical in many cases. Moreover, although the interrupt mechanism facilitates interleaving of I/O operations, it is of little help when concurrent execution of computationally intensive activities is desired.

21

Design of a Kernel of a Multitasking Operating System (KMOS)

In this chapter we investigate some aspects of the operating-system design process by means of designing a kernel of a multitasking operating system (KMOS). Following the common approach to analysis, we treated specific topics therein with a certain degree of isolation from the rest of the system, highlighting the particulars and attenuating the effects of interaction with other components. Our goal now is to explore how the individual building blocks presented so far may be combined to form a working system. In integrating the system, our primary concern is with the interactions among its constituents.

1. *Interprocess communication and synchronization:* A set of mechanisms and related primitives necessary to support both functions
2. *Interrupt management:* Typically, vectoring of interrupts, saving and restoring of state, and management of priority levels, including selective level enabling and disabling
3. *Process management:* Functions described such as creation and deletion of processes and delaying of processes
4. *Booting and startup of the initial system configuration*

In addition, kernel usually handles some supporting activities necessary to provide the services visible to other OS layers. Examples of such internal kernel operations include system time-base management and processor allocation by means of basic process scheduling. The kernel design discussed in this and the following chapter assumes that all user processes are resident in memory when the kernel receives control of the processor. This assumption is valid in many embedded computer systems where the application programs are placed in unalterable, read-only (ROM) memory. In larger, general-purpose systems, the kernel usually relies on other layers to bring the user processes into main memory. Bringing the kernel itself into main memory.

In an embedded application, a run-time subset of a kernel may be all of the system software that is provided on the target machine, whereas in a complex multiprogramming system the kernel is typically enclosed by additional layers of an operating system. Our decision to design a kernel is partly motivated by the fact that it is present in virtually every multiprogramming operating system—from the simplest real-time monitor to the large multiuser system with batch, time-sharing, and possibly real-time and network services provided in parallel. In a sense, a multitasking kernel may be regarded as a common denominator of multiprogramming operating systems, kernel activities and even the functions of its basic primitives are quite similar across a wide range of operating system. At least functionally, a kernel is one of the most stable parts of an operating system. Otherwise, any change in the interface specification of a kernel primitive may necessitate changes in all upper layers that call on it. Being closest to hardware, a kernel may be thought of as the first-level functional extension of the bare machine.

As a consequence of all these properties, most attempts to put the operating system in microcode or in silicon begin with kernel primitives. Several actual products provide operating-system kernels in read-only memory. These "silicon operating system, which can be used with a given microprocessors, are largely invariant to the rest of the system hardware configuration. One microprocessor vendor offers an operating-system firmware (OSF) component, consisting of a real-time multitasking (multiprocess) kernel in ROM, programmable interval timers, and a programmable interrupt controller, all housed in a single chip. An interesting aspect of this kernel on a chip is that it has survived, without modifications, several major revisions of the enclosing operating system, which is quite complex. In terms of the layered approach carved in silicon, the same chip is touted as providing some 30 additional operating-system instructions to the instruction set of the basic microprocessor with which it is used. Indeed, with interrupts off during the execution of a kernel primitive, there is hardly any conceptual difference for the user between "proper" hardware instructions and those handled by the operating-system chip.

In designing a sample multitasking operating-system kernel (KMOS, pronounced "keymos"), we will attempt to mimic the actual design process as much as possible, including the motivation for and evaluation of the various design options and trade-offs as they are encountered. The chapter begins with an informal definition of the ranges of services to be provided by KMOS. This paves the way for the subsequent discussion of major design decisions and for the functional specification of KMOS services. In preparation for implementation, some issues regarding selection of a systems implementation language and a method for invoking system services are discussed in the last section of this chapter.

Defining KMOS Services

In this section we outline the range of KMOS services—both those provided to users, that is, directly callable by other software layers, and the internal supporting activities that may not be in invoked by routines external to the kernel.

The multitasking aspect implies the need to support concurrent execution of processes and to provide services for Interprocess communication and synchronization. Perhaps less visible but equally important kernel functions include management of interrupts and basic process scheduling.

An early decision to be made in the design of an OS kernel involves the selection of the Interprocess synchronization and communication mechanisms. One of the primary considerations here is to make sure that the chosen set of services (and thus system primitives) is functionally complete in the sense of supporting adequately both forms of interprocess exchanges. Messages, which may serve both interprocess synchronization and communication in centralized as well as distributed systems, obviously warrant consideration. Their adoption in KMOS is motivated by the desires to keep the design simple, by virtue of having a single mechanism that can also be used to field interrupts from hardware sources to a user's interrupt service routines.

For the sake of simplicity, and without sacrificing generality, we may opt for event-driven, that is, priority-based, preemptive scheduling of processes. In general, a well-designed kernel should provide flexible mechanisms to be used as building blocks by higher software layers. In particular, a kernel should provide mechanism and defer implementation of policies such as those governing resource allocation. By choosing event-driven scheduling, it may appear that our KMOS violates this principle. However, this is not the case, because some basic scheduling must be done by the kernel in order to control execution of processes. In real-time systems, priority-based scheduling offered by KMOS may be adequate for application to all processes. In system with more varied requirements, OS processes an interrupt-service routines are often scheduled on the basis of priority, whereas user processes and utilities may be handled by another scheduling algoritl m implemented by an upper-level layer of the operating system. The tools for implementing additional scheduling mechanisms, such as time slicing, can be built on the existing support for interval timer and system time-base management. Since our list of kernel activities does not include management of input/output devices, we also leave their implementation to the enclosing software layers, which may make the operating system either a single-user or a multiuser system.

Before deciding on the complete list of services to be provided by KMOS, let us point out that our aim is to illustrate the kernel-design process in a realistic way, but also to keep the outcome simple and comprehensible by, among other things, avoiding unnecessary and distracting details. In this spirit, we strive to provide a small but functionally complete system that combines aspects of all important issues discussed in previous chapters, such as interrupts, process management, scheduling, and interprocess interactions. To make things realistic, our KMOS is very similar and functionally comparable to several multitasking kernels. In addition, the version of KMOS presented here is used to control operation of a remote telemetry unit (RTU) in a commercial data-acquisition and control system.

Having made some major design choices, let us briefly discuss KMOS services in terms of the list of typical OS kernel functions given earlier.

Interprocess communication and synchronization Since messages are to be used for both communication and synchronization purposes, we need to implement some sort of SEND and RECEIVE operations. In order to provide the most general many-to-many mapping between senders and receivers, KMOS should manage mailboxes and support at least their creation, say, by means of a CREATEMBOX system call.

Interrupt management Given that messages are also used to synchronize interrupt-service routines with hardware interrupts, it is sufficient to provide some services for manipulation of the interrupt levels, such as enabling of a level, say, by means of an ENABLEV system call.

Process management Obviously, the first necessary function is to create a process, so we need a CREATEPROC primitive. Suspending and resuming of processes may be indirectly accomplished at the user level by means of message primitives, so a minimal kernel need not provide the specialized system calls for that purpose. Orderly process termination and deletion may be accomplished by a DELETEPROC. In order to support clock-driven forms of scheduling as well as the requirements of real-time applications, we should provide a system call to delay execution of a process for a specified period to time; let us name this KMOS service DELAY.

Booting and startup of the initial system configuration Although they all provide some form of booting and startup, operating systems differ greatly in the details of how system initialization is actually performed. We defer specification of this part of KMOS pending elaboration of some related implementation details.

In summary, we need to implement at least the following system calls in KMOS: SEND, RECEIVE, CREATEMBOMX, ENABLEV, CREATEPROC, DELETEPROC, and DELAY. Before discussing the internals of KMOS necessary to provide these services, let us first point out what KMOS does not do. As specified, KMOS provides the means only for creation of objects, such as mailboxes, not for their termination. For example, services such as DELETE_MAILBOX and DISABLE_LEVEL are missing. These functions, as well as other system services such as the remaining process-management calls should be part of a kernel that is to serve as a foundation for a complex operating system. On the other hand, in some embedded applications where the size or the overhead of the executive may be critical (such as the system in which KMOS is actually used) the proposed KMOS kernel may be adequate as is. System processes and real-time processes tend to be permanent, as opposed to transient processes common in program-development systems. In order to make KMOS useful in such different environments, while keeping it as simple as possible, we opt to implement the kernel as specified, with the added provision of designing system data structures for easy addition of the omitted system calls. As we progress with the implementation, such expansion hooks are pointed out where appropriate. Several problems at the end of the chapter involve the design additional KMOS facilities.

Major Design Decision

Before specifying the functions and formats of KMOS service calls provided to users, we must decide some issues regarding internal KMOS organization, including messages, interrupt processing, and data structures.

We discovered that a message facility may be implemented in several different ways, depending on the particular forms of naming, copying, and buffering used in a given system. In the previous section we adopted the indirect form of message exchange via mailboxes. In order to provide for asynchronous communication between senders and receivers necessary to support the most general forms of signaling and fielding or interrupts, let us opt for message buffering at the kernel level. For generality, variable-length messages should be supported. Finally, in order to avoid the issue of protection and the details of dynamic memory management, message-passing in KMOS may be implemented by passing a pointer rather than by copying the contents of a message from the sender's to the receiver's space.

To support the DELAY function, KMOS must keep track of the elapsed time. This is usually accomplished by means of a dedicated interval timer that is initialized and serviced by the OS. Once started, the timer generates interrupts in approximately regular intervals. If vectored to the operating system, these interrupts may serve as the system time base.

Whenever a computer system is brought up, the operating system must initialize itself and the hardware, and create the environment for the initial configuration of processes. When all this is done, control may be passed to the first user process. From that point on, the system becomes event-driven in the sense that behavioural patterns of executing processes, together with the occurrences of event that cause rescheduling, dictate its further state transitions. In general, an operating system acts both as a watchdog by intervening to do the housekeeping necessary to record and to complete the required state transitions, and as a controller charged with maintaining a certain level of performance. Allocation of resources and more sophisticated scheduling policies are usually delegated to higher-level layers of an operating system, which leaves mostly housekeeping and basic mechanism to kernels. Saves for its simple priority-based scheduler, KMOS is not an exception in that regard.

KMOS can keep track of processes and their individual state changes by maintaining a process control block (PCB) for each active process. The initial form of a PCB can be formed process creation time, which is indicated by invocation of the CREATEPROC primitives. Static process attributes, such as the initial priority and starting address, are commonly entered into the process's PCB at this time.

A newly created process is usually made ready, and its PCB is enqueued on the Ready list to await selection by the scheduler. Following a burst of processor activity, the running process may surrender control to the operating system or be preempted as a result of the occurrence of an interrupt. In either case, the context of the running process must be saved, say, in the related PCB, for subsequent restoring when the process is scheduled to run again. In a multitasking system, such as KMOS, a number of processes may be active and in different stages of execution at any time. Their collective state can be traced by the operating system by means of system lists of PCBs. For this reason, KMOS data structures ought to include some form of Ready and Suspended lists. As we proceed with the functional specification of KMOS, we may uncover the need for some additional lists.

Process-State Transitions in KMOS

On the basis of the general specification of the range of services to be provided by KMOS, and on the basis of the assumptions made in this section, we can construct a KMOS-specific state-transition diagram, which is given in Figure 21.1. As discussed earlier, processes are created by means of the CREATEPROC call. A newly created process is assigned a PCB and made ready, as indicated by an arrow between the Dormant and Ready states in figure 21.1. Whenever an event that causes rescheduling is processed, KMOS schedules the highest-priority ready process to run. A running process has its stream of instructions executed until it is preempted, say, by higher-priority interrupt, or until it voluntarily surrenders control to KMOS by executing a system call. Depending or the state of the system and on the nature of the invoked service, KMOS may or may not subsequently return control to the calling process.

As indicated in Figure 21.1, the running process regains control immediately after creating a mailbox (CREATEMBOX) or creating a process (CREATEPROC). The running process may terminate itself and thereby depart the system by invoking the DELETEPROC call.

The running process any preempt itself by sending a message to a higher-priority process that is already waiting. After the message in question is delivered by KMOS as a result of execution of the SEND primitive, both the sending and the receiving processes are ready, but the receiver is scheduled due to its higher priority. Given asynchronous exchange of messages, sending a message in any other case—such as when there are no waiting recipients, or there are one or more recipients of lower priority than that of the sender—does not cause the running process to lose control of the processors after execution of SEND.

Situations leading to possible suspension of the running process are somewhat more involved. The simplest one results from invocation of the DELAY function, which simply suspends the running process for the specified period of time. The *Delayed* state is introduced in Figure 21.1 to handle this situation. This state is effectively an instance of the more general class of suspended states. It is sometimes desirable to introduce several different instances of the suspended state according to the specific reason for suspension. Another variation of the suspended state suitable for KMOS is the *Waiting-for-message* state, also shown in Figure 21.1. Processes enter this state after invoking the RECEIVE call when no messages, are available at the specified mailbox. Conversely, invocation of the same KMOS service when one or more messages happen to be available at the designated mailbox, results in both a message and control being returned to the running process.

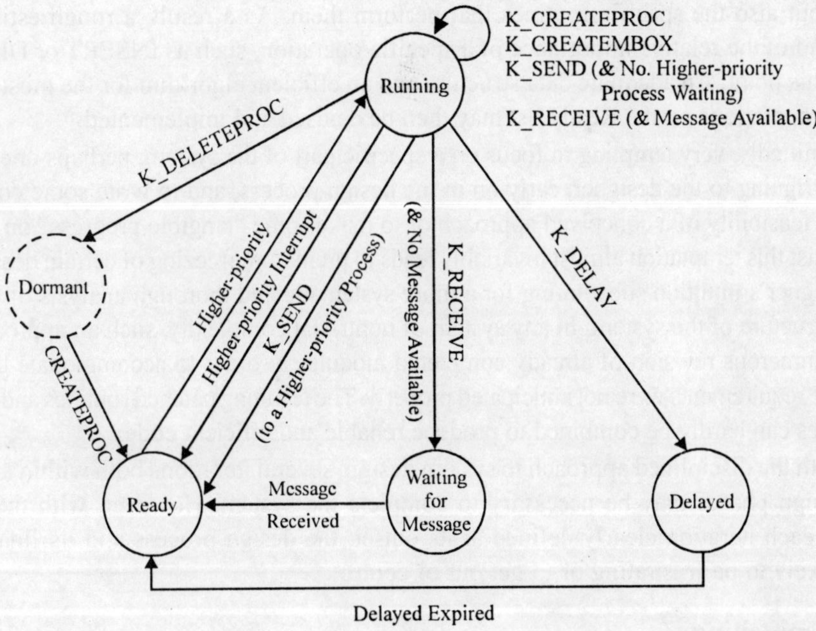

Fig. 21.1. Process state-transition in KMOS.

The final note regarding process-state transitions in KMOS depicted by Figure 21.1 concerns the influence of device interrupts and of external events in general. Given the use of messages to signal occurrences of interrupts to service routines in KMOS, interrupt servers spend their time between activities in the Waiting-for-message state. The arrow marked Interrupt, leading from the Running to the Ready state, refers to the situation when the running process is preempted by a higher-priority interrupt, which causes an ISR of higher priority than that of the running process to become scheduled for execution. Presumably, such an ISR is hibernating in the Waiting-for-message state until an interrupt from its related source arrives. The (lower-priority) process, that happens to be running when the interrupt occurs is preempted, but it remains ready and is thus eligible for subsequent consideration by the scheduler.

Functional Specification of KMOS

Following the usual design procedure, we now proceed with the functional specification of KMOS on the basis of the decisions and assumptions made thus far. This material will serve as a foundation for the subsequent implementation of KMOS. Our primary goal in this section is to organize KMOS activities into a set of routines and to specify their activities, interactions, and interfaces. At this stage of the design process, our main interest is in *what* each routine must do, rather than *how* it does it. In this way we can focus on designing the overall structure of the system, without overcommitment to the particular data structures or to specific algorithms. Once the skeleton of the system is built and major interactions are defined, a detailed specification of data structures can be made with much greater confidence that later "insights" will not necessitate major revisions.

For example, the functional specification should reveal not only the types of operation on the Ready list, but also the specific routines that perform them. As a result, a rough estimate of the frequency and of the relative importance of a specific operation, such as INSERT or DELETE, can be made at this point. An adequate data structure and an efficient algorithm for the most frequent or time-critical operations on the Ready list may then be devised and implemented.

It is, admittedly, very tempting to focus on a specific part of the system, perhaps one that is well known or intriguing to the designer, early on in the design process, and to write some code either to establish the feasibility of a conceived approach or to make some "tangible progress" on the project. Failure to resist this temptation almost invariably leads to premature freezing of certain design choices, with the designer's intuition substituting for a more systematic and thorough analysis of their role in the overall structure of the system. In any system of nontrivial complexity, such an approach is likely to result in numerous revision of already completed modules in order to accommodate the needs of others, whose requirements were not anticipated properly. The resulting patched routines and refurbished data structures can hardly be combined to produce reliable and efficient code.

Even with the disciplined approach to system design, several iterations both within and between different design phases may be necessary to complete the system. However, with the goals and purposes of each iteration clearly defined at its outset, the design process and its final result are much less likely to be frustrating or to get out of control.

Process Dispatching

Let us now return to the functional specification of KMOS. As our earlier discussion and Figure 21.1 suggest, traffic management is an important function of an operating system kernel. Whenever a running process is preempted or suspended, the kernel must save the process's context for proper subsequent resumption. In general, the context of a process encompasses that part of the run-time environment that must be recreated by the operating system to ensure proper operation of the process when it is resumed after a period of inactivity. In particular, each system routine in KMOS whose execution results in rescheduling of processes must save the context of the process that was running when KMOS was entered. As Figure 21.1 reveals, this may be the case with the majority of KMOS calls. When a new running process is selected by the scheduler, KMOS must restore the context of that process before actually surrendering control of the processor to it. This function of an operating system is often called *process dispatching,* so let us entrust it to a DISPATCH routine in KMOS.

DISPATCH is an internal KMOS routine that transfers control to the new running process after restoring its context. In a sense, DISPATCH is an exit routine from KMOS that should be invoked after each rescheduling in order to enforce the scheduling decision. The identity of a new running process must be made known to DISPATCH, so that the related PCB can be found and used to restore the target context. Therefore, a functional specification of the DISPATCH routine may be made in the form presented in Program.

routine DISPATCH (process); {internal, KMOS use only}
{dispatches a new running process}

begin
do {other} housekeeping;
establish run-time environment for the process;
restore context of the process;
surrender control to the process
end;

Program 21.1. Functional specification of DISPATCH.

DISPATCH and subsequent functional specifications of KMOS services are presented in a pseudo high-level language. The word *routine* indicates a tentative structure that later in the design process may evolve into a subroutine, a process, or a part or combination thereof. As indicated earlier in this section, the "statements" of a functional specification are meant to serves as a reminder of what the related routine should do, rather than how it does it. As a result, rules of syntax are not followed closely, and many details are vague or omitted.

Interprocess Communication and Synchronization

As a consequence of the decision to implement a buffered message facility for the purpose of interprocess communication and synchronization, KMOS must support management of mailbox and message objects. In addition, SEND and RECEIVE primitives need to be provided to system and user processes that wish to interact with other processes or system devices.

Mailboxes and Messages

Operation system that support mailbox-based exchange of messages often combine all information necessary for management of a given mailbox into a data structure called a *mailbox descriptor* (MBD). A separate mailbox descriptor is usually dedicated to each active mailbox. An MBD may be formed and initialized at message creation time, indicated by execution of the CREATEMBOX call. Not unlike the relationship between processes and PCBs, the user's concept of a mailbox as a repository of messages is supported at the OS levels by creation and management of a related mailbox object. Let us briefly review the role of a mailbox descriptor and its possible format in KMOS.

As discussed in regard to process-state transitions in KMOS, when a running process sends a message to a specific mailbox by means of the SEND call, the message can be immediately delivered to a waiting process, if any. However, if there are no processes suspended at that mailbox by an unmatched RECEIVE, the message is left in the mailbox, and the running process continues to execute. In this way, several messages can be accumulated in a given mailbox awaiting delivery to the receiver process. Since KMOS is to buffer outstanding messages, a portion each mailbox descriptor may be used as header of the queue of messages awaiting delivery at its related mailbox.

On the other hand, when a running process invokes a RECEIVE system call on a mailbox where no messages are awaiting delivery at that time, the calling process enters the Waiting-for-message state and remains suspended until arrival of a message at the designated mailbox. Due to the nature of message exchanges in KMOS, it is possible that several processes may be awaiting delivery of messages at a given mailbox. Since each such process may be resumed only when a message is delivered to it, mailboxes seem like a good place for matching of processes to messages and vice versa. The idea to queue outstanding messages at a mailbox may thus be extended to include the queuing of processes when receivers temporarily outpace senders of messages to a given mailbox.

In summary, a mailbox serves as a meeting place of processes and messages. KMOS keep track of mailboxes by means of mailbox descriptors. A mailbox descriptor in KMOS must be structured in such a way that either messages (resulting from execution of unmatched SENDs) or control blocks of suspended processes (resulting from execution of unmatched RECEIVEs) can be queued there. Due to the nature of interprocess communication in KMOS, messages or process, but not both, may be queued at a given mailbox descriptor at any time.

Among the numerous possible service disciplines for waiting processes and messages, FIFO and priority queues are quite popular. FIFO is a likely candidate for KMOS because it is simple to implement and it ensures that, with the proper supply of messages, waiting processes cannot be subjected to indefinite postponement. In addition, the strongest implementation of semaphores and some classical problems in concurrency control may best be served by FIFO delivery of waiting messages. Finally, the use of messages to signal interrupt arrivals in KMOS precludes the use of any queuing discipline other that FIFO.

Some multitasking operating systems use priority ordering of waiting processes, thus providing for potentially superior response time to high-priority processes compared with FIFO, but at the expense of the possibility of indefinite postponement and inconvenience in emulating semaphores. An approach adopted in some more complex systems is to support both forms of queuing and to enable system programmers to select the option most appropriate for servicing a particular mailbox.

To allow interprocess message communication, mailbox must first be created by means of the CREATEMBOX call in KMOS. Typically, a sender or the system initialization module is charged with this task. Creating a mailbox in KMOS is a fairly straightforward operation. It normally results in formation of the related mailbox descriptor capable of queuing messages or processes. When a mailbox descriptor is created, both queues are empty, and their headers must be initialized to reflect that fact. As far as message communication in KMOS is concerned, no further operations on a mailbox descriptor need be performed by the CREATEMBOX routine.

In general, however, requests to send messages to, or to receive messages from, a nonexistent mailbox (deleted or not created) should be denied by the operating system. Although the version of KMOS presented here omits this run-time check for reasons of simplicity and performance, we design the mailbox descriptor in KMOS in a way that facilitates subsequent implementation of this feature. Deletion of an existing mailbox is another service that is not offered by KMOS, but that may be desirable in a large operating system. Both of these extensions call for a list of all mailbox descriptors in the system. Entries to this list can be added whenever a new mailbox is created, and entries can be removed when the operating system is required to delete a mailbox. When only a validity check is desired, this list may be searched to find out whether the target mailbox descriptor is in active use, say, by virtue of being created but not deleted. Requests to use active mailboxes can then be granted, and others may be denied with a corresponding error code returned to the calling process. With the Mailboxes list added to KMOS, the functional specification of CREATEMBOX may be devised as presented in Program 21.2.

Mailbox descriptors and the Mailboxes list can be of further use in operating systems that require processes to declare their affiliation with active mailboxes, for example, by means of an ATTACH(MAILBOX) call. In such systems, a process may detach itself from a mailbox that it no longer uses. Similarly, a departing process may be detached from all its mailbox holdings by the operating system as part of the EXIT-call processing.

```
routine CREATEMBOX (mailbox); {user callable}
{creates a mailbox}

begin
    save caller's context;
    allocate storage for the mailbox descriptor;
    with mailbox descriptor do
        begin
            initialize queue of messages to empty;
            initialize queue of processes to empty
        end;
    enter mailbox descriptor in Mailboxes list;
    restore caller's context;
    return control to caller
end;
```

Program 21.2. Functional specification of CREATEMBOX.

With ATTACH/DETACH supported, the operating system is cable to detect unused mailboxes by keeping track of the number of processes actively attached to them. Superfluous mailboxes can then be deleted by the operating system immediately upon detachment of the last related process, reflected by the attached-count in the corresponding mailbox descriptor becoming zero. In this way, the operation system essentially performs event-driven garbage collection of mailboxes. This feature is particularly important in distributed operating systems, where the cost of maintaining an open intersite communication channel may be quite high. KMOS data structures for message exchange allow for addition of the ATTACH/DETACH mechanism when desired.

SEND and RECEIVE Operations

The functional specification of the KMOS facility for sending messages, SEND, is given in Program 21.3. As indicated, SEND needs two parameters: the identity of the mailbox (descriptor) where the message is to be delivered, and the message itself. When SEND is invoked by the running process, either processes or messages may be found waiting at the designated mailbox descriptor. When no processes are waiting, the message cannot be delivered immediately, and SEND enqueues it at the mailbox descriptor before returning control to the caller—the running process in this case. Alternatively, if one or more processes are waiting, SEND delivers the message to the first in line.

```
routine SEND (mailbox, message); {user callable}
{sends message to the mailbox}

    begin
        save caller's context;
        if no processes waiting
            then
                begin
                    queue up the message at the mailbox descriptor; {FIFO}
                    restore caller's context;
                    return control to caller {running process}
                end
            else {processes waiting}
                begin
                    remove message_recipient from the mailbox process queue;
                    deliver the message to the message recipient;
                    make message_recipient ready;
                    running :=schedule the next process to run;
                    dispatch (running)
        end
end;
```

Program 21.3. Functional specification of SEND.

Since delivery of a message results in both the running process and the message recipient becoming ready, the scheduler should be invoked to determine which process should receive control after completion of SEND. Prior to that, the context of the running process must be saved in case it is preempted by the message recipient. In any case, the message recipient is made ready and its PCB is moved from the mailbox queue to the Ready list.

Two subtle but relatively important points can be made about the suggested functional specification of the SEND primitive in KMOS. First, like all system routines callable by users, SEND begins by saving the context of the calling process. The saved context is restored when control is eventually returned to the process that has invoked the system service. In the case of SEND, if the message cannot be delivered immediately and control is returned to the sender, the sender's (caller of SEND) context is restored. Alternatively, if the message is successfully delivered, its sender may or may not be the next process to be dispatched. Thus, SEND cannot blindly restore its caller's context, and the restoring of the proper context is left to the DISPATCH routine, which learns the identity of the next running process from the scheduler. The details of the context save-restore operations are system-specific, and they depend on this such as the format of the system data structures, the type of instruction used to invoke the operating system, the amount of context switch (process switch) done by the underlying hardware, and the memory-management and protection policies in effect.

The second point regards potential selection of the next running process within the body of SEND. When the message is delivered to a waiting process, there are only two viable candidates from which to select the next running process: the caller of SEND (the previously running process) and the message recipient. Given priority-based scheduling in KMOS, probably a more efficient version of SEND may be constructed so that the priorities of the two processes are compared and the scheduling decision is made within SEND. In this way the scheduler need not be invoked, whereas saving the context of the running process and restoring the context of the message recipient is performed only when the priority of the running process is comparatively lower, so that invocation of SEND results in it preemption.

The problem with thus approach is that it would build a policy, rather than a mechanism, into the logic of SEND. Any subsequent change of the scheduling policy would then necessitate corresponding modifications in all routines, such as SEND, that are dependent on it. On the other hand, the functional specification of SEND as given is based on the philosophy that each particular OS function should be entrusted to a separate routine that should have the sole authority to perform the given function. Consequently, SEND is not allowed to make any scheduling decision, even when the algorithm is simple and only two process are involved. By localizing the focus of each activity into a dedicated OS routine, the system is likely to be easier to comprehend, to develop, and to maintain, thus increasing programming productivity and yielding a potentially more reliable product.

```
routine RECEIVE (mailbox) : message; {user callable}
{delivers a message from the specified mailbox}
begin
    save caller's context;
    if messages waiting
        then
            begin
                dequeue the first message from the mailbox descriptor;
                give message to the calling process; {running process}
                restore caller's context;
                return control to caller
            end
        else {no message available}
```

(contd.)

```
            begin
                suspend the calling process at the mailbox descriptor;
                running := schedule new running process;
                dispatch (running)
        end
    end;
```

Program 21.4. Functional specification of RECEIVE.

The insights gained by the functional specification of SEND make the process of devising the logic of RECEIVE, whose functional specification is given in Program 21.4, quite straightforward. RECEIVE takes one parameter, the identity of the mailbox where the message is to be received, and returns a message to the calling process. For this reason, RECEIVE is specified and intended to be called as a function. When invoked by the running process, RECEIVE may find one, more than one, or no messages and perhaps some processes waiting at the designated mailbox. Upon finding at least one message, RECEIVE removes the message from the mailbox and delivers it to the calling process—in this case the running process, which is not preempted. Alternatively, if no message can be delivered, the running process is suspended at the mailbox (descriptor), and a new running process is scheduled and dispatched.

Interrupt Management

Interrupt servicing in KMOS relies heavily on the message-exchange mechanism. Basically, each hardware interrupt is intercepted by KMOS and converted into a corresponding system message, which is then sent to the mailbox dedicated to the interrupt level in question. The operating system should take responsibility for dynamic disabling of lower interrupt levels and enabling of the higher ones, commensurate with the priority level of the running process. Depending on the available hardware support, the hardware/software division of labor for this activity may vary considerably. In order to avoid machine-dependent details, we assume that KMOS is to be implemented on system configurations that include an interrupt controller or equivalent hardware support of all three levels of interrupt making the system-wide level (interrupts on/off), the individual priority level (selective making), and the individual device level (I/O port control register). This assumption is satisfied even by microcomputers when they are fitted with a programmable interrupt controller.

In principle, an operating system should differentiate between *hardware priority* levels that may be assumed by the related interrupt-service routines and *software priority* levels assigned to all other processes. Hardware priorities are commonly used to drive the interrupt enable/disable logic, and they are placed above software priorities to achieves low latency in response to interrupts. In this scheme, processes are scheduled according to their software priorities when no interrupt-related activities are ready to use the processors. Due to is uniform handling of Interprocess communication and of interrupt signalling via messages, strict differentiation between ISRs and other processes, and consequently between hardware and software priority levels, is not mandatory in KMOS. However, some means are required for instructing KMOS which particular interrupt levels should be enable and which disabled when an ISR is running. A simple scheme for accomplishing this may be to partition KMOS priority levels into interrupt-related levels and other (software) levels.

An internal KMOS routine for handling interrupts, ITSERV, is specified in Program 21.5. All hardware interrupts in a KMOS environment are supposed to be vectored to the entry of the ITSERV routine. After saving the context of the pre-empted running process. ITSERV identifies the hardware priority level of the asserted interrupt request. This information is used to send the system interrupt message to the related interrupt mailbox, designated as MAILBOX [LEVEL]. For reasons of portability and hardware independence, KMOS should note be involved in any device-specific interrupt processing and should not communicate directly with any I/O port other than the programmable interrupt controller (PIC).

A PIC, or its functional equivalent, is a highly desirable form of hardware support for multitasking operating systems, especially those intended for real-time. Assuming that a PIC is available to KMOS, ITSERV prevents repetitive processing of the same interrupt by acknowledging the request to PIC. Finally, ITSERV sends the interrupt message to single arrival of the interrupt to the service routine.

```
routine ITSERV; {not software callable}
{processing of hardware interrupts}
    begin
        {entered upon a hardware interrupt}
        save context of the running process;
        mark is state preempted;
        identify the source level to interrupt;
        acknowledge interrupt to interrupt controller; {PIC}
        send interrupt_message to mailbox{level}
        if no process waiting at mailbox [level]
            then
                begin
                    running := schedule new running process;
                    dispatch (running)
                end
    end;
```

Program 21.5. Functional specification of ITSERV.

Naturally, ITSERV should rely on the SEND routine to relay this message and to activate a waiting service process, if any. If no process is waiting for the interrupt message at the related mailbox, SEND returns control to its caller, ITSERV. Since its work is finished, ITSERV surrenders control to the new running process selected by the scheduler.

Although the proposed specification of ITSERV assumes that individual interrupt levels can be enabled and disabled selectively, we have not specified where and how these operations are done in KMOS. Given the possibility of direct mapping of a KMOS priority level into a corresponding hardware priority level, the DISPATCH routine is probably the best candidate to set the PIC or other interrupt-masking registers so that all higher interrupt levels are enable and the lower or equal levels are disabled when the running process receives control of the processor. This operation can be performed as a part of "other housekeeping" in the DISPATCH routine.

In addition to this form of interrupt control, it is customary to allow users to explicitly enable and disable individual levels of interrupt. At system initialization time, user-serviced interrupt levels are typically disabled and mapped to the operating-system routine for detection and handling of false interrupt requests, which could otherwise hang up the system. Some process, most commonly a user-written interrupt-service routine, must then first explicitly enable the interrupt level of the device that it services. One way to implement the user-level interrupt enabling is to maintain an internal system-interrupt mask, which is initially set to all interrupt levels off. The system service to enable a specific level may then simply turn on the corresponding bit or bits in the system mask. Finally, the operating system, when surrendering control to a process, may enable only those interrupt levels that are both higher than that of the running process and enabled by an earlier system call.

```
routine ENABLEV (interrupt_level); {user callable}
{enables a hardware interrupt-level}
begin
    save caller's context;
    if interrupt_level is valid
    then turn on the sysintmask[interrupt_level] bit;
    restore caller's context;
    return control to caller
end;
```

Program 21.6. Functional specification of ENABLEV

The previous discussion provides the basis for the functional specification of a KMOS routine for enabling an interrupt level, ENABLEV, whose functional specification is given in Program 21.6. Routine ENABLEV takes one parameter, the interrupt level to be enabled. The number of interrupt levels in a given system is generally hardware-dependent and may vary among KMOS implementations for different processors. As discussed, ENABLEV simply manipulates the corresponding bit in the system interrupt mask. SYSINTMASK. This implementation implies that SYSINTMASK is set to all levels off at system initialization time. In principle, ENABLEV can also be charged with creating the interrupt mailbox for the enabled level. To keep things simple, the proposed specification assumes that this is done at KMOS initialization time for all interrupt levels in a given hardware configuration.

Process Management

The process-management functions in KMOS are reduced to process creation and to delaying a process for a specified period of time.

Process Creation

Creation of a process entails the initials formation of the process control block, typically followed by the process's transition to the Ready state. When a process departs the system, its PCB is normally returned to the pool of free PCBs.

For reasons similar to those discussed in relation to the Mailboxes list, the run-time validity check of process names passed as parameters to system calls is a useful feature in an operation system. For example, a request for an indefinite suspension or for a forceful abortion of a process normally returns an error indication if the specified process is nonexistent, perhaps because it terminated or was never created. Authentication of process names can be conveniently performed when a list of all nondormant processes names in the system is maintained by the OS. Although the validity of process names is not checked by KMOS, such functional extension is made possible by maintaining the All-processes list. The elements of this list are the process-control blocks, which can be added at process creation time and removed when the related process departs the system. With this addition, the CREATERPROC routine in KMOS may be specified as presented in Program 21.7.

```
routine CREATEPROC (process_ID, process_attributes); {user callable}
{creates a process and makes it ready}
begin
    save caller's context;
    allocate space for a PCB[process_ID];
    enter process_attributes into PCB[process_ID];
    initialize other PCB[process_ID] fields;
    enter PCB[process_ID] into All-processes list;
    enter PCB[process_ID] into Ready list;
    restore caller's context;
    return control to caller
end;
```

Program 21.7. Functional specification of CREATERPROC.

Routine CREATEPROC associates a process-control block with the newly created process; it enters the initial values of process attributes, such as process priority, and enters the PCB into the All-processes and Ready lists. Note that no rescheduling is done following process creation in KMOS, and control is always returned to the calling process. As a result, the newly created process may become the running process only upon occurrence of an event that causes the scheduler to be invoked, such as a timer interrupt.

Deletion of a process is much simpler. The KMOS function DELETEPROC removes the process from all system list and then invokes the scheduler to select the next running process.

Delaying of a Process for a Specified Time

Delaying of a process for a specified amount of time is the second process-management function of KMOS. In principle, a process wishing to delay itself involves the DELAY routine and specifies the duration of the desired delay. The operating system normally services such requests by means of two separate but cooperating activities. The calling process is first suspended and placed in the list of delayed processes, and the number of system clock-ticks corresponding to the duration of the delay is recorded in the related PCB. Second, whenever an interrupt from the interval timer is processed, the operating system decrements the number of remaining intervals in the PCBs of all processes in the Delayed list. Each process whose delay is found to be expired, by virtue of the related count becoming zero, is resumed by being placed into the Ready list.

In keeping with localization of functions within separate routines in KMOS, we may implement the two described activities as two separate routines. The first of them, DELAY, is specified in Program 21.8. After suspending the caller and recording the number of time intervals (clock-ticks) to delay the caller, DELAY causes dispatching of a new running process in a standard way. The functional specification of the routine for processing timer interrupts. KMOSCLOCK, is given in Program 21.9.

The proposed specification of KMOSCLOCK reflects our enhanced understanding of the operation of KMOS. In typical design process, the definition of each new mechanism may require redefinition of other functions to incorporate the new mechanisms into previously specified routines. For example, this was the case with our subsequent augmentation of functions of the DISPATCH routine. In this chapter we take the approach of specifying routines on the basis of the accumulated knowledge about the KMOS system as discussed up to that point, and leave redefinition to the reader. This should provide a realistic illustration of the various stages of the specification process.

In the particular case of KMOSCLOCK, we rely on the interrupt signaling mechanism of KMOS to do context manipulation and to send a message for each timer interrupt. Consequently, KMOSCLOCK can be conceptualized as a process, as all interrupt-service routines under KMOS should be viewed. In its initialization section, KMOSCLOCK initializes the programmable interval timer for the desired duration of a system time unit (clock-tick). Following this, the corresponding interrupt level is enabled in order to allow recognition of timer interrupts. In its repetitive section, KMOSCLOCK is activated upon each timer interrupt (expiration of a clock-tick) to decrement the TICSK_TO_WAIT count of each process in the Delayed list. Processes whose delay period has expired are then effectively resumed by being placed into the Ready list.

```
routine DELAY (time); {user callable}
{places the calling process into Delayed list}
begin
    save caller's context;
    place caller's PCB into Delayed list; {suspend}
    set caller's status to delayed;
    record time as number of clock ticks to wait;
    running := schedule new running process;
    dispatch (running)
end;
```

Program 21.8. Functional specification of DELAY.

```
process KMOSCLOCK; {ISR, running under KMOS}
{timer interrupt processing}
begin
    initialize hardware interval_timer;
    enablev (hardware_timer);
    forever do
```

(contd.)

```
    begin
        {enter upon timer interrupt}
        receive interrupt message at timer mailbox;
        decrement ticks_to_wait of each process in Delayed list;
        for all processes where ticks_to_wait = 0 do
            begin
                remove process from Delayed list;
                insert process into Ready list
            end
    end {forever do}
end;
```

Program 21.9. Functional specification of KMOSCLOCK.

System Startup

Whenever a computer system is "cold-started," say, after being powered or following a system crash, at least a portion of the operating system must be brought into main memory and given control of the processor. This activity is often called *system booting* or *bootstrapping* of an operating system. Typically, the hardware initially transfers control to a known address where a starting routine in ROM is placed. This routine, called the *bootstrap loader,* can be used to bring the rest of the system gradually to main memory, for instance, from secondary storage for from another node in a distributed system. In disk-based systems, the core portion of the operating system if often placed at a known address, called the *boot block* or *boot area,* of a known system disk drive. Thus, the bootstrap-loader routine can include a rudimentary form of a disk driver whose primary function is to load and to activate the initialization section of the operating system. This section can, in turn, load into main memory the rest of the operating system and complete the initialization process. In memory-based systems, such as KMOS, the starting routine can simply transfer control to the operating system, which itself may be residing in ROM.

Initialization of user processes poses a chicken-and-egg problem: if a process must be created in order to start executing, and a process must be executing in order to invoke OS services—including creation of processes—who or what creates the first user process in freshly initialized system? In many interactive multiuser systems this problem is solved by having the operating system create the command-languages interpreter process for at least one terminal. This process can then create other processes in response to user commands. Incidentally, the command-language interpreter is treated as a system process in some operating systems, and as a user process in others.

In embedded systems and in many specialized applications, however, there may not be a single user process—such as the command-line interpreter—that should be present, and therefore activated automatically by the operating system, in every installation. Thus, a more general solution is for the operating system to create a known process, user-definable but system-initiated, whenever the system is started. At least a portion of the program for this process—let us call it INITPROCESS—

can be defined by the system manger or a programmer to include CREATE calls for the initial configuration of user objects, such as processes and mailboxes. By convention, INITPROCESS is always the first user process to receive control from the orating system.

In any case, a working system is needed to define the initial configuration of a target system. For example, a working system is needed to edit the startup command file or to develop the user-specified portion of INITPROCESS. In large, disk-based systems, this problem is often solved by having a version of the operating system that works on the target configuration delivered and installed by the vendor. The system manager can then fine-tune the system and define the desired post-startup configuration of processes by means of *system generation,* a set of programs and procedures for tailoring the operating system for a target configuration. In embedded and other memory-based applications, the target configuration rarely supports program development, and the operating system is usually defined on a different host machine. The configured operating system and application programs are then transferred to the target machine by means of some nonvolatile medium, such as ROM, or downloaded from the host through a communication link or an in-circuit emulator. In the downloading case, a resident program (say, in ROM) is required on the target machine to carry out the necessary communication and loading procedures.

Since KMOS is specified as a memory-based system, we assume that all KMOS code, as well as the code of processes to be run under it, is in memory when control of the processor is initially transferred to KMOS. In the next chapter we explain how this is accomplished in a sample ROM/RAM-based system. The starting routine of KMOS should thus initialize the hardware needed for proper operation of KMOS. Based on our previous discussion, this may include initialization of the programmable interrupt-controller. In order to be as hardware and configuration-independent as possible, KMOS should not initialize any other I/O ports that may be available in a specific system configuration. This task may best of accomplished by the individual interrupt-service routines themselves when they eventually receive control of the processor for the first time, as illustrated by the KMOSCLOCK process presented earlier. Hardware initialization is customarily done with interrupts off, so that no I/O may take place until the system is ready to handle it properly.

Likewise, KMOS must initialize its own data structures before surrendering control to the first user process. These include all system lists and pointers, such as Ready and Delayed list, and global system data, such as SYSMASK. At this point, the initial configuration of user processes and their related mailboxes can be created.

Implementation Considerations

In this section we discuss two issues that must be resolved in any implementation of an operating system: selection of a programming language or languages, and choice of a method for invoking the operating system.

Systems Implementation Languages

Before commencement of coding, a language (or languages) to be used for systems implementation should be selected. By a *system implementation language* we mean a high-level programming language with provisions for systems programming. Although there has not been official standardization of language support for systems programming, there seems to be some agreement among the practitioners as to which features in a language are necessary for systems implementation. Some of those are listed below.

- Facilities for modular program development
- Access to hardware and to physical memory addresses

We briefly review each of these in the subsequent sections.

Facilities for Modular Program Development

Facilities for modular program development generally refer to facilities for individual compilation of modules and for maintenance of module libraries. These facilities are very useful in large programming projects, both for an individual programmer and for programming teams. Depending on whether type checking is preserved or not across module boundaries when different modules belonging to a single program are compiled at different times, module compilation is said to be separate or independent, respectively.

Independent compilation refers to the ability to compile individual modules of a single program independently. Independent compilation does not provide type

```
routine KMOSSTART; {user callability implementation dependent}
{initializes the system}
    begin
        {control passed by hardware}
        disable interrupts;
        initialize hardware
         .PIC;
        initialize KMOS data structures
         .list pointers to nil
         .queue headers to empty
         .global variables to initial values;
        create system processes;
        create system mailboxes;
        provide means for creation of user process (es);
        running := schedule new running process;
        dispatch (running)
    end;
```

Program 21.10. Functional specification of KMOSSTART.

checking across module boundaries; in its basic form, only definition of *public symbols* (defined in one module but used by several) and *external symbols* (used in a given module but defined elsewhere) is supported. Independent compilation is a familiar tool provided, for example, by Fortran and PL/I compiler and by many commercial assemblers. In systems where standard calling and parameter-passing conventions are observed, independent compilation facilitates combination of object modules coded in different programming languages.

For example, combining HLL modules with those written in assembly language is a common practice in system programming. In general, HLLs offer potential for increased programmer productivity, higher product reliability, and comparative ease of maintenance. Assembly language, on the other hand, offers high performance and allows virtually unrestricted access to hardware. In the absence of the appropriate systems implementation language with facilities discussed later in this section, a reasonable approach to systems programming is to code everything initially in a high-level language. After some operational testing to establish the feasibility and correctness of the logic of the particular solution, certain time-critical operations may be identifies and coded in the assembly language. Some hardware and software measuring aids and tools, such as logic analyzers and HLL profilers, are available for pinpointing the areas most likely to benefit from increased speed of execution. In principle, only operation requiring direct access to hardware, and those on which performance of the entire system critically depends, should be considered for coding in assembly language. When used, assembler code should be made as structured as possible. An interesting approach that has been used in some commercial systems is to hand-optimize the code generated by the compiler, as opposed to writing the assembly-language portion from scratch. If local per-statement optimization is done, the HLL code can serve for program documentation and testing purposes.

The inability of independent compilation to enforce typing across module boundaries, that is, to ensure that an external identifier is used in a given module in accordance with its type as declared in the identifier's home module, can be a serious problem. For example, referring to nonexistent fields of an external record structure can create havoc at run-time without even an indication at compile-time. This difficulty is directly attributable to independent compilation, since it is not otherwise encountered in strongly typed languages such as Pascal, when the entire program is compiled as a single unit. Standard Pascal does not allow independent compilation, mainly to enforce the strict compile-time checking of types. As a result, complex Pascal programs can be difficult to develop by a team of programmers, because all of them have to work on a single, large program.

Separate compilation provides for separate compilation of modules constituting a single program, with the significant addition of performing compile-time type checking across the module boundaries. The programming languages Ada and Modula-2, for example, include provision for separate compilation. Basically, both languages require programmers to separate statement of a module (a *package* or *task* in Ada) into a module definition part (the *public part* in Ada) and a module implementation part (the private part in Ada). The definition portion of a module, which is an externally visible part, includes declaration of foreign objects referenced within the given module but defined in some other module, and declarations of objects declared in the related module but available to external users. The implementation part contains declarations of the variables private to the module, and the executable program statements.

Modular program development usually results in a relatively large number of modules that participate in the mechanics of program development, such as editing, compiling, and linking. For this reason, support for separate or independent compilation is often combined with facilities for creation and maintenance of program and module libraries. A module library can be a file that consists of a number of object modules produced by separate or independent compilation. For convenience in linking, a library usually contains a list of names of all public symbols declared or referenced in its constituent modules. A related utility, often called a *librarian*, is commonly provided for the maintenance of program libraries. A typical librarian may provide services for creation and deletion of libraries, for queries about the individual modules or symbols, and for additions or deletions of individual modules.

Separate compilation coupled with library functions is believed to offer some additional advantages, such as reduction of compilation costs and simplified development and management of program corrections. For example, modification of the source code can be simplified by being localized only to one or to very few affected modules. This results in easier editing and selective backup since individual source files are comparatively small. Likewise, compilation costs may be reduced by being limited to fewer lines of code per iteration of the edit, compile, and link cycle. Linking of a large number of modules, which is quite common with modular programming, can become cumbersome in terms of unwieldy command lines where each individual module needs to be specified. Libraries are of great help here, because they can be used to group a number of modules together. Linking commands are then reduced to a few module names and to a single specification of a library where other modules are to be found.

Access to Hardware and to Physical Memory Addresses

Access to hardware is often made possible by means of a special mechanism, rather than by providing specific hardware manipulation statements in the language. The term generally implies some means for vectoring of interrupts to user-written service routines and the ability to manipulate certain machine registers, such as the processor statues word, interrupt masks, and the stack pointer. Access to hardware is often provided by use of the specialized libraries, whose functionality is not defined in the language but is usually informally suggested and often becomes a de facto standard. Independent compilation provides this feature indirectly by allowing object modules produced by compiler to be combined with those produced by the assembler.

Access to physical memory addresses usually refers to the ability to obtain the address of, or to form a pointer to, a static object in memory. For example, this type of operation may include initialization of a pointer to an actual memory address of a named variable. Another common variety is assignment of an address to a variable. For example, a variable of the declared type can be located at a programmer-specified physical address. This feature is useful for accessing I/O ports from a high-level language.

Access to memory words and physical addresses is often coupled with some sort of pointer arithmetic with relaxed type checking, such as comparisons or increments. Pascal, for example, does not aid systems programmers in this respect, because it severely restricts the range of operations allowable on pointer types and permits creation of pointers only to dynamically created objects in memory. Its descendant, Modula-2. provides a range of operations for access to memory words, in addition to a mechanism for controlled type conversion.

Controlled type conversion essentially refers to the ability to occasionally escape, with the compiler's consent, the strong type checking if it is otherwise enforced by the programming language in question. Programming languages that support this feature, such as Modula-2 and Edison, differ in the mechanics of this mechanism. In some languages, a given type can be retyped to another type of equivalent length by invoking a system-provided function or procedure. In other languages, a generic type—such as an unsigned integer or a word—is provided and maked compatible with other types of the same length. Note that controlled type-conversion may substitute for pointer arithmetic mentioned earlier.

Uncontrolled type conversion is often make possible by systems that support independent compilation. Although it is not allowed in standard Pascal, many commercial versions of Pascal compilers provide independent compilation. In such systems, one may simply call a procedure coded in another language, say, assembler, to equate two Pascal variables of different types. We call this approach *uncontrolled* because the compiler is not alerted to potentially dangerous and often nonportable conversion of types.

The portability of programs that access hardware and physical memory addresses is often restricted to a given type of processor, or even to a specific hardware configuration. Although sometimes indispensable for systems programming, machine-dependent operations should be used only when absolutely necessary. Some systems and compilers flag the use of potentially nonportable or nonstandard features of a language. One such example is the *lint* utility for C code available under the Unix operation system. Lint verifies the potential portability of a program coded in C and advises on constructs and usages that might constitute portability problems, bugs, or dead code.

Invoking the Operating System

In this section we briefly discuss the common approaches to invoking the operating system. In genera, system architects must provide a way to invoke OS services from user programs and to pass some parameters when needed by a specific OS routine. In computer systems that provide some hardware support for protection between the operating system and user processes, and additional requirement is to change the level of privilege whenever crossing the OS-user boundary. Three popular methods for invoking the OS are:

1. Procedure call
2. Supervisor call
3. Software interrupt

Each of these is elaborated in the subsequent sections.

Procedure Call

A procedure call, in its ordinary form, assumes that the operating-system routines are coded as procedures. Users may invoke them and pass parameters to the OS by means of the standard procedure call. This method is simple and usable on virtually and computer system, since all that it requires is hardware support for the procedure call/return mechanism.

However, procedure calls are generally unsuitable for changing the level of privilege when transferring between a caller and a callee. An exception to this rule may be claimed by virtual-memory systems in which the operating system is mapped into each user's virtual spaces. Such systems may use the procedure-call mechanism for its efficiency, since they provide protection to common OS routines through address-space isolation, but privileged access to system facilities may still be difficult to implement.

Another, no less serious, problem with invoking the operating system via procedure calls is that of binding. Namely, in most program development systems the operating system is already in place when user programs are being developed and run. When invoking the OS, the question is when and how to bind user-specified names of OS services to the actual addresses of the corresponding OS routines long since loaded in memory. A straightforward solution, employed in some primitive monitors and early microcomputer systems, is to use direct instead of symbolic addressing and to specify the actual address of the desired operating-system routing. A more convenient approach, used in some larger systems, is to allow symbolic referencing of OS services by their prescribed names. Translation of those names into the entry points of the corresponding modules in performed with the aid to a system-supplied library with the public declarations of names of user-callable OS services. The address of each service can be determined and furnished to the OS library by the linker or the linking loader at the time when the executable version of the operating-system code is prepared. User programs that call on operating-system services directly must specify the OS library as one of the input modules during the linking process in order to have the symbolic references to the OS resolved.

Supervisor Call

A supervisor call (SVC) is usually a specialized hardware instruction dedicated to invoking the operating system. Common implementations of the SVC provide at least one operand, the identity of the desired OS service. Thus, the SVC typically provides a common entry point to the operating system. The indicated service may then be invoked on the basis of the supplied parameter by means of a jump or index table. Since it always transfers control to the OS, the SVC instruction may be allowed to switch to Supervisor or to some other privileged OS mode. A context switch, if necessary, can also be performed at this point and perhaps be included in the microcode of the SVC instruction. When returning control to a user process, the operating system can do so by means of some sort of a (privileged) switch-mode instruction.

Another advantage of the SVC instruction is that it alleviates the problem of knowing the addresses of the OS routines at compile-time or at link-time. Users can simply specify the number of the desired OS service as a parameter to the SVC instruction. The key is in the indirect transfer of control by means of the jump table, whereby SVC performs the required run-time binding. Namely, when code of the OS is loaded in memory, the SVC jump table is normally filled with the actual address of each numbered OS routine. As long as service numbers are kept identical between releases, object-code portability of user programs may be accomplished when the SVC instruction is used.

Software Interrupt

A software interrupt (SWI) is a versatile instruction that is finding its way into an increasing number of computer systems, especially microprocessors. Basically, a software interrupt instruction triggers the hardware interrupt-processing sequence. In other words, an SWI has the same effect as if an external interrupt request were asserted. Depending on the supporting architecture, this may include the context-save and transfer of control of the related interrupt-service routine. The SWI instruction is useful for invocation of the operating-system services and for debugging of interrupt-related code.

When used to invoke the operating system, the SWI instruction may provide both the context switch and vectoring directly to the related OS routine. In addition, switching to a privileged mode of operation can also be performed at this time. Similar to the SVC instruction, the operating system or some other program can load the address of the corresponding service into each interrupt vector dedicated to an OS service. Users are thus relieved from knowing anything but the number or the "interrupt level" of the corresponding OS service. Due to the resulting run-time binding, portability of object code can easily be accomplished when the SWI instruction is used to invoke the operating system. By designating a single interrupt vector as an entry point to the operating system, the SWI instruction can be used to emulate the supervisor call described earlier. However, the SWI instruction can alleviate the bottleneck of a single entry point by dedicating a separate vector to each individual operating-system service.

An additional attraction for system architects and programmers is that the SWI instruction can be used to aid in debugging of interrupt-related code, an area where standard debuggers are of little or no use and where generation and stimulation of realistic test cases is difficult. An SWI instruction issued from a test program can be used to simulate an interrupt coming from a physical device and to trigger the entire event-recognition sequence. However, permissive use of this facility can be dangerous in system in normal operation, and some safeguards must be in place to prevent potentially hazardous uses of the SWI instruction, such as triggering false interrupts at the level assigned to an active device.

Summary

In this chapter we have provided a functional specification of a small kernel for a multitasking operating-system (KMOS) in order to stress the interactions between the various parts of the operating system discussed in earlier chapters, and to illustrate certain aspects of the system design process. A kernel is a first-level functional extension of the computer hardware, corresponding to Layer1. Kernels are among the most stable layers of operating systems, and their functionality is similar across a wide range of systems.

KMOS provides a message facility for interprocess communication and synchronization, as well as for the signaling of hardware interrupts. Basic process scheduling in KMOS is event-driven and based on the static process priorities. KMOS also supports delaying of processes for a specified period of time and manages the system time base.

Messages in KMOS are exchanged via mailboxes, where they are buffered if necessary. A mailbox is created in KMOS by invoking the CREATEMBOX system call. The SEND operation is nonblocking, which results in asynchronous exchange of messages. The RECEIVE operation is used to receive a message.

The CREATEPROC service is available of process creation in KMOS. Timed delaying of processes is performed in cooperation of the DELAY system service and of the KMOSCLOCK process, which services timer interrupts.

Support for modular programming is one of the desirable facilities of programming languages for systems implementation. Separate compilation of modules facilitates a structured form of modular programming by providing compile-time type checking across the module boundaries. Module libraries and related utilities are also useful for modular program development. Access to hardware and to physical memory addresses is often needed in systems programs. Some systems implementation languages provide these facilities by means of specialized libraries, pointer arithmetic, and controlled type conversions.

Although widely available, the procedure call/return mechanism is not very suitable for invoking the operating system because of the difficulty in managing the protection hardware and of the often-inflexible binding of operating-system service names to the corresponding addresses. Invocation of operating-system services by means of the specialized instructions, such as the supervisor call and the software interrupt, can alleviate both of these problems.

22

Implementation of KMOS (Kernel of Multitasking Operating System)

This chapter contains a complete design of KMOS based on its functional specification provided in the previous chapter. The resulting KMOS code, provided at the end of this chapter, can be used on IBM PC and compatibles for operating system laboratory exercises or as a stand-alone system for real time applications, such as control and monitoring of a laboratory instruments and automated experiments. Readers not interested in details of KMOS implementation may omit this chapter without loss of continuity.

Our intent in completing the KMOS design is to provide an illustration of the remaining aspects and intricacies of the system design process, and to provide a realistic example of the application of many concepts discussed in this book. A functional specification, because of the lack of standards and notation for its formal definition, can be presented in many ways that may or may not convey all important aspects of the system under consideration. Consequently, many details, such as the specification of data structures, remain to be worked out before the coding phase of the design process may be safely begun. In addition, the usual iterations prompted by increased understanding of the system being designed were left to the reader, resulting in a certain lack of uniformity in terms of the level of detail in the specification of different routines.

On the other hand, a reasonably debugged and documented working implementation is definitely a more objective landmark in the system design process. In proceeding with our design of KMOS, we begin by specifying the KMOS data structures, and then present a detailed implementation of its routines. Continuing to mimic the actual design process, we arrive at some particular solutions by discussing the considerations involved and by analyzing implementation trade-offs as they are encountered.

Standard Pascal does not provide many of the facilities described as necessary or describe for systems implementation. This problem is tackled in the design of KMOS by using an extended Pascal compiler (Turbo Pascal), which provides some extended facilities that simplify systems implementation and also supports inline assembly-language code for full control of the machine when necessary. The extensions for systems implementation provided in this particular compiler follow closely the syntax and semantics of the similar facilities found in popular systems implementation languages.

The implementation of KMOS presented uses the procedure-call mechanism to invoke the OS because of its applicability to a wide range of hardware. The problem of referencing OS routines is solved by requiring user processes to be linked together with the KMOS modules. This approach is reasonable for embedded real-time systems, such as KMOS in its stand-alone versions. In larger operating systems that support memory management and protection, the SVC or the SWI approach is preferable.

KMOS System Lists

The presented functional specification of KMOS routines also defines most of the operations on the related system lists.

1. All-processes (PCBs)
2. Ready (PCBs)
3. Delayed (PCBs)
4. Waiting-for-message (PCBs, one list per mailbox)
5. Waiting messages (messages, one list per mailbox)
6. Mailboxes (mailbox descriptors)

KMOS data structures include one each of the following lists: All-processes, Ready, and Delayed. In addition, there is potentially one list of messages and one list of processes per each active mailbox in the system. There is no Running list, because in uniprocessor systems the list of running processes can contain at most one entry at any time. Instead of maintaining a degenerate Running list, a pointer in KMOS can be dedicated to marking the PCB of a running process, which otherwise remains in the Ready list. Each KMOS list is populated by one type of KMOS object; process-control blocks, messages, or mailbox descriptors.

The process-control block of a newly created process in KMOS is placed into the All-processes list and the Ready list. As indicated by the KMOS process state-transition diagram the process may subsequently oscillate between the Ready, Running, Delayed and Waiting-for-message states. Whenever a process changes its state, KMOS routines record the resulting state of the system by moving the related PCB between the corresponding system lists. Processing of an event that results in a change of the system state thus typically causes a system object, such as a PCB, to be removed from one list and placed into another. Due to the generally high frequency of such events in multitasking systems, the operating system's performance is largely affected by its efficiency in handling the list-processing operations. Careful selection of the data structures suitable for representation and manipulation of system lists is therefore an important part of the operating-system design.

Given the frequent insertions and deletions of their entries, the OS system list are commonly implemented using a linked-list representation. Ignoring messages for a moment, a PCB of a KMOS process must provide link fields for the links required by various system lists. For example, a link field can be dedicated for the All-processes list. Since Ready and Suspended states of a process are mutually exclusive, at any time a given PCB may participate only in either the Ready list or in one of the two forms of the Suspended list. For this reason, a single multipurpose link field in a PCB can suffice for its placement in any of those three lists.

Having multiple link fields—up to one per each type of list—in a PCB makes it possible to weave KMOS system lists through a set of PCBs statically placed in their allocated memory space and never actually moved. When a PCB needs to be "moved" from one list to another, it is sufficient to update pointers of adjacent nodes accordingly without ever having to copy the contents of a PCB from one place in memory into another. This point is illustrated by Figure 22.1, which depicts a sample configuration of PCBs and a snapshot of system lists.

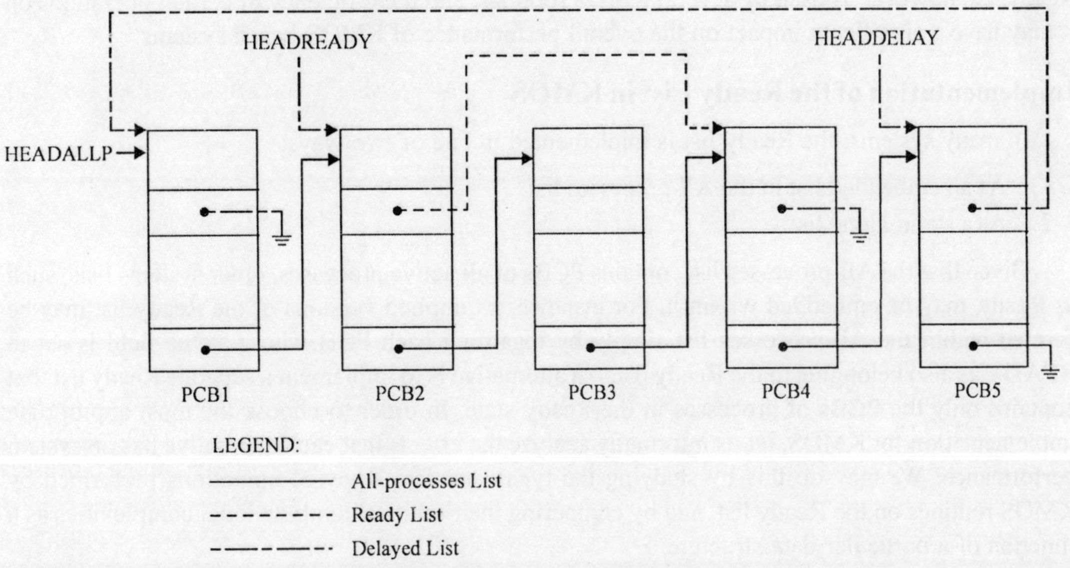

Fig. 22.1. A sample configuration of KMOS lists.

Also shown are KMOS internal pointers to the various lists. For example, the pointer to the All-processes list is designated as HEADALLP (Head of All-processes list). Similarly, HEADREADY and HEADDELAY pointers allows access to Ready and Delayed lists, respectively. In order to facilitate reading of code, the same acronyms are used to name the corresponding KMOS pointer variables.

Five processes are assumed to be active in the system depicted in Figure 22.1. Their corresponding process control blocks, PCB1 through PCB5, are connected in the All-processes list using the link field dedicated to that purposes in each PCB. As indicated, the Ready list is assumed to certain processes P2 and P4, in that order. The corresponding KMOS list pointer, HEADREADY, is therefore set to PCB2. The Delayed list contains PCB5 and PCB1, indicating that processes P5 and P1 are suspended awaiting expiration of their respective timed delayed. Process P3 is assumed to be suspended awaiting a message at some unspecified mailbox. The multipurpose link field of its process control block, PCB3, is left blank pending further elaboration of the structure of Waiting-for-message lists of processes in KMOS.

The Ready List and Its Manipulation

While a process's membership in other list varies with its state transitions, a process remains in the All-processes list from its creation until it terminates. As suggested earlier, this list may be used to satisfy queries about processes. In general, typical operations on this list are searching for a given process, for example, in order to check validity of a parameter supplied to a system call or to read a process's attributes, such as priority. Since our functional specification of KMOS does not provide any services that require such use of the All-processes list, which is maintained solely for the purposes of KMOS extensions, we have no basis for structuring this list in any particular way. The Ready list, however, is used by several KMOS routines, and the efficiency of certain operations on it may have a significant impact on the overall performance of KMOS-based systems.

Implementation of the Ready List in KMOS

In many systems, the Ready list is implemented in one of two ways:

1. As an embedded list in the All-processes list
2. As a stand-alone list

Given that the All-processes list contains PCBs of all active processes, other systems lists, such as Ready, may be embedded within it. For instance, an implied versions of the Ready list may be formed within the All-processes list simply by regarding each PCB whose status field is set to READY as also belonging to the Ready list. An alternative is to implement a separate Ready list that contains only the PCBs of processes in the Ready state. In order to choose the most appropriate implementation for KMOS, let us informally analyze the effects that each alternative has on system performance. We may do this by studying the types and frequency of operations performed by KMOS routines on the Ready list, and by comparing their relative computational complexities as a function of a particular data structure.

From the functional specification of KMOS routines, it follows that the Ready list is updated whenever a process is suspended (removal of the related PCB) or made ready (addition of the related PCB). The Ready list is searched for the highest-priority node whenever a new process needs to be scheduled. Thus, various KMOS routines perform three types of operations on the Ready list: (1) insertion of a node, (2) deletion of a node, and (3) searching to find a node with specific attributes.

If the Ready list is embedded within the All-processes lists, changes of state from Ready to Suspended and from Suspended to Ready can be recorded in place without the need to move the related PCB. Assuming that an operating-system pointer points to the target PCB when a state change needs to be performed, all that is needed is to update the PCB's status field accordingly. With this implementation, a new process can be scheduled by searching all PCBs and selecting the one with the highest priority among those whose STATUS field is set to READY. In terms of complexity, state changes may be recorded in constant time, whereas the time complexity of scheduling is on the order of n_t, which represents the total number of active processes in a given system at the time of scheduling. In this context, an active process is one created but not deleted, whose PCB is recorded in the All-processes list.

A separate Ready list requires the updating of pointers necessary to remove a PCB or to insert a PCB when the corresponding process makes a Ready–Suspended or Suspended–Ready transition, respectively. As illustrated later, these operations may also be performed in constant time independent of the number of nodes in Ready list. Although both approaches exhibits identical asymptotic behaviour (constant time), list manipulations are somewhat more time-consuming than the simple updating of a field required in the embedded implementation of the Ready list. Scheduling of a process with a separate Ready list requires searching of n_r nodes, where n_r is the number of ready processes in a given system at the time of scheduling.

As pointed out, the primary concern is to minimize the time spent searching the Ready list. In order to compare the two alternatives in this respect, observe that in multiprogramming operating systems the following relation between the number of ready processes and the total number of processes holds at all times:

$$n_r \le n_t$$

On the average, the number of active processes is likely to be strictly smaller than the total number of processes in a given system, and it may be considerably smaller when a relatively large number of processes is suspended for some reason. As a result, implementation of a separate Ready list in KMOS is likely to be more efficient than its embedded alternative.

The time complexity of searching can be reduced further, to constant time, when a separate version of the Ready list is sorted by the decreasing priority of participating processes. With this provision, the first PCB in the Ready list always belongs to the highest-priority ready process, and scheduling is reduced to setting a system pointer (running process) to it. However, insertion of a PCB into a sorted Ready list cannot be performed in constant time. On the average, this operation requires searching of ½(n_r) nodes in order to find the proper place to insert a PCB. With deletions and scheduling taking constant time, and scheduling being the most frequent and time-critical operation that directly affects the interrupt-response time, the implementation of a separate, priority-ordered Ready list in KMOS is likely to yield the best performance of all considered alternatives.

Process Control Block

The specification of the overall structure of system lists defines some aspects—links in particular—of the format of a process control block in KMOS. A PCB usually contains a process's attributes and other information that the operating system needs about the process. Some examples of PCB entries include: current status, priority, and allocated resources. In addition, a PCB contains the pointer fields necessary to link it to system lists corresponding to the current status of its related process. A PCB commonly provides some means for storing the context of its process when it is suspended or preempted. This function, as well as the problem of the initial entering of a process's attributes into its PCB, must be specified before we can outline the format of a PCB in KMOS.

Management of Process Stacks

Hardware interrupt-processing sequences and environment-changing instructions often use the stack for storing and retrieving the parts of context that they control. This makes the stack a good place for the operating system to store the remaining part of a process's context that must be saved by software. For reasons of security, it is customary to separate the system stack, used by the operating system, from the stack accessible to user processes. One way to accomplish this is to save and restore the respective stack pointer whenever a transition from a user's process to the operating system, or vice versa, takes place. Some computer systems facilitate this process by providing multiple stack pointer registers in hardware, sometimes augmented with automatic switching between them for executing instructions that make transitions between user and supervisor modes. In this way the integrity of the operating system's stack may be preserved in the presence of erroneous handling of the stack by a user process or processes.

However, maintenance of two separate stacks in a system does not solve the problem of a user process distributing the stack that it shares with other user processes. In particular, if a stack is shared by several user processes, each process making a transition from the Running state must leave the stack exactly as it found it when it was dispatched. Given that a running process may involuntarily be preempted by an external events, this requirement is both difficult to enforce and restrictive in the sense that it effectively precludes the possibility of processes using the stack for storing temporary variables. A much safer approach is to dedicate a separate stack to each user's process. In this way, whenever a user process is running, the stack pointer register (SP) is set to that process's private stack area. Whenever a process switch takes place, the departing process's value of the SP may be stored in its PCB. Likewise, the hardware SP may then be set for the newly inaugurated running process by restoring the saved SP value from the related PCB.

By allocating private stacks to user processes, the negative effects of improper stack manipulation can be localized to affect only offending process. In addition, each user process need not worry about matching the number of stack pushes and pops before surrendering control of the processor to the operating system and, ultimately, to another user process. Other advantages of the private-stack approach regarding context saving and restoring are discussed later in relation to implementation of the ITSERV routine. For obvious reasons, we adopt this form of stacks implementation in KMOS.

Structure of the Process Control Block

PCB format in KMOS is shown in Figure 22.2, which is a graphical representation of the PCB record declared in KMOS code. The first two fields of a PCB in KMOS are links to the Delayed list, which is actually implemented as a doubly linked list for reasons to be explained later. The THREAD field is the multipurpose link field used to place a PCB into the Ready list or into a Waiting-for-message list. The DELAY field is used to record the number of remaining clock-ticks when the process is in the Delayed state. The FRAME field is used to store the stack-frame pointer to the private stack when the process is not running. The STACK field points to the process's stack area whenever the process is not running. For the running process, the hardware stack pointer register and frame pointer register are set to access the process's stack. The MARKER field can be used to indicate the stack limit for a given process. This field is useful for detecting stack overflows and underflows during the system debugging process. Except for the data structure run-time testing of stack boundaries is not otherwise supported by the presented version of KMOS.

The PRI field contains programmer-assigned priority of the process. The STATUS field indicates the current status of the given process, such as Ready or Delayed. The LINKALL field is dedicated for linking the PCB into the All-processes list. The MASK field is used to store the hardware interrupt mask to be applied when the process is dispatched. As discussed later, this mask is machine-dependent, and it may be computed on the basis of process's priority. The HOLDMSG field is used to temporarily hold messages sent to the process. The NAME field contains process's name represented as a string of alphanumeric characters.

Insertions into the Ready List

The version of KMOS provided at the end of this chapter is coded in Pascal. It uses the UNIT construct that the Turbo Pascal compiler provides as a language extension. The notion and much of the syntax of UNIT is borrowed from the programming language Modula-2. As in Modula, UNIT allows separate compilation by strictly separating globally visible interfaces of module from its private implementation.

DELAYED_LINK_FORWARD (NEXT)
DELAYED_LINK_BACK (LAST)
THREAD
DELAY
FRAME_POINTER (FRAME)
STACK_POINTER (STACK)
MARKER
PRIORITY
STATUS
ALL_PROCESSES_LINK (LINK ALL)
MASK
MESSAGE_TO_DELIVER (HOLD MSG)
PROCESS_NAME (NAME)

Fig. 22.2. Structure of a process control block.

The interface portion of the KMOS UNIT contains public KMOS declarations, such as major pointer types, interrupt mailboxes, and names and calling parameters of all user-callable KMOS services and procedures. Public KMOS names are prefixed with the letter *K* followed by an underscore in order to reduce the possibility of naming conflicts with user variables. Thus, for example, the process creation procedure in KMOS is called K_CREATEPROC.

The implementation portion of KMOS contains all private data declarations and actual implementations of public and private KMOS procedures. User processes that call on KMOS services must explicitly specify the usage of UNIT KMOS and thus facilitate compile-time type checking of their calls to KMOS services. In the implementation portion of KMOS, familiar structures include the PCB record and head pointers to the various system lists. Some initial type declarations make use of the unsigned-integer type, UNSINT or WORD, which is discussed in relation to systems implementation languages. Other pointer types defined for KMOS data structures include PTRPCB, which points to a process control block record, and pointers to messages and mailbox descriptors.

The first KMOS routine to be discussed, INSERTREAD, inserts a process into the Ready list. This internal KMOS procedure is called by other KMOS services whenever a process needs to be made ready. As indicated by the functional specification, this operation is quite frequently needed by other parts of KMOS. Incidentally, INSERTREADY itself is not present in the functional specification. The reason is that this procedure implements our decision to maintain a separate, priority-ordered Ready list in KMOS. This decision was made subsequent to completion of the functional specification.

Procedure INSERTREADY inserts a PCB, passed as a parameter, into the Ready list in a manner that preserves its priority ordering. In particular, the new PCB is inserted after all those higher or equal priority, and ahead of all those of lower priority. The priority of a PCB is the value in its PRI field. In KMOS, a smaller number indicates higher priority; thus, 0 is the highest and 255 the lowest priority in the system. Processes of equal priority are placed in the Ready list in first-come, first-served (FCFS) order.

Procedure INSERTREADY uses a standard method of inserting before a given node of a linked list. Two local pointers, CURRENT and PREVIOUS, are used to point to the node currently being visited and to its predecessor, respectively. Both are initially set to the beginning of the Ready list. For coding brevity and convenience, the head node of the Ready list is a dummy PCB structure that does not belong to any process. A search for a lower-priority PCB is then conducted. The search terminates at the first such PCB found, or at the end of the list if none exists. In either case, the new PCB is inserted after the node pointed to by the PREVIOUS pointer.

As discussed earlier, the THREAD field is used to link PCBs to the Ready list. Once the node after which the new PCB is to be inserted (designated by the previous pointer upon exit from the search loop) is identified, the THREAD link of the new PCB is set to point the node before which it is being inserted. The THREAD field of the previous node is set to the new entry, thus completing the insert. The STATUS field of the new entry is set to READY, and the global variable RUNNING is set to the first entry in the Ready list in case an insert before the first node took place. The pointer RUNNING normally points to the running user process, which is the highest-priority ready process in KMOS. When KMOS itself is being executed, RUNNING may take on some transitional states while switching from one running process to another. The pointer to the active user process, RUNNING, essentially marks the only entry, if any, on the Running list.

Two points about the code of INSERTREADY may warrant some explanation. First, the head node of the Ready list is itself declared as a PCB initialized as having priority 0 (highest). Therefore, its THREAD field, that is, HEADREADY THREAD, actually points to the first ready process, and HEADREADY points to the head-node PCB. By designing the head node to have a structure identical to other entries, no special code is needed for insertions into the empty list or for insertions before the first (real) node of the list.

The second point is that INSERTREADY, as implemented, never inserts an entry after the last node. This is because the search loop terminates upon reaching the last node regardless of the relative priorities involved, since then the CURRENT^.THREAD pointer become NIL. This does not seem to be correct, because the new PCB should be inserted *after* the last node whenever the newcomer's priority is lower than that of the last node in Ready list. However, this kind of insertion never occurs in KMOS because the last node of the Ready list is *always* reserved for one special process. We now make a digression in order to explain the role of this rather important special process.

The Null Process

A problem that must be resolved by every multitasking system is what the operating system should do when there is nothing to do. For example, this situation occurs when the running process suspends itself—say, by attempting to receive a message from an empty mailbox—and no other process in the system is ready. As a result of the change of system state necessitating rescheduling (becoming blocked while executing RECEIVE in our example), the scheduler is invoked to select the next running process, but it finds the Ready list to be empty. In principle, this situation requires the system to wait until a process becomes ready, and then to surrender control to that process. A straightforward implementation of this philosophy is for the scheduler to busily test the state of the Ready list until it becomes nonempty as a result of an event that causes a process to become ready. This approach is ineffective in many systems in which the scheduler executes at a higher priority than user processes in order to be protected from potentially harmful preemptions. While in a high-priority wait loop, the operating system may never be able to detect the (lower-priority) event needed to get the user processes back in motion.

This problem is handled in many operating systems with the aid of a special NULL process that is created by the system as a part of the startup sequence. The NULL process never terminates by design and is always ready. As a result, the Ready list is never empty, and the problem is solved. Moreover, execution of the scheduler, a time-critical part of the system, can be made faster by eliminating the need to test for emptiness of the Ready list.

The simplest way to implement the NULL process is as a tight busy-wait loop. As described, NULL monopolizes the processor and therefore must be the lowest-priority processes in the system. This is exactly what is needed to make sure that all other events have higher priority and will thus preempt NULL and be recognized and processed by the system. Being executed only when the processor would otherwise be idle makes the NULL process an excellent vehicle for gathering performance statistics. That is, by NULL's keeping track of the time spent executing it, processor utilization by user processes and by the operating system can be measured. Another useful activity that can be delegated to the NULL process is execution of various diagnostic programs and, thus, assistance in monitoring system integrity.

KMOSNUL is the KMOS version of the do-nothing NULL process. KMOSNUL is the lowest-priority process; it is entirely processor-bound and thus always ready to execute. The body of KMOSNUL consists of an unconditional tight loop of the form.

while *true* **do** {*nothing*};

As indicated, the purpose of KMOSNUL is to ensure that the Ready list is never empty. Since priority ordering of the Ready list and event-driven scheduling result in the scheduler being reduced to a single assignment in the course of process dispatching, the DISPATCH routine selects the next process to run in a KMOS system. Thus, the existence of KMOSNUL process makes the execution of DISPATCH faster, as DISPATCH does not have to test for emptiness of the Ready list. In addition, the presence of at least one PCB in the Ready list, ensured by KMOSNUL, simplifies the work of INSERTREADY as described earlier. This can be important in high-performance applications, since DISPATCH and INSERTREADY are probably the most frequently executed portions of a KMOS system.

Interprocess Communication and Synchronization

As specified, KMOS provides a buffered, indirect message-exchange mechanism via mailboxes. Messages are of variable length, and they are not copied from a sender's to a receiver's space. Each mailbox is visible to KMOS by means of a dedicated message descriptor. A message descriptor must be capable of heading a queue of processes awaiting messages and a queue of messages awaiting delivery to processes. Both queues are serviced in FIFO order. Entries are placed at the rear of the queue and removed from its front. Depending on the relative productivity of senders and receivers on a given mailbox, either the process or the message queue may contain entries, but not both. All mailbox descriptors in the system are contained in the Mailboxes list.

Mailboxes and Messages

The format of a mailbox descriptor in KMOS is given in Figure 22.3 a. It is a graphical representation of the MBD record in KMOS code. As indicated, a mailbox descriptor consists of head and tail pointers to the queue of messages (HEADMES, TAILMES), and head and tail pointers to the Waiting-for-message queue of processes (HEADPROC, TAILPROC). Both sets of head and tail pointers are maintained in order to provide for efficient appending and removal of entries at opposite ends of the queues. The MBOXLINK field is used tc link the descriptcr to the Mailboxes list. When a mailbox is created, all queues are assumed to be empty, and their respective pointers are set to NIL. A process wishing to create a mailbox must provide a pointer to a record of the MBD type and invoke the K_CREATEMBOX routine to allocate memory and to initialize the mailbox descriptor.

Procedure K_CREATEMBOX takes one parameter, a pointer to the mailbox descriptor. Procedure K_CREATMBOX initializes all four pointers of the mailbox descriptor (MBD) to NIL and enqueues the MBD on the Mailboxes list. No particular ordering of this list is required in KMOS, so the simplest and the most efficient method of adding entries to the front is followed. While the created mailbox, descriptor is in the process of being inserted into the Mailboxes list, interrupts are turned off to ensure indivisibility of the operation and, consequently, to provide a consistent update of the global variable HEADMAIL.

A sample configuration of the Mailboxes list with three mailbox descriptors is shown in Figure 22.3b. Descriptor MBDl contains neither processes nor messages. The mailbox descriptor denoted as MBD2 contains two messages, and its messages head and tail pointers are set accordingly. The mailbox whose descriptor is denoted as MBD3 contains three processes in the Waiting-for-message state. As discussed earlier, such processes are linked using their respective THREAD fields.

Support for variable-length messages in KMOS requires some sort of message headers where the length of a given message may be recorded by the sender and referenced by the receiving process. Since KMOS is to provide buffering of messages awaiting delivery (sent but not yet received), we must provide some means for linking them at a mailbox descriptor, as depicted by MBD2 in the Figure 22.3b. The message header is probably the most convenient place for this link field when unlimited message buffering per mailbox is required, as in the case in KMOS.

The resulting format of a message in KMOS is given in Figure 22.4. As indicated, each message consists of a fixed header and an optional data field of variable length. For example, empty messages used for synchronization purposes normally consist of the header field only. The header contains LINK and LENGTH fields, as described earlier. The purpose of its last field, MTYPE, is to allow for differentiation between classes of messages, such as system-sent or user-sent. An example of its use is described in relation to the ITSERV routine. The message header is declared as the MSG record in KMOS code.

In KMOS, a message must be built in the sender's address space before it may be forwarded to a receiving process. Building a message consists of placing data in the data field, if any, and setting the LENGTH field in the header accordingly. After setting the MTYPE field, if necessary, the message is built and may be sent by invoking the K_SEND routine. The LINK field of a message header should not be manipulated by the sending process. This field is used by KMOS for queueing messages at mailbox descriptors.

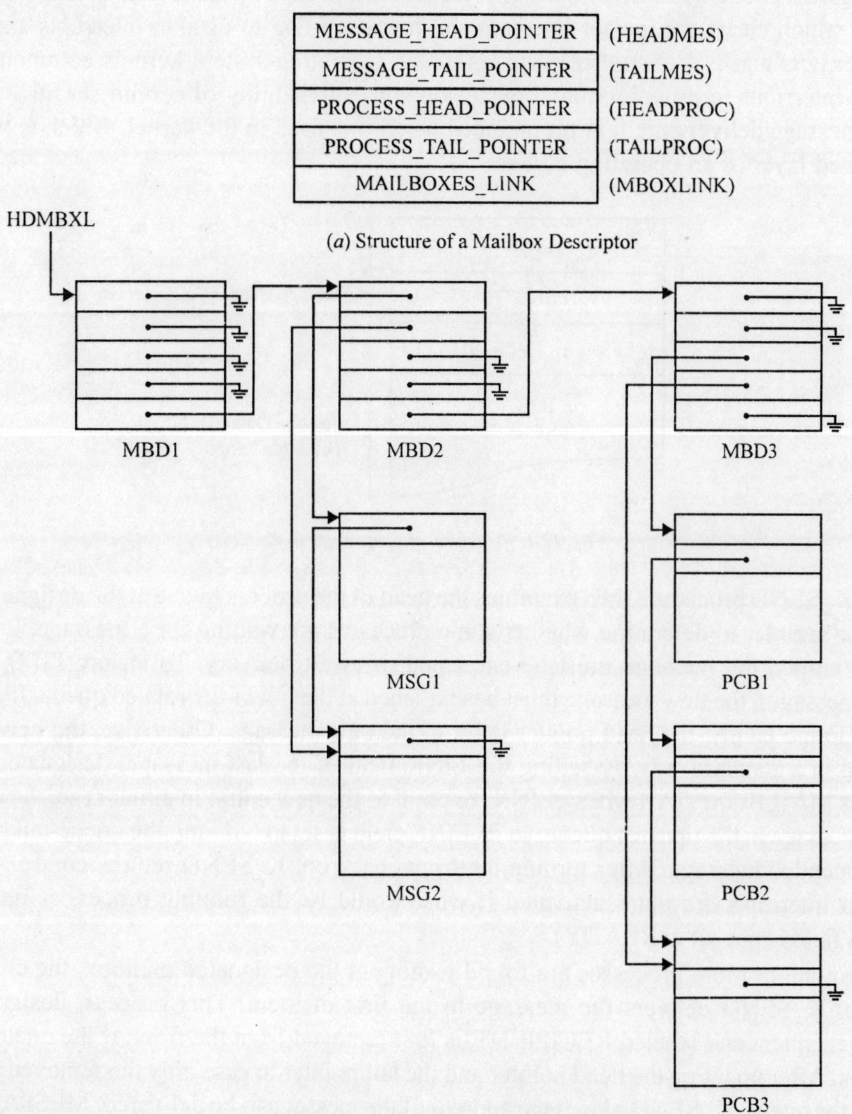

(*a*) Structure of a Mailbox Descriptor

(*b*) A Sample Configuration of KMOS Mailboxes

Fig. 22.3. Mailboxes.

The SEND Operation

As indicated its code, the K_SEND procedure takes two parameters: the address of the mailbox descriptor where the message is to be delivered, MAILBOX, and the address of the message itself, MESSAGE. Procedure K_SEND opens by turning interrupts off in order to ensure mutually exclusive access to global pointers that it manipulates. This is accomplished by the assembly-language procedure INTOFF, which clears the master interrupts-on hardware flag to disable interrupts and leaves all other interrupts masks and control registers intact. Operating-system kernels commonly resort to disabling interrupts to provide mutual exclusion and indivisibility of certain sensitive operations, such as message delivery are less pronounced when it is used in the kernel, which is typically the most trusted layer of an operating system.

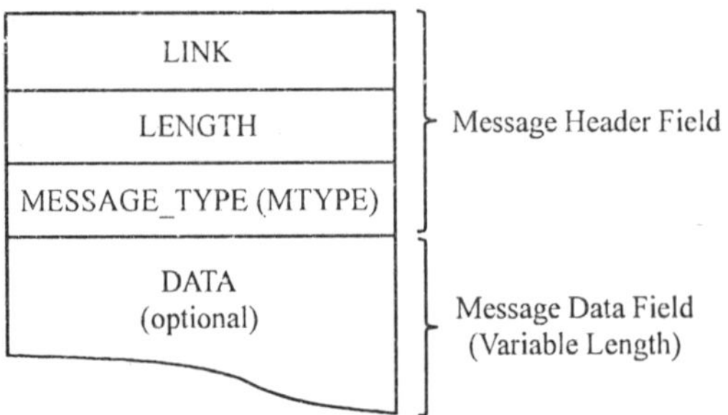

Fig. 22.4. Structure of a message in KMOS.

The K_SEND procedure then examines the head of the process queue at the designated mailbox descriptor in order to determine whether some processes are waiting for a message. If the process queue is empty, the message must be enqueued to await delivery. To ensure FIFO delivery of waiting messages, the new message must be enqueued at the tail of the related queue. If the message queue is found empty, the head pointer is set to the new message. Otherwise, the new message is appended in a standard way by setting the LINK field of the last message, designated by the tail pointer as MAILBOX^.TAILMES^.LINK, to point to the new entry. In either case, the new entry is the last message in the updates queue, so its LINK field is set to NIL and the queue-tail pointer is set to the appended message. After turning interrupts back on, K_SEND returns control to its caller. Note that interrupts are not reactivated if what would be the running process is not active (its STATUS field is not set to READY).

When one or more processes are found waiting at the designated mailbox, the corresponding branch of K_SEND delivers the message to the first of them. This process, designated as the message recipient and labeled RECIPIENT, is first removed from the front of the queue of waiting processes. After updating the head pointer and the tail pointer in case only the removed process was found in the queue, K_SEND places the address of the message to be delivered, MESSAGE, into the HOLDMSG field of the RECIPIENT process's PCB. The MESSAGE remains there until RECIPIENT eventually becomes the running process and the message is actually delivered to it. Message delivery is completed by the DISPATCH routine, which is described later.

Following the saving of the caller's stack, procedure K_SEND makes the message recipient ready by inserting it into the Ready list. The next active process is then scheduled and dispatched.

Given priority ordering, scheduling in KMOS is reduced to a trivial operation of selecting the process at the front of the Ready list. The global variable RUNNING points to this process, making it possible to combine scheduling and dispatching into an invocation of DISPATCH to prepare the environment for and to surrender control to the running process.

The RECEIVE Operation

Receiving of messages in KMOS-based systems is done by means if the K_RECEIVE system call. Since it returns a pointer to a message to the calling process, K_RECEIVE is coded as a function of the PTRMSG type. RECEIVE takes two parameters: a pointer to the mailbox where the message is to be received, MAILBOX, and a time limit, TIMLIM.

When the running process wishing to receive a message invokes the RECEIVE function, either messages or waiting processes may be found at the designated mailbox. In the former case, the calling process receives the first message from the queue. Removal of a message in RECEIVE is a standard deletion from the front of a queue. The address of a removed message is placed in the MESSAGE variable. The LINK field of the removed message is set to itself. This is done in order to allow for differentiation between messages that are in a queue and those that are not, simply by examination of their LINK fields. That is used by the ITSERV routine.

After reenabling interrupts, the pointer to the message is returned to the calling process, which resumes its execution. Similar to K_SEND, K_RECEIVE runs with all interrupts off and, upon exit, reenables only the interrupt levels that were enabled prior to it invocation. This is accomplished by the inline assembler procedure INTON, which sets the master interrupts-on hardware flag and leaves all other interrupt masks and control registers intact.

When K_RECEIVE finds no messages, the calling process designated by the global variable RUNNING is labeled as PROCESS and suspended by virtue of being removed from the Ready list. The removed PROCESS is then placed at the end of the queue of processes waiting for messages at the designated MAILBOX. The context of the PROCESS is saved on its stack using the procedure SSTACK. As indicated, interrupts need not be turned back on in this case, because the DISPATCH procedure will establish the environment of the new running process, including the enabling of qualified interrupt levels.

Process Management

This section present creation, dispatching, deletion, and timed-delaying of processes in KMOS.

Process Creation

Process creation basically consists of initialization of the process control block. The process creator communicates the initial values of process attributes—such as process name, stack size, and priority—as calling parameters to the K_CREATEPROC procedure.

Handling of the stack in somewhat more involved. All process stacks are carved from the same area in the stack segment, whose overall size is specified during KMOS system startup. Each new process stack begins at the end of the last previously built stack marked by the global variable STACKEND. The K_CREATEPROC procedure then prepares the PCB so that KMOS can transfer control of the processor to the newly created process in a manner consistent with the way in which control is surrendered to regular processes. As discussed earlier, a process that is not running always has the address of its next instruction (the value of the PC) on its private stack. When such a process is resumed, DISPATCH eventually surrenders controls to it by emulating a subroutine return with the process's PC on top of the stack. For reasons of uniformity and efficiency, it is desirable to make both regular and new processes look the same to DISPATCH in this regard. This can be accomplished by having K_CREATEPROC place the starting address of the new process onto the process's stack.

In particular, if the starting address of the process is pushed onto the process's stack, the subroutine return used by DISPATCH works for all processes. For this reason, procedure K_CREATEPROC actually places the process's initial starting address, passed as a calling parameter, onto the process's private stack. In addition, the STACK field of the PCB is set to point to the "pushed address" as the current top of stack, making it unnecessary and even impossible for DISPATCH to differentiate newly created and recurring processes. This process is machine dependent, and it generally requires some coding in assembly language.

The IBM PC uses a segmented approach to memory addressing. As a result, addresses of routines are 4 bytes long and consist of two fields; offset and segment, of 2 bytes each. The related, implementation-specific code of K_CREATEPROC initially sets the STACK to the sum of STACKEND and STACKLEN values, reduced by the process address size, PADSIZE (4 in this implementation), to accommodate the initial address to be placed on the stack. Once formed, the STACK is used as a pointer to place the segmented initial address on top of process's stack in memory.

K_CREATEPROC then calculates the value of the interrupt mask, MASK on the basis of the software priority assigned to the process. MASK should have the proper format to be directly writable into the hardware interrupt mask registers in order to enable only the hardware levels of priority higher than that of the process in question. Obviously, this interrupt mask is machine-specific. As discussed in the previous section. MASK is used by the DISPATCH routine in creating the environment for the new running process. Rather than being provided in a separate PCB field, MASK may be calculated by DISPATCH at run-time. However, the lookup method used in KMOS eliminates this run-time calculation and thus results in better performance.

Although the related KMOS calculation is machine-specific and not portable, we explain briefly its logic to give some flavor of this type of operation. As described earlier, the particular hardware on which the presented version of KMOS is implemented provides 8 distinct priority levels of interrupt. The top 128 software priority levels of KMOS are mapped into the 8 hardware levels using a simple 16-to-1 allocation. The corresponding hardware interrupt mask has 8 bits, 1 per level, arranged so that the least significant mask bit corresponds to level 0. Other bits are dedicated to decreasing levels of interrupts, with bit 7 corresponding to hardware level 7.

When a process at a given level of priority is running, only the interrupt levels of higher priority than its own should be enabled. For example, a process running at software level 1 corresponds to hardware priority 0, and all hardware levels must be disabled when it is running. Assuming that a mask bit set to 1 indicates that the corresponding level should be disabled, the MASK for such a process should have the value 0FFH, or 255 decimal. A process having software priority 125 corresponds to a hardware level of 7. When this process runs, all hardware levels excepts for 7 should be enabled. Consequently, the MASK of this process should have the value 80H, or 128 decimal

The K_CREATEPROC code for the calculation of masks uses the following equation for processes in the software range of priorities between 0 and 127:

$$\text{MASK} = 256 - 2^{p \text{ div } 16}$$

where p is the process's software priority. Integer division of software priority by 16 yields the corresponding hardware level of priority. The desired mask may then be obtained by raising base 2 to that power and subtracting the obtained value from 256. The reader may verify this for a few test cases, including the two discussed in the preceding example.

The final responsibility of K_CREATEPROC is to place the newly formed PCB into the All-processes list. Since it is not sorted, insertions into this list are made at its front. The PCB is then inserted into the Ready list using the INSERT-READY procedure described earlier. Both list manipulations are performed with interrupts off in order to protect the global system pointers involved in the process. Note that no scheduling is performed at the process creation time. Consequently, the newly created process will be considered for execution following the next event that causes rescheduling.

Process Deletion

K_DELETEPROC is a KMOS procedure that deletes the caller from the system. In KMOS, a process is not allowed to delete any process other than itself. Thus, K_DELETEPROC accepts no calling parameters and always deletes the running process. In effect, K_DELETEPROC is the KMOS exit procedure.

After disabling interrupts to preserve system integrity while updating global lists, K_DELETEPROC removes the PCB of the running process from the All-processes list and from the Ready list. Memory used by the PCB of the departing process is reclaimed for other uses. In this implementation, the DISPOSE service is used to return the PCB structure to the heap. The next process is then scheduled for execution and activated by calling DISPATCH.

Process Dispatching

The DISPATCH procedure in KMOS contains some assembly language because it directly manipulates certain machine-specific registers and uses special machine instructions, such as interrupt return. The detailed pseudocode equivalent of DISPATCH is given in Program 22.1

The DISPATCH procedure dispatches the highest-priority ready process, designated by the system pointer RUNNING. The first action of DISPATCH is to set the hardware stack and frame pointers to the values recorded in the PCB of the next-to-run process and thus restore the process's stack area. Its next activity is to enable the interrupt levels that should be on when the process being dispatched is running. An interrupt level in KMOS is recognizable when two conditions are satisfied simultaneously: (1) the hardware priority of the request is higher than that of the running process, and (2) the level at which the request is made has been explicitly enabled by means of the K_ENABLEV call.

As discussed earlier, the interrupt mask is derived in such a way that only interrupt levels higher than that of the running process may be enabled. In order to enable only a subset those levels as defined by preceding invocations of K_ENABLEV, procedure DISPATCH combines the process-specific mask with SYSINTMASK. Although variations are possible, depending on the bit polarities of the individual masks, in general the two masks are ANDed together. The corresponding function call in Program 22.1 is meant to suggest the bitwise AND operation on the two masks, which is not available in standard Pascal. As indicated, the value obtained in this way is applied directly to the appropriate PIC register. This compound mask, however, takes effect only when control is surrendered to the user's process, as interrupts remain off throughout DISPATCH.

```
procedure DISPATCH;

begin
    hardware_SP := process^.stack;
    interrupt_mask := and(sysintmask, process^.mask);
    if process^.status = preempted
        then
            begin
                restore_regs
            IRET {end}
        else
            begin
                hardware_FP := process^.frame;
                if process^.holdmsg <> nil
                    then
                        begin
                        message := process^.holdmsg;
                        message^.link := message;
                        receive := message;
                        process^.holdmsg := nil
                        end
            EI;
            RET {end}
    end; {dispatch}
```

Program 22.1. Pseudocode equivalent of DISPATCH.

If the process being dispatched was preempted by an interrupting during its most recent run, DISPATCH restores its context by popping off the contents of register from the stack in the reverse order of their storing by ITSERV. Although no different from other processes at the user level, interrupt-service routines are unique in the sense of being invoked by the hardware interrupt-processing sequence. The effects of this sequence must be undone by the specialized interrupt return instruction, IRET. With the user process's program counter on stack, DISPATCH surrenders control to a preempted process by means of the IRET instruction. In machines where IRET does not restore the value of the hardware interrupt flag, an enable interrupts (EI) instruction should precede IRET.

When a handling process not preempted on its last run, DISPATCH checks whether a message needs to be delivered. This is normally the case when the process being dispatched is exiting the Waiting-for-message state. If so, DISPATCH must retrieve the address of the message from the HOLDMSG field of the related PCB, where it is placed by the K_SEND procedure. After setting the LINK field of the message to point to itself, DISPATCH surrenders control to the user process as if it were returned by the RECEIVE routine. In general, this requires emulation of the function return for delivery of the message destined for the process being dispatched. Many compilers perform a single-value function return, such as RECEIVE, by placing a copy of the variable in question into a specific processor register, so this is all that DISPATCH usually has to do.

Delaying a Process for a Specified Time

An important process-management function of KMOS is delaying of a process for a specified period of time. As indicated by its functional specification, delaying of a process is performed by two separate but related routines. The first routine, DELAY, is called by a user process wishing to be delayed. The calling process is suspended and placed on the list of delayed processes. The second routine, KMOSCLOCK, is actually an interrupt-service routine that decrements the remaining delay of the processes in the Delayed list and makes eligible for execution those processes whose delay is found to be expired.

Timer Management and Delayed List

The Delayed list contains PCBs of processes that are in timed delay. The DELAY procedure basically inserts entries into this list, whereas KMOSCLOCK searches the list and removes qualified entries. The challenge is to choose a data structure that provides for efficient processing of both operations. In most systems the frequency of timer interrupts is higher than that of processes becoming delayed. Consequently, the efficiency of clock-tick processing is usually of primary concern.

The first option to be considered is whether the Delayed list should be sorted or not. Inserts into an unsorted list can be performed in constant time by simply appending new entries. The clock-tick processing with such a list, however, has a time complexity proportional to the total number of delayed processes n_d. On the other hand, insertions into a sorted Delayed list, on the average, take (½) n_d operations. Clock-tick processing with this kind of list apparently has the same time complexity as in the previous case, because the remaining delays of all processes must be decremented upon each timer interrupts. Unfortunately, neither of the two approaches does much for reducing the overhead of the most frequent and time-critical operation. The problem lies with the decrementing of remaining delays of all processes in timed wait. One way to alleviate this problem is to make delays relative to each other, rather than absolute, in terms of remaining time units.

As an example, consider a system in which four processes, P1 through P4 are in Delayed state. Assume that their remaining delays are 5, 20, 20, and 30 time units, respectively. In a classical scheme, KMOSCLOCK decrements all these values upon each timer interrupt and makes ready those processes whose delay becomes 0. In this example, 30 timer interrupts are needed to empty the Delayed list, assuming that no new entries arrive. In the course of processing these interrupts, 75 decrements of the remaining delays have to be made (5 times four entries 15 times three entries, and 10 times one entry).

Alternatively, consider the same system in which delays are recorded and processed relative to each other. Assume that the Delayed list is sorted by increasing absolute delays; a requirement satisfied by our example. Let us now express an individual process's relative delay as the number of clock-ticks that the process is required to wait *after* the delay of that process's predecessor expires. The predecessor's relative delay is, in turn, expressed in terms of its predecessor's delay, yielding the following expression:

$$\text{reld}_i = \text{absd}_i - \sum_{j=1}^{i=1} \text{reld}_j \qquad i = 2,\ldots,n$$

where reld_i is the relative delay of process i, and absd_i is the absolute delay of process i. In other words, the relative delay of process is the increment, expressed in terms of clock-ticks, that must elapse after expiration of all preceding relative delays in order for the process in question to leave the Delayed state. Since the first process in the Delayed list has no predecessor, its relative delay is identical to its absolute delay. In our example, the relative delays of the four sample processes are 5, 15, 0, and 10, respectively.

The primary advantage of this approach is that *only the remaining delay of the first process in the list needs to be decremented upon each timer interrupt*. Since all other delays are relative and additive to it, no PCBs of processes beyond the one at the head of the Delayed list need be processed. This result in a significant reduction of overhead of timer-interrupt processing. In particular, only one node is visited and processed per timer interrupt, which brings the time complexity of that operation down to constant time.

In terms of our running example, the first 5 timer interrupts are serviced by decrementing the delay of the first process. When it becomes 0, the process is removed from the Delayed list. The subsequent 15 timer interrupts result in the second process's delay becoming 0. Since its successor has a relative delay of 0, both processes are removed from the Delayed list at that time. Finally, 10 time interrupts later, the delay of the last process expires, and it makes the transition to the Ready state. Due to the suggested modification, 30 as opposed to 75 decrements are required for the same set of processes. In addition, the node to be processed is accessed in constant time, eliminating the node-traversal overhead imposed by the classical approach.

In summary, the proposed form of the Delayed list is sorted by the relative delay recorded in the DELAY field of each participating process. With this structure, inserts into the Delayed list require, on the average, examination of (½) n_d nodes. Given that a much more frequent companion operation, clock-tick processing, is reduced to constant time, this price is well worth paying for the improved performance.

As indicated earlier, the Delayed list is a doubly linked list. Although not essential for the presented implementation of KMOS, double linking is maintained for a possible extension leading to the addition of a time-limited version of the RECEIVE call. In order to illustrate management of this type of list and of relative delays, we present the appearance of the Delayed list with the four processes introduced in this section in Figure 22.5. Let us briefly outline the steps involved in adding a new process, P*n*, whose absolute delay is 25 time units. Presumably, the process in question invokes KMOS to suspend it for the indicated period of time. As a result, KMOS has to search the Delayed list depicted in Figure 22.5 in order to find where to insert P*n*, that is, behind all processes with shorter remaining delays and ahead of processes with longer remaining delays than that of P*n*. In so doing, the relative delay of process P*n* has to be calculated.

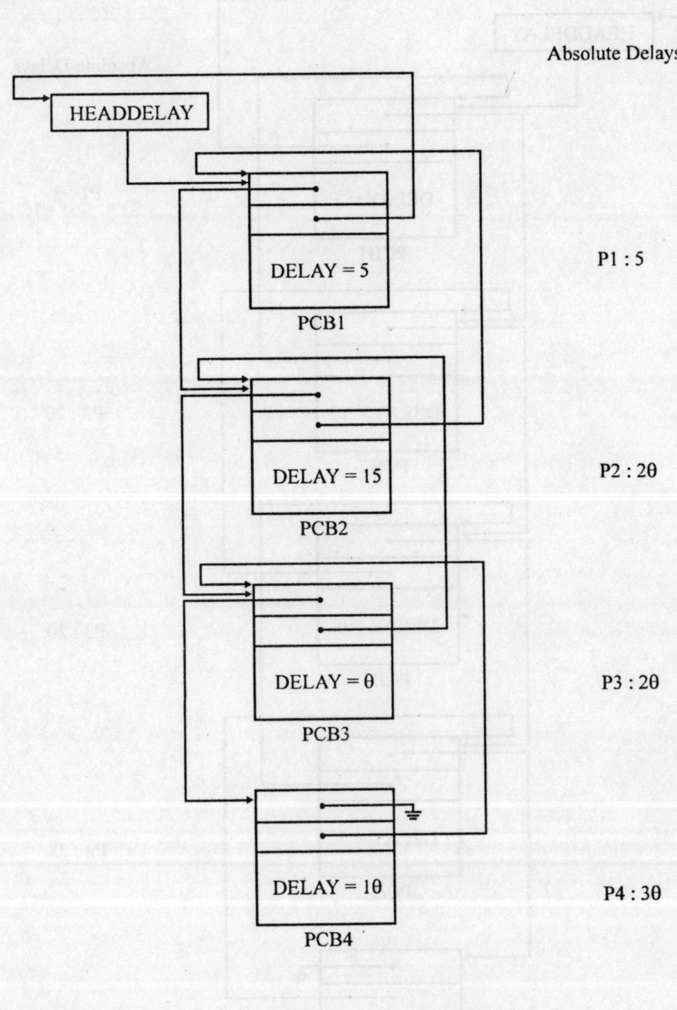

Fig. 22.5. Sample configuration of Delayed list.

P*n*'s delay is first compared to P1's (relative) delay, which is 5. Since P*n*'s delay is larger, the search proceeds to the next node. Before the new comparison, however, the relative delay of P*n* starts being formed by subtracting from it the delay of the examined node, P1. As a result, the running relative delay of P*n*, 20, is compared to that of the current node, P2, which is 15. Since P*n*'s delay is still larger, the process is repeated with P3. When node P4 is reached, P*n*'s delay equals 5. Since it is smaller than the relative delay of P4, process P*n* is to be inserted after the predecessor of P4, which is pointed to by the back-link stored in the field LAST of P4's control block. The state after insertion of P*n* is shown in Figure 22.6.

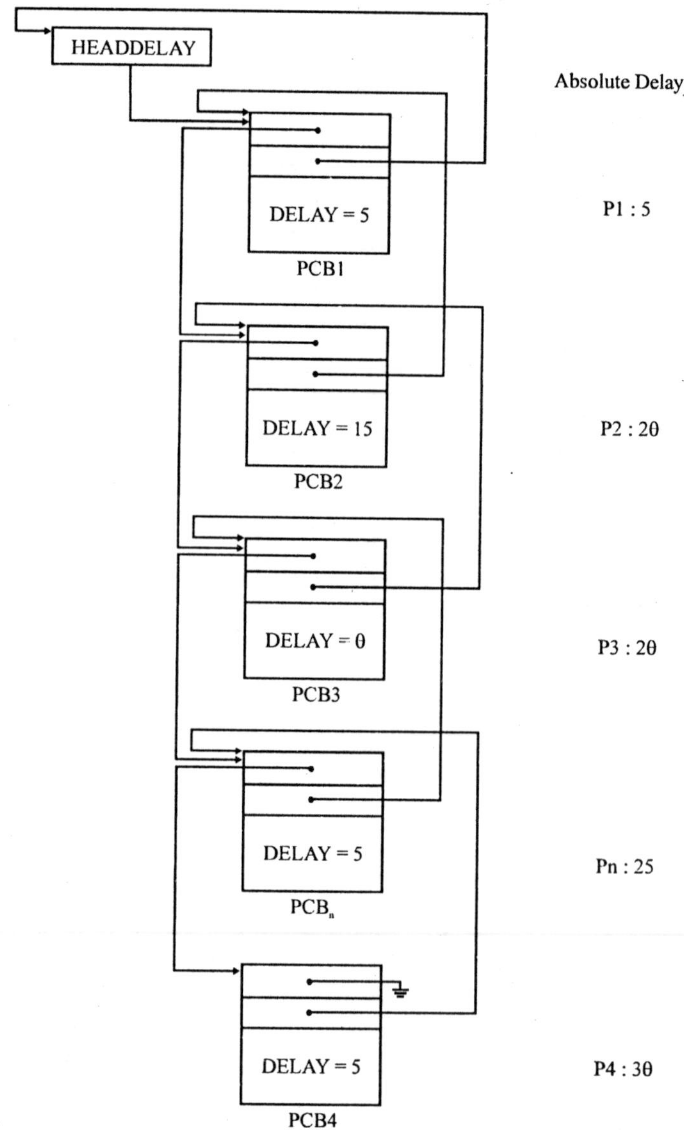

Fig. 22.6. Delayed list after insertion of Pn.

Thus, in addition to updating of the link fields of P3 and P4, the relative delay of P4 is changed. This is because of the cumulative nature of relative delays: the absolute delay of each node is a function of the relative delays recorded for all nodes ahead of it in the Delayed list. In particular, the relative delay P*n* is subtracted from the relative delay of P4, yielding the value of 5. The validity of this operation may be verified by establishing that the absolute remaining delay of P4 remains intact, as it should. In general, whenever a new node is inserted into the Delayed list, the relative delay of its immediate successor must be reduced by the value of the new entry's relative delay.

The DELAY Operation

These ideas are embodied in the K_DEALY procedure provided in KMOS code. The K_DELAY procedure receives as a parameter the amount of desired delay expressed as the number of system clock-ticks. As discussed earlier, specifying the duration of the desired delay in terms of the number of clock-ticks (system time units) is system specific and generally not portable even within the same family of operating systems. The reason is that the time unit is often a system-generation parameter that may vary from installation to installation. Since conversion of standard time units, such as seconds or minutes, into system-specific clock-ticks is straightforward, we opt for the simpler and faster approach of using system clock-ticks in KMOS.

The procedure DELAY acts only on those user calls whose desired delay is greater than one time unit. When called with an illegal argument, such as a negative or zero time to wait, DELAY simply returns to the caller with no error indication. For legal invocations, DELAY turns interrupts off to preserve the integrity of the Delayed list in the presence of concurrent updates.

Following the logic of relative delays outlined earlier, DELAY scans the list to find a place where the new entry is to be inserted. As with the Ready list described earlier, KMOS avoids special processing for inserts to the beginning of the list and into the empty list by structuring the head pointer of the Delayed list as a PCB whose delays is 0. After each node is visited, the relative delay of the new entry is formed by updating the variable TICKS. The related WHILE loop terminates either when a place to insert is found or when the last node is reached. In the latter case, depending on their relative delays, the new entry may have to be inserted before or after the last node

Once its place is found, the new entry is marked as PROCESS (delayed process) and inserted by modifying the forward link of its predecessor and the back link of its successor, if any. Of course, the corresponding links of PROCESS itself are set to its predecessor and successor, respectively. After updating its status and recording its calculated relative delay, TICKS, the stack pointer of the delayed process is saved in its PCB, and the process is suspended by being deleted from the Ready list. Note that the resulting transient state cannot corrupt KMOS, because it is made invisible to other routines by virtue of having the interrupts off. With processing of the significant event completed, the new running process is scheduled and dispatch.

Timer-interrupt Processing

The comparison routine of DELAY, KMOSCLOCK, is a process running under KMOS. It services interrupts from the interval timer by decrementing the remaining delay of the first process, if any, in the Delayed list. If the updated delay becomes 0, the top process and any successors with identical delay are removed from the Delayed list and placed into the Ready list. Since standard Pascal does not support the notion of processes, KMOSCLOCK is coded as a procedure. However, being a process, KMOSCLOCK must never be explicitly invoked by any routine, or the associated timing it produces will be in error, and the system may crash.

In general, when accurate timing desired, the KMOSCLOCK process or its equivalent must have higher priority than any process that delays itself. In the hardware configuration on which the presented version of KMOS is implemented, the interval timer generates its interrupts at hardware level 0. The KMOSCLOCK process is assigned software priority 0, which is commensurate with the hardware level of priority that it services. Consequently, no process can preempt KMOSCLOCK in KMOS-based systems, and the high priority of KMOSCLOCK provides for accurate timekeeping, subject to the accuracy and stability of the hardware clock.

Like most system and real-time processes, KMOSCLOCK consists of the initialization part, which is executed only once, and the forever-do part, which performs the normal processing. The first part of KMOSCLOCK contains a call to enable recognition of hardware interrupts at level 0, and then forms the address of the corresponding interrupt mailbox—K_IMBLV0 in this particular implementation—where KMOSCLOCK receives interrupts-signaling messages from KMOS. An implementation of KMOSCLOCK should normally begin with the initialization of the hardware interval timer so as to specify duration of a clock-tick for the particular system configuration. In the presented implementation this is not done, because the underlying hardware system on which KMOS runs initializes the hardware interval timer to generate interrupts approximately every 55 ms.

Once an interrupt occurs, KMOSCLOCK tests whether there are any delayed processes. If so, the remaining delay of the first one is decremented. Following this, a WHILE loop is entered to remove all processes whose remaining delay is 0, if any. Each qualifying process is made ready and removed from the front position of the Delayed list. If more processes are left, the back pointer of the new first process is set to the list head. Alternatively, if the list is empty, the roving pointer DPROCESS is set to the head node, whose DELAY field is 0, to ensure proper evaluation of the loop condition even when the end of list is reached. Otherwise, a run-time error may occur, since DPROCESS^.DELAY is undefined for a nonexistent node.

In general, when KMOSCLOCK adds one or more entries to the Ready list, the scheduler should be invoked to select the next process to run. In the proposed implementation this is both undesirable and difficult, since a process, such as KMOSCLOCK, should not and cannot invoke an internal system routine, such as DISPATCH. However, scheduling is implicitly accomplished because KMOSCLOCK continues by invoking RECEIVE to await another time interrupt. In normal processing, the interrupt is not asserted until the full tick elapses, and KMOSCLOCK is suspended at the K_IMBLV0 mailbox. The ensuring processing of the change of system state (process KMOSCLOCK moving from the Running to the Waiting-for-message state), results in the rescheduling needed to take newly readied processes into consideration.

Procedure SSTACK

The purpose of SSTACK is to save the stack and frame pointers of a user process about to be suspended by a KMOS service. SSTACK is a specialized procedure that prepares the stage for return two levels up in the hierarchy, that is, to the caller of the caller of the routine that invoked SSTACK. This necessary whenever a user process invokes a KMOS service that causes it to be suspended. When the suspending condition is eventually removed, control should be returned to the user process. However, straightforward storing of the state would cause control to be returned to the KMOS routine where the user was suspended, and not to the user as intended.

The difficulty arises from the fact that KMOS has no stack of its own. As a result, KMOS routines use the stacks of their callers. This is not a problem when a KMOS service returns control to its caller, because each KMOS routine cleans up the stacks and thereby removes the stack record of its invocation. However, if a process is suspended as a result of calling a KMOS service, no return to the user takes place, and the caller's stack retains the record of the KMOS procedure.

To remedy the problem, procedure SSTACK erases the calling frame to the invoking KMOS service from the user's stack and places the user's return address on the top of the stack for proper operation of DISPATCH when the user routine is eventually scheduled for execution.

Procedure SSTACK is highly compiler- and machine-specific. Fortunately, SSTACK is fairly stable on the PC hardware base where most compiler developers follow the procedure call and return conventions recommended by the processor vendor. As indicated, SSTACK takes two parameters: a pointers to the process whose context is to be saved, and the length of the stack space occupied by the input calling parameters of the KMOS routine that invokes SSTACK. For example, K_DELAY supplies the value of 2 for this parameter, because its only calling parameter, TICKS, is a 2-byte integer. K_SEND, on the other hand, supplies the value of 8, as it has two calling parameters, each of which is a 4-byte far pointer in this implementation.

When SSTACK is entered, the stack contains records of at least two nested procedure calls: (1) the user's call to KMOS services and (2) the KMOS service's call to SSTACK—each with calling parameters and a return address. SSTACK uses the frame pointer, called *base pointer* in Intel literature, to erase the calling parameters of the user's call (call-frame 1) and to move the user's return address to the top of the stack; the address is then recorded in the process control block of the user process identified as the first calling parameter of SSTACK. In the course of its operation, SSTACK destroys and partially overwrites the calling parameters and returns address of the KMOS service invoked by the user. This is necessary to ensure proper operation of DISPATCH and to prevent the stack buildup that would otherwise result from orphaned calling parameters. However, SSTACK should be used with extreme caution by those who modify KMOS services, because its invocation has side effects that invalidate some of the caller's stack-based variables.

Interrupt Management

As discussed earlier, preliminary processing of all interrupts in KMOS-based systems is performed within the kernel. Consequently, all interrupts are vectored to the operating system, to the ITSERV routine. When an interrupt request is asserted and accepted, control is transferred to ITSERV. This routine identifies the particular source of interrupt, save the software portion of the preempted process's state, and sends a signaling message to the dedicated mailbox.

Interrupt Mailboxes and Priorities

In KMOS, a separate mailbox is dedicated to each hardware level of interrupt for the exchange of interrupt-signaling messages between the KMOS and the interrupt-service routines. A process wishing to service interrupts from a given source can do so by invoking the RECEIVE function on the corresponding interrupt mailbox. For this reason, interrupt mailboxes in KMOS systems are publicly declared global variables with names of the format K_IMBLVx (*i*nterrupt *m*ailbox *l*evel *x*), where *x* is the number of the corresponding hardware level of interrupt. As a result, KMOS software is capable only of distinguishing between different hardware are levels of interrupt. In systems where interrupt-request lines of several devices are connected to a single level, a software routine must be employed to "demultiplex" requests for service by identifying the specific originating device.

Since a special system message is needed for signaling interrupts occurring at a particular hardware level, one such message is created for each interrupt mailbox. Being used for signaling purposes, only, the message contains only the header field and no data. Its MTYPE field is set to a reserved value, INTERRUPTMSG (=1), to designate the normal, system-sent interrupt message to the receiving process.

In the particular computer system on which the version of KMOS presented in this chapter is implemented (IBM PC), there are 8 distinct hardware levels of interrupt, with level 0 having the highest and level 7 the lowest priority. Due to the lack of difference at the user level between ISRs and ordinary processes in KMOS, some means must be provided to the OS for establishing correspondence between the software priority and the hardware priority of a given process. This is essential, for instance, to the DISPATCH routine, which must enable selected priority levels for the hardware interrupts when creating the environment for a user process. For this reason, software priority levels of this particular implementation are divided in two groups of 128 levels each. The first group, levels 0 through 127 inclusive, is dedicated to interrupt-related processes. With 8 distinct hardware levels of priority, a straightforward allocation of 16 software levels to a hardware level is made using the following expression:

$$software\_level \textbf{ div } 16 = hardware\_level$$

where **div** stands for the ordinary integer division, and *software_level* must be in the range from 0 to 127. For example, processes running at software levels 0 through 15, inclusive, correspond to hardware level 0, and software levels 112 through 127 to hardware level 7. Software priorities in the range 128 through 255 are not associated with hardware priorities.

Processes wishing to service interrupts occurring at a given hardware level of priority must be assigned a software priority level in the corresponding range. In this way a dispatched process is assured that, while it is running, all lower and equal hardware levels of priority are disabled by the operating system. For example, the KMOSCLOCK process, which services timer interrupts occurring at level 0, must be assigned a software priority in the range 0 through 15. when KMOSCLOCK is running in response to a timer interrupt, it cannot be preempted by any other source of interrupt in the described system.

Interrupt Servicing in KMOS

Because it involves several machine-specific manipulation of hardware, ITSERV is coded using a mixture of Pascal and inline assembly language. Its pseudocode equivalent in notation resembling Pascal is given as Program 22.2. As indicated ITSERV is entered whenever a qualified interrupt request, that is, one explicitly enables by means of ENABLEV and of higher priority than that of the running process, is recognized by the Hardware. In order to distinguish hardware sources connected to different levels of interrupt, each level is vectored to its own entry point. After saving the state of the preempted process and recording the identity of the particular hardware interrupt level, a branch to common processing of all interrupt requests, labeled ALLINT, is made.

In KMOS, the hardware SP register points to the private stack area of the running process whose PCB is identified by the global variable RUNNING. Since the hardware interrupt-processing sequence and ITSERV both use the stack to save their respective portions of the preempted process's state, the net effect of these two operations at the beginning of interrupt processing is to save the complete state of the affected processes on its own stack. Subsequent storing of the updated value of the PC into the

PCB of the preempted process completes the state-save operation. When the process in question is eventually resumed and its SP restored, the state-restore sequence may be reduced to simply popping off the saved registers from the process's stack in the reverse order of storing.

After saving the context of the preempted process, ITSERV sets its status to PREEMPTED in order to inform DISPATCH that a full context restore will be needed when the process is to be resumed. Routine ITSERV then acknowledges the interrupt being processed to the programmable interrupt controller (PIC) or to its hardware equivalent. This action normally results in deasserting of the corresponding interrupt-request line to the processor. Note that this does not acknowledge the interrupt to the originating I/O port, whose processing is left to the related ISR. With this division of labour, KMOS handles the processor part of interrupt logic and ISRs the device-specific portions of interrupt processing. This approach relieves users from handling the processor and PIC interrupt flags and, in so doing, has the potential of increasing system reliability by virtue of protecting the common interrupt logic of the system from users. At the same time, KMOS does not become involved in the semantics of the specific sources of interrupt, which could severely restrict its portability.

KMOS uses messages to signal arrivals of interrupts to the related ISRs. With KMOS as an intermediary, asynchronous communication between interrupt occurrences and the related servicing processes is possible. In particular, a service process may conceivably be in some state other than Waiting-for-message when an interrupt message is sent to it. Due to buffering of messages in KMOS, the interrupt message in that case is deposited into the corresponding mailbox pending execution of the matching RECEIVE call by the interrupt-servicing process. When consecutive interrupts from the same source are closely spaced in time, a timing error may cause the servicing process to miss one or more interrupts. Being divorced from the device-specific aspect of interrupt processing, there is little that KMOS can do to remedy this situation. However, it should at least alert the user process when interrupts are lost. This poses the problem of detecting missed interrupts in KMOS without getting involved in details of their processing.

In order to solve this problem, the LINK field if each message is set to point to itself before the message is delivered to a requesting process. The primary reason for doing so is to assist in the detection is missed interrupts. If the LINK field of a given message is set to itself, it may be safely concluded that the message in question is not enqueued at any mailbox. Thus, by examining the LINK field, the system can determine whether or not the message is enqueued at an interrupt mailbox awaiting delivery. Since the same message is sent by the system for each arrival of interrupt at a given hardware level, the only way for an interrupt message to have its LINK field set to itself is as a result of having been delivered to a requesting process. Conversely, if its LINK field has any other value, the interrupt message is awaiting delivery. Due to the symbolic relationship between interrupt mailbox descriptors and interrupt message in KMOS, locating of an interrupt message for inspection is not a problem.

```
routine ITSERV; {entered upon hardware interrupt}
label allint
lev0:    save_state_on_stack;
         level := 0;
         goto allint;
lev1:    save_state_on_stack;
```

(contd.)

```
        level := 1;
        goto allint;
{one vector for each hardware level of priority}
levx:   save_state_on_stack;
        level := s;
        goto allint;
begin
allint: save_state_on_stack;
        running^.stack := hardware_SP;
        running^.status := preempted;
        acknowledge_interrupt_to_PIC;
        if intmsg[level].link = self
            then
            begin
            intmsg[level].mtype := intmessage;
            send (mailbox[level], intmsg[level])
            end
            else intmsg[level].type := missedint;
        dispatch (running)
end; {itserv}
```

Program 22.2. Pseudocode equivalent of Itserv.

Following this line of reasoning, ITSERV checks whether the interrupt message appended to the interrupt mailbox of the level being processed is awaiting delivery or not. If not (LINK = self), the interrupt message is sent to the corresponding mailbox by means of the K_SEND procedure. Otherwise, the message is still awaiting delivery to signal some previous unprocessed interrupt, and a missed interrupt (KMOS cannot tell how many) is detected. To announce that fact, ITSERV sets the TYPE field of the message to the reserved value, 2, which indicates missed interrupts. User processes servicing interrupts are assumed to test the TYPE field of the received message in order to check for missed interrupts. The interrupts message is not when missed interrupts are detected, because doing so does not serve any useful purpose and might corrupt system queues.

In normal processing, a service process is waiting at the interrupt mailbox, and it becomes the running process after receiving the message from K_SEND. However, if service is lagging behind, and no interrupt-service process is suspended at the mailbox, K_SEND enqueues the message and returns control to its caller, ITSERV. In that case ITSERV schedules and dispatches the new running process. It is for this reason that K_SEND does not turn the interrupts back on when running to the caller whose STATUS field differs from READY.

Enabling Hardware Interrupts-Levels

The other interrupt-related service of KMOS, enabling of a hardware interrupt level, is quite straightforward. The K_ENABLEV procedure, coded in assembly language, modifies the system interrupt mask, SYSINTMASK, to allow recognition of a hardware interrupt level passed as a parameter. Enabling an enabled level has no effect.

The variable SYSINTMASK is typically a collection of dedicated bits, each of which indicates whether or not the corresponding hardware level of interrupt has been enabled by means of the K_ENABLEV call. The actual bit settings in SYSINTMASK are machine-specific. They depend on both the number of distinct levels of interrupt in a given system and on the ordering and setting of interrupt enable/disable bits in control registers to the related hardware interrupt controller. SYSINTMASK is used by the DISPATCH routine in creating the interrupt-related part of the environment for the process being dispatched.

Startup and Initial System Configuration

KMOS initialization takes place in two steps. One part of the system in initialized within the KMOS unit, and the remainder is brought up in the KMOSSTART procedure.

Skeletal initialization of KMOS hardware and the Ready list is performed in the KMOS unit initialization section. This basis is used as a foundation to create the two KMOS system processes, KMOSNUL and KMOSCLOCK. Unit initialization code is executed first because it receives control from the loader before execution of the main section of the related user-provided application.

Following initialization of the KMOS unit at run-time, control is transferred to the user's code as illustrated by examples in Appendix A. This allows user code to create the necessary initial processes. KMOS execution begins in earnest when the user code invokes the KMOSSTART procedure, which initializes the rest of the system and transfers control to the highest-priority ready process by invoking DISPATCH.

Summary

In order to facilitate frequent insertions and deletions of nodes resulting from changes of system states, KMOS lists are implemented as linked lists. The Ready list is sorted by decreasing priorities of the participating process control blocks in order to minimize the time complexity of its most frequent and time-critical operation: searching in the course of scheduling the next process to run. Manipulations of the Ready list, as well as the scheduling and dispatching operations, are simplified, and their performance is improved as a result of the KMOSNUL process, whose function is to provide at least one ready process in the system at all times.

The message-exchange facility of KMOS, in addition to supporting interprocess communication and synchronization, is used to signal arrivals of hardware interrupts. As a side effect of message buffering, asynchronous servicing of hardware interrupt requests is made possible in KMOS. Missed interrupts are detected by the system and indicated to service processes. Selective enabling of interrupt levels commensurate with the priority of the running process, as well as explicitly by means of the K_ENABLEV service, is also supported in KMOS.

Programmer-specified process attributes are communicated to the system by means of static process descriptors. The presented KMOS implementation facilities placing of the static portion of the system into read-only memory when desired.

The time complexity of timer-interrupt processing is reduced by ordering the processes in the Delayed list according to increasing relative delays.

23

Multiprocessor System

There are basically two ways to increase the speed of computer hardware: technologically, by means of using high-speed components, and architecturally, whereby new structures are invented or existing ones are put together in new and innovative ways. Very high speed components often rely on exotic technologies and fabrication processes. Such components tend to be expensive and are often less reliable than standard, high-volume parts. Multiprocessors provide an appealing architectural alternative for improving the performance of computer systems by coupling a number of low-cost standard processors.

A well-designed multiprocessor may test the technological speed limit by operating several high-speed processors in parallel. Alternatively, a multiprocessor system composed of widely available standard microprocessors may achieve a better cost/performance ratio than a high-speed uniprocessor based on exotic technology. The relatively high cost of multiprocessor systems may be offset by employing them as compute servers in distributed systems. In such a setup, the overhead of user interface is delegated to the client workstations, while the multiprocessor can concentrate on computationally intensive tasks, which is what it usually does best.

Multiprocessing can be applied to provide:

- *Increased system throughput* by execution a number of different user processes on different processors in parallel
- *Application speedup* by executing some portions of the application in parallel.

Application speedup may be obtained by exploiting parallelism within an application and by creating multiple processes or threads that may be scheduled for execution on different processors. This division may be performed by automatic means, such as a parallelizing compiler, or explicitly by statements in the application program. Automatic parallelization is a difficult problem that has spawned much research, but its wide availability in practice seems to be some time away. In the explicit-tasking approach introduced in the programmer delineates task and thread boundaries and ensures their proper synchronization by invoking the appropriate synchronization primitives. The resulting concurrent programs may be executed concurrently on a uniprocessor, as discussed in or ported to a multiprocessor for truly parallel execution and increased speedup. On the negative side, explicit parallel programming is a complex and sometimes arduous process. In the current state of the art, the resulting programs tend to be machine-specific and are difficult to port due to considerable variation in multiprocessor architectures and programming models.

Portions of a parallelized application usually need to synchronize and to exchange data after completing a stage of computation. Interprocessor communication and synchronization reduces the overall speedup by halting individual computations and by consuming the system interconnect bandwidth. One of the main design challenges of multiprocessor system is to minimize Interprocessor interactions and to provide an efficient mechanism for carrying them out when necessary.

Motivation and Classification

Advantages of Multiprocessors

Some of the arguments in favour of multiprocessing include:

- *Performance and computing power*. Significant speedup of an application may be possible by devoting multiple processors to it. Problems with higher or more frequent Interprocessor interactions can be solved more quickly than in a distributed system because the Interprocessor communication bandwidth is higher.
- *Fault tolerance*. The inherent redundancy in multiprocessors can be employed to increase availability and to eliminate single point of failure.
- *Flexibility*. A multiprocessor system can be made to dynamically reconfigure and tailor itself so as to optimize different objectives for different applications—such as increased throughput, application speedup, or even certain aspects of fault tolerance
- *Modular growth*. Up to a point, a modular system design can be adapted to the needs of a specific installation by adding exactly the type of component most likely to alleviate a major bottleneck—such as processors, memories, or I/O devices.
- *Functional specialization*. Functionally specialized processors can be added to improve performance of particular applications.

Multiprocessor Classification

There are a number of classifications of parallel computer architectures. Flynn introduced a scheme for classifying the architecture of a computer based on how the machine relates its instructions to the data being processed. Basically, there may be a single instruction (IS) stream or a multiple instruction (MI) stream, operating on single data (SD) or on multiple data (MD). This gives rise to the following classification:

- *SISD*: Single instruction stream, single data stream. This category encompasses conventional serial computers.
- *SIMD*: Single instruction stream, multiple data streams. These are typically vector processors and array computers in which a single instruction may operate on different data in different execution units.
- *MIDS*. Multiple instruction streams, single data stream. This is a seldom-used organization in which multiple instructions operate on a single data stream in parallel.
- *MIMD*. Multiple instruction streams, multiple data streams. Simultaneous execution of multiple instructions that operate on data streams. This class includes multiprocessors of different types.

Our focus in this chapter is on the MIMD machines. Based on the relationship of processors and memory, multiprocessors may be classified as:

- *Tightly coupled.* Multiprocessors contain globally shared memory that all processors have access to.
- *Loosely coupled.* Individual processors have private memories, and there is no shared global memory.

This division is not very strict, and there are hybrid systems that have both per-processor private and shared global memory that many or all processors have access to. Shared memory is fundamental for Interprocessor communication and synchronization in tightly coupled systems. Historically, tightly coupled multiprocessors are distinguished by the higher bandwidth and lower delays of their interconnect paths. In purely loosely coupled systems, message passing is usually the primary mechanism for interprocessor communication. In principle, distributed systems fit the description of loosely coupled systems. In the past, loosely coupled systems were typified by the lower bandwidth and higher delay of their interconnection paths. With the advent of optical fibers and other high-speed LAN technologies used to connect loosely coupled systems, this distinction may become blurred.

Hybrid configurations and some loosely coupled systems allow processors to access nonlocal memory and even the private memory of other processors. There is usually a penalty for accessing nonlocal memory in the form of added delays caused by the arbitration contention for, and traversal of the processor-memory interconnection paths. These factors give rise to the following classification of shared-memory multiprocessors on the basis of memory architecture and access delays.

- *Uniform memory access* (UMA): Systems where processors can access all available memory with the same speed; this includes many shared-bus architectures
- *Nonuniform memory access* (NUMA): Systems where there is a time difference in accessing different areas of memory, based on proximity to a given processor and the complexity of the switching fabric between the processor and the target section of the system memory

Sometimes, a third category called *no remote memory access* (NORMA) is added to this classification to designate systems with no shared memory.

Multiprocessor Interconnections

This section outlines the basic architectures of a representative group of common multiprocessor types, including:

- Bus-oriented systems
- Crossbar-connected systems
- Hypercubes
- Multistage switch-based systems

In general, the nature of the multiprocessor interconnection path has a dominant influence on the bandwidth and saturation point for systems communications. In the discussion that follows, we will focus on the complexity, cost, interprocessor communication, and scalability of the presented architectures. *Scalability* refers to the ability of a given architecture to expand in order to support a larger number of processors.

Bus-oriented Systems

One of the simplest ways to construct a multiprocessor is to use a shared bus to connect processors and memories. The basic outline of the shared-bus approach is illustrated in Figure 23.1.

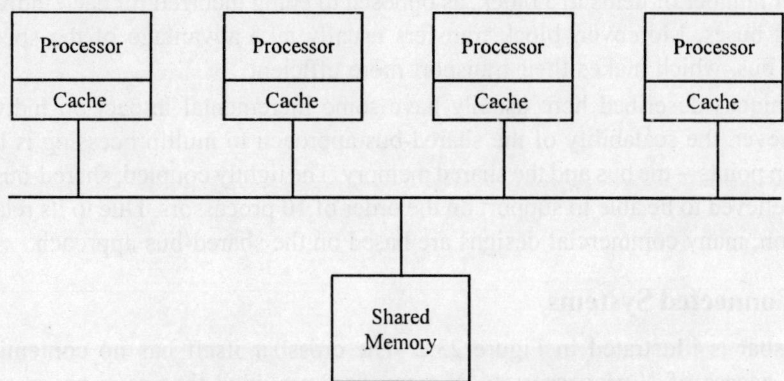

Fig. 23.1. Shared-but multiprocessor organization.

A multitude of processors can communicate with each other and with the globally shared memory over a shared bus. Many variations of this basic scheme are possible: individual processors may or may not have private memory, input/output devices may be attached to individual processors or to the shared bus, and the shared memory itself is usually implemented in the form of multiple physical banks connected to the shared bus.

Two primary points of *contention* in shared-bus systems are the shared bus itself and the shared memory. Cache memory is often employed to reduce contention on the shared bus. In principle, two arrangements of cache are possible in shared-bus systems; (1) cache is associated with the shared memory, and processors access it over the bus; or (2) cache is associated with each individual processor.

Figure 23.1 illustrates the latter approach, which is more popular because processor caches can capture many of the local memory references and thus reduce contention for the common bus. For example, with a cache-hit ratio of 90%, a processor on the average needs to access the shared memory for 1 out of 10 memory references. With uniformly distributed memory access, a 90% cache-hit ratio theoretically enables the shared bus of a given speed to support 10 times as many processors as it would without the processor caches. However, the existence of multiple caches creates problems, when shared writable data are cached. In that case, *cache coherence* must be maintained so that multiple physical copies of a single logical datum are consistent with each other in the presence of update activity. Cache coherence is usually maintained by means of specialized protocols and additional hardware, such as snooping caches. Unfortunately, maintenance of cache coherence tends to increase the bus traffic and thus reduce the benefit that processor caches are designed to provide in the first place.

Several techniques can be employed to decrease the impact of bus and memory saturation in shared-bus systems. For example, the bus can be made wider. A wider parallel bus effectively increases the bandwidth by transferring more bytes in parallel within a single bus cycle. Since bus transactions are usually needed to fetch the missing blocks in processor caches, many systems support block-level reads and writes of main memory. In their way, a missing block is transferred from the main memory into the target cache as a result of a single main-memory (block) read. With block-level access to memory, the overhead of bus arbitration, acquisition, and addressing is amortized over the larger number of items in a block, as opposed to being incurred for each individual word in word-oriented buses. Moreover, block transfers usually take advantage of the specialized burst cycles on the bus, which makes their transport more efficient.

The techniques described here usually have some incremental impact on individual system designs. However, the scalability of the shared-bus approach to multiprocessing is limited by the two contention points—the bus and the shared memory. The tightly coupled, shared-bus organization is generally believed to be able to support on the order of 10 processors. Due to its relatively simple implementation, many commercial designs are based on the shared-bus approach.

Crossbar-Connected Systems

The crossbar is illustrated in Figure 23.2. The crossbar itself has no contention. It allows simultaneous access of *N* processors to *N* memories, provided that each processor accesses a different memory. Thus, the crossbar is the antithesis of the bus.

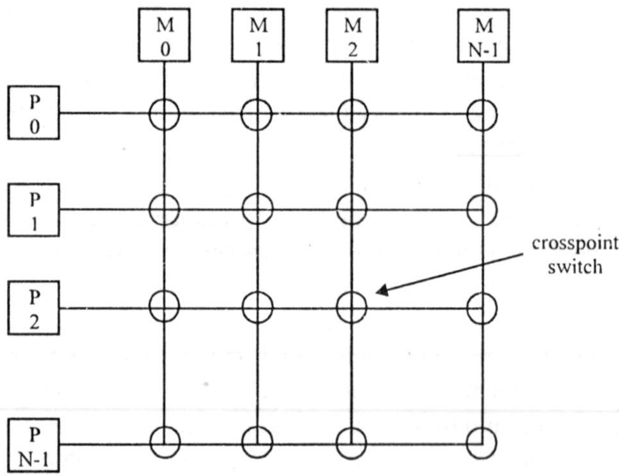

Fig. 23.2. Crossbar connection.

The crosspoint switch is the only source of delay between a processor and a memory. If processors have no private memories, the resulting system is a uniform-memory-access (UMA) multiprocessor.

In crossbar-based multiprocessors, contention may occur only when more than one processor attempts to access the same memory at the same time. Judicious placement of data can help alleviate the memory contention problem in crossbar systems. For example, successive elements may be placed in successive memory modules. if two processors happen to be accessing different data in the same module, one of them will be deferred briefly until the other finished its data reference and moves on to the next memory module. If the two processors access their respective data sequentially, the synchrony will be broken when they contend over a memory module. Thereafter, the two processors will trail each other without conflict for a while.

Unfortunately, this technique does not resolve the contention that arises when several processors attempt to access the same memory location, such as a shared semaphore variable. The crossbar scheme thus allows high degree of parallelism between unrelated tasks, but memory contention is likely if interprocess and interprocessor synchronization are based on shared memory.

The crossbar requires N^2 crosspoint switches to fully connect N endpoints to N other endpoints, such as processors and memory. The quadratic growth of its complexity with the number of components makes crossbars expensive and limits the scalability of the resulting systems.

Hypercubes

Various cube-type multiprocessor topologies address the scalability and cost issues by providing interconnections whose complexity grows logarithmically with the increasing number of nodes. Figure 23.3 illustrates a three-dimensional hypercube.

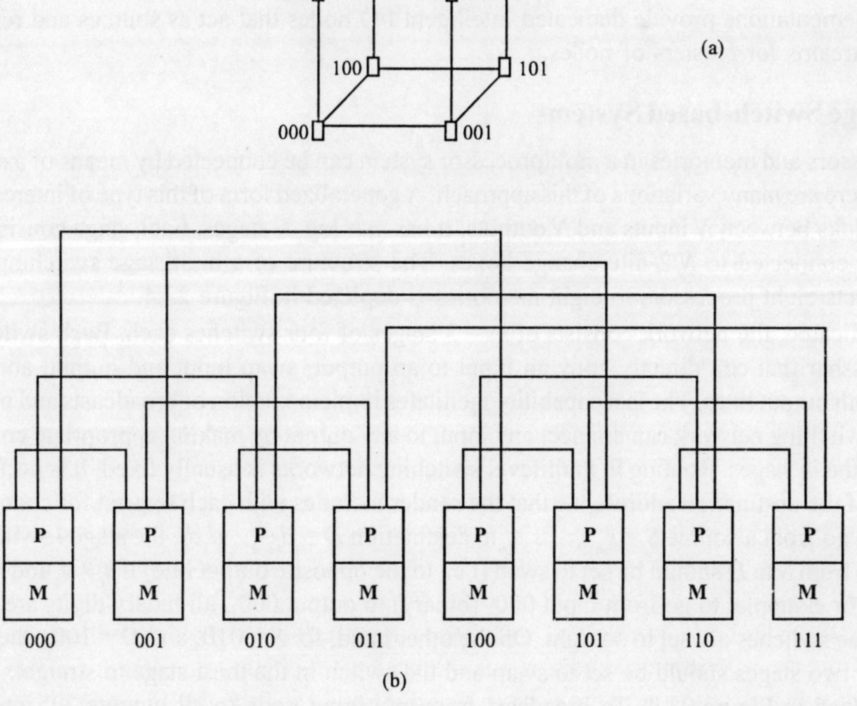

Fig. 23.3. Eight-node hypercube: (a) three-dimensional topology, (b) Interprocessor connections.

As Figure 23.3 a indicates, the system topology is a three-dimensional hypercube, with a node placed at each vertex. This particular configuration yields an eight-node system whose actual interprocessor connections are shown in Figure 23.3 b. Although other arrangements are possible, the multiprocessor system depicted in Figure 23.3 is constructed of nodes that constitute a processor and its private memory. The result is a NORMA-type multiprocessor, which is a rather common hypercube implementation.

Hypercubes have a number of interesting mathematical properties. For example, each processor in a hypercube has direct physical links to $\log_2 N$ other nodes in an N-node system.The maximum distance between any two nodes, measured as the number of physical internode links, is also $\log_2 N$. Hypercubes are recursive structures in the sense that higher-dimensional hypercubes contain the lower-dimensional hypercubes as their proper subsets. Thus a complex hypercube can be partitioned into a number of simpler, lower-dimensional cubes. In the sample system depicted in Figure 23.3, $N = 8$; each node has direct links to $\log_2 8 = 3$ others, the maximum internode distance is 3, and the system can be partitioned into two disjoint two-dimensional hypercubes in three different ways.

Hypercube implementations of the early nineties tend to incorporate private, per-processor, memories. The resulting NORMA architecture dictates message passing as the primary interprocessor communication and synchronization mechanism. In addition to performing processing, individual nodes usually handle communication protocols. They also route and relay external messages to form the indirect communication paths between remote nodes directly connected to each other. Input/output devices may be attached locally to individual nodes. For increased I/O bandwidth, some implementations provide dedicated intelligent I/O nodes that act as sources and repositories I/O data streams for clusters of nodes.

Multistage Switch-based Systems

Processors and memories in a multiprocessor system can be connected by means of a multistage switch. There are many variations of this approach. A generalized form of this type of interconnection provides links between N inputs and N outputs. It has $m = \log_2 N$ stages. Each stage consists of a set of N links connected to $N/2$ interchange boxes. The structure of a multistage switching network that connects eight processors to eight memories is depicted in Figure 23.4.

As indicated, the network consists of $m = 3$ stages of four switches each. Each switch acts as a 2×2 crossbar that can directly copy an input to an output, swap input and output, and copy an input to both output lines. The last capability facilitates implementation of broadcasts and multicasts.

The switching network can connect any input to any output by making appropriate connections in each of the m stages. Routing in multilevel switching networks is usually fixed. It is performed on the basis of the destination address tag that the sender includes with each request for connection. In general, to go from a source $S = s_{m-1} \ldots s_1 s_0$ to destination $D = d_{m-1} \ldots d_1 d_0$, the stage i switching box in the path from S to D should be set to swap (i.e., to the opposite output line) if $s_i \neq d_i$ and to straight if $s_i = d_i$. For example, to go from input 000_2 (binary) to output 000_2, all binary digits are identical, and all three switches are set to straight. On the other hand, for $S = 010_2$ and $D = 100_2$, the switches in the first two stages should be set to swap and the switch in the third stage to straight. This path is emphasized in Figure 23.4. To broadcast from any input node to all outputs, all intermediate switches should be set to copy the input to both outputs. Various combinations of multicasts are possible by using the straight, swap, and copy-both switch functions.

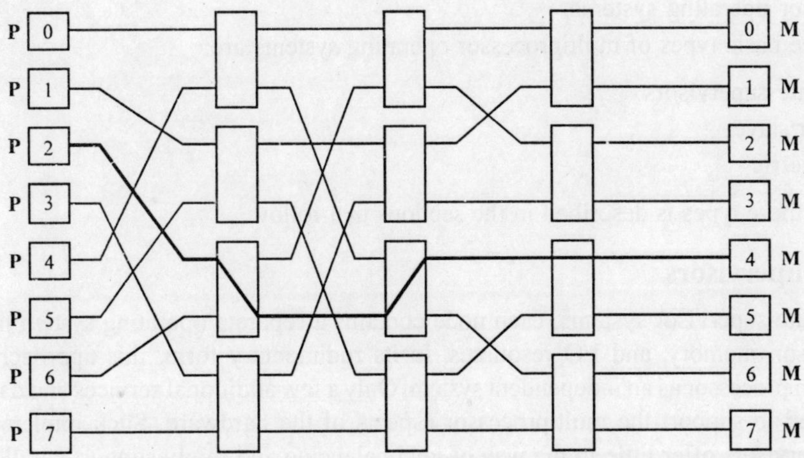

Fig. 23.4. Multistage switching network and path P2-M4.

Multistage switching networks provide a form of circuit switching. Correspondingly, there is a certain setup cost in establishing a path through the switching stages between a source and a destination. Thereafter, the traffic can flow freely using the full bandwidth of the switching network. Obviously, this type of interconnection performs better when blocks of memory are requested at a time. In that way, the setup cost is incurred once per block and it is amortized over the larger number of items in a block.

The multistage switch can simultaneously connect all inputs to all outputs, provided no two processors attempt to access the same memory module at the same time. Otherwise, contention at both the memory module and within the switching network may develop and cause the traffic to back up. A particularly troublesome phenomenon, called *hot-spot* contention, occurs when some memory modules are hotly connected by a number of processors. This can be the case, for example, when a memory module contains a lock for a heavily used resource. Naturally, only one processor is allowed access, and the others must wait. However, the problem is that a hot spot may also block certain switching paths for extended periods of time, impairing the ability of other, unrelated inputs and outputs to establish connections.

Since shared semaphores and locks are primary sources of contention, an interesting alternative is to provide some hardware assists for their implementation in the switching network itself. For example, with the addition of some logic for incrementing and returning of results, the switching network can implement the fetch-and–add instruction. The switching network augmented with processing capability in switches is sometimes referred to as a *combining network.*

Types of Multiprocessor Operating Systems

As is the case with many emerging technologies, the thrust of the early multiprocessor research and implementations was in proving concepts. The primary objects for investigation were the architectures and ways of exploiting parallelism for speedup—often for the specialized, computation-intensive applications. Due to the relative lack of experience with and limited usage of multiprocessors, much work remains to be done in discovering the principles and the design methodology for multiprocessor operating systems.

The three basic types of multiprocessor operating systems are:

- Separate supervisors
- Master/slave
- Symmetric

Each of these types is described in the sections that follow.

Separate Supervisors

In separate-supervisor systems, each node contains a separate operating system that manages local processor, memory, and I/O resources. In its rudimentary form, this approach effectively manages each processor as an independent system. Only a few additional services and data structures may be added to support the multiprocessor aspects of the hardware. Such implementations of separate supervisors offer little in the way of load balancing and rarely support parallelism within applications.

A common example of separate supervisors is provided by hypercube systems, which due, to their regular and repeating structure constructed of identical building blocks, tend to replicate nearly identical copies of a kernel in each node. The kernel provides services such as local process and memory management, and implements the message-passing primitives. Store-and-forward and message-relaying functions may be implemented in the kernel or as a system task. Parallelism within applications is routinely achieved by subdividing them into subtasks that execute on different nodes. The system-level functions, such as allocation of processors to applications and macroscopic scheduling, are delegated to the system executive, which may be implemented in symmetrical or in master/slave fashion. In the early hypercubes, the master operating system was rudimentary or nonexistent. That is, program development and task-to-processor allocation were performed statically on a separate computer and then loaded to the hypercube for execution.

Master/Slave

In the master/slave approach, one processor is dedicated to executing the operating system. The remaining processors are usually identical and form a pool of computational processors. The master processor schedules the work and controls the activity of the slaves. Most of the operating-system data structures are controlled by the master processor and are often stored in its private memory. Slave processors may be able to process directly some simple local queries, but the majority of the operating-system services are provided by the master.

Master/slave systems are relatively simple to develop. With the addition of slave scheduling, a serial uniprocessor operating system can be fairly easily adapted for master/slave multiprocessor operation. The resulting systems have limited scalability, as the single master node often becomes a bottleneck.

Symmetric

In a symmetric organization, all processors are functionally identical. For allocation purposes, they represent a pool of anonymous resources. Other hardware resources, such as memory and

I/O devices, may also be pooled so as to be available to all processors. Otherwise, if only one or just a few processors have access to I/O devices, the system is asymmetric.

In the simplest form of a symmetric organization, called *floating master*, the operating system is more or less a single, large critical section. In response to the workload requirements and processor availability, the OS is executed by different processors at different times. Temporarily, the processor that executes the operating system has a special role and acts as a master in the sense that it schedules the work of others. The operating system is not bound to any specific processor, it floats from one processor to another (hence the name floating master). Since the operating system itself is largely monolithic, very little of its code, if any, is executed in parallel.

The floating master is a natural first step in implementing the operating system for a symmetric multiprocessor. It is relatively easy to port an existing uniprocessor operating system, such as Unix, to a shared-memory UMA multiprocessor. The shared memory contains all of the resident operating system code and data structures. The largely monolithic Unix kernel may be executed in a symmetric environment as the floating master. Any processor can execute the operating system, and process migration is almost trivial if state is saved in shared memory. Parallel execution of different applications is fairly easily achieved by maintaining a queue of ready processes in shared memory. Processor allocation is then reduced to assigning the first ready process to the first available processor until either all processors are busy or the queue is emptied. Thereafter, each idled processor fetched the next work item from the queue.

Some parallelism may be introduced at the operating-system level by identifying routines that can access shared data structures concurrently, and by protecting them with the appropriate interlocks. Concurrency control achieved by uniprocessor shortcuts, such as enabling and disabling interrupts or temporarily raising process priority, usually fails in a multiprocessor environment. Such portions must be recoded to operate correctly when executed in parallel.

Better performance can be expected when the operating system is implemented from scratch as a set of cooperating threads or processes that synchronize by means of the proper mechanisms, such as semaphores or messages. This increases potential parallelism in the operating system and allows mapping to different hardware architectures, such as tightly or loosely coupled. Some implementation issues pertaining to the native multiprocessor operating systems are discussed in the next section.

Multiprocessor OS Functions and Requirements

Like its uniprocessor counterparts, a multiprocessor operating system manages the available resources and augments the hardware functionality to form an abstraction that facilitates program execution and interaction with users. The three basic types of resources that need to be managed are:

- Processors
- Memory
- I/O devices

Processor scheduling is crucial for effective use of multiprocessors. The primary tasks of a multiprocessor scheduler are to:

1. Allocate processors among applications in a manner consistent with system-design objectives
2. Ensure efficient use of processors allocated to an application

The later requirement primarily affects the speedup, and the former affects the system throughput. Depending on the application, speedup or throughput may be given priority. These two objectives are somewhat conflicting, because maximum speedup can call for dedication of a large proportion of a system's processors to a single application.Throughput, on the other hand, can be improved by coscheduling several applications together, thus availing fewer processors to each.

Due to the difficulties of automating the process, exploitation of parallelism within an application usually requires some degree of explicit programmer direction. Most of the support for explicit and automatic parallelism is provided by language translators and preprocessors. Since the operating system is unaware of the semantics of user computations, it usually cannot offer much direct help. However, the operating system should provide the mechanisms and facilities that foster parallelism and aid the efforts of compilers and programmers alike. The two primary facets of OS support for multiprocessing are (1) flexible and efficient interprocess and interprocessor synchronization mechanisms, and (2) efficient creation and management of a large number of threads of activity, such as processes or threads. The latter aspect is important because parallelism is often accomplished by splitting an application into separate, individually executable subtasks that may be allocated to different processors.

Memory management in multiprocessors is highly dependent on the underlying architecture and interconnection scheme. Memory in loosely coupled systems is usually handled independently, on a per-processor basis. In shared-memory systems, the operating system should provide a flexible memory model that facilitates safe and efficient access to shared data structures and synchronization variables. Ideally, a multiprocessor operating system should provide a hardware-independent, unified model of shared memory to facilitate porting of applications between different multiprocessor environments. Shared memory may be simulated by means of a message-passing mechanism in loosely couple systems. Conversely, message passing can be implemented efficiently in tightly coupled systems by relying on physically shared memory. Such a unified memory model consisting of messages and shared memory provides a flexible model and a set of tools for application programmers. The duality of memory management and interprocess communication was exploited by the designers of the Mach operating system.

Device management has received little attention in multiprocessor systems to date. This is partly due to the early focus on speedup in compute-intensive applications that tend to execute for extended periods of time and do not generate much I/O after the initial loading. However, as multiprocessors are applied to more balanced general-purpose applications, one can expect their I/O requirements to increase in proportion with the realized throughput and speedup. Work on disk arrays (Katz et al. 1989) addresses some of these problems, but many other new and innovative techniques will be needed to obtain significantly increased performance using I/O devices whose individual speeds remain essentially unchanged. It is reasonable to expect that the application of multiprocessing techniques to I/O, such as stringing together a multitude of I/O devices and operating them in parallel, should yield good results.

OS Design and Implementation Issues

This section contain a discussion of some major implementation issues and considerations involved in processor and memory management in multiprocessor operating systems.

Processor Management and Scheduling

The main issues in processor management include:

- Support for multiprocessing
- Allocation of processing resources
- Scheduling

Support for Multiprocessing

The operating system can support multiprocessing and parallelism by providing a mechanism for creation and management of a large number of processes and/or threads. The process model can be viewed as providing a virtual-processor abstraction. Each process has a state (register content), a set of allocated resources such as files and memory, and connections to I/O devices. An application consisting of several cooperating processes represents a virtual multiprocessor that consists of virtual processors and the resources that they share. The virtual-multiprocessor abstraction is at a higher level than the hardware, because it includes the services of the operating system, such as a virtual memory and a file system. On uniprocessor, the virtual-multiprocessor abstraction is supported by time-multiplexing the physical processor among the virtual processors. An illusion of multiprocessing is created by allocating the physical processor to a different virtual processor during each time slice. In a multiprocessor environment, true multiprocessing is possible by allocating a separate physical processor to each virtual processor (process). Access to shared resources is usually maintained through the shared memory or by means of some interprocess communication mechanism.

When threads are used, each application is implemented as a separate process, and its concurrent portions are coded as separate threads within the enclosing process. Threads belonging to a single process share the memory and all other resources acquired by the process. Given their close relationship and common goal of executing an application, threads belonging to a process usually have much closer interaction than thread that belong to different processes. Some operating systems provide specialized calls for efficient synchronization of threads that belong to the same process. Communication is normally not an issue since threads share common memory. In addition to facilitating multiprocessing and improving efficiency, threads can also benefit scheduling. By having information about processes and threads, the scheduler can attempt to coschedule the related threads and thus reduce the probability of slowdowns caused by out-of-phase scheduling of closely coupled parties. An example of this problem is given in a later section.

Allocation of Processing Resources

Processor allocation can be a significant problem in massively parallel systems. One way of keeping track of a large number of processes (for economy of expression, the term *process* is used hereafter to refer to a schedulable entity, which, depending on implementation, may be a process or a thread) is to organize them in a logical hierarchy. The proposed hierarchy mimics similar real-world organizations, such as large companies and the military. Basically, some of the processors are workers, and others are managers.

The resulting system, called wave *scheduling*, basically operates as follows. In the MICROS system, which pioneered this approach individual processors are dedicated to one task at a time. Each manager keeps track of the number of workers that it has available. Upon receiving a work request calling for *R* processors, the system must secure *R* or more processors, since some can fail. The work requests can be submitted to a manager at any level of the hierarchy. If the manager chosen does not have a sufficient number of workers, it calls on its boss for help. If the boss does not have enough help available, it can call on its boss. The process continues until a sufficient number of available processors is secured or the top of the hierarchy is reached. If the attempt to allocate processors fails at that level, the request may be delayed pending availability of an adequate amount of resources.

Hierarchical allocation of processes is conceptually appealing because it is conducive to robust implementation and it scales well due to the relatively limited amount of generated traffic. Fault tolerance is possible because the work of a failed manager can be assigned to one of its subordinates or to some other processor designated by its boss. With a committee at the top of the hierarchy tree, failure of a committee member can be handled by the election of a successor. The failure of a worker process need not disrupt the system if its work can be restarted or resumed by another node.

Implementation of wave scheduling creates some practical difficulties. One is that a manager may have an out-of-date estimate of the availability of its workforce. This necessitates the use of estimates, which can result in inefficiencies if they are too conservative, and in allocation failures if they are too optimistic. Moreover, since multiple allocation requests may be in the granting process at the same time, the resources estimated to be available may turn out to be snatched by another client at the time a processor allocation is actually attempted.

Scheduling

The hierarchical approach provides a model for resources control in multiprocessors and in distributed systems. Once the processors are allocated to applications in some manner, they have to be scheduled. A desirable objective in multiprocessor systems is to attempt to coschedule processes that interact so that they run at the same time. Processes at the opposite ends of a pipe, the sender and receiver of a message, and perhaps several threads belonging to a single process, are generally good candidates for coscheduling. Otherwise, considerable time may be wasted as exchanges between out-of–phase parties are attempted.

Figure 23.5 illustrates this problem. In the example, eight processes are scheduled for execution on four processors. Assume that the system under consideration uses time slicing and schedules processes in the *A*, *B*, *C*, *D* group at even time intervals, and processes in the *P*, *Q*, *R*, *S* group at odd time intervals. The particular processor allocated to a particular process in a given time interval is immaterial for the purposes of this example.

Suppose that one or more processes in the first group communicate—say, by means of synchronous messages—with some processes in the second group. For example, after receiving a time slice, process *A* sends a message to process *P*. Since *P* is not running. *A* is blocked for the remainder of its time slice. Assuming that P receives the message at the beginning of its time slice and sends an immediate reply, it will be blocked as well until A runs again. If the time slice lasts 50 ms, scheduling that does not take into consideration process-group relationships could restrict message exchange between A and P to at most one per 100 ms.

Time slot ↓ / Processor →	0	1	2	3
0	A	B	C	D
1	P	Q	R	S
2	B	C	D	A
3	P	R	Q	S
4	B	A	D	C
5	R	S	Q	P

Fig. 23.5. An example of multiprocessor scheduling.

Individual processors in a multiprocessor system may be uniprogrammed or multiprogrammed. In other words, a processor may be devoted to a single task or may multiplex its cycles among a number of tasks allocated to it. In principle, multiprogramming provides the potential for increasing throughput, but it can aggravate the problem of out-of-phase communicate delays. One way of dealing with the problem is to *coschedule* process groups that are known or believed to communicate with each other. In most cases, the initiating party or the operating system known or can find out the identity of the other party. Some means must also be provided to inform the scheduler about group membership and relationship. This information can be deterministic or serve as a scheduling hint. For example, the Mach operating system supports *handoff hints* whereby a process can "handoff" control to another. This can be useful, for example, by having a sender of a message hand off control to its recipient. Another type of hint is the *discouragement hint*, which may be used to inform the scheduler that a process anticipates some delays as a consequence of its action.

In a loosely coupled system, the scheduler should observe the affinity of some processes for certain processors. This may be the case when a process state is stored in the private memory of a specific processor. The scheduler must take into consideration the often-costly migration that would be incurred by reallocation of such processes. Another scheduling consideration is the communication cost. In general, communication cost can be reduced by placing closely interacting processes onto the same processor or into a cluster that has direct interprocessor links. These considerations have to be weighed against the potential for parallelism, which is generally increased when processes are allocated to different processors.

Memory Management

In tightly coupled multiprocessors, the operating system must facilitate and control access to shared memory. In such an environment, the OS usually provides additional primitives for allocation and deallocation of segments of shared memory. In systems that support shared virtual memory, several translation lookaside buffers (TLBs) residing on different processors may contain mappings for pages that belong to a shared segment. In such cases, the operating system must cooperate with hardware to enforce TLB coherence. Otherwise, both memory access and protection can be severely hampered. TLB coherence is generally supported using some variation of the techniques developed for multiprocessor cache coherence.

Shared memory can also be used to improve performance of message passing.This is accomplished by avoiding copying of messages whose senders and receivers have access to the same physical shared memory. Instead, the operating stem can pass the access rights (and sometimes just a pointer) for the message between two processes. However, potential modification of the message by either party would violate the normal semantics of message passing that promises a separate copy for each party.

The copy-on-write technique can be used to alleviate the problem while maintaining high efficiency. In this approach, a single copy of the original message is maintained in shared memory. Message passing is performed by granting the receiver the right to access that copy. However, when either party attempts to modify a part of the message, a trap to the operating system is generated. The operating system in turn makes a fresh copy of the affected page, which is then mapped to the updating process and is used to complete the write. Thus, the sender and the receiver continue to share the unmodified parts of the message, and each has a private copy of the modified portions. This approach capitalizes on the fact that write sharing is relatively infrequent. It strictly preserves the semantics of message passing while maintaining efficiency by performing lazy copying only when it is unavoidable, which is presumably the case for a minority of pages. Copy-on-write has also been successfully applied to reduce the costs of process migration and of message passing in loosely coupled systems. In the Mach operating system, copy-on-write is used for most of the purposes described here.

Some operating systems for loosley coupled multiprocessors provide the shared-memory abstraction and implement it using the message-passing facility.

Introduction to Parallel Programming

Some multiprocessor systems offer automatic tools, usually in the form of compilers or preprocessors, for parallelizing user programs and applications. If the tools fail to exploit potential parallelism, or if the system does not offer such tools, programmers have to provide explicit coding for multiple processors. The programmer typically starts by analyzing the contemplated program for loops, recursions and other iterative structures that are executed often enough to represent significant portions of the execution time. A profiler is often useful in identifying where the program spends most of its time. The innermost complex iterations are usually a good starting point. Following such analysis, the programmer splits the identified regions across N processors, if possible, and adds the necessary synchronization and data transmission statements.

Speedup

In general, the speedup due to parallel execution of a program is limited by three major factors:

- The ratio of sequential to parallel sections of the code

- The available speedup for parallel portions, that is, the smaller of the number of available processors and the maximum degree of parallelism coded in the program
- The setup, synchronization, and communication overhead introduced by parallel operation

The last point refers to overhead for setup and initialization of the shared areas of memory, or for passing data via messages in loosely coupled systems, and to the creation of processes for multiple processors and their run-time communication and synchronization.

The serial portion of the program must be executed serially, so speedup is limited to the parallel sections. This relationship was pointed out early on by Gene Amdahl, who stated that the speedup obtained from introducing a faster component is limited by the fraction of the time that the speedier component is actually in use. More specifically,

$$S = \frac{1}{(1-f)+\frac{f}{k}}$$

where S is the speedup ($S > 1$) relative to the standard (serial) case that results from introduction of a k times faster component ($k > 1$) that is used a fraction of time f ($f \le 1$). Figure 23.6 plots this equation for various values of f, the parallel fraction of a program. Hardware speedup up to tenfold (for k = 1 to 10 processors) and an unlimited number of processes that can run in parallel are assumed. This means that there is always a supply of ready processes for processor allocation.

As suggested by Figure 23.6 the ideal linear speedup is achieved for programs that are fully parallel to a degree that is lesser than or equal to the number of available processors in the system. However, serial portions of the program cause the maximum achievable speedup to fall off sharply. For example, a program that is 90% parallel (f = .9) is limited to speedup of approximately 5.6 on a system with 10 processors.

An Example of Parallel Programming: Matrix Multiplication

As an example of parallel programming, consider matrix multiplication on a multiprocessor. The product of two $n \times n$ matrices A and B yields an $n \times n$ matrix C whose elements can be computed as follows:

$$c_{i,j} = \sum_{k=1}^{n} a_{i,k} \times b_{k,j}$$

One way to perform matrix multiplication in parallel is to compute each row (or each column) on a separate processor. Program 23.1 represents a way of coding matrix multiplication for a multiprocessor.

The program contains a template process, *p_i*, for processes to be spawned for calculation of each row that can be executed on separate processors. The parent program declares the three matrices as global variables to be placed in shared memory for access by all processors. In a loosely coupled system, the parent process would have to send the necessary data in the form of messages to the processors where the specific row-computation processes are to be executed.

The parent process initializes the general semaphore DONE to the negative count of worker processes. Each of them signals the semaphore after completing its computation. When the semaphore receives *N* signals, it becomes free. That fact is used by the parent process to detect the end of the entire matrix multiplication.

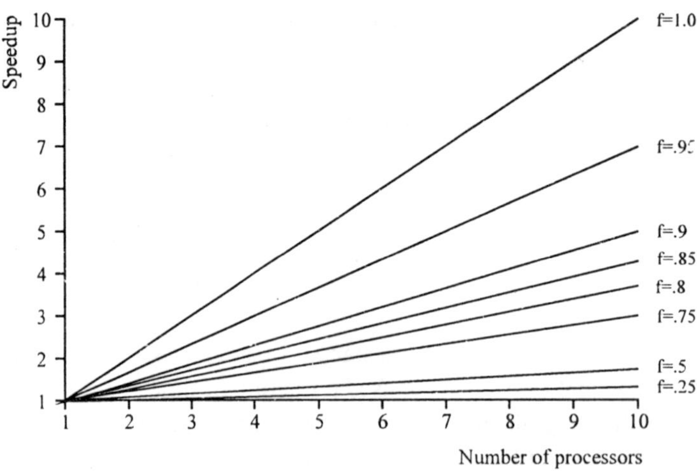

Fig. 23.6. Speedup as a function of parallelism.

After initializing the completion semaphore, the parent process initiates the row-computation processes. Each of them is assumed to receive as a parameter, *i*, a different row number. Thus, rows are computed by separate processes in parallel. The parallelism actually realized depends on the number of available processes and on the degree of parallelism in the application. As coded, the degree of parallelism in the application is *n*, since no subdivision below the row level is made. Figure 23.7 is a timing diagram of an execution scenario of Program 23.1 on a shared-memory multiprocessor with $N = 12$ and five processors.

The diagram assumes that processor 1 runs the parent task, which initializes the system and the shared memory and then initiates the 12 row-computation processes. The first 4 processes are assigned immediately to the free processors, and the remaining 8 processes are placed in the ready list. They are scheduled for execution later as processors become available. The processors are assumed to be multiprogrammed. Consequently processor 1 begins executing the next worker process (5) after the parent process becomes suspended pending opening of the semaphore DONE.

No synchronization beyond the completion semaphore is necessary in the matrix multiplication example as coded in the Program. 23.1. This is because separate processes share the two multiplicand matrices in the read-only mode, and each writes a separate row of the result matrix *C*.

Depending on the process scheduling, on the memory organization, and on the layout of data, three may be some collisions on the hardware level when different processors are attempting to access the same memory cells simultaneously. As Figure 23.7 indicates, the processes are started on various processors at different times. If the arrays are laid out in shared memory in a sequence similar to the order in which the program processes them, it is not very likely that several processors would get into lockstep and collide when accessing shared memory. As an added precaution, the running product, s, is be maintained as the local variable private to each process. Alternatively, the intermediate products could be stored directly in the global copy of the matrix C at the expense of memory contention. Likewise, contention may be aggravated if the data are processed in an order that is at odds with the compiler-produced layout sequence of arrays in memory.

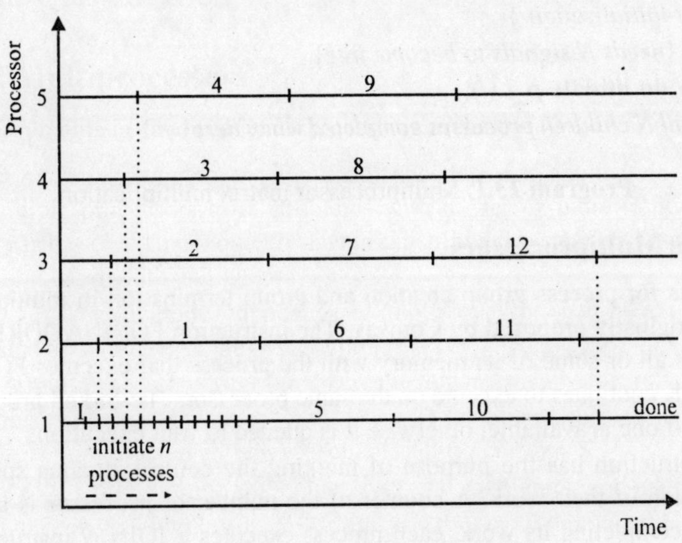

Fig. 23.7. Timing diagram of Program 23.1.

```
Program matrixmul; {parallel matrix multiplication}
const N = ; {# of rows}
var
i : integer; {private, in parent's space}
a : array[1.. N, 1..N] of integer;
{shared global variables}
b : array [1..N,1..N] of integer;
c : array [1..N, 1..N] of integer;
done: semaphore; {general}
process p_i (i : integer);{ N such processes executed}
var
j, k, s : integer; {private local variables}
begin
for j := 1 to N do
begin
```

(contd.)

```
s := 0;
for k := 1 to N do s := s + a[i,k] * b[kj];
c[ij] := s
end; {for j}
signal(done)
end; {process p_i}
begin {parent-initialization }
done := -(N); {needs N signals to become free}
for i := 1 to N do initiate p_i (i);
wait(done); {all N children processes completed when here}
```

Program 23.1. Multiprocessor matrix multiplication.

Fork and Join in Multiprocessors

Two primitives for process group creation and group termination in multiprocessors, FORK and JOIN, were originally proposed by Conway. The instruction FORK-ADDRESS spawn a new process that shares all or some of its memory with the process that executes FORK. The process that executes FORK continues to execute on the same processor. The forked process is assigned to another processor if one is available; otherwise it is queued to wait execution.

The JOIN instruction has the purpose of merging the control streams spawned by FORK following completion of their work. A counter of the number of processes is usually associated with JOIN. Upon completing its work, each process executes a JOIN N instruction. This causes the counter to be incremented and compared to N. If the result is smaller than N, the work is not done, and there are more processes to complete. In addition, execution of JOIN effectively terminates the issuing process, and its resources may be freed and returned to the allocation pool. Eventually, the last spawned process finishes and executes JOIN N. This returns control to the process that issued the FROK instruction.

The FORK and JOIN instructions can be used to implement the intent of Program 23.1 without the use of semaphores. This may be accomplished by having the control (parent) process fork n-1 identical row-computing processes and pass a different value of n to each. The nth row computation may be performed in the body of the control process itself. Each of the spawned processes would end with a JOIN 12 instruction. When all 12 JOINs are executed, the matrix multiplication is completed, and the control process may proceed with its other activities or terminate. This would change the execution diagram in Figure 23.7 by executing Process 11 on processor 1 as a part of the control process. Thereafter, processor 1 would be free for other assignments until successful completion of all JOINs. Application of FORK and JOIN instructions to matrix multiplication may be found in Stone

As indicated, FORK and JOIN instructions are well suited to the needs of multiprocessor programming. The spawned processes retain a close relationship and access to shared data in memory. JOIN instructions provide a way to conclude the computation and to signal production of the result without having to resort to the use of other synchronization mechanisms, such as semaphores. Note that process creation in Unix (and its derivatives) follows the logic of FORK and JOIN to a large extent, but in a uniprocessor environment.

Multiprocessor Synchronization

Interprocessor synchronization and communication are necessary for designing concurrent software that is correct and reliable. Parallel program execution and read/write sharing of data place heavy demands on the synchronization mechanisms in multiprocessors. In loosely coupled multiprocessors both interprocess synchronization and communication are handled via messages. Once the necessary data are transmitted to individual processors for processing, there is usually little need for processed to synchronize while operating on data in local memory. Some synchronization may be needed to communicate results and to consolidate them at whatever node they are to be kept in following completion of a parallel computation.

Access to shared memory can result in speed improvements for many applications, but it also intensifies the need for synchronization. Properly designed uniprocessor instructions, such as test-and-set and compare-and swap implemented using the indivisible read-modify-write (RMW) cycle, can be used as a foundation for interprocess synchronization in multiprocessor systems. In this section we extend some of our earlier discussion and introduce some new mechanisms and techniques suitable for synchronization in multiprocessors.

Test-and-Set

The test-and-set (TS) instruction was introduced and discussed with the aid of the indivisible memory read-modify-write (RMW) cycle extends the TS functionality to shared-memory multiprocessors. One way to implement a semaphore in a multiprocessor system is to declare it as a shared variable and update it as required by the semaphore definition with the aid of test-and-set instructions. In such systems, several processors may be waiting for the semaphore to open by executing TS instructions in parallel. The semaphore WAIT operation may be implemented using either

- Busy-waiting (spin lock) or
- Queuing of waiting processes

Unfortunately, neither alternative is very attractive in multiprocessor systems. Busy-waiting, called spin lock in multiprocessors, wastes processor cycles and consumes the bandwidth of the links that connect processors to shared memory. In addition, several processors spinning on a lock can cause contention at the memory module that contains the semaphore variable and thus impair access by other processors to the enclosing memory bank. In multiprocessor systems with multiple caches, spin locks can cause increased bus traffic needed to maintain consistency among copies of the semaphore variable that reside in caches of the competing processors. Depending on the cache-coherence scheme in effect, additional cache-related problems and performance degradation may develop.

Queuing of waiting processes can alleviate some of these problems, but usually at the expense of significant overhead. Both queueing and subsequent dequeuing and process wakeup entail a series of operations. Worse yet, some of those operations simply access shared data structures—such as the semaphore queue itself—and must be protected by locks. This approach may end up delegating the problem to another implementation layer and reincarnating it there.

Compare-and-Swap

The compare-and-swap (CS) instruction provides a basis for optimistic concurrency control that does not use locking. If implemented using the indivisible read-modify-write memory cycle, the

CS instruction can be used for this purpose these in multiprocessors. These operations are equivalent to enqueue and dequeue operations on a shared queue.

The management of shared lists and queues is an important and often performed task in multiprocessor operating systems. As discussed earlier, a common scheduling technique in shared-memory systems is to maintain a list of ready processes in shared memory for consumption by idle processors. Other instances of shared lists and queues are queuing semaphores, shared-resource queues and mailboxes. Several types of queue and list management operations may be found in KMOS code. Obviously, access to shared queues must be controlled to prevent inconsistent manipulation by concurrent activities initiated by different processors. The compare-and-swap instruction provides a good vehicle for queue manipulation without locking.

A sample appearance of a queue represented in the form of a singly linked list is depicted in Figure 23.8. Two pointers, *Head* and *Tail*, point to the head and tail of the list, respectively. Assuming that elements are added to the tail and removed from the head, the dashed lines in Figure 23.8 show the list appearance after addition of the new element, E_{n+1}. In the KMOS and Pascal notation, a new element item can be added using the following statements.

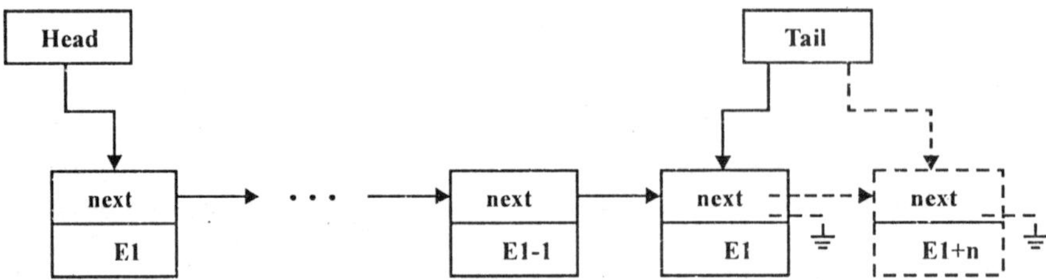

Fig. 23.8. Enqueue operation.

item^.next := nil;

temp := Tail;

Tail := item; {Tail updated to point to inserted item}

temp^.next := item; {next link of formerly last item points to new entry}

Item, *Tail*, and *temp* denote pointers to the corresponding variables. The notation *pointer^.next* refers to the *next* (link) field of the list node that pointer points to.

When several processors attempt to add different elements to the same list concurrently, mishaps such as a lost update or crosslinked pointers can happen when the preceding statements are executed by two or more processors in an interleaved fashion. One way to prevent this is to treat the add (enqueue) operation as a critical section.'The compare-and-swap instruction can be used to add an entry, item, without the overhead of locking and OS invocation as follows:

item^.next := nil;

old_tail := Tail;

LOOP: CS *old_tail, item, Tail;*

if (*old_tail was not = Tail*) **then goto** LOOP; {*else Tail = item*}

Old_tail^.next := item;

The new item will become the last entry in the list, so its *next* link is set to nil. The current value of the *Tail* pointer is copied to the OLD register of CS, denoted as *old_tail* in the code. Then, compare-and-swap is used to try to enqueue the element by setting *Tail* to point to the new item. The CS instruction is used to verify that no additions to the list were performed by other processors in the meantime. If they were, CS will fail and return the new, updated value of *Tail* into the *old_tail* register. Eventually, the update succeeds, and the global variable *Tail* is set to point to the item. At that time, the *next* link of the immediately preceding element in the list (the former tail element) is set to point to the new entry.

The basic removal (dequeue) operation, assuming that the list is nonempty, can be implemented with compare-and-swap as follows:

```
old_head := Head;
LOOP: if old_head <> nil
then
begin
item :=old_head^.next;
CS old_head, item, Head;
if (old_head, was not = Head) then goto LOOP
end
else ...{the list is empty}
```

The possibility of the list being empty causes additional complications and requires more elaborate code. These complexities can be avoided by maintaining a dummy element so that the list is never empty. This technique is used extensively in the KMOS code, for example, to avoid emptying of the ready list.

It can be shown that the first code sequence presented operates correctly in the presence of concurrent enqueue operations. The dequeue sequence operates correctly for concurrent dequeues as long as the list is never emptied. However, the compare-and-swap solution presented is not correct when concurrent enqueue and dequeue operations are allowed on the same shared queue. For example, the enqueue operation assumes that the equality of *old_tail* and *Tail* variables implies that no elements were added to the queue in the interim. With concurrent dequeues and enqueues, this may not be the case. It is possible, for example, that two processes are interleaved so that an item is removed and then immediately put back on the queue. This would leave the *Tail* pointer unchanged and confuse the enqueue sequence in progress so that two processors may perform an erroneous update by placing two different values in the same memory location, *old_tail^.next*, without synchronization.

In summary, the compare-and-swap instruction works in multiprocessors when implemented using the indivisible read-modify-write cycle in shared memory. The instruction assists the implementation of optimistic concurrency control for some applications, such as updating of shared variables and manipulation of shared lists. The primary appeal of the CS approach to concurrency control is the lack of locking, which guarantees that at least one of the contending processes is making progress regardless of their priorities and order of scheduling. Direct application of the CS instruction solves a class of synchronization problem without imposing the overhead of operating-system calls. On the negative side, the compare-and-swap instruction is quite tricky and difficult to use correctly.

Fetch-and-Add

The common performance problem with the read-modify-write memory cycle is the complexity and memory contention caused by the locking protocols. If N processes are trying to access a critical section at the same time, the memory system must execute N basic lock operations, one after another, even though at most one process can be successful.

The fetch-and-add (FA) instruction was introduced in the NYU Ultra-computer project to alleviate the memory contention due to locking. However, the instruction was never implemented in hardware. Unlike other instructions, fetch-and-add is executed by the logic placed in the interconnection (combining) switching network that connects processors with memory. The fetch-and-add primitive is denoted as FA(x,i), where x is a variable in shared memory and i is an increment added to it when the instruction completes. When a single processor requests execution of fetch-and-add on x, the semantics are:

```
Fetch-and-add(x,i) {definition}
begin
temp :=x;
x :=temp + i;
return temp
end;
```

If N processors attempt to execute the fetch-and-add simultaneously on the same location in memory, the increments are added and combined in the switching network so that a single increment—which is the sum of N increments—is applied to the memory location x. In response to this instruction, a single value is returned to each processor. The primary benefit of accumulating increments in the network is reduced contention, since results may be returned to originating processors parallel by nearby switching elements, and the global memory location need be accessed only once to apply the final accumulated result. The individual returned values correspond to some arbitrary serialization of N requests. From the processor and memory point of view, the effect is identical to a serial execution of N fetch-and-add instructions. Since these instructions are actually performed in a one-cycle memory update, the fetch-and-add primitive can be very effective in accessing shared queues and in the management of identical processes that operate on different segments of data.

For example, the matrix multiplication program introduced earlier spreads the work across a multitude of processor, each of which computes a different row. The serial part of that program is the initialization and distribution of a separate row index to each process. With the fetch-and-add instruction, the same effect could be accomplished by having each processor execute the following code for a matrix with N rows:

```
n := FA(R,1);
while (n<=N)do
begin
```

{*computation of row n*};
n :=FA(*R*,1)
end; {*while*}

Each processor initially executes fetch-and-add and obtains a different row index, *n*, which is then used in the code segment. *R* is a global variable that accumulates the count of rows computed. *R* is initially set to 1.

In the code sequence presented, each processor executes the FA(*R*, 1) instruction, obtains a different value on *n*, and thus computes a different row. Upon completion of its computation, the processor executes another FA instruction to obtain the number of the next row that needs to be computed. The processor first tests the value obtained against the size of the matrix, *N*. If it is lower than the constant *N*, the processor repeats the process. However, if the value obtained exceeds *N*, the computation is finished and the processor exits the **while** loop. Since parallel execution of the fetch-and-add instruction returns a unique value of *R* to each processor, each of them computes a different row of the matrix. The test for *N* ensures that the solution works for an arbitrary number of processors that may be smaller or larger than *N*. The beauty of this scheme is that it not only provides the distribution of row indices but also allows processors to schedule themselves effectively without the need to use a shared queue or a ready list.

Summary

Multiprocessing can be used for speedup and for improving throughput of computer systems. Potential benefits of multiprocessing include increased performance and computing power, increased fault tolerance, flexibility, and modular growth.

Several classifications of multiprocessor systems were presented in this chapter. Based on the relationship between instructions and data, computer systems can be characterized as SISD, SIMD, MISD, and MIMD. In tightly coupled systems, multiple processors have access to shared memory. Loosely coupled systems, on the other hand, have no shared memory. The speed of accessing memory may be uniform (UMA) or nonuniform (NUMA).

Multiprocessor interconnect schemes include (1) shared bus, (2) crossbar, (3) hypercube, and (4) multistage switches. Shared-bus systems are relatively simple and popular, but their scalability is limited by bus and memory contention. Crossbar systems allow fully parallel connections between processors and different memories, but their cost and complexity grow quadratically with the number of nodes. Hypercubes and multilevel switches are scalable, and their complexity grows logarithmically with the number of nodes.

The basic types of multiprocessor operating systems are (1) separate supervisors, (2) master/slave, and (3) symmetric. Symmetric is potentially the most flexible of the three because it allows both the operating systems and the applications to be executed in parallel.

The basic facets of operating-system support for multiprocessing include the provision for multiple lightweight processes, such as threads, and efficient implementation of synchronization and communication primitives. Wave scheduling can be applied for allocation of processing in large-scale systems. Processor scheduling in multiprocessor environments must take into consideration process and group relations. It is usually beneficial to coschedule related groups of processes to ensure their timely communication. Processes can use scheduling hints, such as handoff and discouragement, to guide the scheduler.

Automatic tools for parallel programming are available in some multiprocessor compilers and preprocessors. However, explicit programmer-directed parallelism is often a primary vehicle for control of multiprocessors. Many factors conspire to reduce the speedup theoretically possible with multiprocessors. They include a certain dose of sequentiality inherent in many applications, the need to spawn and initialize parallel processes, and the synchronization and communication overhead at run-time.

Hardware primitives to assist synchronization in multiprocessor systems include the test-and-set compare-and-swap instructions. Both can be implemented using the indivisible read-modify-write memory cycle. The compare-and-swap instruction is suitable for optimistic concurrency control in a class of applications such as updating of a shared variable and concurrent enqueue and dequeue operations. The memory contention over shared variables inevitable with the RMW cycle can be solved using innovative approaches such as the fetch-and-add instruction, which is well suited for some common forms of multiprocessor synchronization.

Case Study 1

Windows 2000

Windows 2000 was released in 2000 and incorporated significant changes. It adds an X.500-based directory service, better networking support, support for Plug-and-Play devices, a new file system with support for hierarchical storage, and a distributed file system, as well as support for more processors and more memory.

There are four versions of Windows 2000. The Professional version is intended for desktop use. The other three are server versions: Server, Advanced Server, and Datacenter Server. These differ primarily in the amount of memory and number of processors that they support. They use the same kernel and operating-system code, but Windows 2000 Server and Advanced Server versions are configured for client-server applications and can act as application, servers on NetWare and Microsoft LANs. Windows 2000 Datacenter Server now supports up to 32 processors and up to 64 GB of RAM.

In 1996, more windows NT Server licenses were sold than all versions of UNIX licenses. Interestingly, the code base for Windows 2000 is on the order of 30 million lines of code. Compare this size with the code base of Windows NT version 4.0: about 18 million lines of code.

Design Principles

The design goals that Microsoft has stated for Windows 2000 include extensibility, portability, reliability, compatibility, performance, and international support.

Extensibility refers to the capacity of an operating system to keep up with advances in computing technology. So that changes are facilitated over time, the developers implemented Windows 2000 using a layered architecture. The Windows 2000 executive, which runs in kernel or protected more, provides the basic system services. On top of the executive, several server subsystems operate in user mode. Among them are **environmental subsystems** that emulate different operating systems. Thus, programs written for MS-DOS, Microsoft Windows, and POSIX can all run on Windows 2000 in the appropriate environment.

Because of the modular structure, additional environmental subsystems can be added without affecting the executive, in addition, Windows 2000 uses loadable drivers in the I/O system, so new file systems, new kinds of I/O devices, and new kinds of networking can be added while the system is running. Windows 2000 uses a client-server model like the Mach operating system, and supports distributed processing by remote procedure calls (RPCs) as defined by the Open Software Foundation.

An operating system is **portable** if it can be moved from one hardware architecture to another with relatively few changes. Windows 2000 is designed to be portable. As is true of the UNIX operating system, the majority of the system is written in C and C++. All Processor-dependent code is isolated in a dynamic link library (DLL) called the **hardware-abstraction layers (HAL).** A DLL is a file that gets mapped into a process' address space such that any functions in the DLL appear to be part of the process. The upper layers of Windows 2000 depend on HAL, rather than on the underlying hardware, and that helps Windows 2000 to be portable. HAL manipulates hardware directly, isolating the rest of Windows 2000 from hardware differences among the platforms on which it runs.

Reliability is the ability to handle error conditions, including the ability of the operating system to protect itself and its users from defective or malicious software. Windows 2000 resists defects and attacks by using hardware protection for virtual memory, and software protection mechanisms for operating-system resources. Also, Windows 2000 comes with a native file system—the **NTFS file system**—that recovers automatically from many kinds of file-system errors after a system crash. Windows NT Version 4.0 has a C-2 security classification from the U.S. government, which signifies a moderate level of protection from defective software and malicious attacks. Windows 2000 is currently under evaluation by the government of that classification as well. For more information about security classifications.

Windows 2000 provides source-level **compatibility** to applications that follow the IEEE 1003.1 (POSIX) standard. Thus, they can be compiled to run on Windows 2000 without changes to the source code. In addition, windows 2000 can run the executable binaries for many programs compiled for Intel X86 architectures running MS-DOS, 16-bit Windows, OS/2, LAN Manager, and 32-bit Windows, by using the environmental subsystems mentioned earlier. These environmental subsystems support a veriety of file systems, including the MS-DOS FAT file system, the OS/2 HPFS file system, the ISO9660 CD file system, and NTFS. Windows 2000' binary compatibility, however, is not perfect. In MS-DOS, for example, applications can access hardware ports directly. For reliability and security, Windows 2000 prohibits such access.

Windows 2000 is designed to afford good **performance**. The subsystems that constitute Windows 2000 can communicate with one another efficiently by a local-procedure-call (LPC facility that provides high-performance message passing. Except for the kernel, threads in the subsystems of windows 2000 can be preempted by higher-priority threads. Thus, the system can respond quickly to external events. In addition, Windows 2000 is designed for symmetrical multiprocessing: On a multiprocessor computer, several threads can run at the same time. The current scalability of Windows 2000 is limited, compared to that of UNIX. As of late 2000, Windows 2000 supported systems with up to 32 CPUs, whereas Saloris ran on systems with up 64 processors. Previous version of NT supported only up to 8 processors.

Windows 2000 is also designed for international use. It provides support for different locales via the national language support (NLS) APL. NLS API provides specialized routines to format dates, time, and money in accordance with various national customs. String comparisons are specialized to account for varying character sets. UNICODE is Windows 2000's native character code; Windows 2000 supports ANSI characters by converting them to UNICODE characters before manipulating them (8-bit to 16-bit conversion).

System Components

The architecture of Windows 2000 is a layered system of modules. The main layers are the HAL, the kernel, and the executive, all of which run in protected mode, and a large collection of subsystems that run in use mode. The user-mode subsystems are in two categories. The environmental subsystems emulate different operating systems; the **protection subsystems** provide security functions. One of the chief advantages of this type of architecture is that interactions between modules can be kept simple. The remainder of this section describes these layers and subsystems.

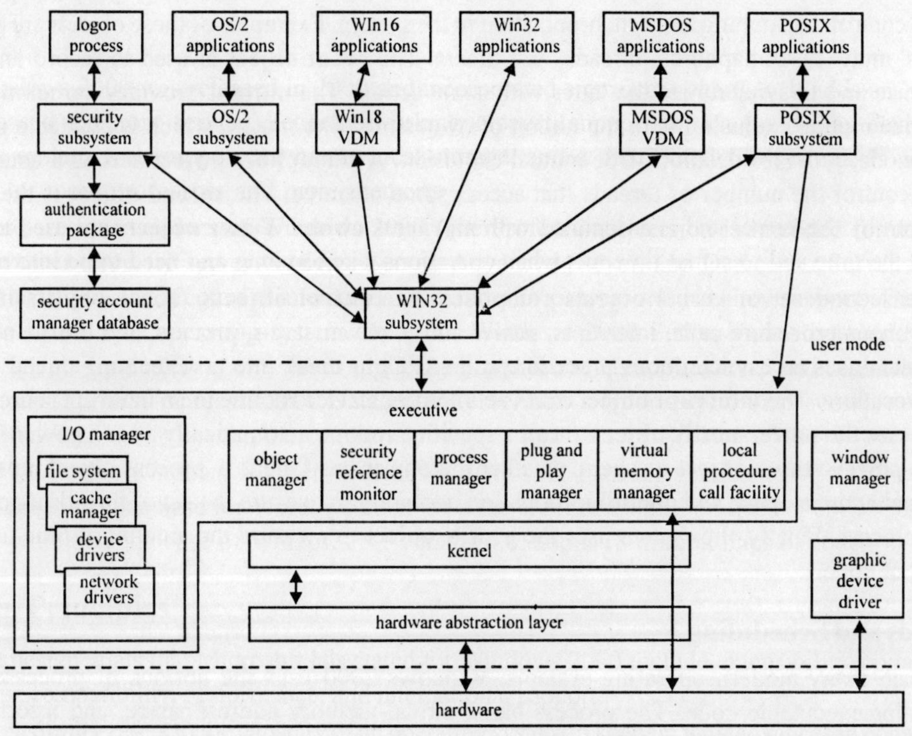

Fig. CS1.1. Windows 2000 block diagram.

Hardware-Abstraction Layer

HAL is the layer of software that hides hardware differences from upper levels of the operating system, to help make Windows 2000 portable. HAL exports a virtual-machine interface that is used by the kernel, the executive, and the device drivers. One advantage of this approach is that only a single version of each device driver is needed—it can run on all hardware platforms without porting the driver code. HAL also provides the support for symmetric multiprocessing. For performance reasons, I/O drivers (and graphics drivers in Windows 2000) can access the hardware directly.

Kernel

The kernel of Windows 2000 provides the foundation for the executive and the subsystems.The kernel is never paged out of memory, and its execution is never preempted. It has four main responsibilities: thread scheduling, interrupt and exception handling, low-level processor synchronization, and recovery after a power failure.

The kernel is object oriented. An object type in Windows 2000 is a system-defined data type that has a set of attributes (or data values) and a set of methods (that, is functions or operations). An **object** is just an instance of a particular object type. The kernel performs its job by using a set of kernel objects whose attributes store the kernel data and whose methods perform the kernel activities.

The kernel uses two sets of objects. The first set comprises the dispatcher objects. **Dispatcher objects** control dispatching and synchronization in the system. Examples of these objects are events, mutants, mutexes, semaphores, threads, and timers. The **event object** is used to record an event occurrence and to synchronize the latter with some action. The **mutant** provides kernel-mode or user-mode mutual exclusion with the notion of ownership. The mutex, which is available only in kernel mode, provides deadlock-free mutual exclusion. A **semaphore object** acts as a counter or gate to control the number of threads that access some resource. The **thread object** is the entity that is run by the kernel and is associated with a **process object**. **Timer objects** are used to keep track of the time and to signal timeouts when operations take too long and need to be interrupted.

The second set of kernel objects comprises the **control objects**. These objects include asynchronous procedure calls, interrupts, power notify, power status, process, and profile objects. The system uses an asynchronous procedure call (APC) to break into an executing thread and to call a procedure. The **interrupt object** binds an interrupt service routine to an interrupt source. The system uses the **power-notify object** to call a specified routine automatically after a power failure, and the **power-status object** to check whether the power has failed. A process object represents the virtual address space and control information necessary to execute the set of threads associated with a process. Finally, the system uses the **profile object** to measure the amount of time used by a block of code.

Threads and Scheduling

As do many modern operating systems, Windows 2000 uses the notions of processes and threads for executable code. The process has a virtual-memory address space, and information such as a base priority and an affinity for one or more processors. Each process as one or more threads, which are the units of execution dispatched by the kernel. Each thread has its own state, including a priority, processor affinity, and accounting information.

This six possible thread states are ready, standby running, waiting, transition, and terminated. **Ready** means waiting to run. The highest-priority ready thread is moved to the **standby** state, which means that it will be the next thread to run. In a multiprocessor system, one thread is kept in the standby state for each processor. A thread is running when it is executing on processor. It will run until it is preempted by a higher-priority thread, until it terminates, until its time quantum ends, or until it calls a blocking system call such as for I/O. A thread is in the **waiting** state when it is waiting for a signal such as an I/O completion. A new thread is in the transition state while it is waiting for the resources necessary for execution. A thread enters the **terminated** state when it finishes execution.

The dispatcher uses a 32-level priority scheme to determine the order of thread execution. Priorities are divided into two classes: The variable class contains threads having priorities from 0 to 15, and the real-time class contains threads with priorities ranging from 16 to 31. The dispatcher uses a queue for each scheduling priority, and traverses the set of queues from highest to lowest until it finds a thread that is ready to run. If a thread has a particular processor affinity but that processor is not available, the dispatcher will skip past it, and will continue looking for a thread that is ready to run. If no ready thread is found, the dispatcher will execute a special thread called the idle thread.

When a thread's time quantum runs out, that thread is interrupted; if the thread is in the variable-priority class, its priority is lowered. The priority is never lowered below the base priority, however. Lowering the thread's priority tends to limit the CPU consumption of compute-bound threads. When a variable-priority thread is released from a wait operation, the dispatcher boosts the priority. The amount of the boost depends on for what the thread was waiting; for example, a thread that was waiting for keyboard I/O would get a large priority increase, whereas a thread waiting for a disk operation would get a moderate one. This strategy tends to give good response times to interactive threads that are using the mouse and windows, and enables I/O-bound threads to keep the I/O devices busy, while permitting compute-bound threads to use spare CPU cycles in the background. This strategy is used by several time-sharing operating systems, including UNIX. In addition, the current window with which the user is interacting also receives a priority boost to enhance its response time.

Scheduling can occur when a thread enters the ready or wait state, when a thread terminates, or when an application changes a thread's priority or processor affinity. If a higher-priority real-time thread becomes ready while a lower-priority thread is running, the lower-priority thread will be preempted. This preemption gives a real-time thread preferential access to the CPU when the thread needs such access. Windows 2000 is not a hard real-time operating system, however, because it does not guarantee that a real-time thread will start to execute within any particular time limit.

Exceptions and Interrupts Handling

The kernel also provides trap handling for exceptions and interrupts that are generated by hardware or software. Windows 2000 defines several architecture independent exceptions, including memory-access violation, integer overflow, floating-point overflow or underflow, integer divide by zero, floating-point divide by zero, illegal instruction, data misalignment, privileged instruction, page read error guard-page violaton paging file quota exceeded, debugger breakpoint, and debugger single step.

The trap handler can handle simple exceptions; others are handled by the kernel's exception dispatcher. The **exception dispatcher** creates an exception record that contains the reason for the exception and finds an exception handler that can deal with it.

When an exception occurs in kernel mode, the exception dispatcher simply calls a routine to locate the exception handler. If no handler is found, a fatal system error occurs and the user is left with the infamous" blue screen of death" that signifies system failure.

Exception handling is more complex for user-mode processes, because an environmental subsystem (such as the POSIX system) can set up a debugger port and an exception port for every process that it creates. If a debugger port is registered, the exception handler sends the exception to that port. If the debugger port is not found or does not handle that exception, the dispatcher then attempts to find an appropriate exception handler. If a handler is not found, the debugger is called again so that it can catch the error for debugging. If a debugger is not running, a message is then sent to the process' exception port to give the environmental subsystem a chance to translate the exception. For example, the POSIX environment translates Windows 2000 exception messages into POSIX signals before sending them to the thread that caused the exception. Finally, if nothing else works, the kernel simply terminates the process that contains the thread that caused the exception.

The interrupt dispatcher in the kernel handles interrupts by calling either an interrupt service routine (such as in a device driver) or an internal kernel routine. The interrupt is represented by an interrupt objects that contains all the information needed to handle the interrupt. Using an interrupt objects makes it easy to associate interrupt service routines with an interrupt without having to access the interrupt hardware directly.

Various processor architectures, such as Intel or DEC Alpha, have different types and numbers of interrupts. For portability, the interrupt dispatcher maps the hardware interrupts into a standard set. The interrupts are prioritized and are serviced in priority order. There are 32 interrupt levels (IRQLs) in Windows 2000. Eight are reserved for the use of the kernel; the other 24 represent hardware interrupts via the HAL (although most ×86 systems use only 16 lines).

The kernel uses an **interrupt dispatch table** to bind each interrupt level to a service routine. In a multiprocessor computer, Windows 2000 keeps a separate interrupt dispatch table for each processor, and each processor's IRQL can be set independently to mask out interrupts. All interrupts that occur at a level equal to or less than the IRQL of a processor get blocked until the IRQL is lowered by a kernel-level thread. Windows 2000 takes advantage of this property to use software interrupts to perform system function. For instance, the kernel uses software interrupts to start a thread dispatch, to handle timers, and to support asynchronous operations.

Interrupt levels	Types of interrupts
31	machine check or bus error
30	power fail
29	interprocessor notification (request another processor to act; eg., dispath a process or update the TLB)
28	clock (used to keep track of time)
27	profile
3–26	traditional PC IRQ hardware interrupts
2	dispatch and defered procedure call (DPC (kernel)
1	asynchronous procedure call (APC)
0	passive

Fig. CS1.2. *Windows 2000 interrupt request levels.*

The kernel uses the dispatch interrupt to control thread context switching. When the kernel is running, it raises the IRQL on the processor to a level above the dispatch level. When the kernel determines that a thread dispatch is required, the kernel generates a dispatch interrupt, but this interrupt is blocked until the kernel finishes what it is doing and lowers the IRQL. At that point, the dispatch interrupt can be serviced, so the dispatcher chooses a thread to run.

When the kernel decides that some system function should be executed eventually, but not immediately, it queues a **deferred procedure call (DPC)** object that contains the address of the function to be executed, and generates a DPC interrupt. When the IRQL of the processor drops low enough, the DPC objects are executed. The IRQL of the DPC interrupt is typically higher than that of user threads, so DPCs will interrupt the execution of user threads. To avoid problems, DPCs are restricted to be fairly simple. They cannot modify a thread's memory; create, acquire, or wait on objects call system services; or generate page faults.

Low-level Processor Synchronization

The third responsibility of the kernel is to provide low-level processor synchronization. The APC mechanism is similar to the DPC mechanism, but for more general sue. The APC mechanism enables threads to set up a procedure call that will happen out of the blue at some future time. For instance, many system services accept a use-mode routine as a parameter. Instead of calling a synchronous system call that will block the thread until the system call completes, a user thread can call an asynchronous system call and supply an APC. The user thread will continue running. When the system service finishes, the user thread will be interrupted to run the APC spontaneously.

An APC can be queued on either a system thread or a user thread, although also user mode APC will be executed only if the thread has decoded itself to be alertable. An APC is more powerful than a DPC, in that it can acquire and wait on objects, cause page faults, and call system services. Since an APC executes in the address space of the target thread, the Windows 2000 executive uses APCs extensively for I/O processing.

Windows 2000 can run on symmetric multiprocessor machines, so the kernel must prevent two of its threads from modifying a shared data structure at the same time. The kernel uses spinlocks that reside in global memory to achieve multiprocessor mutual exclusion. Because all activity on a processor stops when a thread is attempting to acquire a spinlock, a thread that holds a spinlock is not preempted, so it can finish and release the lock as quickly as possible.

Recovery Due to Power Failure

The fourth and final responsibility of the kernel is to provide recovery after a power failure. A power-fail interrupt, which has the second-highest priority, notifies the operating system whenever a power loss is detected. The power notify object provides a way for a device driver to register a routine that will be called on power restoration and ensures that devices get set to the proper state on recovery. For battery-backed-up systems the power-status object is useful. Before it begins, a critical operation, a driver examines the power-status object to determine whether or not the power has failed. If the driver determines that power has not failed, it raises the IRQL of its processor to powerfail, performs the operation, and resets the IRQL. This sequence of actions blocks the powerfail interrupt until after the critical operation completes.

Executive

The Windows 2000 executive provides a set of services that all environmental subsystems can use. The services are grouped as follows: object manager, virtual-memory manager, process manager, local-procedure-call facility, I/O manager, and security reference monitor.

Object Manager

As an object-oriented system, Windows 2000 uses objects for all its services and entities. Examples of objects are directory objects, symbolic link objects, semaphore objects, event objects, process and thread objects, port objects, and file objects. The job of the **object manager** is to supervise the use of all objects. When a thread wants to use an object, it calls the object manager's open method to get a handle to the object. **Handles** are a standardized interface to all kinds of objects. Like a file handle, an object handle is an identifier unique to a process that confers the ability to access and manipulate a system resource.

Since the object manager is the only entity that can generate an object handle, it is the natural place to check security. For instance, the object manager checks whether a process has the right to access an object when the process tries to open that object. The object manager can also enforce quotas, such as the maximum amount of memory that a process may allocate.

The object manager can keep track of which processes are using each object. Each object header contains a count of the number of processes that have handles to that object. When the counter goes to zero, the object is deleted from the name space if it is a temporary object name. Since Windows 2000 itself often uses pointers (instead of handles) to access objects, the object manager also maintains a reference count, which it increments when Windows 2000 gains access to an object and decrements when the object is no longer needed. When the reference count of a temporary object goes to zero, the object is deleted from memory. Permanents object represent physical entities, such as disk drives, and are not deleted when the reference count and the open-handle counter go to zero.

The objects are manipulated by a standard set of methods: create, open, close, delete, query name, parse, and security. The latter three objects need explanation:

- query name is called when a thread has a handle to an object, but wants to know the object's name.
- parse is used by the object manager to search for an object given the object's name.
- security is called when a process opens or changes the protection of an object.

The Windows 2000 executive allows any object to be given a **name**. The name space is global, so one process may create a named object, and a second process can then open a handle to the object and share it with the first process. A process opening a named object can ask for the search to be either case sensitive or case insensitive.

A name can be either permanent or temporary. A permanent name represents an entity, such as a disk drive, that remains even if no process is accessing it. A temporary name exists only while some process holds a handle to that object.

Although the name space is not directly visible across a network, the object manager's parse method is used to help access a named object on another system. When a process attempts to open an object that resides on a remote computer, the object manager calls the parse method, which then calls a network redirector to find the object.

Object names are structured like file path names in MS-DOS and UNIX. Directories are represented by a **directory object** that contains the names of all the objects in that directory. The object name space can grow by the addition of **object domains**, which are self-contained sets of objects. Examples of object domains are floppy disks and hard drives. It is easy to see how the name space gets extended when a floppy disk is added to the system. The floppy has its own name space that is grafted onto the existing name space.

UNIX file systems have **symbolic links**, so multiple nicknames or aliases can refer to the same file. Similarly, Windows 2000 implements a **symbolic link object**. One way that Windows 2000 uses symbolic links is to map drive names to the standard MS-DOS drive letters. The drive letters are just symbolic links that can be remapped to suit the user's preferences.

A process gets an object handle by creating an object, by opening an existing object, by receiving a duplicated handle from another process, or by inheriting a handle from a **parent process**, similar to the way a UNIX process gets a file descriptor. These handles are all stored in the process' **object table**. An entry in the object table contains the object's access rights and states whether the handle should be inherited by **child processes**. When a press terminates, Windows 2000 automatically closes all the process' open handles.

When a user is authenticated by the login process, an access-token object is attached to the user's process. The access token contains information such as the security id, group ids, privileges, primary group, and default access control list. These attributes determine which services and objects can be used by a given user.

In Windows 2000, each object is protected by an access-control list that contains the security ids and access rights granted to each process. When a process attempts to access an object, the system compares the security id in the process' access token with the object's access-control list to determine whether access should be permitted. This check is done only when an object is opened, so internal Windows 2000 services that use pointers, rather than opening a handle to an object, bypass the access check.

Generally, the creator of the object determines the access-control list for that object. If none is supplied explicitly, one may be inherited from the creator object, or a default list may be obtained from the user's access-token object.

One field in the access token controls auditing of the object. Operations that are being audited get logged to the system's audit log with an identification of the user. The audit field can watch this log to discover attempts to break into the system or to access protected objects.

Virtual-Memory Manager

The virtual-memory portion of the Windows 2000 executive is the **virtual-memory (VM) manager.** The design of the VM manager assumes that the underlying hardware supports virtual-to-physical mapping, a paging mechanism, and transparent cache coherence on multiprocessor systems, and allows multiple page-table entries to map to the same page frame. The VM manager in Windows 2000 uses a page-based management scheme with a page size of 4KB. Pages of data that are assigned to a process but are not in physical memory are stored in the **paging file** on disk.

The VM manager uses 32-bit addresses, so each process has a 4GB virtual address space. The upper 2 GB are identical for all processes, and are used by Windows 2000 in kernel mode. The lower 2 GB are distinct for every process, and are accessible by both user- and kernel-mode threads. Note that certain configurations of Windows 2000 reserve only 1 GB for operating system use, allowing a process to use 3 GB of address space.

The Windows 2000 VM manager uses a two-step process to allocate memory. The first step *reserves* a portion of the process' address space. The second step *commit* the allocation by assigning space in the Windows 2000 paging file. Windows 2000 can limit the amount of paging file space that a process consumes by enforcing a quota on committed memory. A process can uncommit memory that it is no longer using to free up its paging quota. Since memory is represented by objects, when one process (the parent) creates a second process (the child), the parent can maintain the ability to access the virtual memory of the child. That is how environmental subsystems can manage the memory of their client processes. For performance, the VM manager allows a privileged process to lock selected pages in physical memory, thus ensuring that the pages will not be swapped out to the paging file.

Two processes can share memory by getting handles to the same memory object, but this approach can be inefficient since the entire memory space of an object must be committed before either process can access that object. Windows 2000 provided an alternative, called a **section object**, to represent a block of shared memory. After getting a handle to a section object, a process can map only the needed portion of the memory. This portion is called a **view**. The view mechanism also enables a process to access an object that is too large to fit into the process' paging file quota. The system can use the view to walk through the address space of the object, open piece at a time.

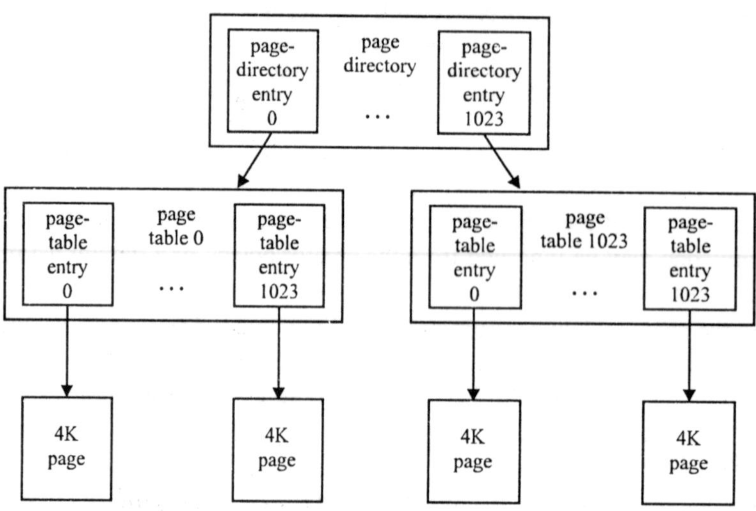

Fig. CS1.3. Virtual-memory layout.

A process can control the use of a shared-memory section object in many ways. The maximum size of a section can be bounded. The section can be backed by disk space either in the system paging file or by a regular file (a **memory-mapped file**). A section can be *based*, meaning that the section appears at the same virtual address for all processes that access it. Finally, the memory protection of pages in the section can be set to read only, read-write, execute only, guard page, or copy on write. The last two of these protection settings need some explanation:

- A guard page raises an exception if accessed; the exception can be used, for example, to check whether a faulty program iterates beyond the end of an array.
- The copy-on-write mechanism allows the VM manager to save memory. When two processes want independent copies of an object the VM manager places only one shared copy into physical memory, but it sets the copy-on-write property on that region of memory. If one of the processes tries to modify data in a copy-on-write page, the VM manager first makes a private copy of the page for that process to use.

The virtual-address translation in windows 2000 uses several data structures. Each process has a **page directory** that contains 1,024 **page-directory entries** of size 4 bytes. Typically, the page directory is private, but it can be shared among processes if the environment so requires. Each page-directory entry points to a **page table** that contains 1,024 **page-table entries (PTEs)** of size 4 bytes. Each PTE points to a 4KB **page frame** in physical memory. The total size of all the page tables for a process is 4 MB, so the VM manager will swap out these tables to disk when necessary.

A 10-bit integer can represent all the values from 0 to 1,023. Thus, a 10-bit integer can select any entry in the page directory, or in a page table.

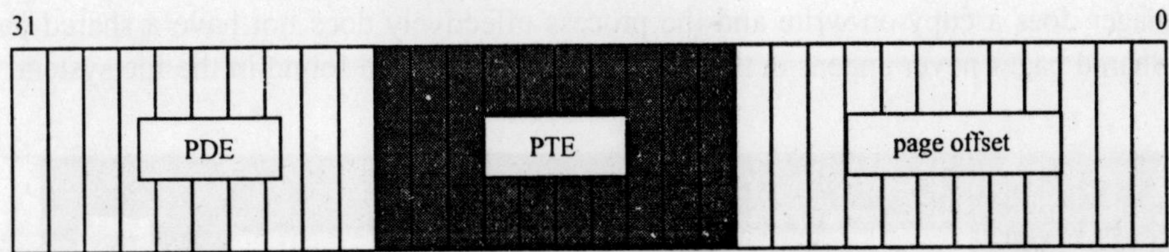

Fig. CS1.4. Virtual-to-physical address translation.

This property is used when a virtual-address pointer is translated to a byte address in physical memory. A 32-bit virtual-memory address is split into three integers. The first 10 bits of the virtual address are used as a subscript in the page directory. This address selects one page-directory entry, which points to a page table. The memory management unit (MMU) uses the next 10 bits of the virtual address to select a PTE from that page table. The PTE points to a page frame in physical memory. The remaining 12 bits of the virtual address point to a specific byte in that page frame. The MMU creates a pointer to that specific byte in physical memory by concatenating 20 bits from the PTE with the lower 12 bits from the virtual address. Thus, the 32-bit PTE has 12 bits left over; these bits describe the page. The Pentium PTE reserves 3 bits for the use of the operating system. The rest of the bits specify whether the page is dirty, accessed, cacheable, read only, write through, kernel mode, or valid; thus they describe the state of the page in memory. For more general information on paging schemes.

A page can be in one of six states: valid, free, zeroed, standby, modified, or bad. A *valid* page is in use by an active process. A *free* page is a page that is not referenced in a PTE. A *zeroed* page is a free page that has been zeroed out and is ready for immediate use. A *standby* page has been removed from the working set of a process. A *modified* page has been written to, but not yet flushed to, disk. Standby and modified pages are considered to be *transition* pages. Finally, a *bad* page is unusable because a hardware error has been detected.

The actual structure of the page-file PTE is shown in Figure CS 1.5. The PTE contains 5 bits for page protection, 20 bits for page-field offset, 4 bits to select the paging file, and 3 bits that describe the page state. This page-file PTE would appear as an invalid page to the hardware. Since executable code and memory-mapped files already have a copy on disk, they do not need space in a paging file. If one of these pages is not in physical memory, the PTE structure is as follows. The most significant bit is used to specify the page protection, the next 28 bits are used to index into a system data structure that indicates a file and offset within the file for the page, and the lower 3 bits specify the page state.

It is difficult to share a page between processes if every process has its own set of age tables, because each process will have its own PTE for the page frame. When a shared page is faulted into physical memory, the physical address will have to be stored in the PTEs that belong to each process that shares the page. The protection bits and page-state bits in these PTEs will all need to be set and updated consistently. To avoid these problems, Windows 2000 uses an indirection. For every page that is shared, the process has a PTE that points to a **prototype page-table entry**, rather than to the page frame. The prototype PTE contains the page-frame address and the protection and state bits. Thus, the first access by a process to a shared page generates a page fault. After the first access, further accesses are performed in the normal manner. If the page is marked read-only, the VM manager does a copy-on-write and the process effectively does not have a shared page any longer. Shared pages never appear in the page file, but are instead found in the file system.

Fig. CS1.5. Page file page-table entry.

The VM manager keeps track of all pages of physical memory in a **page frame database**. There is one entry for every page frame. The entry points to the PTE that points to the page frame, so the VM manager can maintain the state of the page. Page frames are linked to form, for instanced the list of zeroed pages and the list of free pages.

When a page fault occurs, the VM manager faults in the missing page, placing that page into the first frame on the free list. But it does not stop there. Research shows that the memory referencing of a thread tends to have a **locality** property: When a page is used, it is likely that adjacent pages will be referenced in the near future. (Think of iterating over an array, or fetching sequential instructions that form the executable code for a thread.) Because of locality, when the VM manager faults in a page, it also faults in a few adjacent pages. This adjacent faulting tends to reduce the total number of page faults. For more information on locality.

If no page frames are available on the free list, Windows 2000 uses a perprocess FIFO replacement policy to take pages from processes that are using more than their minimum working-set size. Windows 2000 monitors the page faulting of each process that is at its minimum working-set size, and adjusts the working-set size accordingly. In particular, when a process is started under Windows 2000, it is assigned a default working-set size of 30 pages. Windows 2000 periodically tests this size by stealing a valid page from the process. If the process continues executing without generating a page fault for the stolen page, the working set of the process is reduced by 1, and the page is added to the list, of free pages.

Process Manager

The Windows 2000 process manager provides services for creating, deleting, and using threads and processes. It has no knowledge about parent-child relationship or process hierarchies; those refinements are left to the particular environmental subsystem that owns the process.

Local-Procedure-Call Facility

The operating system uses the LPC facility to pass requests and results between client and server processes within a single machine. In particular, it uses LPC to request services from the various Windows 2000 subsystems. LPC is similar in many respects to the RPC mechanisms that are used by many operating systems for distributed processing across networks, but LPC is optimized for use within one Windows 2000 system.

LPC is a message-passing mechanism. The server process publishes a globally visible connection-port object. When a client wants services from a subsystem, it opens a handle to the subsystem's connection-port object, and then sends a connection request to that port. The server creates a channel and returns a handle to the client. The channel consists of a pair of private communication ports: one for client-to-server messages, and the other for server-to-client messages. Communication channels support a callback mechanism, so the client and server can accept requests when they would normally be expecting a reply.

When an LPC channel is created, one of three message-passing techniques must be specified.

1. The first technique is suitable for small messages (up to 256 bytes). In this case, the port's message queue is used as intermediate storage, and the messages are copied from one process to the other.
2. The second technique is for larger messages. In this case, a shared-memory section object is created for the channel. Messages sent through the port's message queue contain a pointer and size information that refer to the section object. Thus, the need to copy large messages is avoided: The sender places data into the shared section, and the receiver can view them directly.
3. The third technique of LPC message passing, called **quick LPC**, is used by graphical display portions of the Win32 subsystem. When a client asks for a connection that will use quick LPC, the server sets up three objects: a dedicated server thread to handle request, a 64 KB section object, and an event-pair object. An *event-pair object* is a synchronization object that is used by the Win32 subsystem to provide notification when the client thread has copied a message to the Win32 server, or vice versa. LPC messages are passed in the section object, and synchronization is performed by the event-pair object. The LPC has several advantages. The section object eliminates message copying, since it represents a region of shared memory. The event-pair object eliminates the overhead of using the port object to pass messages containing pointers and lengths. The dedicated server thread eliminates the overhead of

determining which client thread is calling the server, since there is one server thread per client thread. Finally, the kernel gives scheduling preference to these dedicated server threads to improve performance. The drawback is that quick LPC uses more resources than do the other two methods. So the Win32 subsystem uses quick LPC only for the window-manager and graphics-device interfaces.

I/O Manager

The I/O manager is responsible for file systems, cache management, device drivers, and network drivers. It keeps track of which installable file systems are loaded, are manages buffers for I/O requests. It works with the VM manager to provide memory-mapped file I/O, and controls. The Windows 2000 cache manager, which handles caching for the entire I/O system. The I/O manager supports both synchronous and asynchronous operations, provides timeouts for drivers, and has mechanisms for one driver to call another.

The I/O manager converts the requests it receives into a standard form called an I/O **request packet (IRP).** It then forwards the IRP to the correct driver for processing. When the operation is finished, the I/O manager receives the IRP from the driver that most recently performed an operation, and completes the request.

In many operating systems, caching is done by the file system,. Windows 2000 provides a centralized caching facility, instead. The cache manager provides cache services for all components under the control of the I/O manager, and works closely with the VM manager. The size of the cache changes dynamically, according to how much free memory is available in the system. Recall that the upper 2 GB of a process' address space comprise the system area; it is identical for all processes. The VM manager allocates up to one-half of this space system cache. The cache manager maps files into this address space, and uses the capabilities of the VM manager to handle file I/O.

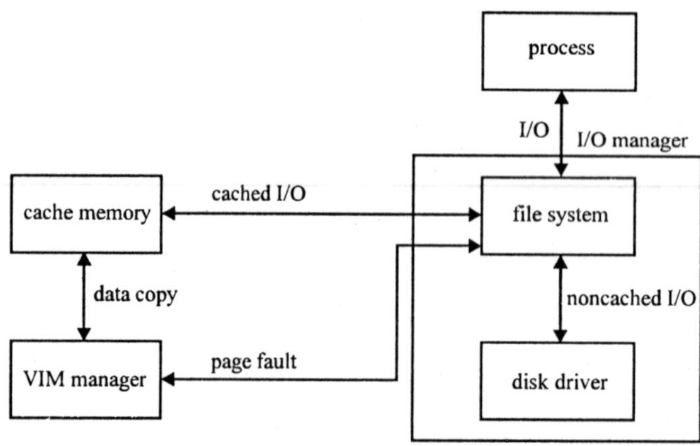

Fig. CS1.6. File I/O.

The cache is divided into blocks of 256 KB. Each cache block can hold a view (that is, a memory-mapped region) of a file. Each cache block is described by a **virtual-address control block (VACB)** that stores the virtual address and file offset for that view, as well as the number of processes that are using the view. The VACBs reside in a single array that is maintained by the cache manager.

For each open file, the cache manager maintains a separate VACB index array. This array has an element for each 256 KB chunk of the file; so, for instance, a 2 MB file would have an 8-entry VACB index array. An entry in the VACB index array points to the VACB if that portion of the file is in the cache; it is null otherwise.

When the I/O manager receives a user-level read request, the I/O manager sends an IRP to the cache manager (unless the request specifically asks for a noncached read). The cache manager calculates which entry of that file's VACB index array corresponds to the byte offset of the request. The entry either points to the view in the cache, or is null. If it is null, the cache manager allocates a cache block (and the corresponding entry in the VACB array), and maps the view into that cache block. The cache manager then attempts to copy data from the mapped file to the caller's buffer. If the copy succeeds, the operation is completed. If the copy fails, it does so because of a page fault, which causes the VM manager to send a noncached read request to the I/O manager. The I/O manager asks the appropriate device driver to read the data, and returns the data to the VM manager, which loads the data into the cache. The data, now in the cache, are copied to the caller's buffer, and the I/O request is completed. When possible, for synchronous, cached, nonlocking I/O, I/O is handled by the **fast I/O mechanism**. This mechanism simply copies data to/from cache pages directly and utilizes the cache manager to perform any needed I/O.

A kernel-level read operation is similar, except that the data can be accessed directly from the cache, rather than being copied to a buffer in user space. To use file-system metadata, or data structures that describe the file system, the kernel uses the cache manager's mapping interface to read the metadata. To modify the metadata, the file system uses the cache manager's pinning interface. **Pinning** a page locks the page into a physical-memory page frame, so the VM manager cannot move or swap out the page. After updating the metadata, the file system asks the cache manager to unpin the page. Since the page has been modified, it is marked dirty, so the VM manager will flush the page to disk. Note that the metadata is actually stored in a regular file.

To improve performance, the cache manager keeps a small history of read requests, and attempts to predict future requests. If the cache manager can find a pattern in the previous three requests, such as sequential access forward or backward, it can prefetch data into the cache before the next request is submitted by the application. Then, the application may find its data already in the cache, and may not need to wait for disk I/O. The Win32 API OpenFile and CreateFile functions can be passed the FILE_FLAG_SEQUENTIAL_SCAN flag, which is a hint to the cache manager to try to prefetch 192 KB ahead of the thread's requests. Typically, Windows 2000 performs I/O operations in chunks of 64 KB or 16 pages; thus, this read-ahead is three times the normal amount.

The cache manager is also responsible for telling the VM manager to flush the contents of the cache. The cache manager's default behaviour is write-back caching: it accumulates writes for 4 to 5 seconds, and then the cache-writer thread wakes up. When write-through caching is needed, a process can set a flag when opening the file, or the process can call an explicit cache-flush function when needed.

A fast-writing process could potentially fill all the free cache pages before the cache-writer thread has a chance to wake up and flush the pages to disk. The cache writer prevented a process from flooding the system in the following way: When the amount of free cache memory gets low, the cache manager temporarily blocks processes that attempt to write data, and wakes the cache-writer thread to flush pages to disk. If the fast-writing process is actually a network redirector for a network file system, blocking it for too long could cause network transfers to time out and be retransmitted. This retransmission would waste network bandwidth. To prevent this waste, network redirectors can tell the cache manager not to let a large backlog or writes accumulate in the cache.

Because a network file system needs to move data between a disk and the network interface, the cache manager also provides a DMA interface to move the data directly. Moving data directly avoids copying data through an intermediate buffer.

Security Reference Monitor

The object-oriented nature of Windows 2000 enables the use of a uniform mechanism to perform run-time access validation and audit checks for every entity in the system. Whenever a process open a handle to an object, the security reference monitor checks the process' security token and the object's access-control list to see whether the process has the necessary rights.

Plug-and-Play Manager

The operating system uses the **plug-and-play (PnP) manager** to recognize and adapt to changes in the hardware configuration. For PnP to work, both the device and the driver must support the PnP standard. The PnP manager automatically recognizes installed devices and detects changes in devices as the system operates. The manager also keeps tracks of resources used by a device, as well as potential resources that could be used, and takes care of loading the appropriate drivers. This management of hardware resources—primarily interrupts and I/O memory ranges—has the goal of determining a hardware configuration in which all devices are able to operate. For example, if device B can use only interrupt 5 but device A could use 5 or 7, then the PnP manager could assign 5 to B and 7 to A. In previous versions, the user might have had to remove device A and reconfigure it to use interrupt 7, before installing device B. The user thus had to study system resources before installing new hardware, and to find out or remember which devices were using which hardware recources. The proliferation of PCCARD and USB devices also dictates that dynamic configuration of resources be supported.

The PnP manager handles this dynamic reconfiguration as follows. First, it gets a list of devices from each bus driver (for example, PCI, USB). It then loads the installed driver (or installs one, if necessary) and sends an add-device command to the appropriate driver for each device. The PnP manager figures out the optimal resource assignments and then sends a start-device command to each driver along with the resource assignment for that device. If a device needs to be reconfigured, the PnP manager sends a query-stop command, which asks the driver whether the device can be temporarily disabled. If the driver can disable the device, then all pending operations are completed and new operations are not allowed to be started. Next, the PnP manager sends a stop command; it can then reconfigure the device with another start-device command. The PnP manager also supports other commands, such as query-remove. This command is used when the user is getting ready to eject a PCCARD device, and operates in a fashion similar to query-stop. The surprise-remove command is used when a device fails or, more likely, when a user removes a PCCARD device without using the PCCARD utility to stop it first. The remove command requests that the driver stop using the device and release all resources that have been allocated to the device.

Environmental Subsystems

Environmental subsystems are user-mode processes layered over the native Windows 2000 executive services to enable Windows 2000 to run programs developed for other operating systems, including 16-bit Windows, MS-DOS, POSIX, and character-based applications for 16-bit OS/2. Each environmental subsystem provides one API or application environment.

Windows 2000 uses the Win32 subsystem as the main operating environment, and thus to start all processes. When an application is executed, the Win32 subsystem calls the VM manager to load the application's executable code. The memory manager returns a status to Win32 that tells what kind of executable the code is. If it is not a native Win32 executable, the Win32 environment checks whether the appropriate environmental subsystem is running; if the subsystem is not running, it is started as a user-mode process. Then Win32 creates a process to run the application, and passes control to the environmental subsystem.

The environmental subsystem uses the Windows 2000 LPC facility to get kernel services for the process. This approach helps windows 2000 to be robust, because the parameters passed to a system call can be checked for correctness before the actual kernel routine is invoked. Windows 2000 prohibits applications from mixing API routines from different environments. For instance, a Win32 application cannot call a POSIX routine.

Since each subsystem is run as a separate user-mode process, a crash in one has no effect on the others. The exception is Win32, which provides all the keyboard, mouse, and graphical display capabilities. If it fails, the system is effectively disabled.

The Win32 environment categorizes applications as either graphical or character based where a *character-based application* is one that thinks that interactive output gets to an 80 by 24 ASCII display. Win32 transforms the output of a character-based application to a graphical representation in a window. This transformation is easy: Whenever an output routine is called, the environmental subsystem calls a Win32 routine to display the text. Since the Win32 environment performs this function for all character-based windows, it can transfer screen text between windows via the clipboard. This transformation works for MS-DOS applications, as well as for POSIX command-line applications.

MS-DOS Environment

The MS-DOS environment does not have the complexity of the other Windows 2000 environmental subsystems. It is provided by a Win32 application called the **virtual DOS machine** (VDM). Sine the VDM is just a user-mode process, it is paged and dispatched like any other Windows 2000 thread. The VDM has an instruction-execution unit to execute or emulate Intel 486 instructions. The VDM also provides routines to emulate the MS-DOS ROM BIOS and "int 21" software-interrupt services, and has virtual device drivers for the screen, keyboard, an communication ports. The VDM is based on the MS-DOS 5.0 source code; it gives the application at least 620 KB of memory.

The Windows 2000 command shell is a program that creates a window that looks like an MS-DOS environment. It can run both 16-bit and 32-bit executables. When an MS-DOS application is run, the command shell starts a VDM process to execute the program.

If Windows 2000 is running on an ×86 processor, MS-DOS graphical applications run in full-screen mode, and character applications can run full screen or in a window. If Windows 2000 is running on a different processor architecture, all MS-DOS applications run is windows. Some MS-DOS applications access the disk hardware directly, but they fail to run on Windows 2000 because disk access is privileged to protect the file system. In general, MS-DOS applications that directly access hardware will fail to operate under Windows 2000.

Since MS-DOS is not a multitasking environment, some applications have been written that hog the CPU—for instance, by using busy loops to cause time delays or pauses in execution.

16-Bit Windows Environment

The Win16 execution environment is provided by a VDM that incorporates additional software called *Windows* or *Windows* that provides the Windows 3.1 kernel routines and stub routines for window manager and GDI functions. The stub routines call the appropriate Win32 subroutines, converting, or *thunking*, 16-bit addresses into 32-bit ones. Applications that rely on the internal structure of the 16-bit window manager or GDI may not work, because Windows on Windows does not really implement the 16-bit API.

Windows on Windows can multitask with other processes on Windows 2000, but it resembles Windows 3.1 in many ways. Only one Win16 application can run at a time, all applications are single threaded and reside in the same address space, and they all share the same input queue. These features imply that an application that stop receiving input will block all the other Win16 applications, just as in Windows 3.×, and one Win16 application can crash other Win16 applications by corrupting the address space. Multiple Win16 environments can coexist, however, by using the command *start /separate win16application* from the command line.

Win32 Environment

The main subsystem in Windows 2000 is the Win32 subsystem. It runs Win32 applications, and manages all keyboard, mouse, and screen I/O. Since it is the controlling environment, it is designed to be extremely robust. Several features of Win32 contribute to this robustness. Unlike the Win16 environment, each Win32 process has its own input queue. The window manager dispatches all input on the system to the appropriate process input queue, so a failed process will not block input to other processes. The windows 2000 kernel also provides preemptive multitasking, which enables the user to terminate applications that have failed or are no longer needed. Win32 also validates all objects before using them, to prevent crashes that could otherwise occur if an application tried to use an invalid or wrong-handle. The Win32 subsystem verifies the type of the object to which a handle points before using that object. The reference counts kept by the object manager prevent objects from being deleted while they are still being used, and prevent their use after they have been deleted.

POSIX Subsystem

The POSIX subsystem is designed to run POSIX applications following the POSIX.1 standard, which is based on the UNIX model. POSIX applications can be started by the Win32 subsystem or by another POSIX application. POSIX application use the POSIX subsystem server PSXSS.EXE, the POSIX dynamic link library PSXDLL.DLL, and the POSIX console session manager POSIX. EXE.

Although the POSIX standard does not specify printing, POSIX applications can use printers transparently via the Windows 2000 redirection mechanism. POSIX applications have access to any file system on the Windows 2000 system; the POSIX environment enforces UNIX-like permissions on directory trees. Several Win32 facilities are not supported by the POSIX subsystem, including memory-mapped files, networking, graphics, and dynamic data exchange.

OS/2 Subsystem

Although Windows 2000 was originally intended to provide a robust OS/2 operating environment, the success of Microsoft Windows led to a change; during the early development of Windows 2000, the Windows environment became the default. Consequently, windows 2000 provides only limited facilities in the OS/2 environmental subsystem. OS/2 1.× character-based applications can run only on Windows 2000 on Intel ×86 computers. Real-mode OS/2 applications can run on all platforms by using the MS-DOS environment. Bound applications, which have dual code for both MS-DOS and OS/2, run in the OS/2 environment unless the OS/2 environment is disabled.

Logon and Security Subsystems

Before a user can access objects on Windows 2000, that user must be authenticated by the logon subsystem. To be authenticated, a user must have an account and provide the password for that account.

The security subsystem generates access tokens to represent users on the system. It calls an **authentication package** to perform authentication using information from the logon subsystem or network server. Typically, the authentication package simply looks up the account information in a local database and checks to see that the password is correct. The security subsystem then generates the access token for the user id containing the appropriate privileges, quota limits, and group ids. Whenever the user attempts to access an object in the system, such as by opening a handle to the object, the access token is passed to the security reference monitor, which checks privileges and quotas. The default authentication package for Windows 2000 domains is Kerberos.

File System (FAT, NTFS)

Historically, MS-DOS systems have used the file-allocation table (FAT) file system. The 16-bit FAT file system has several shortcomings, including internal fragmentation, a size limitation of 2 GB, and a lack of access protection for files. The 32-bit FAT file system has solved the size and fragmentation problems, but its performance and features are still weak by comparison with modern file systems the NTFS file system is much better. It was designed to include many features, including data recovery, security, fault tolerance, large files and file systems, multiple data streams, UNICODE names, and file compression. For compatibility, Windows 2000 provides support for the FAT and OS/2 HPFS file systems.

Internal Layout

The fundamental entity in NTFS is a volume. A volume is created by the Windows 2000 disk administrator utility, and is based on a logical disk partition.

The volume may occupy a portion of a disk, may occupy an entire disk, or may span across several disks.

NTFS does not deal with individual sectors of a disk, but instead uses clusters as the unit of disk allocation. A cluster is a number of disk sectors that is a power of 2. The cluster size is configured when an NTFS file system is formatted.The default cluster size is the sector size for volumes up to 512 MB, 1 KB for volumes up to 1 GB, 2 KB for volumes up to 2 GB, and 4 KB for larger volumes. This cluster size is much smaller than that for the 16-bit FAT file system, and the small size reduces the amount of internal fragmentation. As an example, consider a 1.6GB disk with 16,000 files. If you use a FAT-16 file system, 400 MB may be lost to internal fragmentation because the cluster size is 32 KB. Under NTFS, only 17 MB would be lost when storing the same files.

NTFS uses **logical cluster numbers (LCNs)** as disk addresses. It assigns then by numbering clusters from the beginning of the disk to the end. Using this scheme, the system can calculate a physical disk offset (in bytes) by multiplying the LCN by the cluster size.

A file in NTFS is not a simple byte stream, as it is in MS-DOS or UNIX; rather, it is a structured object consisting of **attributes**. Each attribute of a file is an independent byte stream that can be created, deleted, read, and written. Some attributes are standard for all files, including the file name (or names, if the file has aliases), the creation time, and the security descriptor that specifies access control. Other attributes are specific to certain kinds of files. For instance, Macintosh files have two data attributes, the resource fork and the data fork. A directory has attributes that implement an index for the file names in the directory. In general, attributes may be added as necessary and are accessed using a *file-name:attribute* nomenclature. Most traditional data files have an *unnamed* data attribute that contains all that file's data. Note that NTFS only returns the size of the unnamed attribute in response to file-query operations, such as when running the dir command. Clearly, some attributes are small, and others are large.

Every file in NTFS is described by one or more records in an array stored in a special file called the master file table (MFT). The size of a record is determined when the file system is created; it ranges from 1 to 4 KB. Small attributes are stored in the MFT record itself, and are called **resident attributes**. Large attributes, such as the unnamed bulk data, called **nonresident attributes**, are stored on one or more contiguous **extents** on the disk, and a printer to each extent is stored in the MFT record. For a tiny file, even the data attribute may fit inside the MFT record. If a file has many attributes, or if it is highly fragmented and therefore many pointers are needed to point to all the fragments, one record in the MFT might not be large enough. In this case, the file is described by a record called the **base file record**, which contains pointers to overflow records that hold the additional pointers and attributes.

Each file in an NTFS volume has a unique ID called a **file reference**. The **file reference** is a 64-bit quantity that consists of a 48-bit file number and a 16-bit sequence number. The file number is the record number (that is, the array slot) in the MFT that describes the file. The sequence number is incremented every time that an MFT entry is reused. This incrementation enables NTFS to perform internal consistency checks, such as catching a state reference to a deleted file after the MFT entry has been reused for a new file.

As in MS-DOS and UNIX, the NTFS name space is organized as a hierarchy of directories. Each directory uses a data structure called a **B+ tree** to store an index of the file names in that directory. A B+ tree is used because it eliminates the cost of reorganizing the tree and has the property that the length of every path from the root of the tree to a leaf is the same. The **index root** of a directory contains the top level of the B+ tree. For a large directory, this top level contains pointers to disk extends that hold the remainder of the tree. Each entry in the directory contains the name and file reference of the file, as well as a copy of the update timestamp and file size taken from the file's resident attributes in the MFT. Copies of this information are stored in the directory, so it is efficient to generate a directory listing—all the file names, sizes, and update times are available from the directory itself, so there is no need to gather these attributes from the MFT entries for each of the files.

The NTFS volume's metadata are all stored in files. The first file is the MFT. The second file, which is used during recovery if the MFT is damaged, contains a copy of the first 16 entries of the MFT. The next few files are also special. They are called the log file, volume file, attribute-definition table, root directory, bitmap file, boot file, and bad-cluster file. The *log file* records all metadata updates to the file system. The **volume file** contains the name of the volume, the version of NTFS that formatted the volume, and a bit that tells whether the volume may have been corrupted and needs to be checked for consistency. The **attribute-definition table** indicates which attribute types are used in the volume, and what operations can be performed on each of them. The **root directory** is the top-level directory in the file-system hierarchy. The **bitmap file** indicates which clusters on a volume are allocated to files, and which are free. The **boot file** contains the startup code for Windows 2000 and must be located at a particular disk address so that it can be found easily by a simple ROM bootstrap loader. The boot file also contains the physical address of the MFT. Finally, the **bad-cluster file** keeps track of any bad areas on the volume; NTFS uses this record for error recovery.

Recovery

In many simple file systems, a power failure at the wrong time can damage the file-system data structures so severely that the entire volume is scrambled. Many versions of UNIX store redundant metadata on the disk, and they recover from crashes using the fsck program to check all the file-system data structures, and to restore them forcibly to a consistent state. Restoring them often involves deleting damaged files and freeing data clusters that had been written with user data but have not been properly recorded in the file system's metadata structures. This checking can be a slow process, and can lose significant numbers of data.

NTFS takes a different approach to file-system robustness. In NTFS, all file-system data-structure updates are performed inside transactions. Before a data structure is altered, the transaction writes a log record that contains redo and undo information; after the data structure has been changed, the transaction writes a commit record to the log to signify that the transaction succeeded. After a crash, the system can restore the file-system data structures to a consistent state by processing the log records, first redoing the operations for committed transactions, then undoing the operations for transactions that did not commit successfully before the crash. Periodically (usually every 5 seconds), a checkpoint record is written to the log. The system does not need log records prior to the checkpoint to recover from a crash. They can be discarded, so the log file does not grow without bound. The first time after system startup that an NTFS volume is accessed, NTFS automatically performs file-system recovery.

The log is stored in the third metadata file at the beginning of the volume. It is created with a fixed maximum size when the file system is formatted. It has two sections: the **logging area**, which is a circular queue of log records, and the **restart area**, which holds context information, such as the position in the logging area where NTFS should start reading during a recovery. In fact, the restart area holds two copies of its information, so recovery is still possible if one copy is damaged during the crash.

The logging functionality is provided by the Windows 2000 **log-file service**. In addition to writing the log records and performing recovery actions, the log-file service keeps track of the free space in the log file. If the free space gets too low, the log-file service queues pending transactions, and NTFS halts all new I/O operations. After the in-progress operations complete, NTFS calls the cache manager to flush all data, then resets the log file and performs the queued transactions.

Security

The security on an NTFS volume is derived from the Windows 2000 object model. Each file object has a security-descriptor attribute stored in its MFT record. This attribute contains the access token of the owner of the file, and an access-control list that states the access privileges granted to each user having access to the file.

Volume Management and Fault Tolerance

FtDisk is the fault-tolerant disk driver for Windows 2000. When installed, provides several ways to combine multiple disk drives into one logical volume so as to improve performance, capacity, or reliability.

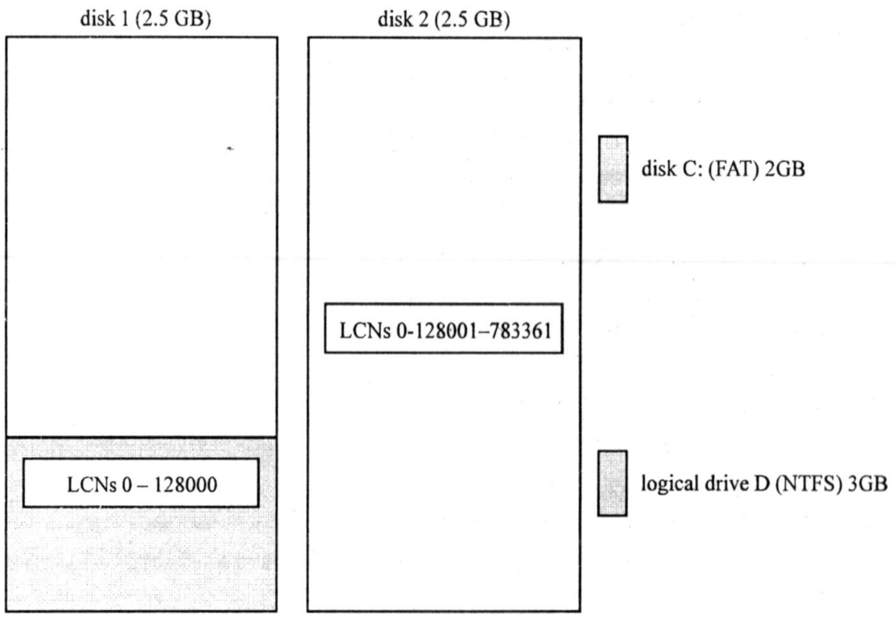

Fig. CS1.7. Volume set on two drives.

One way to combine multiple disks is to concatenate them logically to form a large logical volume. In Windows 2000, this logical volume is called a **volume set**, which can consist of up to 32 physical partitions. A volume set that contains an NTFS volume can be extended without the data already stored in the file system being disturbed. The bitmap metadata on the NTFS volume are simply extended to cover the newly added space. NTFS continues to sue the same LCN mechanism that it uses for a single physical disk, and the FtDisk driver supplies the mapping from a logical volume offset to the offset on one particular disk.

Another way to combine multiple physical partitions is to interleave their blocks in round-robin fashion to form what is called a **stripe set,** This scheme is also called RAID level 0, or **disk striping** FtDisk uses a stripe size of 64 KB: The first 64 KB of the logical volume are stored in the first physical partition, the second 64 KB of the logical volume are stored in the second physical partition, and so on, until each partition has contributed 64 KB of space. Then, the allocation wraps around to the first disk, allocating the second 64 KB block. A stripe set forms one large logical volume, but the physical layout can improve the I/O bandwidth, because, for a larger I/O, all the disks can transfer data in parallel. For more information on RAID.

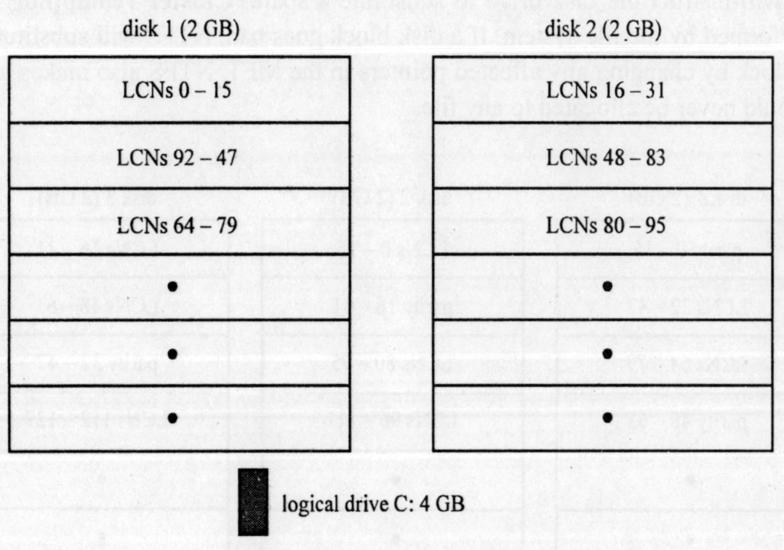

Fig. CS1.8. Stripe set on two drives.

A variation of this idea is the stripe set with parity. This scheme is also called RAID level 5. If the stripe set has eight disks, then, for each of the seven data stripes, on seven separate disks, there will be a parity stripe on the eighth disk. The parity stripe contains the byte-wise exclusive or of the data stripes. If any one of the eight stripes is destroyed, the system can reconstruct the data by calculating the exclusive or of the remaining seven. This ability to reconstruct data makes the disk array much less likely to lose data in case of a disk failure. Notice that an update to one data stripe also requires recalculation of the parity stripe. Seven concurrent writes to seven different data stripes thus would also require seven parity stripes to be updated. If the parity stripes were all on the same disk, that disk could have seven times the I/O load of the data disks. To avoid creating this bottleneck, we spread the parity stripes over all the disks, such as by assigning them round-robin. To build a stripe set with parity, we need a minimum of three equal-sized partitions located on three separate disks.

An even more robust scheme is called **disk mirroring** or RAID level 1. A **mirror set** comprises two equal-sized partitions on two disks, such that their data contents are identical. When an application writes data to a mirror set FtDisk writes the data to both partitions. If one partition fails, FtDisk has another copy safely stored on the mirror. Mirror sets can also improve the performance, because read requests can be split between the two mirrors, giving each mirror half of the workload. To protect against the failure of a disk controller, we can attach the two disks of a mirror set to two separate disk controllers. The arrangement is called a **duplex set**.

To deal with disk sectors that go bad, FtDisk uses a hardware technique called sector sparing, and NTFS uses a software technique called cluster remapping. Sector sparing is a hardware capability provided by many disk drives. When a disk drive is formatted, it creates a map from logical block numbers to good sectors on the disk. It also leaves extra sectors unmapped, as spares. If a sector fails, FtDisk will instruct the disk drive to substitute a spare. **Cluster remapping** is a software technique performed by the file system. If a disk block goes bad, NTFS will substitute a different, unallocated block by changing any affected pointers in the MFT. NTFS also makes a note that the bad block should never be allocated to any file.

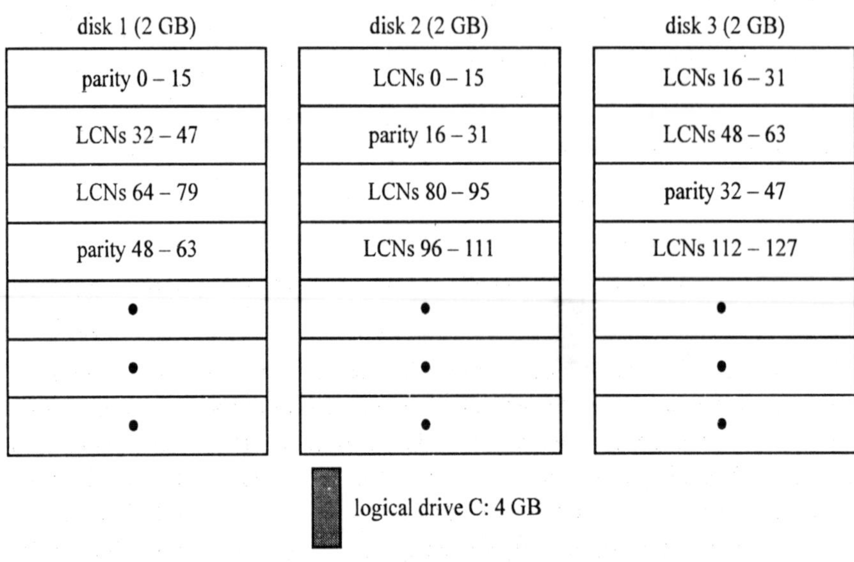

Fig. CS 1.9. Stripe set with parity on three drives.

When a disk block goes bad, the usual outcome is a data loss. But sector sparing or cluster remapping can be combined with fault-tolerant volumes such as stripe sets to mask the failure of a disk block. If a read fails, the system reconstructs the missing data by reading the mirror or by calculating the exclusive or parity in a stripe set with parity. The reconstructed data are stored into a new location that is obtained by sector sparing or cluster remapping.

Compression

NTFS can perform data compression on individual files or on all data files in a directory. To compress a file, NTFS divides the file's data into **compression units**, which are blocks of 16 contiguous clusters. When each compression unit is written, a data-compression algorithm is applied. If the result fits into fewer than 16 clusters, the compressed version is stored. When reading, NTFS can determine whether data have been compressed: If they have been, the length of the stored compression unit is less than 16 clusters. To improve performance when reading contiguous compression units, NTFS perfetches and decompresses ahead of the application requests.

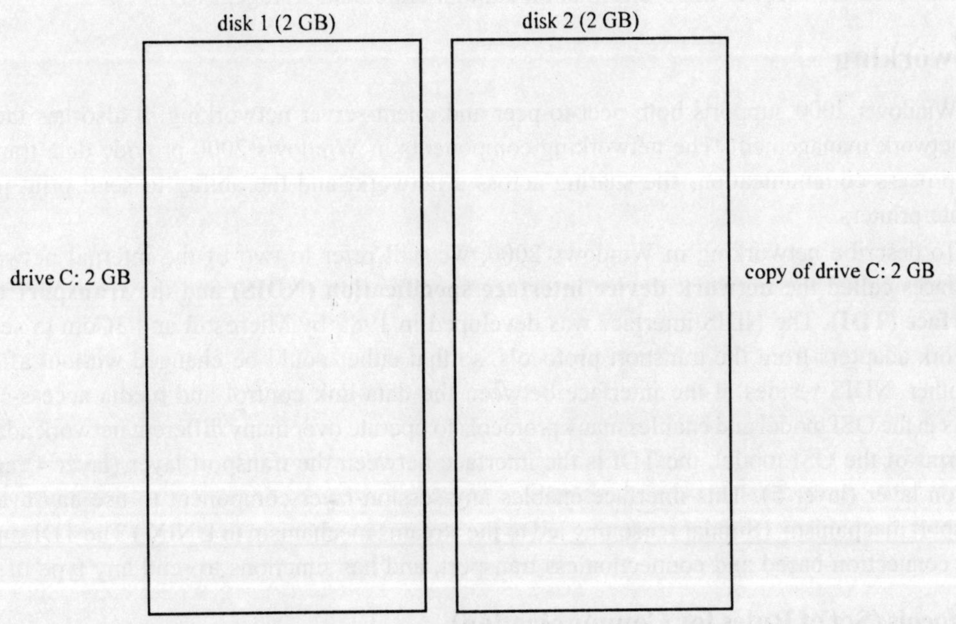

Fig. CS 1.10. *Mirror set on two drives.*

For sparse files or files that mostly contain zeros, NTFS uses another technique to save space. Clusters that contain all zeros are not actually allocated or stored on disk. Instead, gaps are left in the sequence of virtual-cluster numbers stored in the MFT entry for the file. When reading a file, if it finds a gap in the virtual-cluster numbers, NTFS just zero-fills that portion of the caller's buffer. This technique is also used by UNIX.

Reparse Points

Reparse points are a new feature in the file system that in effect return an error code when accessed. The Reparse data then tell the I/O manager what to do.

Mount points are another feature added to Windows 2000; they are a form or reparse points. Unlike UNIX systems, previous Windows versions provided no way to do a logical join of partitions. Each partition was assigned a drive letter that was distinct from every other partition. This meant that, among other things, that if a file system filled, the directory structure would need to be changed to add more space. Mount points would allow you to create a new volume on another drive, move the old data to the new volume, and then mount the new volume in the original place. The data would then still be usable by installed programs since the data would appear to be in the same place as before. The mount point is implemented as a reparse point with reparse data that contains the true volume name.

The remote storage services facility also uses reparse points. When a file is moved to offline storage, the original file data are replaced with a reparse point that contains information about where that file is. When the file is accessed later, the file is retrieved and the reparse point is replaced with the data from the file. For more information about hierarchical storage.

Networking

Windows 2000 supports both peer-to-peer and client-server networking. It also has facilities for network management. The networking components in Windows 2000 provide data transport, interprocess communication, file sharing across a network, and the ability to send print jobs to remote printers.

To describe networking in Windows 2000, we will refer to two of the internal networking interfaces called the **network device interface specification (NDIS)** and the **transport driver interface (TDI).** The NDIS interface was developed in 1989 by Microsoft and 3Com to separate network adapters from the transport protocols, so that either could be changed without affecting the other. NDIS resides at the interface between the data-link control and media-access-control layers in the OSI model and enables many protocols to operate over many different network adapters. In terms of the OSI model, the TDI is the interface between the transport layer (layer 4) and the session layer (layer 5). This interface enables any session-layer component to use any available transport mechanism. (Similar reasoning led to the streams mechanism in UNIX.) The TDI supports both connection-based and connectionless transport, and has functions to send any type of data.

Protocols (Set of Rules for Communication)

Windows 2000 implements transport protocols as drivers. These drivers can be loaded and unloaded from the system dynamically, although in practice the system typically has to be rebooted after a change. Windows 2000 comes with several networking protocols.

The **server message-block (SMB)** protocol was first introduced in MS-DOS 3.1. The system uses the protocol to send I/O requests over the network. The SMB protocol has four message types. The Session control messages are commands that start and end a redirector connection to a shared resource at the server. A redirector uses file messages to access files at the server. The system uses Printer messages to send data to a remote print queue and to receive back status information, and the Message message is used to communicate with another workstation.

The **network basic input/output system (NetBIOS)** is a hardware-abstraction interface for networks, analogous to the BIOS hardware-abstraction interface devised for PCs running MS-DOS

NetBIOS, developed in the early 1980s, has become a standard network-programming interface. NetBIOS is used to establish logical names on the network, to establish logical connections or sessions between two logical names on the network, and to support reliable data transfer for a session via either NetBIOS or SMB requests.

The **NetBIOS extended user interface (NetBEUI)** was introduced by IBM in 1985 as a simple, efficient networking protocol for up to 254 machines. It is the default protocol for Windows 95 peer networking and for Windows for Workgroups. Windows 2000 uses NetBEUI when it wants to share resources with these networks. Among the limitations of NetBEUI are that it uses the actual name of a computer as the address, and that it does not support routing.

The TCP/IP protocol suite that is used on the Internet has become the de facto standard networking infrastructure; it is widely supported. Windows 2000 uses TCP/IP to connect to a wide variety of operating systems and hardware platforms. The Windows 2000 TCP/IP package includes the simple network-management protocol (SNMP) dynamic host-configuration protocol (DHCP), Windows Internet name service (WINS), and NetBIOS support.

The **point-to-point tunneling protocol (PPTP)** is a protocol provided by Windows 2000 to communicate between remote-access server modules running on Windows 2000 Server machines and other client systems that are connected over the Internet. The remote-access servers can encrypt data sent over the connection, and they support multiprotocol virtual private networks over the Internet.

The Novell NetWare protocols (IPX datagram service on the SPX transport layer) are widely used for PC LANs. The Windows 2000 NWLink protocol connects the NetBIOS to NetWare networks. In combination with a redirector (such as Microsoft's Client Service for Netware or Novell's NetWare Client for Windows 2000), this protocol enables a Windows 2000 client to connect to a NetWare server.

Windows 2000 uses the **data-link control (DLC) protocol** to access IBM mainframes and HP printers that are connected directly to the network. This protocol is not otherwise used by Windows 2000 systems.

The **AppleTalk protocol** was designed as a low-cost connection by Apple to allow Macintosh computers to share files. Windows 2000 systems can share files and printers with Macintosh computers via AppleTalk if a Windows 2000 server on the network is running the Windows 2000 Services for Macintosh package.

Distributed-Processing Mechanisms

Although Windows 2000 is not a distributed operating system, it does support distributed applications. Mechanisms that support distributed processing on Windows 2000 include NetBIOS, named pipes and mailslots, windows sockets RPCs, and network dynamic data exchange (NetDDE).

In Windows 2000, NetBIOS applications can communicate over the network using NetBEUI, NWLink, or TCP/IP.

Named pipes are a connection-oriented messaging mechanism. Named pipes were originally developed as a high-level interface to NetBIOS connections over the network. A process can also use named pipes to communicate with other processes on the same machine. Since named pipes are accessed through the file-system interface, the security mechanisms used for file objects also apply to named pipes.

The name of a named pipe has a format called the **uniform naming convention (UNC).** A UNC name looks like a typical remote file name. The format of a UNC name is \\server_name\share_name\x\y\z, where the server_name identifies a server on the network; a share_name identifies any resource that is made available to network users, such as directories, files, named pipes and printers; and the \x\y\z part is a normal file path name.

Mailslots are a connectionless messaging mechanism. They are unreliable, in that a message sent to a mailslots may be lost before the intended recipient receives it. Mailslots are used for broadcast applications, such as for finding components on the network; they are also used by the Windows 2000 Computer Browser service.

Winsock is the Windows 2000 sockets API. Winsock is a session-layer interface that is largely compatible with UNIX sockets, with some Windows 2000 extensions. It provides a standardized interface to many transport protocols that may have different addressing schemes, so that any Winsock application can run on any Winsock-compliant protocol stack.

An RPC is a client-server mechanism that enables an application on one machine to make a procedure call to code on another machine. The client calls a local procedure—a **stub routine**—that packs its arguments into a message and sends them across the network to a particular server process. The client-side stub routine then blocks. Meanwhile, the server unpacks the message, calls the procedure, packs the return results into a message, and sends them back to the client stub. The client stub unblocks, receives the message, unpacks the results of the RPC, and returns them to the caller. This packing of arguments is sometimes called **marshalling**.

The Windows 2000 RPC mechanism follows the widely used distributed-computing environment standard for RPC messages, so programs written to use Window 2000 RPCs are highly portable. The RPC standard is detailed. It hides many of the architectural differences between computers, such as the sizes of binary numbers and the order of bytes and bits in computer words, by specifying standard data formats for ROC messages.

Windows 2000 can send RPC messages using NetBIOS, or Winsock on TCP/IP networks, or named pipes on LAN Manager networks. The LPC facility, discussed earlier, is similar to RPC, except that in the LPC case the messages are passed between two processes running on the same computer.

It is tedious and error-prone to write the code to marshal and transmit arguments in the standard format, to unmarshal and execute the remote procedure, to marshal and send the return results, and to unmarshal and return them to the caller. Fortunately, however, much of this code can be generated automatically from a simple description of the arguments and return results.

Windows 2000 provides the **Microsoft Interface Definition Language** to describe the remote procedure names, arguments, and results. The compiler for this language generates header files that declare the stubs for the remote procedures, and the data types for the argument and return-value messages. It also generates source code for the stub routines used at the client side, and for an unmarshaller and dispatcher at the server side. When the application is linked, the stub routines are included. When the application executes the RPC stub, the generated code handles the rest.

COM is a mechanism for interprocess communication that was developed for Windows. COM objects provide a well defined interface to manipulate the data in the object. Windows 2000 has an extension called **DCOM** that can be used over a network utilizing the RPC mechanism to provide a transparent method of developing distributed applications.

Redirectors and Servers

In Windows 2000, an application can use the Windows 2000 I/O API to access files from a remote computer as though they were local, provided that the remote computer is running an MS-NET server, such as is provided by Windows 2000 or Windows for Workgroups. A **redirector** is the client-side object that forwards I/O requests to remote files, where they are satisfied by a server. For performance and security, the redirectors and servers run in kernel mode.

In more detail, access to a remote file occurs as follows:

- The application calls the I/O manager to request that a file be opened with a file name in the standard UNC format.
- The I/O manager builds an I/O request packet.
- The I/O manager recognizes that the access is for a remote file, and calls a driver called a **multiple universal-naming-convention provider (MUP).**
- The MUP sends the I/O request packet asynchronously to all registered redirectors.
- A redirector that can satisfy the request responds to the MUP. To avoid asking all the redirectors the same question in the future, the MUP uses a cache to remember which redirector can handle this file.
- The redirector sends the network request to the remote system.
- The remote-system network drivers receive the request and pass it to the server driver.
- The server driver hands the request to the proper local file-system driver.
- The proper device driver is called to access the data.
- The results are returned to the server driver, which sends the data back to the requesting redirector. The redirector then returns the data to the calling application via the I/O manager.

A similar process occurs for applications that use the Win32 network API, rather than the UNC services, except that a model called a multiprovider router is used, instead of a MUP.

For portability, redirectors and servers use the TDI API for network transport. The requests themselves are expressed in a higher-level protocol, which by default is the SMB protocol. The list of redirectors is maintained in the system registry database.

Domains

Many networked environments have natural groups of uses, such as students in a computer laboratory at school, or employees in one department in a business. Frequently, we want all the members of the group to be able to access shared resources on their various computers in the group. To manage the global access rights within such groups, Windows 2000 uses the concept of a domain. Previously, these domains has no relationship whatsoever to the domain name system DNS that maps Internet host names to IP addresses; now, however, they are closely related. Specifically, a Windows 2000 domain is a group of Windows 2000 workstations and servers that shares a common security policy and user database. Since Windows 2000 now uses the Kerberos protocol for trust and authentication, a Windows 2000 domain is the same thing as a Kerberos realm. Previous versions of NT used the idea of primary and backup domain controllers.; now all servers in a domain are domain controllers. In addition, previous versions required the setup of one-way trusts between domains. Windows 2000 utilizes uses a hierarchical approach based on DNS, and allows transitive trusts that can flow up and down the hierarchy. This approach reduces the number of trusts required for n domains for $n * (n - 1)$ to $O(n)$. The workstations in the domain trust the domain controller to give correct information about the access rights of each user (via the user's access token). All users retain the ability to restrict access to their own workstations, no matter what any domain controller may say.

Because a business may have many departments and a school may have many classes, it is often necessary to manage multiple domains within a single organization. A **domain tree** is a contiguous DNS naming hierarchy. For example, *bell-labs.com* might be the root of the tree, with *research.bell-labs.com* and *pez.bell-labs.com* as children—domains *research* and *pez*. A **forest** is a set of non-contiguous names. An example would be the trees *bell-labs.com* and/or *lucent.com.* A forest may be comprised of only one domain tree, however.

Trust relationships may be set up between domains in three ways, one-way, transitive, and cross-link. Versions of NT through Version 4.0 allowed only one-way trusts to be set up. A **one-way trust** is exactly what its name implies: Domain A is told it can trust domain B. However, B would not trust A unless another relationship is configured. Under a **transitive trust**, if A trusts B and B trusts C, then A, B, and C all trust one another since transitive trusts are two-way by default. Transitive trusts are enabled by default for new domains in a tree and can be configured only among domains within a forest. The third type, a **cross-link trust**, is useful to cut down on authentication traffic. Suppose that domains A and B are leaf nodes, and that users in A often use resources in B. If a standard transitive trust is used, authentication requests must traverse up to the common ancestor of the two leaf nodes; but if A and B have a cross-linking trust established, the authentications would be sent directly to the other node.

Resolution in TCP/IP Networks

On an IP network, **name resolution** is the process of converting a computer name to an IP address, such as resolving *www.bell-labs.com* to 135.104.1.14. Windows 2000 provides several methods of name resolution, including Windows Internet Name Service (WINS), broadcast name resolution, domain name system (DNS), a hosts file, and an LMHOSTS file. Most of these methods are used by many operating systems, so we describe only WINS here.

Under WINS, two or more WINS servers maintain a dynamic database of name-to-IP address bindings, and client software to query the servers. At least two servers are used, so that the WINS service can survive a server failure, and so that the name-resolution workload can be spread over multiple machines.

WINS uses the dynamic host-configuration protocol (DHCP). DHCP updates address configurations automatically in the WINS database, without user or administrator intervention, as follows. When a DHCP client starts up, it broadcasts a discover message. Each DHCP server that receives the message replies with an offer message that contains an IP address and configuration information for the client. The client then chooses one of the configurations and sends a request message to the selected DHCP server. The DHCP server responds with the IP address and configuration information it gave previously, and with a lease for that address. The lease gives the client the right to use that IP address for a specified period of time. When the lease time is half expired, the client will attempts to renew the lease for that address. If the lease is not renewed, the client must get a new one.

Programmer Interface

The Win32 API is the fundamental interface to the capabilities of Windows 2000. This section describes five main aspects of the Win32 API: access to kernel objects, sharing of objects between processes, process management, interprocess communication, and memory management.

Access to Kernel Objects

The Windows 2000 kernel provides many services that application programs can use. Application programs obtain these services by manipulating kernel objects. A process gains access to a kernel object named XXX by calling the CreateXXX function to open a handle to XXX. This handle is unique to that process. Depending on which object is being opened, if the create function fails, it may return 0, or it may return a special constant named INVALID_HANDLE_VALUE. A process can close any handle by calling the CloseHandle function, and the system may delete the object if the count of processes using the object drops to 0.

Windows 2000 provides three ways to share objects between processes. The first way is for a child process to inherit a handle to the object. When the parent calls the CreateXXX function, the parent supplies a SECURITIES_ATTRIBUTES structure with the bInheritHandle field set to TRUE. This field creates an inheritable handle. Then, the child process can be created, passing a value of TRUE to the CreateProcess function's bInheritHandle argument.

Assuming that the child process knows which handles are shared, the parent and child can achieve interprocess communication through the shared objects. The child process would get the value of the handle from the first command-line argument, and could then share the semaphore with the parent process.

```
...
SECURITY_ATTRIBUTES sa;
sa.nlength = sizeof(sa);
sa.lpSecurityDescriptor = NULL;
sa. bInheritHandle =TRUE;
Handle a_semaphore = CreateSemaphore(&sa,1,1,NULL);
char command_line [132] ;
ostrstream ostring(command_line,sizeof(command_line));
ostring<< a_semaphore <<ends;
CreateProcessor ("another_process.exe", command_line,
                    NULL, NULL, TRUE, ...);
```

Fig. CS1.11. Code for a child to share an object by inheriting a handle.

```
//process A
...
Handle a_semaphore = CreateSemaphore(NULL,1,1,"MySEM1");
...
//process B
```

```
...
Handle b_semaphore = OpenSemaphore(SEMAPHORE_ALL_ACCESS,
                     FALSE,"MySEM1");
```

Fig. CS1.12. Code for sharing an object by name lookup.

The second way to share objects is for one process to give the object a name when that object is created, and for the second process to open that name. This method has tw0 drawbacks. One is that Windows 2000 does not provide a way to check whether an object with the chosen name already exists. A second drawback is that the object name space is global, without regard to the object type. For instance, two applications may create an object named *pipe* when two distinct—and possibly different—objects are desired.

Named objects have the advantage that unrelated processes can share them readily. The first process would call one of the CreateXXX functions and supply a name in the 1pszName parameter. The second process can get a handle to share this object by calling OpenXXX (or CreateXXX) with the same name.

The third way to share objects is via the DuplicateHandle function. This method requires some other method of interprocess communication to pass the duplicated handle. Given a handle to a process and the value of a handle within that process, a second process can get a handle to the same object, and thus share it.

Process Management

In Windows 2000, a process is an executing instance of an application, and a thread is a unit of code that can be scheduled by the operating system. Thus, a process contains one or more threads. A process is started when some other process calls the CreateProcess routine. This routine loads any dynamic link libraries that are used by the process, and creates a **primary thread**. Additional threads can be created by the CreateThread function. Each thread is created with its now stack, which defaults to 1 MB unless specified otherwise in an argument to CreateThread. Because some C run-time functions maintain state in static variables, such as errno, a multithread application needs to guard against unsynchronized access. The wrapper function beginthreader provides appropriate synchronization.

```
...
// process A wants to give process B access to a semaphore
// process A
Handle a_semaphore = CreateSemaphore (NULL,1,1,NULL);
//send the value of the semaphore to process B
//using a message or shared memory
...
//process B
Handle process_a = OpenProcess(PROCESS_ALL_ACCESS,FALSE,
                   process_id_of_A);
Handle b_semaphore;
Duplicatehandle(process_a,a_semaphore,
```

```
GetCurrentProcess(),&b_semaphore,
0,FALSE,DUPLICATE_SAME_ACCESS);
//use b_semaphore to access the semaphore
...
```

***Fig. CS1.13.** Code for sharing an object by passing a handle.*

Every dynamic link library or executable file that is loaded into the address space of a process is identified by an instance handle. The value of the **instance handle** is actually the virtual address where the file is loaded. An application can get the handle to a module in its address space by passing the name of the module to GetModuleHandle. If NULL is passed as the name, the base address of the process is returned. The lowest 64 KB of the address space are not used, so a faulty program that tires to dereference a NULL pointer will get an access violation.

Priorities in the Win32 environment are based on the Windows 2000 scheduling model, but not all priority values may be chosen. Win32 uses four priority classes: IDLE_PRIORITY_CLASS (priority level 4), NORMAL_PRIORITY_CLASS (priority level 8), HIGH_PRIORITY_CLASS (priority level 13) and REALTIME_PRIORITY_CLASS (priority level 24). Processes are typically members of the NORMAL_PRIORITY_CLASS unless the parent of the process was of the IDLE_PRIORITY_CLASS,or another class was specified when CreateProcess was called. The priority class of a process can be changed with the SetPriorityClass function, or by an argument being passed to the START command. For example, the command START /REALTIME cbserver. exe would run the observer program in the REALTIME_PRIORITY_CLASS. Note that only users with the increase scheduling priority privilege can move a process into the REALTIME_PRIORITY_CLASS. Administrators and power users have this privilege by default.

When a user is running an interactive program, the system needs to provide especially good performance for that process. For this reason, Windows 2000 has a special scheduling rule for processes in the NORMAL_PRIORITY_CLASS. Windows 2000 distinguishes between the foreground process that is currently selected on the screen, and the background processes that are not currently selected. When a process moves into the foreground, Windows 2000 increases the scheduling quantum by some factor—typically by 3. (This factor can be changed via the performance option in the system section of the control panel.) This increase gives the foreground process three times longer to run before a timesharing preemption occurs.

A thread starts with an initial priority determined by its class, but the priority can be altered by the SetThreadPriority function. This function takes an argument that specifies a priority relative to the base priority of its class:

- `THREAD_PRIORITY_LOWEST:base - 2`
- `THREAD_PRIORITY_BELOW_ NORMAL:base - 1`
- `THREAD_PRIORITY_NORMAL:base +0`
- `THREAD_PRIORITY_ABOVE_NORMAL :base + 1`
- `THREAD_PRIORITY_HIGHEST:base + 2`

Two other designations are also used to adjust the priority. 16-31 for the real-time class, and 0-15 for the variable-priority class. THREAD_PRIORITY_IDLE sets the priority to 16 for real-time threads, and to 1 for variable-priority threads. THREAD_PRIORITY_TIME_CRITICAL sets the priority to 31 for real-time threads, and to 15 for variable-priority threads.

The kernel adjusts the priority of a thread dynamically depending on whether the threads is I/O bound or CPU bound. The WIN32 API provides a method to disable this adjustment, via SetProcessPriorityBoost and Set ThreadPriorityBoost functions.

A thread can be created in a **suspended state**: The thread will not execute until another thread makes it eligible via the ResumeThread function. The SuspendThread function does the opposite. These functions set a counter, so if a thread is suspended twice, it must be resumed twice before it can run.

To synchronize the concurrent access to shared objects by threads, the kernel provides synchronization objects, such as semaphores and mutexes. In addition, synchronization of threads can be achieved by using the WaitForSingleObject or WaitForMultipleObjects functions. Another method of synchronization in the Win32 API is the critical section. A critical section is a synchronized region of code that can be executed by only one thread at a time. A thread establishes a critical section by calling InitializeCritical–Section. The application must call EnterCriticalSection before entering the critical section, and LeaveCriticalSection after exiting the critical section. These two routines guarantee that, if multiple threads attempt to enter the critical section concurrently, only one thread at a time will be permitted to proceed, and the others will wait in the EnterCriticalSection routine. The critical-section mechanism is slightly faster than the kernel-synchronization objects.

A **fiber** is user-mode code that gets scheduled according to a user-defined scheduling algorithm. A process may have multiple fibers in it, just as it can have multiple threads. A major difference between threads and fibers is that threads can execute concurrently, but only one fiber at a time is permitted to execute, even on multiprocessor hardware. This mechanism is included in Windows 2000 to facilitate the porting of those legacy UNIX applications that were written for a fiber-execution model.

The system creates a fiber by calling either ConvetThreadTo Fiber or CreateFiber. The primary difference between these functions is that CreateFiber does not being executing the fiber that was created. To being execution, the application must call SwitchToFiber. The application can terminate a fiber by calling Delete Fiber.

Interprocess Communication

One way that Win32 applications can do interprocess communication is by sharing kernel objects. Another way is by passing messages, an approach that is particularly popular for Windows GUI applications.

One thread can send a message to another thread or to a windows by calling PostMessage, PostThreadMessage, SendMessage, SendThreadMessage, or SendMessageCallback. The difference between *posting* a message and *sending* a message is that the post routines are asynchrpnous: They return immediately, and the calling thread does not know when the message is actually delivered. The send routines are synchronous—they block the caller until the message has been delivered and processed.

In addition to sending a message, a thread can also send data with the message. Since processes have separate address space, the data must be copied. The system copies them by calling SendMessage to send a message of type WM_COPYDATA with a COPYDATASTRUCT data structure that contains the length and address of the data to be transferred. When the message is sent, Windows 2000 copies the data to a new block of memory and gives the virtual address of the new block to the receiving process.

Unlike the 16-bit Windows environment, every Win32 thread has its own input queue from which the thread receives messages. (All input is received via messages.) This structure is more reliable than the shared input queue of 16-bit windows, because, with separate queues, one stuck application cannot block input to the other applications. If a Win32 application does not call GetMessage to handle events on its input queue, the queue will fill up, and after about 5 seconds the system will mark the applications as "Not Responding."

Memory Management

The Win32 API provides several ways for an application to use memory: virtual memory, memory-mapped files, heaps, and thread-local storage.

An application calls VirtualAlloc to reserve or commit virtual memory, and VirtualFree to decommit or release the memory. These functions enable the application to specify the virtual address at which the memory is allocated. They operate on multiples of the memory page size, and the starting address of an allocated region must be greater than 0×10000.

A process may lock some of its committed pages into physical memory by calling VirtualLock. The maximum number of pages that a process can lock is 30, unless the process first calls SetProcessWorkingSetSize to increase the maximum working-set size.

Another way for an application to use memory is by memory mapping a file into its address space. Memory mapping is also a convenient way for two processes to share memory: Both processes map the same file into their virtual memory. Memory mapping is a multistage process.

If a process wants to map some address space just to share a memory region with another process, no file is needed. The process can call CreateFileMapping with a file handle of 0×ffffffff and a particular size. The resulting file-mapping object can be shared by inheritance, by name lookup, or by duplication.

```
...
// allocate 16 MB at the top of our address space
void *buf = VirtualAlloc(0,0×1000000,MEM_RESERVE | MEM_TCP_DOWN,
        PAGE_READWRITE);
// commit the upper 8 MB of the allocated space
VirtualAlloc(buf + 0×800000,0×800000,MEM_COMMIT,PAGE_READWRITE);
// do some stuff with it
//decommit
VirtualFree(buf + 0×800000,0×800000,MEM_DECOMMIT);
//release all the allocated address space
VirtualFree(buf,0,MEM_RELEASE);
```

Fig. CS1.14. *Code fragments for allocating virtual memory.*

```
...
// open the file or create it if it does not exist
HANDLE hfile =CreateFile("somefile",GENERIC_READ | GENERIC_WRITE,
FILE_SHARE_READ | FILE-SHARE_WRITE,NULL,OPEN ALWAYS,
FILE_ATTRIBUTE_NORMAL,
NULL);
//create the file mapping 8 MB in size
HANDLE hmap = CreateFileMapping(hfile,PAGE_READWRITE,
SEC_COMMIT,0,0'800000, "SHM_1");
// get a view to the space mapped
void *buf = MapViewOfFile(hmap,FILE_MAP_ALL_ACCESS,0,0,0×800000);
//do some stuff with it
// unmap the file
//UnmapViewOfFile(buf);
CloseHandle(hmap);
CloseHandle(hfile);...
```

Fig. CS1.15. Code fragments for memory mapping of a file.

The third way for applications to use memory is a heap. A heap in the Win32 environment is just a region of reserved address space. When a Win32 process is initialized, it is creates with a 1 MB **default heap**. Since many Win32 functions use the default heap, access to the heap is synchronized to protect the heap's space-allocation data structures from being damaged by concurrent updates by multiple threads. Win32 provides several heap-management functions so that a process can allocate and manage a private heap. These functions are HeapCreate,HeapAlloc, HeapRealloc, HeapSize, HeapFree, and HeapDestroy. The Win32 API also provides the HeapLock and HeapUnlock functions to enable a thread to gain exclusive access to a heap. Unlike VirtualLock, these functions perform only synchronization; they do not lock pages into physical memory.

The fourth way for applications to use memory is a thread-local storage mechanism. Functions that rely on global or static data typically fail to work properly in a multithreaded environment. For instance, the C run-time function strtok uses a static variable to keep track of its current position while parsing a string. For two concurrent threads to execute strtok correctly, they need separate *current position* variables. The thread-local storage mechanism allocates global storage on a per-thread basis. It provides both dynamic ands static methods of creating thread-local storage.

To use a thread-local static variable, the application would declare the variable as follows to ensure that every thread has its own private copy:

```
_declspec(thread) DWORD cur_pos = 0;
// reserve a slot for a variable
SWORD var_index = T1sAlloc();
//set it to some value
T1sSetValue(Var_index,10);
//get the value back
int var = T1sGetValue(var_index);
```

```
//release the index
TlsFree(var_index);
```

Fig. CS 1.16. Code for dynamic thread-local storage.

Summary

Microsoft designed Windows 2000 to be an extensible, portable operating system—one able to take advantage of new techniques and hardware. Windows 2000 supports multiple operating environments and symmetric multiprocessing. The use of kernel objects to provide basic services, and the support for client-server computing, enable Windows 2000 to support a wide variety of application environments. For instance, Windows 2000 can run programs compiled for MS-DOS, Win16, Windows 95, Windows 2000, and /or POSIX. It provides virtual memory, integrated caching, and preemptive scheduling. Windows 2000 supports a security model stronger than those of previous Microsoft operating systems, and includes internationalization features. Windows 2000 runs on a wide variety of computers, so users can choose and upgrade hardware to match their budgets and performance requirements, without needing to alter the applications that they run.

Case Study 2

MS-DOS

Early History of MS-DOS

MS-DOS appeared in 1981. It was the first 16-bit microcomputer operating system. As of 1988, over 10 million copies had been sold, and this number is growing rapidly as the IBM Personal System/2 assumes its position in the marketplace. The growth and access of MS-DOS cannot be separated from IBM's development of its personal computer, the IBM PC.

The first real personal computer was the Altair, developed in 1975 by MITS (Micro Instrumentation Telemetry Systems) of Albuquerque, New Mexico. It was based on the 8-bit Intel 8080 microprocessor and had 256 bytes of memory. It sold for $397 without keyboard, screen, disk or tape. It was intended primarily for hobbyists. Bill Gates and Paul Allen of Microsoft developed a version of BASIC for the Altair. Allen went to work at MITS and asked Gates to develop a version of BASIC to work with floppy disks. This effort forced the creation of a file management system based on the use of a memory-resident (rather than disk-resident) *file allocation table (FAT)* that eventually because the basis of MS-DOS.

At the time, CP/M was dominating what was an 8-bit microcomputer operating system market. But 16-bit microcomputers were emerging. Although the 16-bit chips were much faster and more powerful, they were extremely expensive and it was not clear that the personal computing marketplace could bear these costs. Microsoft licensed UNIX from Bell Labs and evolved it into XENIX in 1980 as a multiuser, multitasking operating system for 16-bit micros. When the Intel 8080 appeared in 1974, there was a small microcomputer marketplace. But when the Intel 8086 appeared in 1978, the microcomputer marketplace (albeit for 8-bit micros) was well established.

In 1979, Tim Paterson of Seattle Computer Products, a company that produced memory boards, needed software to test an 8086-based product. Microsoft had 8086 BASIC. Digital Research was working on CP/M-86 but was running behind schedule. Paterson developed his 86-DOS operating system to mimic CP/M because CP/M had become the de facto standard microcomputer operating system for 8080/8086-based systems. He used the file allocation table approach, and his first version of 86-DOS required only 6K bytes of memory.

Meanwhile, IBM Boca Raton was developing a microcomputer. For some years, IBM had watched the personal computing industry evolving, and saw it as a "toy" industry that would not generate significant enough sales. But eventually IBM decided to enter the industry and to do so in a big way. The problem was that an entry machine and software had to be developed quickly. IBM knew that its normal product development cycle was too slow. They did not have time to develop all their components themselves, so they decided to use off-the-self hardware components. They needed to offer existing software packages rather than develop new ones.

IBM asked Microsoft to develop a ROM BASIC for an 8-bit microcomputer design. Microsoft suggested using a 16-bit machine, instead. IBM considered both the 8086 and 8088 16-bit microprocessors available from Intel. The 8086 handles data internally and externally, 16 bits at a time. The 8088 handles internal transfers 16 bits at a time, but communicates with peripherals 8 bits at a time. IBM chose the Intel 8088 microprocessor rather than the more powerful 8086 because the 8088 was considerably less expensive and because most of the peripherals available at the time communicated 8 bits at a time.

IBM wanted other programming languages to be available quickly. BASIC had the advantage of being a standalone product with a built-in operating system. Other languages would have needed the support of an operating system. Bill Gates suggested that IBM use CP/M-86; if IBM had done so, Gates might well be a few hundred million dollars today (Ut86)! IBM met with Digital Research, but it didn't work out. CP/M-86 was running late. Microsoft decided to write its own operating system. Microsoft purchased 86-DOS from Seattle Computer Products. Microsoft felt that it has to develop the operating system as well as the languages in order to deliver the languages on time. IBM agreed in November of 1980, and Microsoft went to work. Paterson made changes while at Seattle Computer Products; he had no idea that IBM was Microsoft's key client until he joined Microsoft in April. IBM's secrecy requirements were stringent; the development was done in a secure 6-foot-by-10-foot room with no windows and a locked door. MS-DOS ran on the IBM PC prototype in February of 1981, and it appeared with the announcement of the IBM PC in August of 1981. It quickly became the world's most widely-used operating system.

MS-DOS Version 1.0

The IBM PC was introduced in August 1981. Its operating system, called DOS by IBM but really MS-DOS version 1.0, consisted of 4000 lines of assembly language code requiring 12K of memory. It was organized into three files. The *IBMBIO.COM* had the disk and character input/output system. The *IBMDOS.COM* file contained the disk file manager character I/O handler, and the program interface. The *COMMAND.COM* file contained the external command processor. The system was CP/M compatible; this was important in the market place at that time. The command syntax was essentially the same as CP/M's.

Reserved file names for the devices were used to implement device independence *CON* for the console (the keyboard for input and the screen for output), *PRN* for the printer and *AUX* for auxiliary serial ports. I/O was to files, but if the reserved names were used, the I/O was directed to the appropriate devices. CP/M had logical and physical record length of 128 bytes, but IBM disks had 512-bytes sectors. Version 1.0 supported single-sided floppy disk drives with 160K capacity, while IBM's DOS Version 1.1 handled double-sided floppy disks of capacity 320K.

Relocatable program files were allowed. The *.COM files* were like CP/M binary absolute files. The *.EXE* files were relocatable. The COMMAND.COM file was relocatable and replaceable; it could be replaced by a menu-driven command processor, for example.

The file allocation table was kept in memory for speed. This greatly reduced the amount of disk accessing involved in managing files (in contrast to the scheme used is CP/M).

The command processor had a *resident part* and a *transient part*. The transient part consisted of portions that would ordinarily reside on disk but that could be brought into memory as needed, thus conserving main memory.

MS-DOS 1.0 had trapping of hardware errors, automatic disk logging, data and time stamping, and batch processing of *command files* (i.e., prestored sequences of commands). Meaningful error messages were provided to help users determine what was wrong and how to respond properly for each type of error. Programs could be locked into memory and could call other programs on termination.

There was confusion about which operating system PC users should choose. IBM announced it would support Microsoft's MS-DOS, Digital Research's CP/M-86, and SofTech Microsystem's P-system. MS-DOS was thought to be a losing gamble against CP/M by the trade press, but CP/M-86 was delivered six months late, giving MS-DOS a large head start. There was name confusion between 86-DOS, MS-DOS, PC-DOS, and others. Microsoft insisted that licensees use the name MS-DOS to help promote the standard, but IBM chose to call the operating system DOS, and the industry promptly labeled it PC-DOS.

MS-DOS Version 2.0

Originally, IBM had wanted a small operating system of approximately 16K. XENIX, Microsoft's version of UNIX systems, was already 100K and needed a hard disk to be effective. IBM announced that its PC/XT personal computer was forthcoming and that it would include a 10MB hard disk. Microsoft insisted on a hierarchical file structure. Users wanted to be able to incorporate *device drivers* easily for new devices, and they wanted multitasking (a strength of UNIX systems).

MS-DOS Version 2.0 appeared in March 1983. It used a hierarchical file system to organize information on the 10MB disk; the hierarchy consisted of directories, subdirectories, and files. The hierarchical file system is necessary for a hard disk system. With lower capacity floppy disks, the number of files on one volume is usually small enough that a linear search capability suffices. But with the 10MB disk provided with the IBM PC/XT, the disk volume could hold a hundred times as many files as the original floppy disks provided with the first versions of the IBM PC. So a hierarchical file system like that used with XENIX was incorporated. The MS-DOS designers did consider using a CP/M-like *disk partitioning* scheme, but this would have made MS-DOS too dependent on the physical layout of the disk and would have made it less flexible from the programmer's standpoint. The hierarchical file system helps promote device independence and some degree of XENIX compatibility. A unique *pathname* identifies each file (as in UNIX systems).

The move toward a XENIX-like system was intentional. UNIX systems were receiving a great deal of attention. Microsoft's XENIX system was too large and powerful for the personal computers of the time, but with the move from floppy disks to hard disks, and with the knowledge that larger hard disks, faster processors, and larger main memories were on the horizon, Microsoft felt that it was logical to evolve MS-DOS toward XENIX. The challenge was to make the hierarchical file system physically consistent with the MS-DOS file allocation table and logically consistent with the XENIX file structure.

MS-DOS 1.0 used file control blocks for CP/M-86 compatibility. But this approach did not allow for dealing with files in different directories. Versions 2.0 used *file handles*. When a file is opened, MS-DOS returns a file handle. All further manipulations on the file are with the handle; MS-

DOS then automatically manipulates the file control block (FCB). MS-DOS 2.0 (and later versions) supported both *FCB calls* and *file handle calls* for accomplishing input/output. File input and output could be *redirected* by using file handles. Redirection, for example, allows the user to switch output from a file to a printer. Data from a file could be *piped* to a *sort filter*, for example, which would input a stream of unscored data and output a stream of stored data.

MS-DOS 2.0 allowed for *installable device drivers*. The *open architecture* of the IBM PC encouraged new devices. Open architecture means that the vendor makes the detailed hardware and software specifications available to anyone who wants them; this encourages the development of third-party hardware devices and software applications, and can ultimately help the vendor sell many more computers. The user could add a new device by sliding a hardware card into a slot. The hardware architecture was indeed open, but the operating system really was not. The *BIOS (Basic Input/Output System)* contained all the code to run all the hardware devices. But this code was highly integrated. A hardware manufacturer that wanted to supply new devices to IBM PC users would have to produce a completely new BIOS, a nontrivial task, or would have to supply patches to the existing BIOS. The patches for one new device would often conflict with those for another. It was difficult to add multiple devices, and upgrading to the next version of MS-DOS was often a difficult transition for users with heavily patched systems. Microsoft solved the problem by making the device drivers modular. IBMBIO.COM was converted in 2.0 to a linked list of device drivers. New device drivers could be installed easily at run time through the *CONFIG.SYS file*.

Many customers were interested in having multitasking capabilities (Fo86). But providing multitasking greatly complicates an operating system and requires considerably more memory. Microsoft studied the manner in which the vast majority of personal computers were being used in business environments, and discovered that *background print spooling* was the most needed multitasking capability. Few users needed to be running multiple applications concurrently, but most could benefit greatly by using background print spooling to print the results of one application session while moving on to the next. The *print spooler*, *PRINT.COM*, was designed to run when MS-DOS was not busy. When MS-DOS had nothing to do, it would automatically generate an interrupt to run the print spooler. When a parent application again became active, it would interrupt the print spooler. This kind of capability is easily extended to allow for background communications such as electronic mail systems require.

MS-DOS Version 2.0 had grown to 20,000 lines of code, yet it was still being maintained by only three or four staff programmers. Version 2.0 secured MS-DOS as the standard operating system for 16-bit microcomputers with hard disks. Six months later, Digital Research delivered support for the PC/XT in the form of CP/M-86 but it was too late to stem the tide to MS-DOS 2.0. This could have been one of the costliest delays in Digital Research's history, and may well be responsible for eliminating CP/M based systems from contention as a standard.

The availability of the hard disk IBM PC/XT established personal computers firmly in the business marketplace and established MS-DOS 2.0 as the industry standard personal computer operating system. At this point, it become clear to Microsoft that it had the important responsibility of maintaining and evolving an industry standard, and that this would require a considerably larger commitment of resources than the company had previously given to MS-DOS. But the potential rewards certainly justified an increased commitment. Microsoft came under pressure from a diversity of users to provide the features that would help those users meet their individual needs; it had to walk a fine line between satisfying all those users and not making the system too cumbersome.

The IBM PC/XT was released into a strong business market. Many *PC clones* appeared. These are computers compatible with the IBM PC, but normally sold at a lower price or with some enhanced features in order to draw buyers away from the IBM PC. Microsoft was now in the position of having to maintain an industry standard. IBM found it increasingly difficult to offer its hardware at competitive prices as the PC clones rapidly increased their market share. MS-DOS 2.05 provided *international support* to help Microsoft meet the surging worldwide demand for MS-DOS. This version enabled date, time, decimal symbol, and currency symbol formats to change, and facilitated translation of error messages to many foreign languages. It supported Japanese Kanji characters. IBM refused this version. MS-DOS 2.1 handled the *PCjr*, IBM's ill-fated lowend version of the PC; this version went to the IBM only. MS-DOS 2.11 combined versions 2.05 and 2.1; this was not used by IBM, but Microsoft sold millions of copies internationally as 2.11 was translated into more than 60 languages. MS-DOS 2.2 supported the Korean character set, and 2.25 supported both the Korean and Japanese character sets.

MS-DOS Version 3.0

MS-DOS 3.0 appeared in August 1984 to support IBM's new *PC/AT* with a 20MB hard disk and 1.2 MB floppy disks. It had grown to 40,000 lines of code, and the support team had increased to 30 people. IBM was looking toward networking, but Microsoft preferred a multitasking approach. IBM had developed its *IBM PC Network Adapter*, a hardware card with a communications controller chip. Microsoft was not able to deliver networking features in time for Version 3.0

The PC/AT used Intel's 80286 microprocessor, which supports *protected mode* with a 16MB address space. There is a four-level *ring protection mechanism* (Sc72). The address spaces of applications may be separated from one another, so the 80286 can run many concurrent applications reliably. Data is transmitted or received 16 bits at a time. The 80286 supports virtual memory and multitasking. In real address mode there is a 1MB address space and the machine operates essentially as a fast 8086. In protected mode, 24-bit addresses allow a 16MB real address space. With 32-bit addresses, the 80286 supports virtual addresses, consisting of a 16-bit segment number and a 16-bit displacement within each segment.

Version 3.0 supported CMOS clock and configuration information. It had international support. It also supported *virtual disks* in RAM. It provided a standard set of I/O calls used by both FCB calls and file handle calls. It enabled users to declare files as read only (for security), and provided facilities for recovering erased data.

MS-DOS 3.1 was introduced in November 1984 and included *Microsoft Networks*. It was the first version of MS-DOS that was truly identical for IBM users and non-IBM users. It supported networking with "well-behaved" programs. One general problem with open architecture is that users can know too much. They work around the operating system and directly with the hardware to pull of tricks for increasing the efficiency of their applications. Unfortunately, this can destroy compatibility, and it makes it extreme difficult for these users to upgrade to newer versions of MS-DOS. MS-DOS 3.1 supported multiple file systems on the network. It provided for file sharing and for data locking, and had file security features for local area networking.

MS-DOS 3.2 appeared in 1986. It supported 3-1/2 inch disks. It moved the disk formatting function from the format utility to the device driver. The IBM PC had become the workstation of choice in the automated office. Version 3.2 supported the *IBM token ring local area network* MS-DOS 3.2 provided some additional commands: The REPLACE command allows the user to change between versions of applications and the operating system, XCOPY allows the user to copy entire directories and their subdirectories between disks of either the same or different types, and DRIVER.SYS enables the user to copy files within the same internal drive.

The IBM Personal System/2

IBM developed the Personal System/2, its new generation of personal computers, to handle a changing environment. Applications now demand more memory and processing power, and require connectivity between all an organization's computers. Multitasking is essential to enables users to perform many applications concurrently, and users must be able to switch easily between applications. Space limitations demand that personal computers and their peripherals occupy a minimal amount of desk top space. And a company's personal computers must integrate smoothly with its minicomputers, its mainframe computers, and its networks.

The PS/2 Model 30 uses an 8MHx Intel 8086 processor, has 640KB of RAM, a 720 KB diskette drive, and a 20MB Hard disk. The Model 50 uses a 10 MHz Intel 80286 processor, has 1MB of RAM (expandable to 7MB), a 1.44MB diskette drive, and has a maximum disk storage capacity of 20MB. The Model 60 is similar to the Models 50, but its RAM is expandable to15MB, and its maximum disk storage capacity is 185MB. The model 50 and 60 can add the 80287 Math Coprocessor for higher speed floating point mathematical operations.

The Model 80 uses a 16MHz Intel 80386 processor (20MHz is also available) with 1MB RAM (expandable to 16MB), and a maximum disk storage capacity of 230MB. It uses the same high-speed (80ns) one-megabit memory chip technology of IBM's 3090 mainframe processors. The Intel 80386 has 32-bit addressing with 4gigabyte (billion byte) real address space and a 64-terabyte virtual address space. This is incredible considering that IBM mainframes have commonly supported 32-bit addressing only since 1983. The 80386 can process as many as four million instructions per second. It offers the protected mode needed for multitasking. It passes data back and forth to memory 32 bits at a time. The Model 80 can add the 80387 Math Coprocessor. The Models 60 and 80 each have seven Micro Channel expansion slots.

The Micro Channel

The Micro Channel™ parallel bus (multichannel) architecture is used in PS/2 model 50, 60, and 80. It provides for multitasking support, support of concurrent multiple intelligent processors, 32-bit data path capability, and an analog channel for complex voice and analog signals.

The Micro Channel is not compatible with the PC's bus. It can synchronize multiple concurrent 16-bit transfers or 16-bit/32-bit transfers (80386 machine only). It can support multiple DMA channels. It provides dedicated service for occasional high-volume, high-speed transmissions such as occur when reading or writing entire tracks of fast hard disks.

The Micro Channel allows the use of a new fixed disk storage management technique called *one-to-one sector interleave*. With the original IBM PC bus, it was not possible to write to contiguous sectors, so data was written to every third sector (three-to-one sector interleave), thus requiring three passes to write a full track. The PS/2 can write to contiguous sectors so it can write a full track in a single pass, thus greatly improving system performance.

The Micro Channel is specifically designed to be shared effectively by dissimilar processors. Each device that plugs into the bus must have a unique identification code for the bus to recognize it. The Micro Channel supports environments where the computer's hardware may consist of many microprocessors performing various hardware device control functions. It can carry many simultaneous communications.

MS-DOS 3.3

MS-DOS 3.3 extended MS-DOS 3.2 to add functions and capabilities to run on the PS/2. It is compatible with IBM's PC family. It allows an increased number of open files. It supports four communications port, 1.44MB diskette drives, and multiple 32MB hard disk partitions. It facilitates connectivity with IBM's 3270 communications family and with IBM's local area network products.

MS-DOS 3.3 is the entry-level operating system for the PS/2 (the PS/2 does not support earlier MS-DOS versions). MS-DOS 3.3 is a single-tasking, MS-DOS-compatible operating system. MS-DOS 3.3 runs under the real mode of the 80286 and 80386, making a PS/2 appear to be an 8086-based IBM PC. MS-DOS 3.3 provided some new commands: FASTOPEN keeps a list of recently accessed files to help locate and open these files more quickly than is possible when having to search a large hierarchical directory structure; and CALL lets one batch file execute another, return, and continue executing from the point of the call. MS-DOS 3.3 also has significant improvements in the area of foreign language support—a long standing goal of Microsoft and IBM. MS-DOS 4.0, the release most current as this book went to press.

Operating System/2 Standard Edition

Operating system/2 (OS/2) is intended as a new family of operating systems to support the more powerful capabilities of IBM's Personal System/2 computers. Microsoft calls the operating system, MS OS/2. It has agreed to make MS OS/2 available to OEMs, but Microsoft does not intend to sell MS OS/2 directly to end users (nor does it sell MS-DOS to end users). It enables users to access the full capabilities of 80286 based and 80386-based systems). It can handle much larger programs and can process many programs concurrently. It is designed to operate in IBM's *Systems Application Architecture* (SAA) environments. Which foster friendlier user interfaces and facilitate applications portability across IBM's full range of computing, and communications products. The Application Program Interface (API) of OS/2 enables users to develop SAA-compatible applications. OS/2 is a very large and complex operating system; its first version has approximately a million and a half lines of code.

OS/2 Standard Edition Version 1 breaks the IBM PC's 640K memory barrier and can run multiple applications concurrently. Version 1.1 includes the *Presentation Manager* (based on Microsoft Windows), which provides graphics and windowing capabilities conforming to IBM's Systems Application Architecture, and it features pop-up menus and contextual help. It has 16MB memory addressability and handles multitasking. It supports several 32MB disk partitions. It is compatible with MS-DOS 3.3 and provides various migration aids for users who wish to convert between the operating systems. It offers device independence.

In real mode, the 80286 and 80386 processors provide a MS-DOS 3.3 environment that makes the PS/2 appear to be an 8086 with simple real addressing and the ability to execute only a single application at once (i.e. no multitasking). Thus real mode allows backward compatibility with earlier versions of the PC.

In the protected mode provided by both the 80286 and the 80386, users may run multitasking and tasks are protected from one another. Protected mode allows 16MB addressing on the 80286 and 4 GB (4 billion byte) addressing on the 80386. Programs originally written for the IBM PC will generally not run under protected mode without modification. OS/2 can run a PS/2 in real mode, protected mode, or both at once.

The PS/2 ROM contains both a *compatibility BIOS,* which ensures compatibility for programs developed for the IBM PC, and an *advanced BIOS*, which supports the new capabilities of the PS/2.

The OS/2 kernel handles file input/output, character mode display output, multitasking, and interprocess communication. OS/2 supports dynamic link libraries; this feature facilitates adding new program modules to extend the operating system's capabilities, and allows programs to share code in external libraries. Microsoft also supplies the LAN Manager for supporting local area networks. Processes located at different nodes of a network may intercommunicate easily.

OS/2 uses a superset of the commands of DOS. The key difference is that in OS/2 many programs may run concurrently. OS/2 running under protected mode handles the memory management, file locking, file sharing and task isolation necessary to provide reliable multitasking. In real mode, such protection is not available, so multitasking could easily fail as an errant program destroys other programs.

OS/2 supports virtual memory, so programs can be larger than the amount of available real memory; memory segments are replaced using the least-recently-used algorithm.

One program may initiate another to run with it asynchronously. The new OS/2 command, DETACH, can initiate any program to run in the background. Programs can have multithread execution. Threads may be assigned different priorities or they may be suspended. Threads can synchronize their operation through semaphores.

OS/2 uses the same file system as DOS. Although the current versions of OS/2 runs on the 80386. They still do not fully use the 80386's 32-bit addressing range. OS/2 provides a rich variety of means for interprocess communication.

Operating System/2 Extended Edition

The OS/2 Extended Edition provides a wide range of communications capabilities and a database manager that supports IBM's relational database model. IBM created the OS/2 Extended Edition; this version will not be available to other OEMs through Microsoft.

OS/2's communications capabilities include concurrent multiple protocol support, concurrent emulation of multiple terminal types, communication and system management support, and a variety of programming interfaces.

The relational database management subsystem features interactive query and report writing, consistency with IBM DB2 (a mainframe relational database), consistency with Structured Query Language/Data System (SQL/DS), and local area network support.

Systems Application Architecture

Systems Application Architecture (SAA) is an IBM strategy for having its wide range of systems become more compatible with regard to user interfaces, application program interfaces, and communications procedures. IBM currently offers three major lines of computers, namely the System/370 mainframe computers, the System/3X minicomputers, and the Personal System/2 microcomputers. IBM has created Systems Application Architecture, a set of programming guidelines, to enables programmers to develop applications compatibles with all three kinds of systems.

Programs designed to conform to SAA are more portable—they can be moved between the different lines of computers with minimal changes. Programmers benefit because they can spend less on software development, and can have common applications running on many different types of computers in their organizations. As an organization grows and its computing needs increase, it can move up to more powerful computing systems without incurring major reprogramming costs. Software development companies also benefit because they can market their products to the huge base of installed IBM and IBM-compatible equipment

SAA includes protocols for how programs should communicate with one another within the same computer, between the same types of computers, and between different types of computers. Programs written to conform to these guidelines can intercommunication more easily with a wide range of computers in various kinds of computer networks.

SAA also includes guidelines for defining the user interface for any type of program. This ensures that all applications will have similar or even identical interfaces. It enables users to learn new applications faster, and helps users avoid mistakes that occur when they use a wide range of software packages with different conventions for a accomplishing similar tasks.

The User's View of MS-DOS

This section is intended to give the reader a sense of what the user can accomplish with the MS-DOS commands. It is not intended as a user's manual. There are many fine publications for that purpose. Read this only for a general understanding of MS-DOS's capabilities.

The *command processor* interprets user commands. The command processor is stored in the file COMMAND.COM, which is loaded automatically when MS-DOS is started. Internal Commands are part of this file. External commands are brought into memory from disk as needed. The command processor also executes programs files. Executable files have one of the extension .COM, .EXE, and .BAT.

MS-DOS prompts the user to enter commands. The standard prompt is the letter of the current drive followed by the greater than sign (>). The next several sections contain a detailed listing of MS-DOS's commands.

Communicating with the System

- COMMAND—Load a new copy of the command processor (COMMAND.COM).
- DATE—Set or display the system date.
- EXIT—Terminate a copy of the command processor (return to parent copy).
- PROMPT—Define the system prompt.

- SET—Define an environmental variable.
- SHARE—Load support for file sharing (required for Microsoft Networks).
- TIME—Set or display the current system time.
- VER—Display the version number of the active MS-DOS command interpreter.

Working with Disks

- ASSIGN—Route request for disk operations from one drive to another.
- CHKDSK—Check the allocation of storage space on the disk for errors in directory entries or the file allocation table, or for physical damage to the disk. Also check the allocation of sectors to individual files.
- DISKCOMP—Compare two floppy disks track-for-track and report any differences.
- DISKCOPY—Copy a floppy disk track-for-track (does not consolidate fragmented files).
- FDISK—Configure a fixed disk (hard disk) for use with MS-DOS.
- FORMAT—Format a disk for use with MS-DOS by initializing the directory and the file allocation table (FAT).
- JOIN—Make a disk a subdirectory of another disk (join a disk in one drive to a directory in another drive).
- LABEL—(Version 3.0 or higher) Modify, create, or delete a volume label.
- SUBST—Substitute a drive letter for a subdirectory pathname, thus making a subdirectory a virtual-disk drive.
- SYS—Transfer MS-DOS system files (IO.SYS and MSDOS.SYS) to an application disk.
- VERIFY—Verify data as it is written to a disk.
- VOL—Display the volume label of a disk.

Working with Directories

The top-level directory is called the root directory. The root directory holds entries. An entry is a file or a subdirectory. A subdirectory is a file that holds directory entries. Each subdirectory and file has a unique pathname.

- CHDIR or CD—Make a directory the current directory.
- DIR—Display information about directory entries (file name, extensions, size in bytes, date and time created of last changed).
- MKDIR or MD—Create a new subdirectory.
- PATH—Define pathnames that MS-DOS uses to search for .COM, .EXE, and .BAT files that are not in the current directory.
- RMDIR or RD—Remove an empty directory.
- TREE—Display the hierarchical directory structure.

Managing Files

- ATTRIB—Define a file as a read-only file (this can help prevent accidental destruction) or a read-and-write file.
- BACKUP—Make backup copies of files and their directory structure.

- COPY—Copy one or more files; copy from one device to another. (Copy removes any existing fragmentation by placing data on consecutive sectors and adjacent tracks.)
- EDLIN—Create or modify an ASCII text file (EDLIN is a line editor).
- ERASE (or DELETE)—Erase a file.
- EXE2BIN—Convert an executable file in the .EXE format to a memory-image file (usually .COM, .BIN, or .SYS).
- FC—Compare two files and display the differences.
- RECOVER—Reconstruct files from a disk that has damaged sectors.
- RENAME or REN—Change the name of one or more files.
- RESTORE—Restore files created by the BACKUP command to a disk with the same directory structure as the original.

Managing Input and Output

MS-DOS normally reads input from the standard input (usually the keyboard), and normally writes output to the standard output (usually the display screen). The standard input or output may be *redirected* to a file or a device. Devices are treated as files by MS-DOS. The output of a command or program can be *piped* to another command or program.

- CLS—Clear the screen.
- CTTY—Change the device to be used for standard input and standard output.
- FIND—Search for a string. (FIND is a filter that searches a specified file or standard input for a character string; it displays the lines that contain the character string on the standard output.)
- GRAFTABL—Define the IBM extended character set.
- GRAPHICS—Print a display created in graphics mode.
- MODE—Control the mode of the output device. (MODE sets the display characteristics, sets the line length and spacing for a parallel printer port, connects a serial printer by redirecting parallel printer output to an asynchronous communications port, and sets the communications parameters for an asynchronous communications port.
- MORE—The MORE command is a filter that displays the contents of the files one screenful at a time.
- PRINT—Print a file in the background (while the user performs other tasks).
- SORT—The SORT command is a filter that sorts records alphabetically.
- TYPE—Send a file to the standard output.

Setting up the Environment

The user can tailor the working environment via the CONFIG.SYS file that defines the operating characteristics of an MS-DOS system. When MS-DOS starts, it automatically executes the commands in the CONFIG.SYS file if one is available.

- ANSI.SYS—This is a device driver that implements the American National Standards Institute (ANSI) Standard escape codes for screen and keyboard control.

- BREAK—Control how often MS-DOS checks for a Control-C interrupt. (When MS-DOS encounters a Control-C, it interrupts the current process and returns to the system prompt.)
- BUFFERS—Specify the number of in-memory disk buffers that MS-DOS allocates each time it starts.
- COUNTRY—Specify the country, thus indicating the appropriate date, decimal sign and currency symbol to be used.
- DEVICE—Install a device driver.
- DRIVPARM—Redefine the default characteristics defined by a device driver for a block device.
- FCBS—Specify the maximum number of FCB-controlled file that can be open while file sharing is in effect.
- FILES—Specify the maximum number of open files controlled by file handles.
- LASTDRIVE—Determine the maximum number of drives by setting the highest drive latter that MS-DOS recognizes.
- SHELL—Specify a command processor to be used in place of COMMAND.COM.
- VDISK.SYS—Create a memory-resident virtual disk. This is a file containing the device driver that actually creates the virtual disk in RAM. VDISK.SYS is placed in the CONFIG.SYS file with DEVICE command. A virtual disk is much faster than a real disk, but the data is lost when the power is turned off. CHKDSK reports the storage allocated to the virtual disk.

Using Batch File

A batch file is an executable file that contains a group of commands that the user wants to execute in sequence. The user types the name of the file and MS-DOS executes the commands in the file. A batch file has the extension .BAT. To have a batch file executed automatically every time MS-DOS starts, create an AUTOEXEC.BAT file in the root directory.

- CALL—Call another batch file with parameters.
- ECHO—Display command names or messages as commands are executed from a batch file.
- FOR—Execute an MS-DOS command iteratively for each file in a set of files.
- GOTO—Execute a command in a batch file other than the next in sequence.
- IF—Test a condition and execute a command in a batch file, depending on the result.
- PAUSE—Stop execution of the batch file temporarily.
- REM—Include remarks in a batch file and display them when the file is executed.
- SHIFT—Extend the number of possible command line parameters.

Working with the Assembler

The Microsoft Macro Assembler translates assembly language source programs into object modules that can then be linked to produce an executable program to run under MS-DOS.

- CODEVIEW—Window-oriented debugger that lets user view source code, unassembled machine code, register values, and watch variables while program execution is being traced.
- CREF—Generate a cross-reference file of the symbols in an assembled program.
- DEBUG—Load and execute assembly language programs in a test environment.

- LIB—Maintain a library of object modules for use by the LINK program.
- LINK—Combine object modules into a single executable program that MS-DOS can load anywhere in available memory.
- MAKE—Maintain related program files at the same level of development.
- MAPSYM—Create a symbol map to test an executable file with SYMDEB's symbolic debugging features.
- MASM—Translate assembly language source programs into object modules.
- SYMDEB—Use symbols in testing programs written in assembly and high-level languages. (This is a symbolic debugging program that sets up an environment in which the user can load, examine, text, alter, and store any file.)

The System's View of MS-DOS

In this section we consider the internal organization of the MS-DOS operating system. Disks are comprised of sides, tracks and sectors. Sectors are grouped into *clusters*. The *File Allocation Table (FAT)* shows how clusters are allocated to files. The *master directory* for each disk shows for each file the starting location, the size, when the file was created, and any special file attributes. *Subdirectories* may be used to organize files on disk. Most applications need not be familiar with this level of detail; they simply call the appropriate operating system routines to accomplish desired tasks without having to worry about precisely how the tasks are performed and how the data is organized.

On booting, the first disk sector, called the *boot sector*, is transferred to memory. This boot program then loads in the first portion of DOS, the *initialization routine*. This routine organizes memory and then overlays the next portion of DOS on top of the initialization code. The *resident code* is then loaded into low memory; it includes the *interrupt handlers* and *system calls*. The *transient code* is loaded into high memory; it contains the *command processor* and the *internal commands*. The transient code may be overlaid as applications run; MS-DOS brings in new copies of the transient code as needed.

MS-DOS provides a *terminates but stay resident* capability; this allows uses to write programs that may remain in memory, for example, to be able to respond quickly to various keystroke combinations.

Communicating with the System

Users enter *commands* to communicate with the system; applications programs use *system calls*. The command processor, COMMAND.COM, contains the resident part, the initialization part, and the transient part. The resident part handles standard errors, processes the *terminate on control-C interrupt*, and contains code to reload the transient part as needed. The initialization part determines where to begin program loading, and loads and processes the *AUTOEXEC.BAT file* (a file containing a prestored sequence of commands that the system executes automatically each time it is booted or rebooted) if there is one; it is overlaid after it completes. The transient part contains the *batch file processor* and the *internal commands;* it issues the *system prompt* to tell the user the system is ready to accept the next command, reads commands (from the keyboard or from a batch file), and executes commands. It controls the loading and execution of *external commands*. Internal commands reside in memory so that they can be executed quickly; external commands are brought in from disk as needed.

System calls initiate the variety of MS-DOS services. Users can write their own programs to access the hardware and the operating system, but this creates "misbehaved" programs that may not run properly on future versions of MS-DOS. The two types of system calls are *interrupts* (Du83) and *function requests*.

A *software interrupt* enables a program to issue an interrupt that will cause an interrupt handler routine to execute and process the interrupt; the program loads needed values into appropriate registers and then issues the *INT instruction*, including the appropriate interrupt number. MS-DOS keeps a list of all the interrupt handler address in a vector table in memory.

Working with Disks

Formatting disks with the *FORMAT command* prepares them to be read or written by MS-DOS routines. The FORMAT command (DOS 3.0 and later versions) simply calls the device driver which contains the code to perform the formatting of its particular device. Newly installed device drivers must contain the code to format the devices they control.

A *volume* is a floppy disk or a partition of a fixed disk. Volumes are divided into *logical sectors*. Logical sectors reside on parts of physical tracks. The tracks are determined by the various fixed positions of the read-write heads. Sectors are grouped into clusters; the file allocation table chains the clusters to define the contents of the file. Each volume has an identifying *volume label*. Volume labels may be created, modified, or deleted with the *LABEL command*. Each logical volume includes five control areas and a files area as follows:

1. Boot sector
2. Reserved area
3. File allocation table #1
4. File allocation table #2
5. Root directory
6. Files area.

The boot sector contains all the information MS-DOS needs to interpret the structure of the disk. The FAT allocates disk clusters to files. Each cluster may contain many sectors, but this number is fixed when the disk is formatted and it must be a power of 2. A file's clusters are chained together in the FAT. The extra copy of the FAT is for integrity and reliability. The root directory organizes the files on the disk into entries and subdirectories. The *files area* (also called the *data area*) is where the files' information is stored. File space is allocated one cluster at a time as needed.

The FORMAT command causes the following information to be placed in the *BIOS parameter block (BPB)* in the boot sector:

1. sector size in bytes
2. sector on the disk
3. sector per track
4. cluster size in bytes
5. number of FATs

6. sectors per FAT
7. number of directory entries
8. number of heads
9. hidden sectors
10. reserved sectors
11. media identification code.

CHKDSK comparems the two FATs to make sure they are identical. MS-DOS maintains a copy of the FAT in memory to be able to search it quickly. Each cluster entry in the FAT contains codes to indicate the following:

1. The cluster is available.
2. The cluster is in use.
3. The cluster is bad (i.e., it has a bad sector); CHKDSK reports these.
4. The cluster is a file's last one.
5. A pointer (cluster number) to the file's next cluster. (The directory points to the file's first cluster.)

Clusters are allocated to files one at a time on demand. Because of the continuing addition. modification, and deletion of files, the disk tends to become fragmented with free clusters dispersed throughout the disk. Clusters are allocated sequentially, but in-use clusters are skipped. No attempt is made to reorganize the disk so that files would consist only of sequential clusters, but this can be accomplished via the MS-DOS commands.

MS-DOS uses memory buffers the disk input/output. With file handle calls, the location of the buffer may be specified in the call. With FCB calls, MS-DOS uses a preset buffer called the *disk transfer area*, which is normally in a program's *program segment prefix* and is 128 bytes long.

Working with Directories

Initial versions of MS-DOS had a simple linear directory listing all files. Version 2.0 incorporated a hierarchical file structure with directories and subdirectories. A root directory and subdirectories form the hierarchical structure, and directory entries describe individual files.

The 32-byte directory entry contains the following:

1. File name (8 bytes)
2. Extension (3 bytes)
3. File attribute byte (1 byte)
4. Reserved (10 bytes)
5. Time created or last updated (2 bytes)
6. Date created or last updated (2 bytes)
7. Starting cluster (2 bytes)
8. File size (4 bytes)

The first byte of the file name may contain special codes indicating the following:

1. A directory entry that has never been used

2. The entry is a subdirectory
3. File has been used, but is now erased.

The file attribute byte may indicate the following:

1. Read-only file (an attempt to open the file for writing or deletion will fail)
2. Hidden file (excluded from normal searches)
3. System file (excluded from normal searches)
4. Volume label (can exist only in the root directory)
5. Subdirectory (excluded from normal searches)
6. Archive bit (set to "on" whenever a file is modified)

Each disk is formatted to have at least one directory, but there can be many directories. A directory may include other directories. Formatting creates an initial root directory. Each fixed disk partition has its own root directory. With versions 2.0 and higher, the root directory may contain directories in addition to files. Directories may contain one or more file entries or more directories, thus generating a hierarchical file system directory structure. The volume label, if present, appears in the root directory.

MS-DOS function calls are available to search directories for files in a hardware independent manner. FCB functions require that files be specified by a pointer to an unopened FCB; these functions do not support the hierarchical file system. With the file handle function request, it is possible to search for a file by specifying an ASCII string; it is possible to search within any subdirectory on any drive, regardless of the current subdirectory, by specifying a pathname.

Managing Files

Data is organized into files whether that data is in memory or on disk. Files may be data files or executable files. A file is simply string of bytes; no record structure or access technique is assumed. Applications impose their own record structure on the string of bytes. MS-DOS requires only a pointer to the data buffer, and a count of the number of bytes to be read or written in order to do I/O. Executables files must be in either the .COM formats or the .EXE format. Objects modules are maintained in the Intel Corporation object-record format.

Files may be accessed with FCB calls or file handle calls (Version 2.0 and later); the file handle calls are designed to work with a hierarchical file system. File handle calls are preferable, but FCB calls are provided for compatibility with previous versions of MS-DOS. File handle call support record locking and sharing. Users interested in writing programs that will be compatible with future versions of MS-DOS should use the file handle calls rather than the FCB calls.

The FCB function requests are as follows:

1. Open file with FCB
2. Close file with FCB
3. Delete file with FCB
4. Read block sequentially
5. Write block sequentially
6. Create file with FCB
7. Rename file with FCB

8. Read block directly
9. Write block directly
10. Get file size with FCB
11. Set relative record field
12. Read multiple blocks directly
13. Write multiple blocks directly

The FCB data structure occupies a portion of the application's memory and contains 37 bytes of data as follows:

1. Drive identifier (1 byte) (0=default drive, 1=drive A, 2=drive B, and so on)
2. File name (8 bytes)
3. Extension (3 bytes)
4. Current block number (2 bytes) (for sequential reads and writes)
5. Record size (2 bytes) (MS-DOS sets to 128, but this may be changed.)
6. File size (4 bytes)
7. Date created/updated (2 bytes)
8. Time created/updated (2 bytes)
9. Reserved (8 bytes)
10. Current record number (1 byte) (for sequential reads and writes)
11. Relative record number (4 bytes)

A file handle is a 16-bit integer (usually 0 to 20) created by MS-DOS and returned to a program that creates or opens a file or device. A file may be opened with a handle by passing a pathname and attribute to MS-DOS, which then returns the 16-bit handle. The program saves the handle and uses it to specify the file in future operations on the file. An FCB-like data structure is built by MS-DOS for the file, but this is strictly controlled by the operating system. The file handle function calls are as follows:

1. Create file
2. Open file
3. Close file
4. Read from file or device
5. Write to file or device
6. Move file pointer
7. Duplicate file handle (creates a new handle that refers to the same file as an existing handle)
8. Match file handle (cause one handle to refer to the same file as another)
9. Create temporary file
10. Create file if name is unique (fails if a file with the same name already exists)

MS-DOS maintains a table that relates handles to files or devices. Eight handles are normally available to programs, but this can be increased to 20 via the CONFIG.SYS file. Five of the handles are preassigned to standard devices as follows:

Handle	Standard Device	Device Name
0	Standard input device	CON (reads characters from the keyboard)
1	Standard output device	CON (writes characters to the video display)
2	Standard error device	CON (writes characters to the video display)
3	Standard auxiliary device	AUX (controls serial port I/O)
4	Standard printer device	PRN (controls parallel port output; usually to the printer)

A .COM file consists of absolute machine code and data. It is not relocatable. It loads faster than an .EXE file. An .EXE file is a relocatable executable file; it contains a header with relocation information, and the actual load module. The .EXE files separate the code and data portions. This feature is designed to facilitate the sharing of "pure procedures" among several tasks in evolving MS-DOS systems that support concurrent tasks. The Microsoft Macro Assembler translates source code files into object files with the .OBJ extension.

Managing Input and Output

Device drivers are programs that control input and output. They manage communication between the hardware devices and the operating system. Regardless of the specific details of performing input/output on particular devices, device drivers all communicate in a standard manner with the rest of the operating system. Five resident device drivers control the standard devices. Other device drivers may be installed at the command level as needed. The two types of devices are *character devices* that handle one byte at a time, and *block devices* that can access blocks of information on random access devices such as disks. Device drivers are treated as files. The IO.SYS file consists of the five resident device drivers that form the MS-DOS BIOS.

New or replacement device drivers may be installed (version 2.0 and later) by using the DEVICE command followed by the driver's file name in a CONFIG.SYS file on the boot disk. Thus, the input/output system may be reconfigured at the command level. MS-DOS uses character device drivers and block device drivers. CON, AUX, and PRN are character device drivers. The CONFIG.SYS file may be used to notify the operating system of hardware device changes such as additional hard disks, a clock chip, a RAM disk, or additional memory.

A device driver is composed of a *device header*, a *strategy routine*, and an *interrupt routine*. The device header contains a pointer to the next device driver in the chain of device drivers in IO.SYS, and it points to the strategy routine and the interrupt routine. The request header is the data structure that MS-DOS uses to give the driver the information necessary to perform a requested input/output operation. The strategy routine saves a pointer to the request header data structure. The interrupt routine performs the I/O and passes status and completion information back to MS-DOS in the request header. Each driver has a *strategy routine* entry point and an *interrupt routine* entry point. For asynchronous I/O, the strategy routine is called upon to enqueue a request and return to the caller quickly. The interrupt routine then performs the I/O when it can.

A *filter* is a program that processes input data in some particular way to produce output data directed to some file or device. Three filters are built in to MS-DOS. *SORT* sorts text data. *FIND* searches for a character string. *MORE* displays one screen of data at a time. Other filters may be created. Filters may be piped together (with the | symbol) so that the output of one forms the input to another. Inputs or outputs may be *redirected.*

Background programs are dormant until they are activated by a signal from the keyboard. A *hot key*, or combination of keys, signals a program to take control of keyboard input.

Managing Memory

Memory is organized as follows in MS-DOS (from low memory to high memory locations):

1. Interrupt vector table
2. Optional extra space (used by IBM for ROM data area)
3. IO.SYS
4. MSDOS.SYS
5. Buffers, control areas, and installed device drivers
6. Resident part of COMMAND.COM
7. External commands or utilities (.COM and .EXE files are loaded here)
8. User stack for .COM Files (256 bytes)
9. Transient part of COMMAND.COM

The interrupt vector table contains the addresses of the interrupt handler routines IO.SYS is the basic input/output system; it is the MS-DOS/hardware interface. MSDOS.SYS contains most of the interrupt handlers and function requests. The resident part of COMMAND.COM contains certain interrupt handlers and the code that reloads the transient part of COMMAND.COM as needed; the transient part of COMMAND.COM includes the batch processor, the internal commands, and the command processor.

MS-DOS begins the user's *program segment* in the lowest address free memory area. The program segment prefix (PSP) occupies the first 256 bytes of the program segment area. The PSP points to various memory locations the program requires as it executes.

MS-DOS creates a *memory control block* at the start of each memory area it allocates. This data structure specifies the following:

1. the size of the area
2. the program name (if a program owns the area)
3. a pointer to the next allocated area of memory

MS-DOS may allocate a new memory block to a program, free a memory block, or change the size of an allocated memory block. If a program tries to allocated memory block of a certain size, MS-DOS searches for an appropriate block. If such a block is found, it is modified to belong to the requesting process. If the block is too large, MS-DOS parcels it into an allocated block and a new free block. When a block of memory is released by a program, MS-DOS changes the block to indicate that it is available. When a program, reduces the amount of memory it needs, MS-DOS creates a new memory control block for the memory being freed. The first memory block of a program always begins with a program segment prefix. Normally when a program terminates, its memory is released. The program can retain its memory by issuing function 31, TERMINATE BUT STAY RESIDENT.

Controlling Program Flow

COMMAND.COM uses the EXEC function to load and execute program files. A program issuing EXEC causes MS-DOS to allocate memory, write a program segment prefix, load the new program, and transfer control to it. The calling program is the *parent program*, the called program is the *child program*. A child program may use EXEC to load and execute its own child programs. Each child automatically inherits its parent's active handles, so it can access its parent's active files. MS-DOS allows programs to load and execute overlays.

MS-DOS handles hardware interrupts from devices and software interrupts caused by executing instructions. An interrupt vector table causes control to transfer to the appropriate interrupt handlers. User may write their own interrupt handlers. The Control-C interrupt normally terminates the active process and returns control to the command interpreter.

Certain types of critical errors may occur that prevent a program from continuing. For example, if a program tries to open a file on a disk drive without a disk, or a disk drive whose door is open, a critical error is signalled. MS-DOS contains a *critical error handler*, but users may which to provide their own routines for better control over errors in specific situations.

Setting Up the Environment

The operating system environment is configurable. Users can modify the system data and time, the number of buffers allocated, and so on. These can be modified at the command level with the CONFIG.SYS file, or they can be modified with appropriate function requests. The MS-DOS command processor constructs an environment block. MS-DOS provides capabilities for varying date and time formats, decimal formats, and currency formats for foreign countries; it handles Korean and Japanese (Kanji) character sets.

The Programmer's View of MS-DOS System Calls

MS-DOS provides the programmer with a rich collection of system calls. These calls accomplish various manipulations that would be extremely time-consuming and difficult to program and debug if the operating system were not available. The calls manipulate files, disks and directories; return information about the hardware and software environment; and obtain additional memory and relinquish memory no longer needed. By using MS-DOS calls, programmers realize several advantages. Applications programming becomes faster and less error prone, and application that use system calls are easier to upgrade to new versions of the operating system. Microsoft is committed to providing upward compatibility for programs that use system calls properly. The next several sections enumerate most of MS-DOS's system calls.

Working with Disks

- Check Status of Verify Flag—Returns the value of the Verify Flag, which determines whether or not DOS verifies write operations to the disk.
- Get Default Drive Data—Returns information about the current default drive, namely the number of sectors per cluster, information about the type of disk in the current default drive, bytes per sector, and cluster per drive.

- Get Disk Transfer Address—Returns the pointer to the current Disk Transfer Area (the DTA is the buffer that DOS uses to transfer data to-and-from the disk).
- Get Free Disk Space—Determines how many bytes are free on the specified drive.
- Get Specified Drive Data—Returns information about the specified drive, namely the number of sectors per cluster, the offset to the FAT ID byte, the number of bytes per sector, and the number of clusters per drive.
- Identify Current Drive—Returns the default drive ID.
- Read Absolute Disk Sectors (*Int.*)—Reads the specified number of disk sector from the disk drive, starting at a given location.
- Reset Disk—Flushes all buffers to the media and marks them "free."
- Select Drive—Sets the default drive to the specified drive.
- Set Disk Transfer Address—Sets the Disk Transfer Address to the specified value.
- Set or Reset Verify Flag—Sets the value of the Verify Flag to a specified value. The Verify Flag determines whether or not DOS verifies write operations to the disk.
- Write Absolute Disk Sectors (*Int.*)—This interrupt handler writes the specified number of sectors to the disk drive, starting at a given location.

Working with Directories

- Change Current Directory—Changes the current directory to the directory in the user's pathname.
- Create Directory—Creates a directory using the name in the user's pathname.
- Get Current Directory—Returns the pathname of the current directory on a specified drive.
- Remove Directory—Removes the directory specified in the user's pathname.

Managing Files

- Change File Attributes—Gets or sets the attributes of the file specified in the user's pathname.
- Close File—Closes the specified handle.
- Close File with FCB—Closes the file pointed to by the user's FCB.
- Create File—Creates and assigns a handle to the file in the user's pathname.
- Create File if Name is Unique—Creates a new file if a file by that name does not exist in the specified directory.
- Create File with FCB—Creates a file in the current directory using the file name in the user's FCB.
- Create Temporary File—Uses the clock device to provide a unique file name and appends it to the pathname provided by the user.
- Delete File—Deletes the directory specified in the user's pathname.
- Delete File with FCB—Deletes a file named in the user's FCB, and removes the specified file from the directory buffer for the drive specified in the user's FCB.
- Duplicate File Handle—Copies the handle of an open file.
- Find First Matching File—Searches the specified or current directory for the first entry that matches the user's pathname.

- Find First Matching File with FCB—Searches the current directory for the first file name matching the file name contained in the user's FCB.
- Find Next Matching File—Searches for the next entry that matches the name and attributes specified in a previous Find First Matching File.
- Find Next Matching File with FCB—Searches for the file named in the user's FCB. The file name was used originally to conduct the "Find First Matching with FCB" function.
- Get File Size with FCB—Returns the size of the file specified in the FCB.
- Lock or Unlock Region of File—Lock (deny access to) or unlock a specified region of a file.
- Match File Handle—Forces a specified handle to refer to the same file as another handle already associated with an open file.
- Move File Pointer—Moves the read/write pointer of the open file associated with the specified handle.
- Open File—Opens a file and assigns it a handle using the file name specified in the user's pathname
- Open File with FCB—Opens the file named in the user's FCB.
- Parse File Name— Searches the specified string for a valid name. If the file name is valid, the function returns a pointer to an unopened FCB.
- Read Block Directly—Reads the record pointed to by the user's FCB Relative-Record field.
- Read Block Sequentially—Reads the next block from the file named in the user's FCB.
- Read from File or Device—Reads from the specified open file handle.
- Read Multiple Blocks Directly—Reads a specified number of records from the file starting at the block named in the user's FCB relative-record field.
- Rename File—Renames the file specified in the user's pathname by changing the directory entry.
- Rename File with FCB—Renames a file in the current directory using the two file names in the user's modified FCB; the first name is the file in the current directory, and the second is the new name for the file.
- Set Relative Record Field—Sets the relative record field in the user's FCB to the value of the current record field in the FCB. The relative record field is used by the Read (or write) Block Directly functions.
- Write Block Directly—Writes the record pointed to by the relative record field (in the user's FCB), to the file named in the user's FCB.
- Write Block Sequentially— Writes to the file named in the user's FCB. The FCB also contains the current block and the record to be written.
- Write Multiple Blocks Directly—Writes a specified number of records to the file named in the user's FCB. The FCB also contains the current relative record number where writing will start.
- Write to File or Device—Writes to the open file associated with the specified handle.

Managing Input and Output

- Check Keyboard Status—Returns a code to indicate if characters are available from standard input.
- Display Character—Sends the specified character to standard output.

- Display String—Sends the specified string to standard output.
- I/O Through Standard Device—Either reads or sends a character to standard input or output, depending on the specified value.
- Input from Auxiliary Device—Waits for a character to be read from standard auxiliary, and returns the character.
- IOCTL—The IOCTL function is a group of 16 related subfunctions that manipulate character and block-device control data. These subfunctions can be used to set or return the attributes of a certain device, send or receive control data with either character or block devices, checks the status of a device, or check if a device or file handle has been redirected with Microsoft Networks.
- Output to Auxiliary Device—Sends the specified character to the standard auxiliary device.
- Print Character—Sends the specified character to the standard printer device.
- Read Keyboard—Waits for a character to be read from the standard input device and returns the character.
- Read Keyboard after Clearing Buffer—First clears the input buffer and then executes the specified function.
- Read Keyboard and Echo—Waits for a character to be read from the standard input device, then echos it to the standard output device and returns the character.
- Read Keyboard to Buffer—Gets a string (terminated with a carriage return) from the standard input device and puts it in the user-specified buffer.

Managing Memory

- Allocate Memory—Attempts to allocate the specified amount of memory to the current process. DOS coalesces unowned blocks, if necessary, to provide enough room for the user's requested block size.
- Change Memory Allocation Block Size—Puts the user's specified block back into the memory pool, coalesces it with other unowned blocks, and then tries to allocate the requested block size; the function returns the size of the resultant block to the user.
- Free Allocated Memory—Releases the specified block of memory.
- Get or Set Memory Allocation Strategy—Gets or sets the strategy used by MS-DOS to allocate memory when a process requests it; the three different strategies are first fit, best fit and last fit.

Controlling Program Flow

- Abort Program—Aborts the current process.
- Check Control-C—Either returns or sets DOS's internal Control-C checking flag; the Control-C is used by DOS to determine before which function requests it should check for a Control-C.
- Create New program Segment Prefix—Creates a new program segment prefix (PSP) at the specified address. (This is an obsolete function except for compatibility with pre-2.0 versions of DOS.)
- Execute program—Loads and executes a program.

- Get Current Program Segment Prefix—Returns the contents of the DOS "Current PSP" variable. (A PSP is a block of memory that immediately precedes a .COM or .EXE program.)
- Get Extended Error Codes—Returns an extended error code for the function that immediately preceded it. The extended error code contains details about the type and location of the error, and the recommended course of action to take when the error occurs.
- Get Interrupt Vector—Returns the address of the specified interrupt handler.
- Get Return Code of Child Process—Returns the exit code specifying the reason for termination, such as normal, Control-C, or critical device error.
- Set Interrupt Vector—Sets the address of the specified interrupt in the Interrupt Vector Table.
- Terminate But Stay Resident—Returns control to the parent process (usually COMMAND.COM), but keeps the current process resident after it terminates.
- Terminates But Stay Resident (*Int.*) —Terminates a program of up to 64K in size, but keeps it in memory. (This interrupt is obsolete.)
- Terminate on Control-C—(*Int.*)—Used by DOS to deal with a control-C being typed on the keyboard.
- Terminate on Fatal Error (*Int.*)—Used by DOS if a critical error occurs during I/O.
- Terminate Process—This is the proper way for a program to terminate when finished.
- Terminate Program (*Int.*)—Terminates the current process and returns control to the parent process. (This is an obsolete interrupt.)

Setting up the Environment

- Get Date—Returns the current system date (year, month, day, and day of the week).
- Get MS-DOS Version Number—Returns the version number of COMMAND.COM.
- Get or Set Country-Dependent Data—Returns the country-dependent information sets the country code using the specified information.
- Get or set File Date or Time—Gets or sets the time and date of the last write to a file, using the specified handles to reference the file.
- Get Time—Returns the current system time.
- Set Date—Set the year, month, and day using the specified information, and updates the DOS clock driver's count of days since January 1st, 1980.
- Set Time—Sets the hour, minutes, seconds, and hundredths of seconds from the specified information, and updates the DOS clock device driver's time information.

DOS 4.0

As Microsoft and IBM introduced OS/2, they expected a major rush of DOS users converting to OS/2. This has occurred, but not quite to the extent envisioned. In fact, millions of users remain committed to DOS, so IBM and Microsoft have provided a steady stream of enhancements to DOS. Many of these are designed to smooth the migration path to OS/2 for users who may eventually wish to convert. The first of these is *DOS 4.0*, released in 1988.

DOS 4.0 is the first DOS operating system to implement IBM's *Common User Access* specification—the user interface component of IBM's System Application Architecture. This is a graphic-oriented user interface that supports windows, menus, and a mouse; it is similar to the Presentation Manager used with OS/2.

Previous versions of DOS supported hard disks up to 32 megabytes; DOS 4.0 extends this limit to 2 gigabytes. FDISK can now create these very large hard disk partitions. DOS 4.0 adds a unique volume serial number to each disk to help users manage their collection of disks; OS/2 does this, too. The *File Allocation Table (FAT)* can be four times the size of that allowed in earlier versions of DOS.

Dos 4.0 supports the LIM expanded memory specification developed by Lotus, Intel and Microsoft; this feature also supported in other recent DOS versions, enables programs to break the 640K memory barrier. Program code must remain in 640K, though data can be in expanded memory. To speed I/O, as many as 10000 buffers may be used; these buffers can be placed in the expanded memory.

The SELECT program enables novices to install DOS 4.0. The TREE command displays the file system directory in a neat graphic format which nicely illustrates hierarchical structure. The MEM utility produces a memory map. The BUFFERS and VDISK commands now also work with various forms of expanded memory not provided by IBM. The /P option may be used with the DEL (or ERASE) command; with this option, the system forces the user to verify each item to be erased.

The "Start Programs" screen appears first when the shell is executed. It enables the user to select various utilities or the File System file handling module. The File System screen shows two windows. The first is a directory tree structure which may be scrolled. The second window lists the current directory's files.

The DOS shell enables users to combine an application with its data so that when a data file is selected, the application automatically becomes active. Selecting a file produced by a word processor, for example, brings up that file opened and ready to be edited using that word processor. This capability (associated with object-oriented programming) is available under OS/2 as well.

The Future of MS-DOS and OS/2

This chapter has presented the evolution and details of the most widely used series of operating systems in the history of computing. In its earliest implementations, MS-DOS was a small, simple system with primitive capabilities. But its recent versions are large, complex, and extremely powerful. When it first appeared, MS-DOS provided an acceptable system for an incidental market for IBM. Today, it is a main-line system that has had a significant impact on IBM's planning for its hardware, software and communications systems designs for the 1990s. Microsoft and IBM have developed a strong partnership devoted to evolving MS-DOS and OS/2 as the standards of the IBM-compatible personal computing industry. The UNIX and Macintosh operating systems have their large and loyal followings. Can all these standards prosper? Will one of them displace the others and dominate the marketplace, or will they all merge to produce one system that will satisfy the requirements of today's diverse user communities? We may have to wait until the mid 1990s to answer these questions. In the interim, personal computer users continue to benefit by the increasingly powerful, more user-friendly, and lower-cost systems produced in this intensely competitive environment.

Case Study 3

OS/2

Introduction

Microsoft had already developed the XENIX operating system, a UNIX-like system licensed from AT&T, when IBM originally approached Microsoft to produce a new operating system for the IBM PC XENIX was too large and powerful for the 8086/8088-based processors of the PC (which did not offer memory management and memory protection hardware), so Microsoft had to develop a simpler operating system.

Microsoft bought the rights to SCP-DOS, developed by Tim Paterson at Seattle Computer Products and used this CP/M-80 clone as the basis of *MS-DOS version 1.0* for the IBM PC, introduced in 1981.

MS-DOS version 2.0 was released in 1983 to support the hard-disk IBM PC XT. The primary innovation was a tree-structured *hierarchical file system.*

MS-DOS version 3.0 appeared with the IBM PC AT in 1984. The AT uses an Intel 80286 microprocessor, which provides extended addressing capability and *protected mode* for running multiuser operating systems (and ensuring that users don't interfere with one another). But MS-DOS 3.0 simply runs the microprocessor in 8086 emulation mode (*real mode*) so that the 80286 functions merely as a more powerful 8086.

Microsoft created a real mode multitasking operating system called *MS-DOS version 4.0.* This system was designed for the 8086 and therefore had only one 640KB storage area to hold all processes. Because the 8086 lacks protected mode, processes can collide and destroy one another. Therefore version 4.0 was not a useful general-purpose multiuser operating system. It is important to note here that there is some confusion about the name MS-DOS 4.0.The system we mentioned here was never released in the United States. But a different MS-DOS version 4.0 has subsequently been released to enhance support for MS-DOS users; this new version is described in the MS-DOS case study.

Microsoft and IBM entered into a joint agreement in 1985 to develop a general-purpose multitasking operating system that would take advantage of the protected mode of the 80286, which provides secure environments for separate processes. This product was renamed *DOS version 5.0* and then *CP/DOS*; its name was eventually changed to OS/2.

The initial version of OS/2 was the standard edition version 1.0 which included a text-oriented interface similar to that of MS-DOS. This edition utilized the features of the Intel 80286 microprocessor and run on the Intel 80386 (Mc88) (Da89) as well, but it did not use the more advanced features of the 80386 Standard edition 1.1 was eventually released and included a graphical interface called the *Presentation Manager* Extended edition 1.0, also with a text-oriented interface, included the *Communications Manager* and the *Database Manager*; it, too, was replaced with a version, extended edition 1.1 which included the Presentation Manager. The extended edition provides connectivity to the IBM product line and to IBM's *SQL relational database* standard. We refer to MS-DOS as DOS from this point in the text.

Design Overview

The major goals of OS/2's designers were to create an ideal office automation operating system, provide device-independent graphics drivers, allow applications to have direct access to high-bandwidth peripherals, provide multitasking, provide a customized environment for each program and its descendants, and provide a protected environment to ensure system stability.

Graphical display devices that can be used with PS/2s already exist in wide varieties and the technology is evolving quickly, so OS/2 is designed to control displays in a device-independent fashion. Device-specific code is handled in *device drivers* for the various kinds of devices; adding a new type of display device requires adding a corresponding new device driver to hide from the operating system the details of controlling the screen.

OS/2 uses *preemptive scheduling;* it can take the CPU away from one process and give it to another it considers more important. OS/2 supports *virtual memory* management so that each user controls its own private address space. Virtual address spaces may be much larger than available real storage. It reclaims memory no longer needed by a process so that this memory can be given to other processes. OS/2 manages *memory overcommit*; it allows a set of programs to run even if the total memory requirements (within reasonable limits) are larger than the real memory of the computer.

The early versions of OS/2 (designed primarily for the 80286 microprocessor environment) use pure *segmentation*; later versions based on the 80386 microprocessor will use *paging*.

OS/2 *uses the least-recently-used (LRU) segment replacement algorithm* for choosing segments to swap to secondary storage to make room for incoming segments. Managing swapping carefully is important; if OS/2 were to allow the swap space in secondary storage to become full, a deadlock could occur if primary memory became full and a segment had to be swapped out to make room for an incoming segment.

OS/2 protects applications from one another and from damaging the operating system. Protection is especially critical in computer networks in which large numbers of users interact through the network OS/2 uses the *ring protection mechanism* of the 80286. Applications run in *ring 3* (nonprivileged), the kernel and device drivers run in *ring* 0 (privileged), and certain routines requiring *I/O privilege* run in *ring 2.* A program in any ring has access to data in that ring or in higher numbered rings.

In a single-tasking environment, a program must include all the capabilities it needs that are not directly provided by the operating system. This tends to encourage the growth of large, complex programs. In a multitasking OS/2, it is better to build smaller programs, each which performs one function or a related set of functions well, and then have these programs intercommunicate to accomplish the user's goals. This is sometimes referred to as the *software tools* approach.

The conventional *device driver* model used in OS/2 can be too slow for devices that require high-speed interaction, particularly when passing relatively small amounts of information each time. OS/2 allows applications to directly access a device's *I/O ports* and its *device memory* (if it has any); such access, however, is allowed in a carefully controlled manner, through the *I/O privilege mechanism.*

It is essential that new generations of hardware and software be compatible with existing widely used hardware and software if vendors want users to upgrade. The user investment in hardware and software is generally too large for an installation to start from scratch each time a new generation appears. OS/2 therefore was designed to be compatible with the 8086/8088 architectures used in the early IBM PC models, and with the 80286 architecture made prevalent with the IBM PC AT models. It is also compatible with DOS (Gi87).

The 80286 architecture was designed to provide compatibility with 8086/8088 computers, but it did this in a manner that was eventually "corrected" by the 80386 architecture, as will soon be explained *Real mode* (also called *compatibility mode*) on the 80286 runs program exactly the same as they run on the 8086/8088, except faster. But the 80286 was designed to support multitasking, and this requires the use of *protect mode*. So the 80286 can either run as a fast 8086/8088 or a multitasking 80286, but it *was not designed to switch back and forth between the two modes.* The 80286 starts in real mode and can be switched into protect mode, but it cannot be switched back. OS/2 was designed to allow a single machine to run both modes and switch easily and efficiently back and forth between the modes in spite of limitations in the 80286 hardware; later in this case study we'll see how designers attacked this difficult problem.

DOS programs assume that they can access all of memory. If they are not currently using all the memory they can ask for more, and such additional requests within the limits of available memory cannot be refused. Because there are no other users on the system, the one user is guaranteed to receive the additional memory, and therefore users rarely provide for handling a "request denied" possibility. But requests can be denied in OS/2 since a request for memory returns what is available at that moment; before a program can actually obtain the memory, another user may grab it.

OS/2 provides a *file locking* capability to prevent users from clashing during concurrent file references. An application attempting to reference a locked file receives an indication that the file is locked and acts accordingly, probably retrying the request later. In real mode applications, users never expect to receive such errors so they rarely provide for handling them. OS/2 thus expects that DOS users will not take the proper actions, so it has to decide what is best in each case.

It is possible to write *downward compatible* programs under OS/2 that will run directly on a DOS version 3.X system. This is important for software developers making major investments in new products; it enables them to ensure a large marketplace for their products. Downward compatibility is facilitated by the *family applications program interface (family API),* which has been incorporated into OS/2. The family API provides an environment comfortable for both DOS 3.X program and OS/2 programs; it consists of a subset of OS/2 calls (the full set being the *applications programming interface or API)* that will also work in DOS. Users who write to the family API are assured that their programs will run on both OS/2 systems and DOS systems. A program may call the system function *DosGetMachineMode* to determine whether it is running *DOS mode or OS/2 mode*; based on this it can determine whether to limit itself to the family API calls or the full set of OS/2 API calls.

OS/2 is intended to run in networked environments in which OS/2 machines intercommunicate flexibly and easily with DOS machines, and in which multiple versions of OS/2 may be present at once. A program may determine the OS/2 version number by calling *DosGetVersion*.

In OS/2, an application may not access or modify another application's memory. The execution of one application will not affect the proper operation of another. When errors of happen, OS/2 localizes them to avoid disrupting other aspects of the system. It also helps the user determine the source of the error. No program may individually crash the system, or cause any *screen group* other than its own to fail.

Multitasking

In multitasking operating systems more than one program may operate at once. Users may switch between applications. OS/2 provides for *multiple thread execution* (Pe88b). Each *thread* is an active path through a program. OS/2 threads are similar to lightweight processes as used in Sun's UNIX there may be several threads per process, and each of these threads shares the process's address space. The OS/2 scheduler is priority-based and preemptive. Processes have priorities. The CPU is always assigned to the highest priority thread that is ready to run.

Under DOS, the user essentially runs a single task or process. OS/2, however, provides three forms of multitasking. The user may run several different *sessions*—also called *screen groups*. Each screen group may have several *processes*. Each process may have several *threads*. A new session may be started with the START command. In a sense, each screen group may be considered a virtual compute with its own keyboard and its own screen. Processes and threads are forms of multitasking that the programmer controls. Screen groups are controlled by the user. The *foreground session* is the one in control of the keyboard and the screen; any other sessions are called *background sessions*.

OS/2 assigns a unique *process identification (PID)* to each process. A parent process has no way to tell if its children create their own descendants. Therefore, a parent that wants to know if the task to be performed by a child is finished cannot determine this because even though the parent can ask if the child is still alive, the child could in fact have delegated its work to descendants and then terminated itself.

When a parent creates child, the parent is informed of the child's PID. This may be treated as a *command subtree* ID that identifies the entire tree of processes for which the child is the *root process*. Various OS/2 functions can either work with PIDs or with command subtrees. With a PIDs,only that one process is affected with a command subtree form, the named process and its entire set of descendants is affected.

OS/2 uses *file handles* as do the more recent versions of DOS. OS/2 returns a unique 16-bit integer file handle whenever a process opens a file. The process then passes that value to OS/2 to identify the file for which it wishes to do input or output. Handles are also used when a program creates a *semaphore*; the program uses the handle in subsequent *semaphore request and semaphore release* calls. Handle references are much faster than using long text names. There are three standard handles; normally all OS/2 programs read their inputs from *STDIN* (*standard input*), write their output to *STDOUT* (*standard output*), and list their errors on *STDERR* (*standard error*). Programs inherit these handles automatically; they do not need to open them. Opening is normally done with *DosOpen*, reading with *DosRead*, and writing with *DosWrite*.

Named pipes were not provided in OS/2 version 1.0. A process that opens an *anonymous pipe* (unnamed pipe) receives a file handle for reading from the pipe (with *DosRead*), and another file handle for writing to the pipe. Data written to a pipe is stored in RAM (so reading and writing is much faster than with disk files), and is accessed FIFO. When a parent process creates a child process, the child inherits open pipe handles; the child can pass information to the parent by writing to the pipe, and the parent can read from it. OS/2 is like UNIX in the sense that pipes, files, and devices operate in a similar manner with similar calls.

Processes

The *DosExecPgm* call is used to execute a child process. The *exec* function in DOS simply loads a file, but with the OS/2 *dynamic linking* facility things become more complex. An application may reference many dynamic link libraries and these, in turn, may reference others. On an error return from *DoExecPgm,* OS/2 explicitly returns the name of the object causing the trouble such as a missing or defective dynamic link library, or some other load object.

DosExecPgm allows the caller to specify execution options such as

- The child program should be executed *synchronously*, i.e., the thread issuing the call suspends execution until the child terminates. This is most like the DOS method of handling *exec* and is provided to facilitate DOS 3.X to OS/2 conversions; this option should generally be avoided in the development of new OS/2 applications.
- The child program should be executed *asynchronously*, i.e., the calling thread returns immediately the child process is created and proceeds independently. When the child terminates, no return codes are supplied. This form of the call is used when it is desired to create a child to perform a certain task, but when the calling thread is not particularly interested in the result of the child's execution.
- The child program should be executed asynchronously, and on return the child's exit code should be saved for examination by *DosCWait* so that it can be determined if the child process succeeded or failed.
- The child process may be examined or modified by a debugger such as *CodeView* which uses the *DosPTrace* function to control the process or to *peek* (view) or *poke* (modify) it.
- The child process should be executed asynchronously, and it should be detached from the parent process (thus running as an orphan). This *DosExecPgm* option is most commonly used to create background *daemon* programs that do not interact with the user.
- The child process is loaded into memory in a suspended state, and does not execute until it is "thawed out" by the session manager.

DosCWait enables a parent process to determine when a child process has completed and whether its operation was successful. A child process may create its own children and so on. Therefore, if a parent wants to know that all the work being done by a child has finished, it should use the *command subtree option* of *DosCWait*. Also, one parent process may have many children to monitor. *DosCWait* may be used to monitor an individual child process, or it may be used to monitor the entire command subtree with a given child at its root. The functionality provided here is similar to that in UNIX.

OS/2 provides an environment in which processes, even parents and children, are quite independent of one another. A parent exercises only limited control over its command subtrees; it can either adjust their CPU priorities, or it can kill (terminate) them. A parent may wish to terminate a child prematurely as a result of a user command or in response to the user typing Ctrl-Break. *DosKillProcess* can terminate a process, or it can terminate a process and each of its descendant processes. Each process terminates only when all its threads have returned from there system calls. Calls such as "read a keyboard character," which might require a great deal of time to complete, are automatically aborted by the system to facilitate rapid termination.

A child process inherits the priority of its parent; the parent may change the child's priority with a system call, and should do so with the command subtree option.

Threads

The path of execution of the CPU through the instructions of a program is called a *thread of execution*. OS/2 allows for the simultaneous presence of many threads of execution in an application. In systems with multiple CPUs, many threads may be truly active at once. With single CPU systems, it is still reasonable to have multiple threads of execution. Multiuser systems certainly support multiple treads in a system-wide sense, but OS/2 actually supports multiple threads per process.

In OS/2, processes own resources (such as memory, files, system semaphores, pipes and queues), and every thread within a process shares all that process's resources. Threads have some private data such as their own copies of the CPU registers.

A process's first thread is created automatically by OS/2 when the process is created; additional threads are created with the *DosCreateThread* call. All a process's threads are siblings on an equal basis; there are no parent/child relationship among threads regardless of which create which. *DosGetPID* retrieves various identification information for the calling thread, namely the current thread ID, the current process ID, and the parent's process ID.

The first thread created for a process is called *thread 1* and it has some special properties. Threads can be created and destroyed faster than processes. It is easy to share data between the threads of a process because they all share the memory of the parent process. The thread is the dispatchable unit of execution and has priority associated with it.

There is a separate stack area for each thread. OS/2 automatically provides the stack area for thread 1, but the caller of *DosCreateThread* must provide a process memory area for the stack space for the new thread. Unfortunately, this memory is accessible and modifiable by all threads so the programmer must be careful to prevent threads from modifying these stack areas inadvertently. Because stacks can grow arbitrarily large, they can exceed the designated segment size, causing a *stack fault* and consequent thread termination.

Programmers in an OS/2 environment use threads for a variety of reasons. A common application is to provide one thread for *foreground* work, which controls interaction with the user, and another thread to control *background* work, which performs the bulk of the work in support of the user's application. Modifiable data structures accessed by multiple threads in the same process need to be protected by RAM semaphores to prevent indeterminate results.

Threads provide a convenient way to handle portions of a job that are most naturally handled asynchronously. For example, a thread may be assigned the job of periodically backing up critical information automatically; it can call *DosSleep* to rest for a designated time interval, be awakened, perform its backups, and then sleep again. A thread should be used to avoid the need for high-overhead polling loops; it can go blocked waiting for an event to occur and be awakened when the event occurs. A *server* process can use multiple threads to monitor and perform the services being requested by multiple *client* processes.

Software engineering has become increasingly important as programs have grown in size and complexity. Most programs in use today are sequential rather than parallel in nature. But, as solving problems with inherent parallelism becomes more common, structuring parallel programs to make them more reliable, maintainable, and likely to be correct on the first try becomes increasingly difficult with sequential programming languages. Multiple-thread programming makes it convenient to mirror the structure of a parallel problem with parallel programming. This promotes ease of programming, ease of design, and maintainability. Parallel problems can certainly be solved with sequential programming languages that provide the ability to poll and detect the occurrence of parallel events, but these programs tend to be complex and difficult to debug.

Uncontrolled common access to shared information can cause indeterminate results. We repeatedly emphasized that no assumptions may be made about the relative speeds of asynchronous concurrent processes (or threads). Therefore it is essential that threads use semaphores or other means to avoid simultaneous access to shared data (when one or more of the threads is updating the data).

When multiple threads need to access shared data, possibly for updating, the shared data access should be included in a critical section protected by RAM semaphores to ensure that only one thread at a time accesses the data.

One way to guarantee the integrity of shared data in a critical section within a process is to suspend all other threads that might want to enter the section; this can be done with successive calls to *DosSuspendThread.* This, of course, requires that the thread about to enter a critical section knows the identities of the other threads that might want to enter their own critical sections. *DosSuspendThread* can only suspend other threads that belong to the same process. A suspended thread is resumed with *DosResumeThread.* Normally, critical sections within a process should be protected with RAM semaphores rather than with *DosSuspendThread.*

DosSuspendThread suspends one thread. *DosEnterCritSec* suspends all a process's threads except for the one calling *DosEnterCritSec*; this process may then enter a critical section. Note that *DosEnterCritSec* is not quite the same as the ENTERMUTUALEXCLUSION call which only suspends other threads as they attempt to enter their critical sections. *DosExitCritSec* resumes only threads that *DosEnterCritSec* suspended; it does not resume threads suspended by *DosSuspendThread.* A weakness of using *DosEnterCritSec* is that a process could be suspended while in a critical section.

Threads can die or be killed by an external event. A thread terminates itself (dies) by calling *DosExit.* A thread terminates all threads belonging to its process by calling *DosExit* and specifying the "exit entire process" option; application threads are terminated immediately, while threads executing system calls are terminated at appropriate points in their execution, possibly not immediately. If a single thread remains in a process and that thread calls *DosExit*, the entire process is terminated.

Scheduling

There is considerable overhead associated with creating and maintaining processes; threads are intended to be a low overhead means for implementing parallelism within a process.

OS/2 assigns priorities to each thread and runs the highest priority, ready-to-run thread. The OS/2 scheduler is *preemptive*; if a higher-priority thread becomes ready to run, then the CPU will be taken away (preempted) from a lower priority thread immediately, and given to the higher-priority thread.

The highest priority thread run for as long as it wants to, or until its time slice expires. Then the next highest priority thread executes A blocked process that becomes ready to run gets the CPU if its priory is higher than the running process. The scheduler causes threads, not processes, to be dispatched; but all threads of a process have the same priority. Most threads run in the *general priority* (or *regular*) category in which they are categorized as either *interactive*, *foreground*, or *background*.

OS/2 is more concerned with optimizing response than it is with optimizing through-put. A process that controls a screen group not being displayed is a background process; background is the lowest of the general priorities. A foreground thread always gets the CPU first; background threads execute only when there are no active foreground threads. If a foreground thread becomes ready to run while a background thread is operating, the CPU is preempted and given to the foreground thread.

OS/2 tends to increase the priority of I/O-bound processes and decrease the priority of CPU-bound processes to ensure good device utilization while keeping CPU-bound jobs progressing. But OS/2 will not allow any background thread to attain a higher priority than any foreground thread.

Some applications, because of their nature, are *time critical*; they need to run at high priorities possibly contrary to the normal priority allocation algorithms (Le88). A print spooler ideally wants to keep the printer going at full speed; printers don't use much CPU time anyway, so giving the printer high priority rarely impacts the progress of other threads. Networks need to respond quickly to network events or possibly lose information. Identifying a thread as time critical can affect the response to other threads, so this designation should be used with care. It is important to try to keep the interactive process serviced at top speed. Ready-to-run time-critical threads are given priority over *regular* threads and *idle-time* threads. Threads of equal priority are scheduled round robin.

Normally, a thread inherits the priority of its creator. The intent of future releases of OS/2 is to give processes in the general priority category *base priorities* (Le88). New threads will inherit the base priorities of their creators. All a process's threads in the general priority category will be expressed relative to that process's base priority. If the process's base priority changes, then the priorities of all its threads change accordingly. Time-critical threads and low-priority threads are not affected by changes in their process's base priority. A process may alter its own priority, the priorities of its threads, or the priorities of its descendant processes either *DosSetPrty*; the priority of a process or thread is determined with *DosGetPrty*.

Dynamic Linking

Dynamic linking enables a program to call a subroutine that has not been linked into its executable image. OS/2 resolves the references automatically at either load time or run time. *Dynamic link libraries (DLLs)* contain many common subroutines, especially the huge number that support OS/2's applications programming interface (API).

In *static linking*, external references are fully resolved at link time prior to loading or running the program. With dynamic linking, references to DLLs are not fully resolved by combining the code, but instead a *dynamic link reference* is included in the .EXE file (Pe88c). This informs the loader where to find the missing code (the DLL) when the linked program is loaded. This is called *load-time dynamic linking*, and it requires the references a program will make to be clear when the program is written and translated.

Dynamic linking delays binding until after the initial linking process. Unresolved external references are resolved either at load time or at run time.

A real advantage to dynamic linking over static linking is that it is much easier to incorporate new versions of subroutines. With static linking, each new version requires relinking. With dynamic linking, new versions are simply incorporated into the dynamic link libraries without any need to change the applications programs. Dynamic linking makes it easy to extend the operating system; software developers can write DLL packages without having to directly modify the operating system. This is in line with the philosophy of an *open systems architecture.*

With run-time dynamic linking, programs need not know in advance of execution the names of all the dynamic link packages they'll need. Of course, as systems become more complex and more dynamic it becomes increasingly difficult for programmers to have this information or even to predict it reliably. With run-time dynamic linking, programs determine what dynamic link packages they'll need as they execute; only the needed packages are then made available.

DosLoadModule loads a dynamic link module and returns a module handle. This handle is given to *DosFreeModule* to free the module so its memory can be released, to *DosGetProcAddr* to determine procedure addresses in the module, or to *DosGetModName* to determine the fully-qualifies module name including the drive, path filename, and extension of the module in the file system. *DosGetModHandle* returns a handle to a dynamic link module if, in fact, that module is loaded.

The File System

The initial release of OS/2, version 1.0 included a file system quite similar to that in DOS in an effort to preserve compatibility with DOS and facilitate the gradual transition to OS/2.

OS/2 provides asynchronous I/O accessible through the functions *DosReadAsync* and *DosWriteAsync*. These are similar to *DosRead* and *DosWrite* with the exception that they return to the caller immediately rather than waiting for the call to complete. Both asynchronous I/O operations require as an argument a semaphore that is cleared upon I/O completion. Process threads can wait for operation completion or they can check the semaphore for completion. The *DosMuxSemWait* call is used to wait on multiple semaphore events.

OS/2 also offers *extended partitioning*, which allows it to view a hard disk as several smaller hard disks each containing a FAT (file allocation table) and a full file system.

A volume is a nonremovable disk in a disk drive, or a removable disk in a disk drive. To prevent duplication of volume IDs, OS/2 checksums the user-supplied name, combines this with the seconds since 1980, and uses this as a seed for a random number generator, which then returns a random number up to four billion. This helps ensure that created volumes are unique. OS/2 provides blocking and deblocking for disk I/O requests.

OS/2 uses common naming conventions for objects such as files, system semaphores, named shared memory, named pipes and so on. DOS uses file names of as many as eight characters followed by a period followed by an extension of up to three characters. OS/2 uses installable file systems (IFSs) rather than a built-in-file system. In a sense, an IFS is like a device driver in that it is loaded at boot time. An IFS provides the code it takes to control a complete file system on a device, including all common file system management takes such as creating and maintaining file directories, allocating space on disks, and so on. An IFS communicates with OS/2 across a standard interface. By using names in the "8.3 format" of DOS (i.e., a file name as long as 8 characters, followed by a period, followed by file extension as long as 3 characters), applications can ensure compatibility with future versions of OS/2. In future versions of OS/2, access permissions will be included in the file system name space along with other security features.

Memory Management Technique

The OS/2 *memory manager* allocates physical memory and virtual memory to processes DOS is a real memory, single-process operating system. OS/2 is a virtual memory, multiple-process operating system with multiple protected address spaces. Every memory reference results in a *segment selector* reference. The segment selector references an entry in either the *GDT* (*global descriptor table*) or the *LDT* (*local descriptor table*). A memory location can only be referenced after it has been described in an LDT or GDT entry; the selector for that entry must be loaded into one of the four *segment registers.*

OS/2 protects processed from interfering with one another. Programs in OS/2 may access memory only through the LDT or the GDT. Segment descriptors in these tables contain both the physical address of each segment and the segment length. Programs are prevented from attempting to execute portions of a data segment. Programs may not write in procedure segments.

In DOS, programs may *hook* interrupt vectors by replacing the addresses of interrupt handlers with addresses in the program; OS/2 prohibits this because it could corrupt the security of the multitasking environment.

OS/2 processes cannot directly call into ROM BIOS code. Application programs cannot execute in ring 0 (privileged mode).

OS/2 supports both *named shared memory* and *giveaway shared memory.* For each type, the shared entity is a segment. No names are assigned to giveaway shared segments. Access is granted only to an intended process with no chance that unauthorized processes can reference the segment. Giveaway shared memory segments may be created faster than named shared memory segments.

The maximum segment size on the 80286 processor is 64K; this problem goes away with the enormous capacities of the 80386. OS/2 provides a capability called *huge segments* to enable users to create and manipulate segments larger than 64K. A huge segment may consist of several 64K segments plus a last segment of 64K or smaller. Huge segments are created with the *DosAllocHuge* call; they may be made larger or smaller via the *DosReallocHuge* call.

OS/2 File System Calls

DosBufReset	Commit File's Cache Buffers
DosChDir	Change Current Directory
DosChgFilePtr	Change (Move) File Read/Write Pointer
DosClose	Close File Handle
DosDelete	Delete File

(contd.)

DosDevConfig	Get Device Configuration
DosDevIOCtl	I/O Control for Devices
DosDupHandle	Duplicate File Handle
DosFileLocks	File Lock Manager
DosFindClose	Close Find Handle
DosFindFirst	Find First Matching File
DosFindNext	Find Next Matching File
DosMkDir	Make subdirectory
DosMove	Move a File
DosNewSize	Change File size
DosOpen	Open File
DosPhysicalDisk	Partitionable Disk Support
DosQCurDir	Query Current Directory
DosQCurDisk	Query Current Disk
DosQFHandState	Query File Handle State
DosQFileInfo	Query File Information
DosQFileMode	Query File Mode
DosQFSInfo	Query File System Information
DosQHandType	Query Handle Type
DosQVerify	Query Verify Setting
DosRead	Read from File
DosReadAsync	Asynchronous Read from File
DosRmDir	Remove Subdirectory
DosSearchPath	Search Path for File Name
DosSelectDisk	Select Default Drive
DosSetFHAndState	Set File Handle State
DosSetFileInfo	Set File Information
DosSetFileMode	Set File Mode
DosSetFsInfo	Set File System Information
DosSetMaxFH	Set Maximum File Handles
DosSetVerify	Set/Reset Verify Switch
DosWrite	Synchronous Write to File
DosWriteAsync	Asynchronous Write to File

Fig. CS3.1. OS/2 file system calls.

OS/2 ordinarily allocates memory in segments, but it has the capability to allocate portions of segments via its *memory suballocation* facility. This enables the system to satisfy frequent requests for small amount of memory more efficiently than is possible through the system's standard segment allocation procedures, which incur substantial overhead. *DosSubSet* initializes a segment for suballocation, or increases the size of a suballocated segment. *DosSubAlloc* suballocates memory within a segment; *DosSubFree* frees suballocated memory. It is important to note that the 80286 is segment based, but the 80386 supports paging and segmentation.

Swapping is performed by segment; a process may lose its segments to secondary storage as the space they occupy is demanded by the system. A process runs smoothly as long as it references in-memory segments. When an out-of-memory segment is referenced, a *segment fault* occurs, requiring a delay as the required segment is read in from disk, and possibly an additional delay as one or more segments are swapped out to make room for the incoming segment. OS/2 swaps out the *least-recently-used* (*LRU*) segment (or segments) to make room for an incoming segment. The early releases of OS/2 swap by segment; later releases based on the 80386 processor will use paging. The priorities or processes or threads are not considered by the swapping algorithm; once a process is marked to be swapped it is equally eligible with all such marked processes to be swapped Certain portions of system code cannot be swapped for efficiency and response reasons, or because swapping is simply not possible, such as with real mode code.

Memory overcommit occurs when the total size of all current programs is large than real memory; this is normal in virtual storage systems. Managing memory overcommit is important; OS/2 will not initiate another process if the degree of memory overcommit would result in too little RAM to run a swapped-out process or too little disk space to swap out a process to make room for other processes (could this lead to deadlock?).

Every system is different in the sense that the job mix is dependent on the goals and purposes of a particular system. Individual users may deal with inefficient operation by placing fewer demands on the system, or by providing more memory or faster processors to run the desired demand more efficiently.

OS/2 tries to swap out segments that are not needed soon. Because swapping is done by segment, programmers should be careful as they decide what will be included in each segment. If a segment is brought to memory, that segment should ideally contain code likely to be used. Infrequently used error-processing routines should be placed in separate segments from frequently used mainline code. In general, items used together should appear in the same segment; items unlikely to be used together should be in separate segments.

OS/2 provides two special segments, one global and one local, that hold system information. The *global information segment* contains system data such as time and date information; the *local information segment* contains process data. The global information includes *RAS* (*reliability, availability*, and *serviceability*) data that aids in determining and correcting system problems. The local data contains information about processes and threads.

With protect mode, each process has one local descriptor table (LDT) for all its threads. The global descriptor table enables a process to address system-wide information and procedures shared by all processes.

DosAllocSeg allocates a segment of a requested size to a process; the memory is both *movable* (when *compacting* main storage) and *swappable*. Storage compaction and swapping are selectable features that can be disabled when the system is configured. *DosReallocSeg* adjusts the size of an allocated segment; segments can be increased or decreased in size, but shared segments can only be increased. *DosFreeSeg* frees a memory segment (for a shared segment, the *reference count* is reduced; the segment is freed when the count reaches 0).

DosAllocHuge allocates multiple segments of memory to form a *huge segment*; this is a means of overcoming the 80286 limitation of 64K bytes per segment. *DosGetHugeShift* returns the shift value for determining the selectors to access a huge memory area allocated by *DosAllocHuge*. *DosReallocHuge* adjusts the size of a huge memory segment originally allocated by *DosAllocHuge*. *DosMemAvail* determines the size of the largest available memory block.

OS/2 creates an LDT for each application. An entry is made in the LDT for each segment loaded, including segments from dynamic link libraries. Only one copy of any segment is in memory although it may be shared by several applications each with an entry for that segment in its own LDT.

OS/2 allows segments to be any size up to 64K, so as segments are allocated and freed, memory tends to become *fragmented*. When a sufficiently large block of memory is not available to satisfy a request for memory, OS/2 uses *segment motion* to form a large enough block; only when this fails does swapping occur.

Segments may be marked for *demand loading*; this feature is particularly useful for segments that are not likely to be referenced on each execution of a program (such as error routines for obscure errors). Demand-loaded segments are not brought into memory when a program is initially loaded; this conserves memory and enables programs to execute sooner.

The *DosCreateCSAlias* call enables a process to place executable code in a data segment and call this as a code segment This call is used by the debuggers to circumvent protection in the 80286 that disallows modifying code.

OS/2 provides a feature called *discardable segments*. Segments marked as discardable are used to hold objects to be accessed only briefly and which can be recreated quickly. When the system gets low on available memory it reclaims discardable segments. Discardable segments can be swapped or moved. *DosLockSeg* prevents a discardable segment from being discarded; *DosUnlockSeg* makes the segment discardable again.

Interprocess Communication

OS/2 is a multitasking operating system; many processes may be active at once. This section describes how processes communicate through OS/2's *interprocess communication (IPC)* facilities. OS/2 provides a variety of means for interprocess communication including *signals, pipes, queues, semaphores*, and *shared memory*. Applications use calls to create semaphores, pipes, and queues; these calls return unique handles to be used in calls that manipulate and eventually destroy the created objects.

Shared Memory

Shared memory is implemented in two ways, namely with *giveway shared memory* or with *named shared memory*. With *giveaway shared memory* the owner awards access to another process. To use giveaway shared memory, a process creates a segment with *DosAllocSeg*, and informs the system (via *DosGiveSeg*) of the segment selector and the intended sharer's process ID. The system returns the segment selector to be used by the intended sharer; the process granting access then passes this selector to the share via an interprocess communication mechanism. The intended sharer then accesses the segment by providing this selector in the *DosGetSeg* call.

A named shared segment is created with *DosAllocShrSeg*; the process supplies the name and the desired segment size, and a segment selector is returned. The segment name must begin within \SHAREMEM\. The sharer requests access via *DosGetShrSeg* by supplying the segment name given to the process when it was created.

Semaphores

Semaphores are normally used to ensure mutual exclusion. OS/2 supports *RAM semaphores* and *system semaphores* RAM semaphores are four-byte data structures intended for use by the threads of one process. A RAM semaphore is claimed with a test-and-set operation. The handle for a RAM semaphore is the address of its double word in the local address space of the process.

When several processes are involved, system semaphores are needed to ensure integrity. System semaphores have their data structures in system memory rather than in the address spaces of processes, so accessing system semaphores is slower because the operating system boundary must be crossed and this is a relatively time-consuming operation.

The *DosCreateSem* call creates a system semaphore and returns a *semaphore handle*. Each subsequent semaphore call requires a semaphore handle as an argument. A system semaphore is opened by the *DosOpenSem* call (RAM semaphores have no explicit open). A RAM semaphore must be in shared memory segment; it is initialized simply by zeroing its memory.

Semaphores are normally used to protect critical sections. To use a critical section, the process first calls *DosSemRequest*. This call returns when it has claimed the semaphore and then the process can proceed. After accessing the critical section, the process should call *DosSemClear* to release the semaphore and allow threads waiting on it to proceed. A weakness of this scheme is that a process may indeed access a critical resource without first claiming the semaphore; a process may do this maliciously or even accidentally.

Many threads can be waiting on a semaphore; when the semaphore becomes available, the thread with the highest CPU priority gets it.

Semaphores may also be used to signal threads that events have occurred. With the *DosMuxSemWait* call, a process may wait on several events and be awakened whenever any of them occurs.

DosSemClear releases the semaphore; any blocked threads waiting on the semaphore can proceed. *DosSemSet* sets a semaphore to *owned*; it is most often used in signalling situations in which a blocked thread is to be awakened when a semaphore is cleared. *DosSemWait* waits for a semaphore to be cleared. *DosSemSetWait* sets a semaphore and then waits for it to be cleared. *DosMuxSemWait* waits for any of several semaphores to clear. *DosCreateSem* creates a system semaphore, *DosOpenSem* opens it, and *DosCloseSem* closes it.

One problem with semaphores is that they are sometimes not released and thus left "orphaned," a situation that could lead to deadlock among processed still dependent on being able to claim the semaphores before entering their critical sections. This can occur in several ways

- A signal handler may fail to return to the point at which a thread was interrupted by a signal. This may prevent the semaphore from being released.
- A process that has set a semaphore may be killed.
- A process can incur a fatal error.
- A process may simply malfunction because of a logic bug.

A process can use *DosHoldSignal* to prevent a signal from preempting the processor while the process is in a critical section, but this technique does not preclude all possible causes of preemption.

When a process dies, so do its semaphores. When a process owning a system semaphore dies, the next process to use the semaphore receives a message indicating the death of the owner.

Anonymous Pipes

One form of message communication is *anonymous pipes*, which allow processes to communicate in a manner similar to file I/O. Anonymous pipes are used by closely related processes. Anonymous pipes are like UNIX pipes.

An anonymous pipe is created via *DosMakePipe*, which specifies a pipe size up to 64Kb, and which return a *read handle* and a *write handle*. When an anonymous pipe is full, a write waits until space is available; when an anonymous pipe is empty, a read waits until data is available

Processes communicate via anonymous pipes with standard *DosRead* and *DosWrite* calls. Anonymous pipes need not be opened prior to their use; they are closed with *DosClose*. An anonymous pipe is destroyed after all its processes issue *DosClose* calls. Anonymous pipes are maintained in main storage buffers. Data read from a file is still in the file; data read from an anonymous pipe is no longer accessible. A child process inherits access to its parent's pipes; a parent will often communicate with a child over an inherited pipe. One weakness of pipes is that the data being passed is copied from the writer to the pipe and from the pipe to the reader; this multiples copying is inefficient for high volume data transfers. Pipes operate FIFO; the order in which the data is written to the pipe is the order in which it is read from the pipe.

Named Pipes

A *named pipe* is a serial communication channel between processes which use the *DosRead* and *DosWrite* calls to communicate.

Users of a named pipe need to know the name of the pipe but the users need not be related. Named pipes work equally well on a local machine and across a network. When a named pipe is opened, a single handle is returned that may be both read and written.

A named pipe is created with the call *DosMakeNmPipe*. Servers and clients use the *DosConnectNmPipe* call to make the pipe operative; the server issues the call and this enables a client to open the pipe. *DosMakeNmPipe* returns a handle to the server; *DosOpen* returns a handle to the client.

When a process at one end of a pipe closes it, writers receive an error and readers receive an end-of-file indication. The server that sees a client has closed a pipe issues *DosDisconnectNmPipe*.

There are several operations for client processes. *DosTransactNmPipe* is like a *DosWrite* followed by a *DosRead*. On an unopened pipe, *DosCallNmPipe* is equivalent to a *DosOpen*, *DosTransactNmPipe*, and *DosClose*. The *DosCallNmPipe* is like a remote procedure call across a network.

The *DosPeekNmPipe* call can peek at data to be read in the pipe without actually reading the data and removing it from the pipe. A server can use this call to determine if it wants to handle a client's request.

Queues

Queues are also used for interprocess communication. Queues use the file system name space. They pass *messages* rather than stream of bytes. Multiple writers are allowed. Pipes are read FIFO, but queues may be read in various orders. Queues use shared memory so they are faster than pipes for high volume data transfers, but queues do not work across a network. Queues normally require more involved programming than pipes.

Each queue has one owner who creates the queue. The client process must use the calls *DosReadQueue* and *DosWriteQueue*. Each queue has a single owner but may have many clients.

A queue message consists of the message itself, the process ID of the sender, and a word value supplied by the sender to be used by servers and clients as they see fit to facilitate communication.

Queues also contain a *peek* capability. But since queues can be read in a variety of orders, and since higher priority records may arrive, when the queue is *peeked* a value is returned that guarantees the same information will be read by a subsequent *DosReadQueue*.

A queue is created with *DosCreateQueue*, opened with *DosOpenQueue*, and closed with *DosCloseQueue*. An element is added to a queue with *DosWriteQueue*, removed from a queue with *DosReadQueue*, and examined by *DosPeekQueue*. The number of elements in a queue may be determined by *DosQueryQueue*, and all entries may be purged by *DosPurgeQueue*.

Queue elements are message packages. Queue data is stored in shared memory segments, which must of course be accessible to readers and writers. Queues can vary in size and can be quite large because messages need not be confined to a single 64Kb segments as with pipes.

Signals

Signals are a software-initiated asynchronous means of interprocess communication. A signal is the software parallel to a hardware interrupt. OS/2 signals are similar to UNIX signals. As the result of a signal, various application registers are saved to the stack and an appropriate *signal handler* automatically begins executing; the signal handler saves anything else that needs to be preserved.

DosSetSigHandler informs OS/2 that a particular handler is to respond to a particular signal number. The call may also specify that the signal is to be ignored, or that the system's default action should apply.

OS/2 supports three common signals and three general-purpose signals. The common signals are *Ctrl-C (SIGINTR)*, *Ctrl-Break (SIGBREAK)* and *program termination* (*SIGTERM*) (which occurs when a parent process kills a child process with *DosKill*). The general-purpose signals are *process flag A (SIGPFA)*, *process flag B (SIGPFB)*, and *process flag C (SIGPFC);* a process signals a *flag event* in a target process by calling *DisFlagProcess* processes may interpret these flags any way they wish. There are some problems with *DosFlagProcess*: Signals only pass a single word of information beside their number, they can disrupt system calls, and they may arrive faster than they can be serviced and hence can be lost. Processes may install signal handlers to respond to flag signals. A process may send a Ctrl-C or a Ctrl-Break signal to another process via *DosSendSignal*.

An arriving signal interrupts the process's *thread 1* (i.e., the process's primary thread); the process calls the signal handler with an argument provided to it by the sender of the signal. While the signal handler is operating, further signals are blocked to prevent the handler from being reentered.

The signal handler eventually issues a *DosSetSigHandler* call to allow further signals. The *DosHoldSignal* call protects a critical section from being interrupted by a signal.

When a signal to a process occurs, if that process is executing, the signal causes the process to switch to its signal handler immediately. But if another process is running, the signal merely causes the operating system to *post* the signal to the process; the current process is not interrupted, but the next time the signalled process becomes active, the signal causes that process to switch to its signal handler.

Signal handlers run nonprivileged in ring 3. Only thread 1 of a process receives signals and executes signal handlers. Therefore multithreaded applications often dedicate thread 1 to this purpose and use other threads to accomplish most of their work.

Applications can only receive signals after they have indicated their desire to do so. A signal that arrives while thread 1 is in a critical section protected by a semaphore could cause the signal handier to execute; if the handler does not return to the interrupted code, then the semaphore is left on ("orphaned"), which could eventually cause a deadlock.

The Presentation Manage and VIO

Personal computers produced before 1984 generally had text-oriented interfaces that required little CPU support. The development of mouse-oriented, graphics-oriented user interfaces is generally attributed to research work done at Xerox PARC in the 1970s. With the appearance of the Apple Macintosh in January 1984, the industry focused on the advanced capabilities of graphical interfaces. They were faster, easier to learn, more fun to use, and better for novices while simultaneously offering an appropriate interface for experts.

IBM and Microsoft have responded to the success of graphical interfaces with the introduction of the *Presentation Manager* for OS/2. The Presentation Manager is the OS/2 version of enhanced *Microsoft Windows*. It uses windows, menus, buttons, scroll bars, dialog boxes, and other graphics to implement a user-friendly interface. The original Microsoft Windows product used *tiled windows* (displayed side-by-side) rather than *overlapped windows*. The presentation manager may receive its inputs from a mouse, the keyboard, or both.

A graphical interface is far more complex to implement that a text-oriented interface, but the advantages to users are many. OS/2 version 1.1 added over 500 additional function calls to support the graphical interface; about half of these are to control windowing, while most of the rest support the *graphics programming interface (GPI)* which is closely related to IBM's *graphical data display manager (GDDM)*. The Presentation Manager is a complex one for developing new applications.

The Presentation Manager is a key to IBM's *Systems Application Architecture (SAA),* and it could well become the standard graphical interface across all level of IBM mainframes and minicomputers.

OS/2 also provides the *VIO interface*, a character-oriented interface that appears similar to the ROM BIOS video interface. The first release of OS/2 (1.0) included only the VIO interface; the Presentation Manager is included in subsequent releases. The VIO interface and the Presentation Manager are like device drivers. They are device dependent. VIO is character oriented. It is replaceable; VIO-oriented applications may eventually be managed by the Presentation Manager. Users will generally prefer the Presentation Manager to VIO. Applications written for the real mode environment may find the VIO interface preferable. Applications may use the VIO interface in character mode, work around VIO and directly manipulate the screen in either character or graphics mode, or use the Presentation Manager. Background processes do not interact directly with the user. When using VIO, a process is relegated to the background when a user selects another screen group.

Device Monitors

In ensuring compatibility with the huge base of DOS applications programs, the designers of OS/2 decided to include features that would enable programs to examine and modify device data streams. Many DOS programs, for example, hook (edit) interrupt vectors to gain control when a device interrupt comes in; they examine the interrupt and decide if they want to process it for some application-specific reason rather than allowing the interrupt to go directly to DOS. OS/2 includes *device monitors* to provide such capabilities. A *printer spooler*, for example, might use a device monitor to intercept a process's printer output, spool it to disk, and route the data to the printer at an appropriate time.

OS/2 Video Function Calls

VioDeRegister	DeRegister Video Subsystem
VioEndPopUp	Deallocate Pop-Up Display Screen
VioGetAnsi	Get ANSI Status
VioGetBuf	Get Logical Video Buffer
VioGetConfig	Get Video Configuration
VioGetCp	Get Code Page
VioGetCurPos	Get Cursor Position
VioGetCurType	Get Cursor Type
VioGetFont	Get Font
VioGetMode	Get Display Mode
VioGetPhysBuf	Get Physical Display Buffer
VioGetState	Get Video State
VioModeUndo	Restore Mode Undo
VioModeWait	Restore Mode Wait
VioPopUp	Allocate a pop-up Display Screen
VioPrtSc	Print Screen
VioPrtScToggle	Toggle Print Screen
VioReadCellStr	Read Char/Attr String
VioReadCharStr	Read Character String
VioRegister	Register Video subsystem
VioSavRedrawUndo	Screen Save Redraw Undo
VioSavRedrawWait	Screen Save Redraw Wait
VioScrLock	Lock Screen
VioScrollDn	Scroll Screen Down

(contd.)

VioScrollLf	Scroll Screen Left
VioScrollRt	Scroll Screen Right
VioscrollUp	Scroll Screen Up
VioScrUnLock	Unlock screen
VioSetAnsi	Set ANSI On or Off
VioSetCp	Set Code Page
VioSetCurPos	Set Cursor Position
VioSetCurType	Set Cursor Type
VioSetFont	Set Font
VioSetMode	Set Display Mode
VioSetState	Set Video State
VioShowBuf	Display Logical Buffer
VioWrtCellStr	Write Char/Attr String
VioWrtCharStr	Write Character String
VioWrtCharStrAtt	Write Char String with Attr
VioWrtNAttr	Write N Attributes
VioWrtNCell	Write N Char/Attrs
VioWrtNChar	Write N Character
VioWrtTTY	Write TTY String
Vio Functions Supporting the Presentation Manager	
VioAssociate	Associates Vio presentation space with device context
VioCreateLogFont	Creates logical font for use with Vio presentation space
VioCreatePS	Allocates Vio presentation space
VioDeleteSetId	Released logical font identifier
VioDestroyPS	Destroys Vio presentation space
VioGetDeviceCellSize	Returns character cell height and width
VioGetOrg	Returns Screen coordinates for origin of Vio presentation space
VioQueryFonts	Returns list of Available fonts for specified typeface
VioQuerySetIds	Returns list of loaded fonts
VioSetDeviceCellSize	Sets character cell height and width
VioSetOrg	Sets screen coordinates of origin for Vio presentation space
VioShowPS	Updates display from Vio presentation space

Fig. CS3.2. OS/2 video function calls.

OS/2 does not let applications hook interrupt vectors; this could be disastrous in a multitasking system as users could then corrupt the system. A program that wishes to examine and modify a device data stream uses an OS/2 *device monitor* while executing in ring 3; this is done in such a manner that the device driver is aware of the use of the device monitor and grants permission for its use.

A process indicates its intent to be a device monitor first by issuing *DosMonOpen* to obtain a handle for the device, and then by calling the device driver via *DosMonReg*. The process provides a buffer to receive incoming monitor data and another buffer to hold outgoing monitor data. A process can call OS/2 easily, but OS/2 really can't call a process, so it uses an interesting technique to communicate with the process: A monitoring process must call OS/2 via one of its threads immediately after indicating its intent to be a monitoring process; OS/2 holds this thread until data is in the incoming buffer, and then releases the thread to the monitoring process. The device monitor writes outgoing data via *DosMonWrite*. *DosMonClose* terminates device monitoring on a particular device.

Multiple device monitors are allowed for certain devices; OS/2 chains these monitors together so they all see the device data stream. Inefficient monitors, or too many monitors in the chain, could slow a device's throughput. Device monitors should not suspend or block: they must be written and tested carefully to be error-free for obvious reasons.

Data Integrity

OS/2 provides *file sharing* and *record locking* for protecting critical sections that update files and records. File sharing enables the owner to specify if readers are allowed or if writing is allowed. Record locking enables a process to lock out other processes from accessing a range of bytes within the file. The file sharing and record locking features lock out all other processes whether these intend to be cooperative or not (as with semaphores, for example). File sharing and record locking do not provide for blocking until the file or record once again becomes accessible; an application wishing to wait for this can do so with a polling loop (and should use *DosSleep* between polls to reduce wasted CPU time).

OS/2 buffers its data to be written to disk, so when the system crashes it is possible that some data is till in the buffers rather than on the disk. *DosBufReset* immediately writes all buffers with modified data to the disk.

Timer Services

OS/2 provides a number of features that enable applications to monitor real time with reasonable precision. These services in version 1.0 are generally based on a 32Hz periodic clock system interrupt (i.e., that interrupt approximately 30 times per second). This granularity is appropriate for timing human-related events, but is too coarse for timing events occurring at microsecond computer speeds. No matter how fine-grained the timing eventually becomes in future systems, the use of preemptive scheduling means that a thread waiting on a timer event may not run immediately anyway if there are higher priority ready-to-run-threads.

The *DosGetDataTime* call returns the current data and time; these are set with *DosSetDateTime*.

The program may determine the duration of a clock tick by using *DosGetInfoSeg* to gain access to the *global information segment* (which contains this, and other, information of system-wide interest).

DosSleep works synchronously; the thread that calls *DosSleep* is held in the operating system until the time elapses, then the thread is released.

DosTimerAsync works asynchronously. The call takes an interval and a system semaphore handle; it then returns immediately. The system semaphore is cleared when the time has expired.

The process can poll the semaphore to determine if the time has expired, or it can block on the semaphore and wait to be awakened. *DosTimerStart* is similar to *DosTimeAsync*, but it clears the semaphore periodically each time the interval specified in the call elapses; *DosTimerStop* stops the timer (specified by a semaphore handle) that had been started by either of these calls.

Applications that require more precision than these alternatives provide should reference the time values in the global information segment. Applications that need to respond quickly to timeouts should assign a high-priority thread to handling timer events; the bulk of their work should, however, be done by their normal priority threads.

Device Drivers

Device drivers essentially encapsulate their devices (and device-specific information) so that the details of operating the device need not be of concern to a program that simply wants to read data from the device or write data to the device.

Device drivers could be part of the operating system, but this would require new releases of the operating system each time a new device became available. Instead, OS/2 installs device driver at boot time; this makes it easy to incorporate new devices onto an OS/2 system.

Each OS/2 device driver has a *device strategy routine* and *device interrupt routine.* The strategy routine queues the request, and, if the device is available, initiates the I/O; it then returns to the kernel, which blocks the device driver pending I/O completion. The interrupt routine handles the I/O completion interrupt; it keeps the device busy by initiating the next waiting request, it posts the I/O completion, and it unblocks threads waiting on the I/O that has completed.

DOS device drivers return when they have successfully performed their designated function or when an error has occurred. The multitasking nature of OS/2 requires more complex device drivers. Multiple threads can simultaneously call a device driver.

OS/2 is reentrant so that its code may be executed simultaneously by many processes. The OS/2 scheduler will not preempt a thread executing the kernel. Critical sections within the kernel need to be protected, but it is known that preemption will not occur while inside the kernel, so the CPU is lost only on voluntary blocking; this makes protecting critical sections within the kernel easier.

Device drivers are for either *character mode devices or block mode devices.* Character mode devices perform I/O synchronously (in FCFS order); block mode devices can perform the I/O asynchronously (in an order possibly different from that in which the calls were made). Requests to a disk, for example, can be processed in any order; OS/2 block device drivers queue arriving requests and sort the queues to minimize disk head movement.

Device drivers also manage the devices they control. They are called on every open and *close* operation. They can allow processes to access the *I/O ports* and the *mapped memory* of a device directly.

OS/2 device drivers are written in *dual mode* and they are said to be *bimodal*; this means the drivers are designed to execute in real mode or in protected mode.

Hard Errors

Errors such as the user leaving the door open on a floppy disk drive are called *hard errors*; these are not corrected by the system retrying the operation. The single-tasking DOS operating system handles hard errors simply: it suspends operation, displays a message, waits for the user to take an appropriate action, and continues. But OS/2 is a multitasking system that cannot afford to suspend all operations while waiting on a particular process or thread. In DOS it is trivial to identify the process that caused the error because there is only one; in OS/2 it is sometimes difficult to determine the source of the error because any of several processes could have caused it. Also, OS/2 uses buffering techniques that may make a hard error appear when no process is, in fact, doing I/O. An error caused by an application in a screen group other than the one controlling the screen and the keyboard would prevent the application from informing the user of the problem.

OS/2 permanently runs a special process called the *hard error daemon*, which monitors hard errors. When a hard error occurs, the daemon switches to the hard error screen group, which displays an appropriate message and reads inputs. The process with the hard error blocks waiting for the hard error daemon to receive the user's response. The hard error daemon relays the response to the kernel, which allows the thread encountering the error to take the indicated action. That thread retries or generates an appropriate error. The hard error daemon then causes the system to return to the original process in the screen group in which this all began.

There are situations in which an application's hard errors should not be automatically handled by the system. A network server operating in an unattended mode may simply want to send information about a hard error to a remote node rather than hanging indefinitely.

Device Helper Services

Because device drivers execute in the kernel, they cannot use the OS/2 API calls. Instead, they may use a special set of *device helper (DevHlp) routines.* These are interfaces to low-level kernel services for accomplishing device service. A variety of services are provided.

Queue management services enable device drivers to chain I/O request packets into a linked list, and manage circular character buffers used with serial data streams. *Synchronization services* enable device drivers to synchronize their operation with threads. *Memory management services* enable drivers to control memory used in buffers during interrupt handling, and allocate (deallocate) additional memory as needed. *Process management services* enable drivers to block and unblock threads to effect overlapped I/O. *Interrupt management services* enable device drivers to receive device interrupts. *Timer services* enable device drivers to specify routines to handle timer ticks, to adjust the period between timer ticks, and to program for timeouts. *Monitor services* enable character-oriented device drivers to support OS/2 device monitors. A listing of OS/2 DevHlp services, their function codes, and descriptions appears in Fig. CS 3.3.

Device Helper Services

DevHlp Service	Description
System Clock Management	
SchedClockAddr	Get system clock routine
Process Management	
Block	block thread on event

(contd.)

DevDone	Device I/O complete
Run	Unblock thread
TCYield	Yield the CPU to time-critical
Yield	Yield the CPU
Semaphore Management	
SemClear	Release a semaphore
SemHandle	Get a semaphore handle
SemRequest	Claim a semaphore
Request Queue Management	
AllocReqPacket	Get a request packet
FreeReqPacket	Free a request packet
PullParticular	Remove a specific request from list
PullRedPacket	Remove a request from list
PushReqPacket	Add a request to list
SortReqPacket	Insert request in sorted order to list
Character Queue Management	
QueueFlush	Clear character queue
QueueInit	Initialize character queue
QueueRead	Get a character from the queue
QueueWrite	Put a character in the queue
Memory Management	
AllocGDTSelector	Allocate GDT Selectors
AllocPhys	Allocate physical memory
FreePhys	Free physical memory
Lock	Lock segment
PhysToGDTSelector	Map physical to virtual address
PhysToUVirt	Map physical-to-user virtual
PhysToVirt	Map physical-to-virtual address
Unlock	Unlock segment
UnPhysToVirt	Mark Phys To Virt complete
Verify Access	Verify memory access
VirtToPhys	Map virtual-to-physical address
Interrupt Management	
EOI	Issue an End-Of-Interrupt
Set1RQ	Set a hardware interrupt handler
SetROMVector	Set Software interrupt vector
UnSetRQ	Reset a hardware interrupt handler

Timer Services	
ResetTimer	Remove a timer handler
SetTimer	Set a timer handler
TickCount	Modify timer
Monitor Management	
DeRegister	Remove a monitor
MonFlush	Remove all data from stream
MonitorCreate	Create a monitor
MonWrite	Pass data records to monitor
Register	Install a monitor
System Services	
RegisterSatckUsage	Notifies the kernel's interrupt dispatcher of the driver's interrupt-time stack requirements
AttachDD	Obtains inter-driver communication point (IDC) for another driver
GetDOSVar	Return pointer to DOS variable
SendEvent	Indicate an event
ROMCritSection	ROM BIOS critical section
Processor Mode Services	
ProtToReal	Protect Mode to Real Mode
RealToProt	Real Mode to Protect Mode
Advanced BIOS Services	
ABIOSCall	Invoke ABIOS Function
ABIOSCommonEntry	Invoke ABIOS Common Entry Point
FreeLIDEntry	Release Logical ID
GetLIDEntry	Get Logical ID

Fig. CS3.3. Device helper (DevHlp) services.

OS/2 Mouse Support

The mouse is a readonly device that provides the computer with information approximately 30 times per second. The data indicates the position of the mouse on the screen, whether the mouse button is up or down, and the like.

Each time a mouse interrupt arrive, the position of the screen mouse pointer is adjusted if necessary. Commands are available to specify the shape of the mouse printer, to specify a *collision area* where the mouse pointer will not be displayed, and to free a *collision* area. The mouse driver does not manipulate the screen directly to adjust the mouse pointer, rather it calls the screen driver.

Mouse coordinates are relative to (0,0) at the upper left of the screen. In *graphics mode*, the coordinates are in pixels; in *text mode* the coordinates are in character units. Mouse movements may be specified either absolutely or as relative displacements called *mickeys* (honestly!). *Mickeys* are mouse movement units relative to the current mouse position. The mouse may be accessed through the *IOCTL interface* but most applications will generally call the mouse driver.

Mouse events are reported in a data structure containing an event mask identifying the event(s) in the record, the time (in milliseconds since the system was started), the row absolute (or mickeys), and the column absolute. Coordinates are ordinarily reported in pixels or character units, so the *MouSetDevStats* call is used to indicate reporting in mouse Mickey units.

The application supplies the pointer image. Only foreground applications receive mouse events. A device monitor may be used to read and process the mouse events; some applications use this capability to consume, discard, or replace mouse events.

Let's walk through the mouse calls in the Mouse API. Ordinarily, mouse processing is handled by the base mouse subsystem. An alternative handler may be specified via the *MouRegister* call; *MouDeRegister* causes the system to revert to the base mouse subsystem.

MoulnitReal initializes the DOS mode mouse driver. *MouOpen* opens the mouse for the current session and sets its initial state (including, for example, setting the mouse pointer position to the centre of the screen), and *MouClose* closes the mouse for the current session, *MouRemovePtr* defines the *collision area*, an area of the screen reserved for the application; the mouse driver cannot draw pointer images there. *MouDrawPtr* nullifies the collision area and makes the area available to the mouse driver.

Calls may be used to set and to get information. *MouSetPtrPos* sets new coordinates for the mouse pointer. *MouSetPtrShape* sets the mouse pointer shape and size. *MouSetScaleFact* sets the scale factors of mickeys to pixels; this essentially controls the sensitivity of the mouse, determining how fast the mouse pointer moves around the screen in response to the speed at which the mouse device moves. *MouSetDevStatus* sets status flags in the mouse driver (such as specifying that mousse events should report mickeys rather than absolute coordinates). *MouSetEventMask* sets event mask bits to specify which types of mouse events should be reported on the event queue.

MouGetDevStatus reads the mouse driver status flags. *MouGetEventMask* reads the mouse event queue mask. *MouGetNumButtons* determines the number of buttons that the mouse driver supports. *MouGetNumMickeys* determines the number of mouse movement units (mickeys) per centimeter on the screen. *MouGetNumQueE1* returns the current number of mouse events in the event queue and the maximum number allowed. *MouGetPtrPos* determines the current mouse position coordinates. *MouGetPtrShape* returns a copy of the mouse pointer shape. *MouGetScaleFact* determines the row and column coordinates scaling factors.

OS/2 Keyboard Support

Programs may control the keyboard through the keyboard KBD API calls. High-level KBD services are string oriented; low-level KBD services are character oriented.

KbdStringIn reads a character string. *KbdCharIn* reads a single character, *KbdPeek* examines, but does not remove, the character in the keyboard buffer. *KbdFlushBuffer* purges the keyboard buffer, *KbdSetStatus* sets various keyboard parameters such as the keyboard mode to ASCII (senses carriage return then sends data to the program immediately), to BINARY ("raw" input mode which returns data to the program when the buffer is full), or ECHO (which each characters to the display as they are typed). *KbdGetStatus* returns the status settings.

There are various *code page support* calls that enable the user to control international character set options. *KbdSetCP* sets the code page, *KbdGetCP* determines which code page is currently active.

The keyboard generates *scan codes*, which are then translated to various character sets. *KbdSetCustXT* sets a custom translation table. *KbdXlate* translates a single scan code into ASCII.

Users may replace keyboard function calls. *KbdRegister* registers an alternate keyboard subsystem. *KbdDeRegister* causes the base keyboard subsystem to be used.

For each session, a logical keyboard buffer is shared by the applications in the session. *KbdOpen* initializes the logical keyboard. *KbdGetFocus* connects the logical keyboard to the physical keyboard. *KbdFreeFocus* disconnects the logical keyboard from the physical keyboard. *KbdClose* disconnects the application from the logical keyboard. *KbdSync* enables a keyboard subsystem to synchronize its access to the keyboard driver. *KbdSetFgnd* enables a subsystem to increase the priority of the thread handling the foreground keyboard.

Font and Code Page Support

Os. 2 provides font and code page support features to enable OS/2-based computers to handle languages other than English. *DosPFSActivate* is for applications that specify an alternate spooler and perform *code page switching*; it activates a *code page* and font for a specific printer and process. *DosPFSCloseUser* indicates that a process closed the file it was using for spooling. *DosPFSlint* initializes a printer for code page and font switching. *DosPFSQueryAct* returns the code page and font for a printer and process. *DosPFSVerifyFont* determines if a code page and font are available in printer's font file.

DosSetProcCp sets the code page of the calling process. *DosSetCp* sets the code page of the calling process, the sessions display code page, and the keyboard code page; *DosGetCp* queries this information. *DosGetCtryInfo* returns various country-dependent information including code page information. *DosCaseMap* performs case mapping related to specifications in the country mapping file. *DosGetCollate* gets a collating sequence (for sorting purposes) from the country information file. *DosGetDBCSEv* gets the DBCS (double-byte character set) environmental vector from the *country information file*; the double-byte Pairs provide for the wide variety of character used in various international character sets.

I/O Privilege Mechanism

Giving applications the right to access devices directly can result in very high speed transfers, but it can jeopardize system stability and cause conflicts between applications that want to control the device simultaneously. OS/2 has an *I/O privilege* mechanism to deal with these issues. This mechanism allows a process to request from a device driver that it be allowed to access the device and its dedicated or mapped memory directly. This tends to make an application device-dependent.

The DOS Compatibility Box

OS/2 runs the huge installed base of DOS applications. To support DOS, OS/2 provides what is called the *real mode screen group* (or the *compatibility box*, or the 3 *.x box*). This gives a program the environment of an 8086PC running DOS 3.3. Programs running under DOS execute in real mode. OS/2 actually switches into real mode to execute DOS programs rather than attempting to emulate real mode from inside protected mode (which is slow).

OS/2 designates one screen group as the *real mode screen group*. The user can switch to the protected mode environment by selecting a different screen group. OS/2 version 1.0 supports only a single real mode screen group. Later versions of OS/2 may support multiple real mode screen groups, a feature the 80386 is capable of supporting.

The DOS compatibility box is supported by the 80286's real mode. The 80286 processor starts up in real mode and can be switched to protect mode, but there is no natural provision for switching from protect mode to real mode. The processor may switch from protected mode to real mode with a special technique that essentially simulates complete resetting of the system.

System Configuration

The user may customize the OS/2 environment by placing appropriate commands in the *CONFIG.SYS* file OS/2 locates the CONFIG.SYS file at initialization time in the startup drive's root directory. The file comes preloaded with values generally appropriate for OS/2 systems, but users may wish to edit the file to customize their systems for optimal performance with particular applications. A summary of CONFIG.SYS statements appears in Fig CS 3.4.

DOS Mode Configuration Statements	
BREAK	Detect Ctrl+Break in DOS mode (always on in OS/2 mode)
FCBS	Set FCB (File Control Block) management information
RMSIZE	Set memory size for DOS mode
SHELL	Specify alternate DOS command processor

OS/2 Mode Configuration Statements	
BUFFERS	Specify the number of 512-byte buffers for disk I/O
CODEPAGE	Select code pages for using international character sets
COUNTRY	Specify country for country-dependent information
DEVICE	Name the path and filename of a device driver (to install)
DEVINFO	Ready device for code page switching
DISKCACHE	Set the number of storage blocks for the disk cache
IOPL	Permits program with I/O privilege (ring 2) to execute I/O instructions directly
LIBPATH	Specify the directories in which DLLs are located
MAXWAIT	Set time delay after which waiting process gets priority boost
MEMMAN	Enable or disable swapping and/or compaction
PAUSEONERROR	Enables/disables pausing for CONFIG.SYS error display
PRIORITY	Specifies whether priorities of regular calls threads are to be varied dynamically or are to remain fixed
PROTECTONLY	Enables either OS/2 mode only, or both OS/2 and DOS mode

(contd.)

PROTSHELL	Allows replacement of the OS/2 command processor
REM	Insert a remark in the CONFIG.SYS file
RUN	Start a system program during system initialization
SWAPPATH	Specify the path to the swap file
THREADS	Specify the maximum number of OS/2 threads that may exist
TIMESLICE	Set minimum and maximum values of the quantum
TRACE	Specify system tracing (generally for use by a service person)
TRACEBUF	Specify system traced circular buffer size

Fig. CS3.4. CONFIG.SYS statements.

OS/2 Software Developers Kit

The personal computing industry depends on a steady flow of powerful and innovative software applications developed by independent software vendors (ISVs). Microsoft makes available a *software developers* kit to encourage and facilitate the development of independent software.

A recent version of the kit included OS/2, Microsoft Windows and the Windows Toolkit, an optimizing Microsoft C compiler and the Microsoft Macro Assembler that can produce real mode DOS or protected mode OS/2 programs, various utilities and sample programs, and the presentation manager. Thousands of developers bought the package at its initial $3000 price, which include a technical developers conference at Microsoft and a year's subscription to Microsoft's on-line support system. Videotapes were included for those who could not attend the developers conference.

This kind of support provided early in the life cycle of a major personal computer operating system, such as OS/2, can be essential to the operating system's widespread acceptance.

Handling Errors and Exceptions

The *DosBeep* call generates a beep sound of specified frequency and duration; programs may signal the user that an error has occurred by issuing a beep.

DosError can prevent hard error messages and program exception messages from being issued to users; if these types of errors then occur, the process is terminated.

DosSetVec enables a process to specify (register) the address of a handler routine to be used when a certain type of machine exception (such as divide overflow or invalid opcode) occurs.

DosErrClass is a general-purpose error-handling routine that helps users interpret the errors that occur, and determine how to correct them. The user supplies an *error code* (returned by a previous function call), and OS/2 returns an *error classification*, a *recommended action*, and an *error locus*. The class, action, and locus definitions appear in Fig. CS3.5.

The Future

There are so many firmly established trends that it is relatively straightforward to write this section, but with one exception: the personal computing systems that will derive from OS/2 will be ever larger and ever more complex than the standard edition 1.0, so it becomes increasingly difficult to predict *when* key milestones will occur.

The field of software engineering is concerned with fostering on-time, within-budget systems development efforts, but it generally presumes the availability of detailed, high-quality specifications. Because future designs will affect so many people working in such a diversity of applications and geographical areas, the specifications process itself is becoming increasingly prolonged. The key to the future is open systems interconnection, and this implies the involvement of standards groups throughout the world as new directions in computing and communications take shape.

Class Definitions

Value	Mnemonic	Description
1	OUTRES	Out of resources
2	TEMPSIT	Temporary situation
3	AUTH	Authorization failed
4	INTRN	Internal error
5	HRDFAIL	Device hardware failure
6	SYSFAIL	System failure
7	APPERR	Probable application error
8	NOTFND	Item not located
9	BADFMT	Bad format for call/data
10	LOCKED	Resource/data locked
11	MEDIA	Incorrect media, CRC error
12	ALREADY	Resource/action already taken/done/exists
13	UNK	Unclassified
14	CAN'T	Can't perform requested action
15	TIME	Timeout

Actions Definitions

Value	Mnemonic	Description
1	RETRY	Retry immediately
2	DLYRET	Delay and retry
3	USER	Bad user input-get new values
4	ABORT	Terminate in an orderly manner
5	PANIC	Terminate immediately
6	IGNORE	Ignore error
7	INTRET	Retry after user intervention

(contd.)

Locus Definitions

Value	Mnemonic	Description
1	UNK	Unknown
2	DISK	Random access device such as a disk
3	NET	Network
4	SERDEV	Serial Device
5	MEM	Memory

Fig. CS3.5. *OS/2 error class, action, and locus definitions.*

For the next few years, it is anticipated that IBM will concentrate on taking full advantage of the 80386 architecture. The 80386 offers the protection features of the 80286, paging, and segments as large as 4 million KB (4GB). On the 80386, programs can use such large segments that they can run in only one data segment and one procedure segment (if they wish); this is called the *flat model* and it return programs considerably faster than if they are heavily segmented. The 80386 architecture provides *virtual real mode* which runs program in an 8086-compatible real mode but with protection; this will enable 80386-based computers to support multipled real mode applications at once. The 80386 architecture can allow or disallow I/O access prot-by-prot, a feature that may be exploited in future OS/2 versions to provide more secure systems.

What will the personal computer (or advanced workstation, if you will) look like at the turn of the century. It will have a huge primary storage probably on the order of 100Mb. It will have high-speed parallel processors (and eventually massive parallelism). It will use rewritable optical disks with capacities of tens of billions of bytes. Its display will be high resolution colour of near-photographic quality. Printout will be of true typeset quality on ultra-high-resolution laser printers, and colour printing will become common. Ultra-high-speed communications through fiber optics will enable computers to intercommunicate at computer speed rather than at today's slow telephone line speeds. Application will be integrated to interoperate smoothly with other applications, the operating system, and with remote systems. Operating systems vendors will provide increasing applications functionality "wrapped" within the operating system itself. Advanced graphics interfaces will become the norm as innovations in the user interface make it increasingly easy for the general public to use computers. Operating systems vendors will participate actively in the international standards area as open systems predominate; this will fundamentally change the marketplace as vendors used to providing and sustaining their own proprietary architectures will now adhere to the open standards. Users will ultimately be able to purchase the hardware and software they need from many different companies and these products will interoperate smoothly. All of these trends will affect the evolution of OS/2 and its competitors and successors.

As the previous edition of this text went to press, an interesting question was whether MS-DOS or CP/M would become the personal computer operating system of choice for IBM PCs and compatibles, and whether either operating system would emerge as the standard for the entire industry. MS-DOS won the battle primarily because IBM chose it as the standard and because Microsoft and IBM kept evolving it in response to architectural trends and increasing user demands.

Now the stage is set for round two in which OS/2 and UNIX systems will compete for supremacy on PS/2s and in the entire industry. To hazard a prediction, it seems that OS/2 will dominate on PS/2s while UNIX systems will dominate on advanced workstations and in the open systems marketplace. To hazard a more distant prediction, UNIX systems seem likely to become the industry standard by the mid-to-late 1990s, even on the generation of IBM personal computers that will eventually supersede the PS/2s. Regardless of which operating system dominate, if indeed one ever does, the competition fostered by having several valid contenders continues to provide users with declining costs, greater ease of use, and increasing operating system functionality.

Case Study 4

UNIX System

Introduction

The first version of UNIX was developed in 1969 by Ken Thompson of the Research Group at Bell Laboratories to use an otherwise idle PDP-7. He was soon joined by Dennis Ritchie. Thompson, Ritchie, and other members of the Research Group produced the early versions of UNIX.

Ritchie has previously worked on the MULTICS project, and MULTICS had a strong influence on the newer operating system. Even the name UNIX is merely a pun on *MULTICS*. The basic organization of the file system, the idea of the command interpreter (the shell) as a user process, the use of a separate process for each command, the original line-editing characters (# to erase the last character and @ to erase the entire line), and numerous other features came directly from MULTICS. Ideas from various other operating systems, such as from MIT's CTSS and the XDS-940 system, were also used.

Ritchie and Thompson worked quietly on UNIX for many years. Their work on the first version allowed them to move it to a PDP-11/20, for a second version. A third version resulted from their rewriting most of the operating system in the systems-programming language C, instead of the previously used assembly language. C was developed at Bell Laboratories to support UNIX. UNIX was also moved to larger PDP-11 models, such as the 11 / 45 and 11 / 70. Multiprogramming and other enhancements were added when it was rewritten in C and moved to systems (such as the 11/45) that had hardware support for multiprogramming.

As UNIX developed, it became widely used within Bell Laboratories and gradually spread to a few universities. The first version widely available outside Bell Laboratories was Version 6, released in 1976. (The version number for early UNIX systems corresponds to the edition number of the *UNIX Programmer's Manual* that was current when the distribution was made; the code and the manuals were revised independently.)

In 1978, Version 7 was distributed. This UNIX system ran on the PDP-11/70 and the Interdata 8/32, and is the ancestor of most modern UNIX systems. In particular, it was soon ported to the other PDP-11 models and to the VAX computer line. The version available on the VAX was known as 32V. Research has continued since then.

After the distribution of Version 7 in 1978, the UNIX Support Group (USG) assumed administrative control and responsibility from the Research Group for distributions of UNIX within AT&T, the parent organization for Bell Laboratories. UNIX was becoming a product, rather than simply a research tool. The Research Group has continued to develop their own version of UNIX, however, to support their own internal computing. Next came Version 8, which included a facility called the stream *I/O system* that allows flexible configuration of kernel IPC modules. It also contained RFS, a remote file system similar to Sun's NFS. Next came Versions 9 and 10 (the latter version, released in 1989, is available only within Bell Laboratories).

USG released System V in 1983; it is largely derived from System III. The divestiture of the various Bell operating companies from AT&T has left AT&T in a position to market System V aggressively. USG was restructured as the UNIX System Development Laboratory (USDL), which released UNIX System V Release 2 (V.2) in 1984. UNIX System V Release 2, Version 4 (V.2.4) added a new implementation of virtual memory with copy-on-write paging and shared memory. USDL was in turn replaced by AT&T Information Systems (ATTIS), which distributed System V Release 3 (V.3) in 1987. V.3 adapts the V8 implementation of the stream I/O system and makes it available as *STREAMS*. It also includes RFS, an NFS-like remote file system.

The small size, modularity, and clean design of early UNIX systems led to UNIX-based work at numerous other computer-science organizations, such as at Rand, BBN, the University of Illinois, Harvard, Purdue, and even DEC. The most influential of the non-Bell Laboratories and non–AT&T UNIX development groups, however, has been the University of California at Berkeley.

The first Berkeley VAX UNIX work was the addition in 1978 of virtual memory, demand paging, and page replacement to 32V; this work was done by Bill Joy and Ozlap Babaoglu to produce 3BSD UNIX. This version was the first implementation of any of these facilities on any UNIX system. The large virtual-memory space of 3BSD allowed the development of very large programs, such as Berkeley's own Franz LISP. The memory-management work convinced the Defense Advanced Research Projects Agency (DARPA) to fund Berkeley for the development of a standard UNIX system for government use; 4BSD UNIX was the result.

The 4BSD work for DARPA was guided by a steering committee that included many notable people from the UNIX and networking communities. One of the goals of this project was to provide support for the DARPA Internet networking protocols (TCP/IP). This support was provided in a general manner. It is possible in 4.2BSD to communicate uniformly among diverse network facilities, including local-area networks (such as Ethernets and token rings) and wide-area networks (such as NSFNET). This implementation was the most important reason for the current popularity of these protocols. It was used as the basis for the implementations of many vendors of UNIX computer systems, and even other operating systems. It permitted the Internet to grow from 60 connected networks in 1984 to more than 8000 networks and an estimated 10 million user in 1993.

In addition, Berkeley, adapted many features from contemporary operating systems to improve the design and implementation of UNIX. Many of the terminal line-editing functions of the TENEX (TOPS-20) operating system were provided by a new terminal driver. A new user interface (the C Shell), a new text editor (ex/vi), compilers for Pascal and LISP, and many new systems programs were written at Berkeley. For 4.2BSD, certain efficiency improvements were inspired by the VMS operating system.

UNIX software from Berkeley is released in *Berkeley Software Distributions*. It is convenient to refer to the Berkeley VAX UNIX systems following 3BSD as 4BSD, although there were actually several specific releases, most notably 4.1BSD and 4.2BSD. The generic numbers BSD and 4BSD are used for the PDP-11 and VAX distributions of Berkeley UNIX. 4.2BSD, first distributed in 1983, was the culmination of the original Berkeley DARPA UNIX project. 2.9BSD is the equivalent version for PDP-11 systems.

In 1986, 4.3BSD was released. It was so similar to 4.2BSD that its manuals described 4.2BSD more comprehensively than the 4.2BSD manuals did. It did include numerous internal changes, however, including bug fixes and performance improvements. Some new facilities also were added, including support for the Xerox Network System protocols.

4.3BSD Tahoe was the next version, released in 1988. It included various new developments, such as improved networking congestion control and TCP/IP performance. Also, disk configurations were separated from the device drivers, and are now read off the disks themselves. Expanded time-zone support is also included. 4.3BSD Tahoe was actually developed on and for the CCI Tahoe system (Computer Console, Inc., Power 6 computer), rather than for the usual VAX base. The corresponding PDP-11 release is 2.10.1BSD, which is distributed by the USENIX Association, which also publishes the 4.3BSD manuals. The 4.32BSD Reno release saw the inclusion of an implementation of ISO/OSI networking.

The last Berkeley release, 4.4BSD, was finalized in June of 1993. It includes new X.25 networking support, and POSIX standard compliance. It also has a radically new file system organization, with a new virtual file system interface and support for *stackable* file systems, allowing file systems to be layered on top of each other for easy inclusion of new features. An implementation of NFS is also included in the release, as in a new log-based file system. The 4.4BSD virtual memory system is derived from Mach. Several other changes, such as enhanced security and improved kernel structure, are also included. With the release of version 4.4, Berkeley has halted its research efforts.

4BSD was the operating system of choice for VAXes from its initial release (1979) until the release of Ultrix, DEC's BSD implementation. 4BSD is still the best choice for many research and networking installations. Many organizations would buy a 32V license and order 4BSD from Berkeley without even bothering to get a 32V tape.

The current set of UNIX operating systems is not limited to those by Bell Laboratories (which is currently owned by Lucent Technology), and Berkeley, however. Sun Microsystems helped popularize the BSD flavor of UNIX by shipping it on their workstations. As UNIX has grown in popularity, it has been moved to many different computers and computer systems. A wide variety of UNIX, and UNIX-like, operating systems have been created. DEC supports its UNIX (called Ultrix) on its workstations and is replacing Ultrix with another UNIX-derived operating system, OSF/1; Microsoft rewrote UNIX for the Intel 8088 family and called it XENIX, and its new Windows/NT operating system is heavily influenced by UNIX; IBM has UNIX (AIX) on its PCs, workstations, and mainframes. In fact, UNIX is available on almost all general-purpose computers; it runs on personal computers, workstations, minicomputers, mainframes, and supercomputers, from Apple Macintosh IIs to Cray IIs. Because of its wide availability, it is used in environments ranging from academic to military to manufacturing process control. Most of these systems are based on Version 7, System III, 4.2BSD, or System V.

The wide popularity of UNIX with computer vendors has made UNIX the most portable of operating systems, and has made it possible for users to expect a UNIX environment independent of any specific computer manufacturer. But the large number of implementations of the system has led to remarkable variation in the programming and user interfaces distributed by the vendors. For true vendor independence, application-program developers need consistent interfaces. Such interfaces would allow all "UNIX" applications to run on all UNIX systems, which is certainly not the current situation. This issue has become important as UNIX has become the preferred program-development platform for applications ranging from databases to graphics and networking, and has led to a strong market demand for UNIX standards.

There are several standardization projects underway, starting with the */usr/group 1984 Standard* sponsored by the UniForum industry user's group. Since then, many official standards bodies have continued the effort, including IEEE and ISO (the POSIX standard). The X/Open Group international consortium completed XPG3, a Common Application Environment, which subsumes the IEEE interface standard. Unfortunately, XPG3 is based on a draft of the ANSI C standard, rather than the final specification, and therefore needs to be redone. The XPG4 is due out in 1993. In 1989, the ANSI standards body standardized the C programming language, producing an ANSI C specification that vendors were quick to adopt. As these projects continue, the variant flavors of UNIX will converge and there will be one programming interface to UNIX, allowing UNIX to become even more popular. There are in fact two separate sets of powerful UNIX vendors working on this problem: the AT&T-guided UNIX International (UI) and the Open Software Foundation (OSF) have both agreed to follow the POSIX standard. Recently, many of the vendors involved in those two groups have agreed on further standardization (the COSE agreement) on the Motif window environment, and ONC+ (which includes Sun RPC and NFS) and DCE network facilities (which includes AFS and an RPC package).

AT&T replaced its ATTIS group in 1989 with the UNIX Software Organization (USO), which shipped the first merged UNIX, System V Release 4. This system combines features from System V, 4.3BSD, and Sun's SunOS, including long file names, the Berkeley file system, virtual memory management, symbolic links, multiple access groups, job control, and reliable signals; it also conforms to the published POSIX standard, POSIX.1. After USO produced SVR4, it became an independent AT&T subsidiary named Unix System Laboratories (USL); in 1993, it was purchased by Novell, Inc.

Figure CS4.1 summarizes the relationships among the various versions of UNIX.

The UNIX system has grown from a personal project of two Bell Laboratories employees to an operating system being defined by multinational standardization bodies. Yet this system is still of interest to academia. We believe that UNIX has become and will remain an important part of operating-system theory and practice, UNIX is an excellent vehicle for academic study. For example, the Tunis operating system, the Xinu operating system, and the Minix operating system are based on the concepts of UNIX, but were developed explicitly for classroom study. There is a plethora of ongoing UNIX-related research systems, including Mach, Chorus, Comandos, and Roisin. The original developers, Ritchie and Thompson, were honored in 1983 by the Association for Computing Machinery Turing award for their work on UNIX.

The specific UNIX version used in this chapter is the VAX version of 4.3BSD. This system is used because it implements many interesting operating-system concepts, such as demand paging with clustering, and networking. It has also been influential in other UNIX systems, in standards, and in networking developments. The VAX implementation is used because 4.3BSD was developed on the VAX and that machine still represents a convenient point of reference, despite the recent proliferation of implementations on other hardware (such as the Motorola 68040 and 88000, the Intel i486, the Sun SPARC, DEC Alpha, HP Precision, and the MIPS R4000 CPUs).

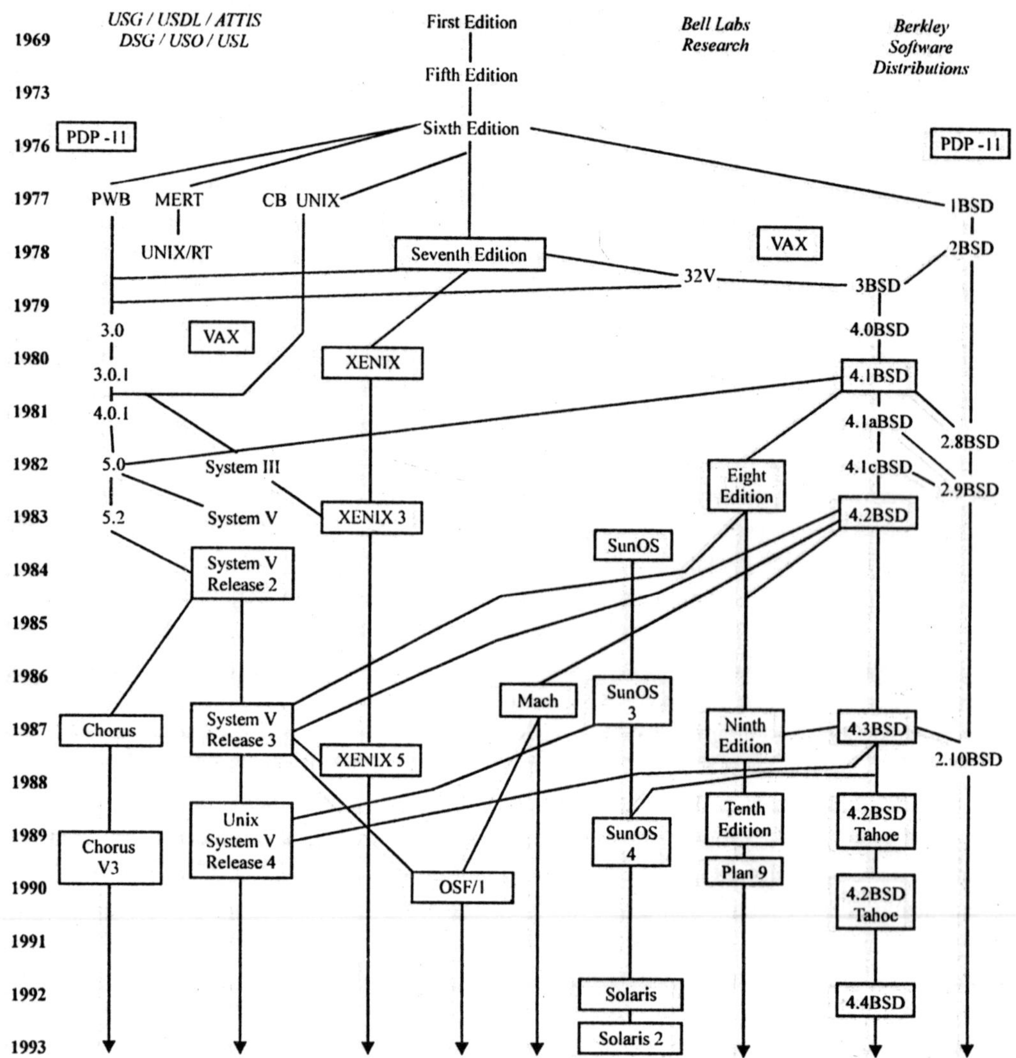

Fig. CS4.1. History of UNIX versions.

Design Principles

UNIX was designed to be a time-sharing system. The standard user interface (the shell) is simple and can be replaced by another, if desired. The file system is a multilevel tree, which allows users to create their own subdirectories. Each user data file is simply a sequence of bytes.

Disk files and I/O devices are treated as similarly as possible. Thus, device dependencies and peculiarities are kept in the kernel as much as possible; even in the kernel, most of them are confined to the device drivers.

UNIX supports multiple processes. A process can easily create new processes. CPU scheduling is a simple priority algorithm. 4.3BSD uses demand paging as a mechanism to support memory-management and CPU-scheduling decisions. Swapping is used if a system is suffering from excess paging.

Because UNIX was originated first by one programmer, Ken Thompson, and then by another, Dennis Ritchie, as a system for their own convenience, it was small enough to understand. Most of the algorithms were selected for *simplicity*, not for speed or sophistication. The intent was to have the kernel and libraries provide a small set of facilities that was sufficiently powerful to allow a person to build a more complex system if one were needed. UNIX's clean design has resulted in many imitations and modifications.

Although the designers of UNIX had a significant amount of knowledge about other operating systems, UNIX had no elaborate design spelled out before its implementation. This flexibility appears to have been one of the key factors in the development of the system. Some design principles were involved, however, even though they were not made explicit at the outset.

The UNIX system was designed by programmers for programmers. Thus, it has always been interactive, and facilities for program development have always been a high priority. Such facilities include the program make (which can be used to check to see which of a collection of source files for a program need to be compiled, and then to do the compiling) and the *Source Code Control* System (SCCS) (which is used to keep successive versions of files available without having to store the entire contents of each step).

Te operating system is written mostly in C, which was developed to support UNIX, since neither Thompson nor Ritchie enjoyed programming in assembly language. The avoidance of assembly language was also necessary because of the uncertainty about the machine or machines on which UNIX would be run. It has greatly simplified the problems of moving UNIX from one hardware system to another.

From the beginning, UNIX development systems have had all the UNIX sources available on-line, and the developers have used the systems under developments as their primary systems. This pattern of development has greatly facilitated the discovery of deficiencies and their fixes, as well as of new possibilities and their implementations. It has also encouraged the plethora of UNIX variants existing today, but the benefits have outweighed the disadvantages: if something is broken, it can be fixed at a local site; there is no need to wait for the next release of the system. Such fixes, as well as new facilities, may be incorporated into later distributions.

The size constraints of the PDP-11 (and earlier computers used for UNIX) have forced a certain elegance. Where other systems have elaborate algorithms for dealing with pathological conditions, UNIX just does a controlled crash called panic. Instead of attempting to cure such conditions, UNIX tries to prevent them. Where other systems would use brute force or macro-expansion, UNIX mostly has had to develop more subtle, or at least simpler, approaches.

These early strengths of UNIX produced much of its popularity, which in turn produced new demands that challenged those strengths. UNIX was used for tasks such as networking, graphics, and real-time operation, which did not always fit into its original text-oriented model. Thus, changes were made to certain internal facilities and new programming interfaces were added. These new facilities, and others—particularly window interfaces—required large amounts of code to support them, radically increasing the size of the system. For instance, networking and windowing both doubled the size of the system. This pattern in turn pointed out the continued strength of UNIX—whenever a new development occurred in the industry, UNIX could usually absorb it, but still remain UNIX.

Programmer Interface

As do most computer systems, UNIX consists of two separable parts: the kernel and the systems programs. We can view the UNIX operating system as being layered, as shown in Figure CS4.2. Everything below the system-call interface and above the physical hardware is the *kernel.* The kernel provides the file system, CPU scheduling, memory management, and other operating-system functions through system calls. Systems programs use the kernel-supported system calls to provide useful functions, such as compilation and file manipulation.

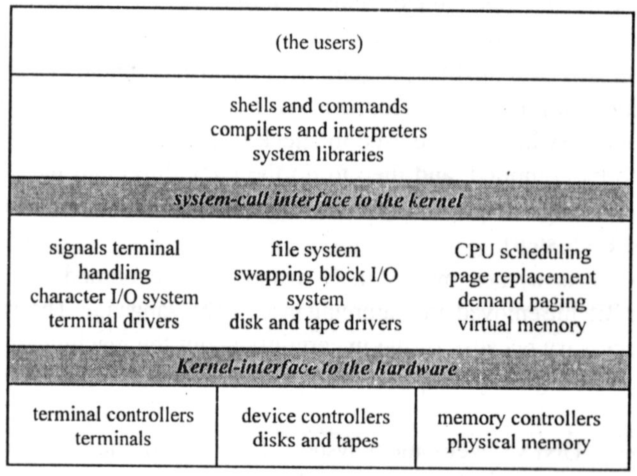

Fig. C.S4.2. 4.3BSD layer structure.

System calls define the *programmer interface* to UNIX; the set of systems programs commonly available defines the *user interface*. The programmer and user interface define the context that the kernel must support.

System calls in VAX 4.2BSD are made by a trap to location 40 of the VAX interrupt vectors. Parameters are passed to the kernel on the hardware stack; the kernel returns values in registers R0 and R1. Register R0 may also return an error code. The carry bit distinguishes a normal return from an error return.

This level of detail is seldom seen by a UNIX programmer, fortunately. Most systems programs are written in C, and the *UNIX Programmer's Manual* presents all system calls as C functions. A system program written in C for 4.3BSD on the VAX can generally be moved to another 4.3BSD system and simply recompiled, even though the two systems may be quite different. The details of system calls are known only to the compiler. This feature is a major reason for the portability of UNIX programs.

System calls for UNIX can be roughly grouped into three categories: file manipulation, process control, and information manipulation. We listed a fourth category, device manipulation, but since devices in UNIX are treated as (special) files, the same system calls support both files and devices (although there is an extra system call for setting device parameters).

File Manipulation

A *file* in UNIX is a sequence of bytes. Different programs expect various levels of structure, but the kernel does not impose a structure on files. For instance, the convention for text files is lines of ASCII characters separated by a single newline character (which is the linefeed character in ASCII), but the kernel knows nothing of this convention.

Files are organized in tree-structured directories. Directories are themselves files that contain information on how to find other files. A *path name* to a file is a text string that identifies a file by specifying a path through the directory structure to the file. Syntactically, it consists of individual file-name elements separated by the slash character. For example, in */usr/local/font*, the first slash indicates the root of the directory tree, called the *root* directory. The next element, *usr*, is a subdirectory of the root, *local* is a subdirectory of *usr*, and *font* is a file or directory in the directory *local.* Whether *font* is an ordinary file or a directory cannot be determined from the path-name syntax.

The UNIX file system has both *absolute path names* and *relative path names*. Absolute path names start at the root of the file system and are distinguished by a slash at the beginning of the path name; */usr/local/font* is an absolute path name. Relative path names start at the *current directory*, which is an attribute of the process accessing the path name. Thus, *local/font* indicates a file or directory named *font* in the directory local in the current directory, which might or might not be */usr*.

A file may be known by more than one name in one or more directories. Such multiple names are known as links, and all links are treated equally by the operating system. 4.3BSD also supports *symbolic links*, which are files containing the path name of another file. The two kinds of links are also known as *hard links* and *soft links*. Soft (symbolic) links, unlike hard links, may point to directories and may cross file-system boundaries.

The file name "." In a directory is a hard link to the directory itself. The file name ".." is a hard link to the parent directory. Thus, if the current directory is */user/jlp/programs*, then. */bin/wdf* refers to */user/jlp/bin/wdf.*

Hardware devices have names in the file system. These *device special files* or *special files* are known to the kernel as device interfaces, but are nonetheless accessed by the user by much the same system calls as are other files.

Figure CS4.3 shows a typical UNIX file system. The root (/) normally contains a small number of directories as well as */vmunix*, the binary boot image of the operating system; */dev* contains the device special files, such as */dev/console*, */dev/lpo*, */dev/mt0*, and so on; */bin* contains the binaries of the essential UNIX systems programs. Other binaries may be in */usr/bin* (for applications systems programs, such as text formatters), */usr/ucb* (for systems programs written by Berkeley rather than by AT&T), or */usr/local/bin* (for systems programs written at the local site). Library files—such as the C, Pascal, and FORTRAN subroutine libraries—are kept in */lib* (or */usr/lib* or */usr/local/lib*).

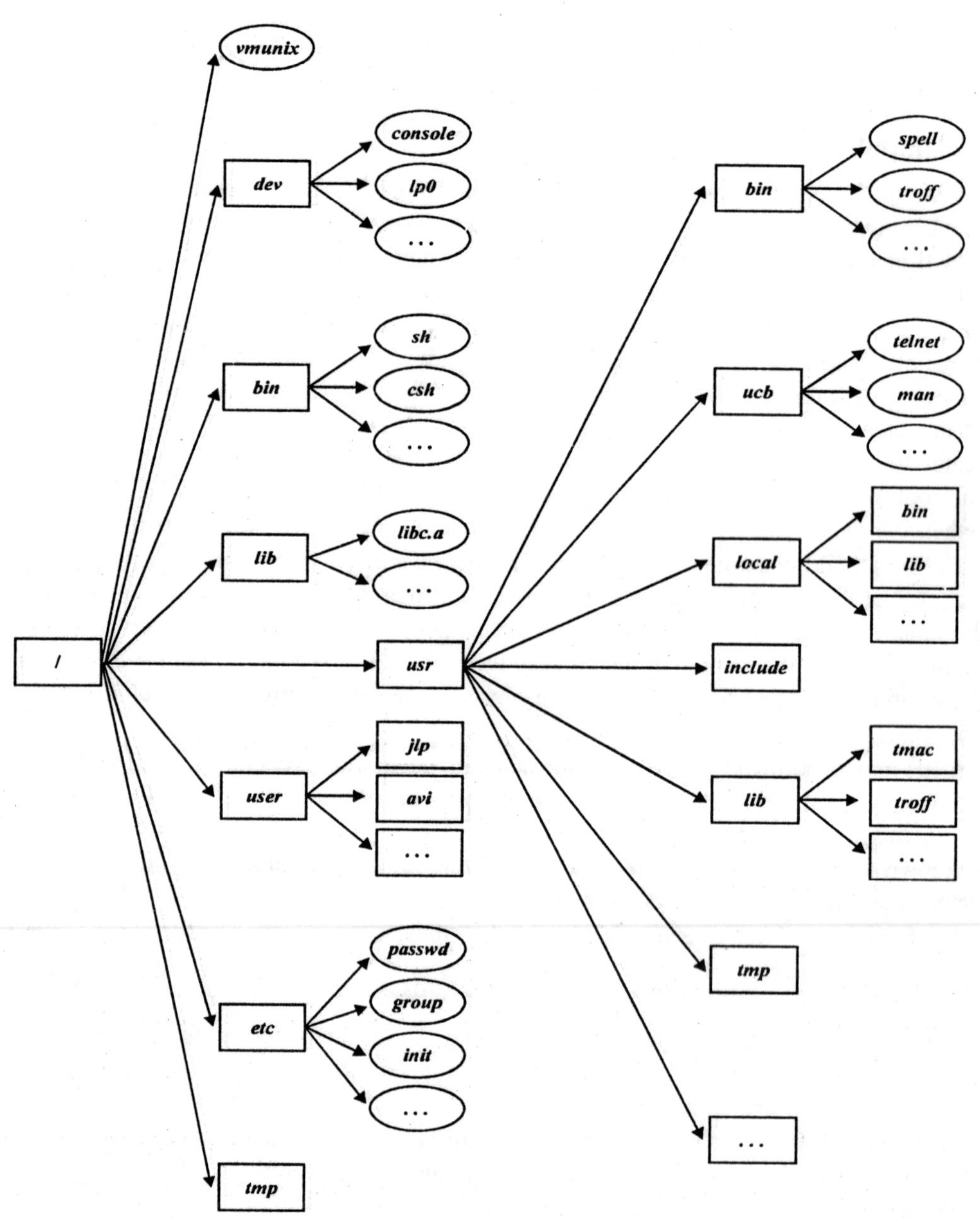

Fig. CS4.3. Programmer Interface.

The files of users themselves are stored in a separate directory for each user, typically in */user*. Thus, the user directory for *carol* would normally be in */user/carol*. For a large system, these directories may be further grouped to ease administration, creating a file structure with */user/prof/avi* and */user/staff/carol*.

Administrative files and programs, such as the password file, are kept in */etc*. Temporary files can be put in*/tmp*, which is normally erased during system boot, or *in/usr/tmp*.

Each of these directories may have considerably more structure. For example, the font/description tables for the troff formatter for the Merganthaler 202 typesetter are kept in */usr/lib/troff/dev202*. All the conventions concerning the location of specific files and directories have been defined by programmers and their programs: the operating-system kernel needs only */etc/init*, which is used to initialize terminal processes, to be operable.

System calls for basic file manipulation are **creat, open, read, write, close, unlink**, and **trunc**. The **creat** system call, given a path name, creates an (empty) file (or truncates an existing one). An existing file is opened by the **open** system call, which takes a path name and a mode (such as read, write, or read-write) and returns a small integer, called a *file descriptor*. A file descriptor may then be passed to **read** or **write** system call (along with a buffer address and the number of bytes to transfer) to perform data transfers to or from the file. A file is closed when its file descriptor is passed to the **close** system call. The **trunc** call reduces the length of a file to 0.

A file descriptor is an index into a small table of open files for this process. Descriptors start at 0 and seldom get higher than 6 or 7 for typical programs, depending on the maximum number of simultaneously open files.

Each **read** or **write** updates the current offset into the file, which is associated with the file-table entry and is used to determine the position in the file for the next **read** or **write**. The **lseek** system call allows the position to be reset explicitly. It also allows the creation of sparse files (files with "holes" in them). The **dup** and **dup2** system calls can be used to produce a new file descriptor that is a copy of an existing one. The **fcntl** system call can also do that, and in addition can examine or set various parameters of an open file. For example, it can make each succeeding **write** to an open file append to the end of that file. There is an additional system call, **ioctl**, for manipulating device parameters. It can set the baud rate of a serial port, or rewind a tape, for instance.

Information about the file (such as its size, protection modes, owner, and so on) can be obtained by the **stat** system call. Several system calls allow some of this information to be changed: **rename** (change file name), **chmod** (change the protection mode), and **chown** (change the owner and group). Many of these system calls have variants that apply to file descriptors instead of file names. The **link** system call makes a hard link for an existing file, creating a new name for an existing file. A link is removed by the **unlink** system call; if it is the last link, the file is deleted. The **symlink** system call makes a symbolic link.

Directories are made by the **mkdir** system call and are deleted by **rmdir**. The current directory is changed by **cd**.

Although it is possible to use the standard file calls on directories, it is inadvisable to do so, since directories have an internal structure that must be preserved. Instead, another set of system calls is provided to open a directory, to step through each file entry within the directory, to close the directory, and to perform other functions; these are **opendir, readdir, closedir**, and others.

Process Control

A process is a program in execution. Processes are identified by their *process identifier*, which is an integer. A new process is created by the **fork** system call. The new process consists of a copy of the address space of the original process (the same program and the same variables with the same values). Both processes (the parent and the child) continue execution at the instruction after the **fork** with one difference: The return code for the **fork** is zero for the new (child) process, whereas the (nonzero) process identifier of the child is returned to the parent.

Typically, the **execve** system call is used after a fork by one of the two processes to replace that process' virtual memory space with a new program. The **execve** system call loads a binary file into memory (destroying the memory image of the program containing the **execve** system call) and starts its execution.

A process may terminate by using the **exit** system call, and its parent process may wait for that event by using the **wait** system call. If the child process crashes, the system simulates the exit call. The wait system call provides the process id of a terminated child so that the parent can tell which of possibly many children terminated. A second system call, **wait3**, is similar to **wait** but also allows the parent to collect performance statistics about the child. Between the time the child exits, and the time the parent completes one of the wait system calls, the child is *defunct*. A defunct process can do nothing, but exists merely so that the parent can collect its status information. If the parent process of a defunct process exits before a child, the defunct process is inherited by the *init* process (which in turn waits on it) and becomes a *zombie* process. A typical use of these facilities is shown in Figure CS 4.4.

The simplest form of communication between processes is by pipes, which may be created before the **fork,** and whose endpoints are then set up between the **fork** and the **execve.** A pipe is essentially a queue of bytes between two processes. The pipe is accessed by a file descriptor, like an ordinary file. One process writes into the pipe, and the other reads from the pipe. The size of the original pipe system was fixed by the system. With 4.3BSD, pipes are implemented on top of the socket system, which has variable-sized buffers. Reading from an empty pipe or writing into a full pipe causes the process to be blocked until the state of the pipe changes. Special arrangements are needed for a pipe to be placed between a parent and child (so only one is reading and one is writing).

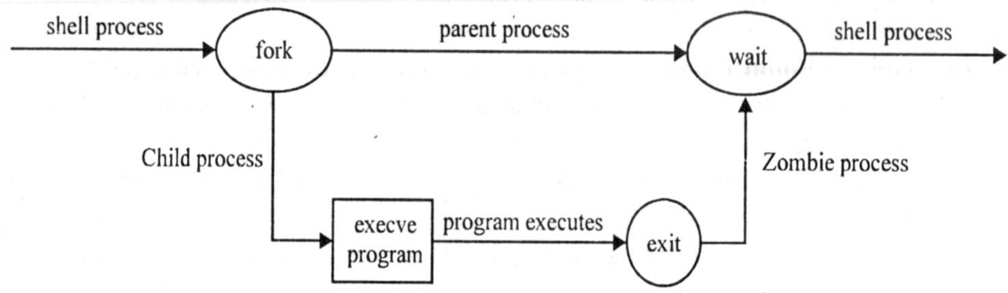

Fig. CS4.4. A shell forks a subprocess to execute a program.

All user processes are descendants of one original process, called *init*. Each terminal port available for interactive use has a *getty* process forked for it by *init*. The *getty* process initializes terminal line parameters and waits for a user's *login* name, which it passes through an **execve** as an argument to a *login* process. The *login* process collects the user's password, encrypts the password, and compares the result to an encrypted string taken from the file */etc/passwd*. If the comparison is successful, the user is allowed to log in. The *login* process executes a *shell*, or command interpreter, after setting the numeric *user identifier* of the process to that of the user logging in. (The shell and the user identifier are found in */etc/passwd* by the user's login name.) It is with this shell that the user ordinarily communicates for the rest of the login session; the shell itself forks subprocesses for the commands the user tell it to execute.

The user identifier is used by the kernel to determine the user's permissions for certain system calls, especially those involving file accesses. There is also a *group identifier*, which is used to provide similar privileges to a collection of users. In 4.3BSD a process may be in several groups simultaneously. The *login* process puts the shell in all the groups permitted to the user by the files */etc/passwd* and */etc/group*.

There are actually two user identifiers used by the kernel: the *effective user identifier* is the identifier used to determine file access permissions. If the file of a program being loaded by an **execve** has the **setuid** bit set in its inode, the effective user identifier of the process is set to the user identifier of the owner of the file, whereas the *real user identifier* is left as it was. This scheme allows certain processes to have more than ordinary privileges while still being executable by ordinary users. The **setuid** idea was patented by Dennis Ritchie (U.S. Patent 4,135,240) and is one of the distinctive features of UNIX. There is a similar **setgid** bit for groups. A process may determine its real and effective user identifier with the **getuid** and **getuid** calls, respectively. The **getgid** and **getgid** calls determine the process identifier and group identifier, respectively. The rest of a process' groups may be found with the **getgroups** system calls.

Signals

Signals are a facility for handling exceptional conditions similar to software interrupts. There are 20 different signals, each corresponding to a distinct condition. A signal may be generated by a keyboard interrupt, by an error in a process (such as a bad memory reference), or by a number of asynchronous events (such as timers or job-control signals from the shell). Almost any signal may also be generated by the **kill** system call.

The interrupt signal, SIGINT, is used to stop a command before that command completes. It is usually produced by the ^C character (ASCII 3). As of 4.2BSD, the important keyboard characters are defined by a table for each terminal and can be redefined easily. The *quit* signal, SIGQUIT, is usually produced by the ^bs character (ASCII 28). The *quit* signal both stops the currently executing program and dumps its current memory image to a file named *core* in the current directory. The core file can be used by debuggers. SIGILL is produced by an illegal instruction and SIGSEGV by an attempt to address memory outside of the legal virtual-memory space of a process.

Arrangements can be made either for most signals to be ignored (to have no effect), or for a routine in the user process (a signal handler) to be called. A signal handler may safely do one of two things before returning from catching a signal: call the **exit** system call, or modify a global variable. There is one signal (the *kill* signal, number 9, SIGKILL) that cannot be ignored or caught by a signal handler. SIGKILL is used, for example, to kill a runaway process that is ignoring other signal such as SIGINT or SIGQUIT.

Signals can be lost: If another signal of the same kind is sent before a previous signal has been accepted by the process to which it is directed, the first signal will be overwritten and only the last signal will be seen by the process. In other words, a call to the signal handler tells a process that there has been at least one occurance of the signal. Also, there is no relative priority among UNIX signals. If two different signals are sent to the same process at the same time, it is indeterminate which one the process will receive first.

Signals were originally intended to deal with-exceptional events. As is true of the use of most other features in UNIX, however, signal use has steadily expanded. 4.1BSD introduced job control, which uses signals to start and stop subprocesses on demand. This facility allows one shell to control multiple processes: starting, stopping, and backgrounding them as the user wishes. 4.3BSD added the SIGWINCH signal, invented by Sun Microsystems, for informing a process that the window in which output is being displayed has changed size. Signals are also used to deliver urgent data from network connections.

Users also wanted more reliable signals, and a bug fix in an inherent race condition in the old signals implementation. Thus, 4.2BSD also brought with it a race-free, reliable, separately implemented signal capability. It allows individual signals to be blocked during critical sections, and has a new system call to let a process sleep until interrupted. It is similar to hardware-interrupt functionality. This capability is now part of the POSIX standard.

Process Groups

Groups of related processes frequently cooperate to accomplish a common task. For instance, processes may create, and communicate over, pipes. Such a set of processes is termed a *process* group, or a job. Signals may be sent to all processes in a group. A process usually inherits its process groups from its parent, but the **setpgrp** system call allows a process to change its group.

Process groups are used by the C shell to control the operation of multiple jobs. Only one process group may use a terminal device for I/O at any time. This *foreground* job has the attention of the user on that terminal while all other nonattached jobs (*background* jobs) perform their function without user interaction. Access to the terminal is controlled by process group signals. Each job has a *controlling terminal* (again, inherited from its parent). If the process group of the controlling terminal matches the group of a process, that process is in the foreground, and is allowed to perform I/O. If a nonmatching (background) process attempts the same, a SIGTTIN or SIGTTOU signal is sent to its process group. This signal usually results in the process group freezing until it is foregrounded by the user, at which point it receives a SIGCONT signal, indicating that the process can perform the I/O. Similarly, a SIGSTOP may be sent to the foreground process group to freeze it.

Information Manipulation

System calls exist to set and return both an interval timer (**getitimer/setitimer**) and the current time (**gettimeofday / settimeofday**) in microseconds. In addition, processes can ask for their process identifier (**getpid**), their group identifier (**getgid**), the name of the machine on which they are executing (**gethostname**), and many other values.

Library Routines

The system-call interface to UNIX is supported and augmented by a large collection of library routines and header files. The header files provide the definition of complex data structures used in system calls. In addition, a large library of functions provides additional program support.

For example, the UNIX I/O system calls provide for the reading and writing of blocks of bytes. Some applications may want to read and write only 1 byte at a time. Although it would be possible to read and write 1 byte at a time, that would require a system call for each byte—a very high overhead. Instead, a set of standard library routines (the standard I/O package accessed through the header file *<stdio.h>*) provides another interface, which reads and writes several thousand bytes at a time using local buffers, and transfers between these buffers (in user memory) when I/O is desired. Formatted I/O is also supported by the standard I/O package.

Additional library support is provided for mathematical functions, network access, data conversion, and so on. The 4.3BSD kernel supports over 150 system calls; the C program library has over 300 library functions. Although the library functions eventually result in system calls where necessary (for example, the *getchar* library routine will result in a **read** system call if the file buffer is empty), it is generally unnecessary for the programmer to distinguish between the basic set of kernel system calls and the additional functions provided by library functions.

User Interface

Both the programmer and the user of a UNIX system deal mainly with the set of systems programs that have been written and are available for execution. These programs make the necessary system calls to support their function, but the system calls themselves are contained within the program and do not need to be obvious to the user.

The common systems programs can be grouped into several categories; most of them are file or directory oriented. For example, the system programs to manipulate directories are *mkdir* to create a new directory, *rmdir* to remove a directory, *cd* to change the current directory to another, and *pwd* to print the absolute path name of the current (working) directory.

The *ls* program lists the names of the files in the current directory. Any of 18 options can ask that properties of the files be displayed also. For example, the *-l* option asks for a long listing, showing the file name, owner, protection, date and time of creation, and size. The *cp* program creates a new file that is a copy of an existing file. The *mv* program moves a file from one place to another in the directory tree. In most cases, this move simply requires a renaming of the file; if necessary, however, the file is copied to the new location and the old copy is deleted. A file is deleted by the *rm* program (which makes an **unlink** system call).

To display a file on the terminal, a user can run *cat*. The *cat* program takes a list of files and concatenates them, copying the result to the standard output, commonly the terminal. On a high-speed cathode-ray tube (CRT) display, of course, the file may speed by too fast to be read. The *more* program displays the file one screen at a time, pausing until the user types a character to continue to the next screen. The head program displays just the first few lines of a file; *tail* shows the last few lines.

These are the basic systems programs widely used in UNIX. In addition, there are a number of editors (*ed*, *sed*, *emacs*, *vi*, and so on), compilers (C, Pascal, FORTRAN, and so on), and text formatters (troff, TEX, scribe, and so on). There are also programs for sorting (*sort*) and comparing files (*cmp*, *diff*), looking for patterns (*grep*, *awk*), sending mail to other users (*mail*), and many other activities.

Shells and Commands

Both user-written and systems programs are normally executed by a command interpreter. The command interpreter in UNIX is a user process like any other. It is called a shell, as it surrounds the kernel of the operating system. Users can write their own shell, and there are, in fact, several shells in general use. The *Bourne shell*, written by Steve Bourne, is probably the most widely used—or, at least, it is the most widely available. The *C shell*, mostly the work of Bill Joy, a founder of Sun Microsystems, is the most popular on BSD systems. The Korn shell, by Dave Korn, has become popular because it combines the features of the Bourne shell and the C shell.

The common shells share much of their command-language syntax. UNIX is normally an interactive system. The shell indicates its readiness to accept another command by typing a prompt, and the user types a command on a single line. For instance, in the line

% *ls-l*

the percent sign is the usual C shell prompt, and the *ls-l* (typed by the user) is the (long) list-directory command. Commands can take arguments, which the user types after the command name on the same line, separated by white space (spaces or tabs).

Although there are a few commands built into the shells (such as *cd*), a typical command is an executable binary object file. A list of several directories, the *search path*, is kept by the shell. For each command, each of the directories in the search path is searched, in order, for a file of the same name. If a file is found, it is loaded and executed. The search path can be set by the user. The directories */bin* and */usr/bin* are almost always in the search path, and a typical search path on a BSD system might be

(*./home/prof/avi/bin /usr/local/bin /usr/ucb/bin/usr/bin*)

The *ls* command's object file is */bin/ls* and the shell itself is */bin/sh* (the Bourne shell) or */bin/csh* (the C shell).

Execution of a command is done by a **fork** system call followed by an **execve** of the object file. The shell usually then does a **wait** to suspend its own execution until the command completes (Figure CS4.4). There is a simple syntax (an ampersand [&] at the end of the command line) to indicate that the shell should *not* wait for the completion of the command. A command left running in this manner while the shell continues to interpret further commands is said to be a *background* command, or to be running in the background. Processes for which the shell does wait are said to run in the foreground.

The C shell in 4.3BSD systems provides a facility called *job control* (partially implemented in the kernel), as mentioned previously. Job control allows processes to be moved between the foreground and the background. The processes can be stopped and restarted on various conditions, such as a background job wanting input from the user's terminal. This scheme allows most of the control of processes provided by windowing or layering interfaces, but requires no special hardware. Job control is also useful in window systems, such as the X Window System developed at MIT. Each window is treated as a terminal, allowing multiple processes to be in the foreground (one per window) at any one time. Of course, background processes may exist on any of the windows. The

Korn shell also supports job control, and it is likely that job control (and process groups) will be standard in future versions of UNIX.

Standard I/O

Processes can open files as they like, but most processes expect three file descriptors (numbers 0, 1, and 2) to be open when they start. These file descriptors are inherited across the **fork** (and possibly the **execve**) that created the process. They are known as *standard input* (0). Thus, the program can read what the user types by reading standard input, and the program can send output to the user's screen by writing to standard output. The standard-error file descriptor is also open for writing and is used for error output; standard output is used for ordinary output. Most programs can also accept a file (rather than a terminal) for standard input and standard output. The program does not care where its input is coming from and where its output is going. This is one of the elegant design features of UNIX.

The common shells have a simple syntax for changing what files are open for the standard I/O streams of a process. Changing a standard file is called I/O redirection. The syntax for I/O redirection is shown in Figure CS4.5. In this example, the *ls* command produces a listing of the names of files in the current directory, the *pr* command formats that list into pages suitable for a printer, and the *lpr* command spools the formatted output to a printer, such as */dev/lp0*. The subsequent command forces all output and all error messages to be redirected to a file. Without the ampersand, error messages appear on the terminal.

Command	Meaning of command
% ls > filea	direct output of *ls* to file *filea*
% pr < filea > fileb	input from *filea* and output to *fileb*
% lpr < fileb	input from *fileb*
% % make program >& error	save both standard output and standard error in a file

Fig. CS4.5. *Standard I/O redirection.*

% *ls* | *pr* | *lpr*

Each vertical bar tells the shell to arrange for the output of the preceding command to be passed as input to the following command. A pipe is used to carry the data from one process to the other. One process writes into one end of the pipe, and another process reads from the other end. In the example, the write end of one pipe would be set up by the shell to be the standard output of *ls*, and the read end of the pipe would be the standard input of *pr*; there would be another pipe between *pr* and *lpr*.

A command such as *pr* that passes its standard input to its standard output, performing some processing on it, is called a *filter*. Many UNIX commands can be used as filters. Complicated functions can be pieced together as pipelines of common commands. Also, common functions, such as output formatting, do not need to be built into numerous commands, because the output of almost any program can be piped through *pr* (or some other appropriate filter).

Both of the common UNIX shells are also programming langugaes, with shell variables and the usual higher-level programming-language control constructs (loops, conditionals). The execution of a command is analogous to a subroutine call. A file of shell commands, a shell script, can be executed like any other command, with the appropriate shell being invoked automatically to read it. *Shell programming* thus can be used to combine ordinary programs conveniently for sophisticated applications without the necessity of any programming in conventional languages.

This external user view is commonly thought of as the definition of UNIX, yet it is the most easily changed definition. Writing a new shell with a quite different syntax and semantics would greatly change the user view while not changing the kernel or even the programmer interface. Several menu-driven and iconic interfaces for UNIX now exist, and the X Window System is rapidly becoming a standard. The heart of UNIX is, of course, the kernel. This kernel is much more difficult to change than is the user interface, because all programs depend on the system calls that it provides to remain consistent. Of course, new system calls can be added to increase functionality, but programs must then be modified to use the new calls.

Process Management

A major design problem for operating systems is the representation of processes. One substantial difference between UNIX and many other systems is the ease with which multiple processes can be created and manipulated. These processes are represented in UNIX by various control blocks. There are no system control blocks accessible in the virtual address space of a user process; control blocks associated with a process are stored in the kernel. The information in these control blocks is used by the kernel for process control and CPU scheduling.

Process Control Blocks

The most basic data structure associated with processes is the *process structure*. A process structure contains everything that the system needs to know about a process when the process is swapped out, such as its unique process identifier, scheduling information (such as the priority of the process), and the pointers to other control blocks. There is an array of process structures whose length is defined at system linking time. The process structures of ready processes are kept linked together by the scheduler in a doubly linked list (the ready queue), and there are pointers from each process structure to the process' parent, to its youngest living chills, and to various other relatives of interest, such as a list of processes sharing the same program code (text).

The *virtual address space* of a user process is divided into text (program code), data, and stack segments. The data and stack segments are always in the same address space, but may grow separately, and usually in opposite directions: most frequently, the stack grows down as the data grow up toward it. The text segment is sometimes (as on Intel 8086 with separate instruction and data space) in an address space different from the data and stack, and is usually read-only. The debugger puts a text segment in read-write mode to be able to allow insertion of breakpoints.

Every process with sharable text (almost all, under 4.3BSD) has a pointer from its process structure to a *text structure*. The text structure records how many processes are using the text segment, including a pointer into a list of their process structures, and where the page table for the text segment can be found on disk when it is swapped. The text structure itself is always resident in main memory: an array of such structures is allocated at system link time. The text, data, and stack segments for the processes may be swapped. When the segments are swapped in, they are paged.

The *page tables* record information on the mapping from the process' virtual memory to physical memory. The process structure contains pointers to the page table, for use when the process is resident in main memory, or the address of the process on the swap device, when the process is swapped. There is no special separate page table for a shared text segment; every process sharing the text segment has entries for its pages in the process page table.

Information about the process that is needed only when the process is resident (that is, not swapped out) is kept in the *user structure* (or *u structure*), rather than in the process structure. The *u* structure is mapped read-only into user virtual address space, so user processes can read its contents. It is writable by the kernel. On the VAX, a copy of the VAX PCB is keep here for saving the process' general registers, stack pointer, program counter, and page-table base registers when the process is not running. There is space to keep system-call parameters and return values. All user and group identifiers associated with the process (not just the effective use identifier kept in the process structure) are kept here. Signals, timers, and quotas have data structures here. Of more obvious relevance to the ordinary user, the current directory and the table of open files are maintained in the user structure.

Every process has both a user and a system phase. Most ordinary work is done in *user mode*, but, when a system call is made, it is performed in *system mode*. The system and user phases of a process never execute simultaneously. When a process is executing in system mode, a *kernel stack* for that process is used, rather than the user stack belonging to that process. The kernel stack for the process immediately follows the user structure: The kernel stack and the user structure together compose the *system data segment* for the process. The kernel has its own stack for use when it is not doing work on behalf of a process (for instance, for interrupt handling).

Figure CS4.6 illustrates how the process structure is used to find the various parts of a process.

The **fork** system call allocates a new process structure (with a new process identifier) for the child process, and copies the user structure. There is ordinarily no need for a new text structure, as the processes share their text; the appropriate counters and list are merely updated. A new page table is constructed, and new main memory is allocated for the data and stack segments of the child process. The copying of the user structure preserves open file descriptors, user and group identifiers, signal handling, and most similar properties of a process.

The **vfork** system call does not copy the data and stack to the new process; rather, the new process simply shares the page table of the old one. A new user structure and a new process structure are still created. A common use of this system call is by a shell to execute a command and to wait for its completion. The parent process uses **vfork** to produce the child process. Because the child process wishes to use an **execve** immediately to change its virtual address space completely, there is no need for a complete copy of the parent process. Such data structures as are necessary for manipulating pipes may be keep in registers between the **vfork** and the **execve**. Files may be closed in one process without affecting the other process, since the kernel data structures involved depend on the user structure, which is not shared. The parent is suspended when it calls **vfork** until the child either calls **execve** or terminates, so that the parent will not change memory that the child needs.

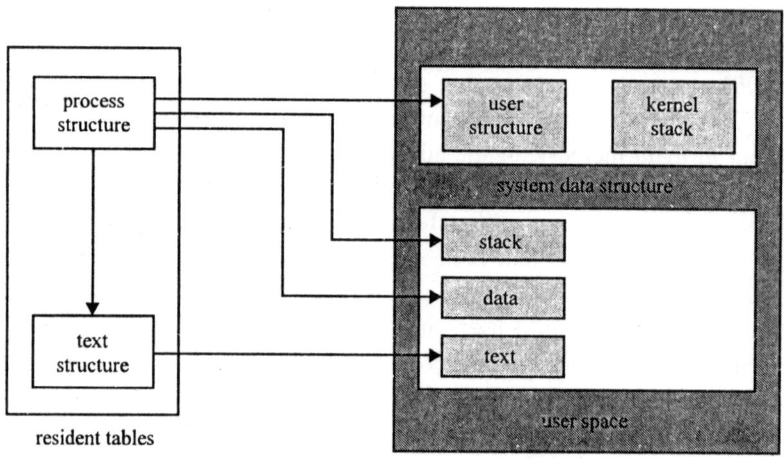

Fig. CS4.6. Finding parts of a process using the process structure.

When the parent process is large, **vfork** can produce substantial savings in system CPU time. However, it is a fairly dangerous system call, since any memory change occurs in both processes until the **execve** occurs. An alternative is to share all pages by duplicating the page table, but to mark the entries of both page tables as *copy-on-write*. The hardware protection bits are set to trap any attempt to write in these shared pages. If such a trap occurs, a new frame is allocated and the shared page is copied to the new frame. The page tables are adjusted to show that this page is no longer shared (and therefore no longer needs to be write-protected), and execution can resume.

An **execve** system call creates no new process or user structure; rather, the text and data of the process are replaced. Open files are preserved (although there is a way to specify that certain file descriptors are to be closed on an **execve**). Most signal-handling properties are preserved, but arrangements to call a specific user routine on a signal are canceled, for obvious reasons. The process identifier and most other properties of the process are unchanged.

CPU Scheduling

CPU scheduling in UNIX is designed to benefit interactive processes. Processes are given small CPU time slices by a priority algorithm that reduces to round-robin scheduling for CPU-bound jobs.

Every process has a *scheduling priority* associated with it; larger numbers indicate lower priority. Processes doing disk I/O or other important takes have priorities less than "pzero" and cannot be kills by signals. Ordinary user processes have positive priorities and thus are all less likely to be run than are any system process, although user processed can set precedence over one another through the *nice* command.

The more CPU time a process accumulates, the lower (more positive) its priority becomes, and vice versa, so there is negative feedback in CPU scheduling and it is difficult for a single process to take all the CPU time. Process aging is employed to prevent starvation.

Older UNIX systems used a 1-second quantum for the round-robin scheduling. 4.3BSD reschedules process every 0.1 second and recomputes priorities every second. The round-robin scheduling is accomplished by the *timeout* mechanism, which tells the clock interrupt driver to call a kernel subroutine after a specified interval; the subroutine to be called in this case causes the rescheduling and then resubmits a *timeout* to call itself again. The priority recomputation is also timed by a subroutine that resubmits a *timeout* for itself.

There is no preemption of one process by another in the kernel. A process may relinquish the CPU because it is waiting on I/O or because its time slice has expired. When a process chooses to relinquish the CPU, it goes to sleep on an event. The kernel primitive used for this purpose is called *sleep* (not to be confused with the user-level library routine of the same name). It takes an argument, which is by convention the address of a kernel data structure related to an event that the process wants to occur before that process is awakened. When the event occurs, the system process that knows about it calls *wakeup* with the address corresponding to the event, and *all* processes that had done a *sleep* on the same address are put in the ready queue to be run.

For example, a process waiting for disk I/O to complete will *sleep* on the address of the buffer header corresponding to the data being transferred. When the interrupt routine for the disk driver notes that the transfer is complete, it calls *wakeup* on the buffer header. The interrupt uses the kernel stack for whatever process happened to be running at the time, and the *wakeup* is done from that system process.

The process that actually does run is chosen by the scheduler. *Sleep* takes a second argument, which is scheduling priority to be used for this purpose. This priority argument, if less than "pzero," also prevents the process from being awakened prematurely by some exceptional event, such as a signal.

When a signal is generated, it is left pending until the system half of the affected process next runs. This event usually happens soon, since the signal normally causes the process to be awakened if the process has been waiting for some other condition.

There is no memory associated with events, and the caller of the routine that does a *sleep* on an event must be prepared to deal with a premature return, including the possibility that the reason for waiting has vanished.

There are *race conditions* involved in the event mechanism. If a process decides (because of checking a flag in memory, for instance) to sleep on an event, and the event occurs before the process can execute the primitive that does the actual sleep on the event, the process sleeping may then sleep forever. We prevent this situation by raising the hardware processor priority during the critical section so that no interrupts can occur, and thus only the process desiring the event can run until it is sleeping. Hardware processor priority is used in this manner to protect critical regions throughout the kernel, and is the greatest obstacle to porting UNIX to multiple processor machines. However, this problem has not prevented such ports from being done repeatedly.

Many processes such as text editors are I/O bound and usually will be scheduled mainly on the basis of waiting for I/O. Experience suggests that the UNIX scheduler performs best with I/O-bound jobs, as can be observed when there are several CPU-bounds jobs, such as text formatters or language interpreters, running.

What has been referred to here as *CPU scheduling* corresponds closely to the *short-term scheduling* of although the negative-feedback property of the priority scheme provides some long-term scheduling in that it largely determines the long-term *job mix*. Medium-term scheduling is done by the swapping mechanism described in previously.

Memory Management

Much of UNIX's early development was done on a PDP-11. The PDP-11 has only eight segments in its virtual address space, and each of these are at most 8192 bytes. The larger machines, such as the PDP-11/70, allow separate instruction and address spaces, which effectively double the address space and number of segments, but this address space is still relatively small. In addition, the kernel was even more severely constrained due to dedication of one data segment to interrupt vectors, another to point at the per-process system data segment, and yet another for the UNIBUS (system I/O bus) register. Further, on the smaller PDP-11s, total physical memory was limited to 256K. The total memory resources were insufficient to justify or support complex memory-management algorithms. Thus, UNIX swapped entire process memory images.

Swapping

Pre-3BSD UNIX systems use swapping exclusively to handle memory contention among processes: If there is too much contention, processes are swapped out until enough memory is available. Also, a few large processes can force many small processes out of memory, and a process larger than nonkernel main memory cannot be run at all. The system data segment (the *u* structure and kernel stack) and the user data segment (text [if nonsharable], data, and stack) are kept in contiguous main memory for swap-transfer efficiency, so external fragmentation of memory can be a serious problem.

Allocation of both main memory and swap space is done first-fit. When the size of a process' memory image increases (due to either stack expansion or data expansion), a new piece of memory big enough for the whole image is allocated. The memory image is copied, the old memory is freed, and the appropriate tables are updated. (An attempt is made in some systems to find memory contiguous to the end of the current piece, to avoid some copying.) If no single piece of main memory is large enough, the process is swapped out such that it will be swapped back in with the new size.

There is no need to swap out a sharable text segment, because it is read-only, and there is no need to read in a sharable text segment for a process when another instance is already in core. That is one of the main reasons for keeping track of sharable text segments: less swap traffic. The other reason is the reduced amount of main memory required for multiple processes using the same text segment.

Decisions regarding which processes to swap in or out are made by the *scheduler process* (also known as the *swapper*). The *scheduler* wakes up at least once every 4 seconds to check for processes to be swapped in or out. A process is more likely to be swapped out if it is idle, has been in main memory a long time, or is large; if no obvious candidates are found, other processes are picked by age. A process is more likely to be swapped in if it has been swapped out a long time, or is small. There are checks to prevent thrashing, basically by not letting a process be swapped out if it has not been in memory for a certain amount of time.

If jobs do not need to be swapped out, the process table is searched for a process deserving to be brought in (determined by how small the process is and how long it has been swapped out). If there is not enough memory available, processes are swapped out until there is.

In 4.3BSD, swap space is allocated in pieces that are multiples of a power of 2 and a minimum size (for example, 32 pages), up to a maximum that is determined by the size of the swap-space partition on the disk. If several logical disk partitions may be used for swapping, they should be the same size, for this reason. The several logical disk partitions should also be on separate disk arms to minimize disk seeks.

Many systems still use the swapping scheme just described. All Berkeley UNIX systems, on the other hand, depend primarily on paging for memory-contention management, and depend only secondarily on swapping. A scheme similar in outline to the traditional one is used to determine which processes get swapped, but the details differ and the influence of swapping is less.

Paging

Berkeley introduced paging to UNIX with 3BSD. VAX 4.2BSD is a demand-paged virtual-memory system. External fragmentation of memory is eliminated by paging. (There is, of course, internal fragmentation, but it is negligible with a reasonably small page size.) Swapping can be kept to a minimum because more jobs can be kept in main memory, because paging allows execution with only parts of each process in memory.

Demand paging is done in a straightforward manner. When a process needs a page and the page is not there, a page fault to the kernel occurs, a frame of main memory is allocated, and the proper disk page is read into the frame.

There are a few optimizations. If the page needed is still in the page table for the process, but has been marked invalid by the page-replacement process, it can be marked valid and used without any I/O transfer. Pages can similarly be retrieved from the list of free frames. When most processes are started many of their pages are prepaged and are put on the free list for recovery by this mechanism. Arrangements may also be made for a process to have no prepaging on startup, but that is seldom done, as it results in more page-fault overhead, being closer to pure demand paging.

If the page has to be fetched from disk, it must be locked in memory for the duration of the transfer. This locking ensures that the page will not be selected for page replacement. Once the page is fetched and mapped properly, it must remain locked if raw physical I/O is being done on it.

The *page-replacement* algorithm is more interesting. The VAX architecture has no hardware memory page-reference bit. This lack of hardware support makes many memory-management algorithms, such as page-fault frequency unusable. 4.2BSD uses a modification of the *second chance* (clock) algorithm. The map fall nonkernel main memory (the *core map* or *cmap*) is swept linearly and repeatedly by a software *clock hand*. When the clock hand reaches a given frame, if the frame is marked as in use by some software condition (for example, physical I/O is in progress using it), or the frame is already free, the frame is left untouched, and the clock hand sweeps to the next frame. Otherwise, the corresponding text or process page-table entry for this frame is located. If the entry is already invalid, the frame is added to the free list; otherwise, the page-table entry is made invalid but reclaimable (that is, if it does not get paged out by the next time it is wanted, it can just be made valid again).

4.3BSD Tahoe added support for systems which do implement the reference bit. On such systems, one pass of the clock turns the reference bit off, and a second pass places those pages whose reference bits remain off onto the free list for replacement. Of course, if the page is dirty (the VAX does have a dirty bit), it must first be written to disk before being added to the free list. Pageouts are done in clusters to improve performance.

There are checks to make sure that the number of valid data pages for a process does not fall too low, and to keep the paging device from being flooded with requests. There is also a mechanism by which a process may limit the amount of main memory it uses.

The LRU clock hand scheme is implemented in the *pagedaemon*, which is process 2 (remember that the *scheduler* is process 0, and *init* is process 1). This process spends most of its time sleeping, but a check is done several times per second (scheduled by a *timeout*) to see if action is necessary; if it is, process 2 is awakened. Whenever the number of free frames falls below a threshold, *lotsfree*, the *pagedaemon* is awakened; thus, if there is always a large amount of free memory, the *pagedaemon* imposes no load on the system, because it never runs.

The sweep of the clock hand each time the *pagedaemon* process is awakened (that is, the number of frames scanned, which is usually more than the number paged out), is determined both by the number for frames lacking to reach *lotsfree* and by the number of frames that the *scheduler* has determined are needed for various reasons (the more frames needed, the longer the sweep). If the number of frames free rises to *lotsfree* before the expected sweep is completed, the hand stops and the *pagedaemon* process sleeps. The parameters that determine the range of the clock-hand sweep are determined at system startup according to the amount of main memory, such that *pagedaemon* does not use more than 10 percent of all CPU time.

If the *scheduler* decides that the paging system is overloaded, processes will be swapped out whole until the overload is relieved. This swapping usually happens only if several conditions are met: load average is high, free memory has fallen below a low limit, *minfree*; and the average memory available over recent time is less than a desirable amount, *desfree*, where *lotsfree* > *desfree* > *minfree*. In other words, only a chronic shortage of memory with several processes trying to run will cause swapping, and even then free memory has to be extremely low at the moment. (An excessive paging rate or a need for memory by the kernel itself may also enter into the calculations, in rare cases.) Processes may be swapped by the *scheduler*, of course, for other reasons (such as simply for not running for a long time).

The parameter *lotsfree* is usually one-quarter of the memory in the map that the clock hand sweeps, and *desfree* and *minfree* are usually the same across different systems, but are limited to fractions of available memory.

Every process' text segment is by default shared and read-only. This scheme is practical with paging, because there is no external fragmentation, and the swap space gained by sharing more than offsets the negligible amount of overhead involved, as the kernel virtual space is large.

CPU scheduling, memory swapping, and paging interact: the lower the priority of a process, the more likely that its pages will be paged out and the more likely that it will be swapped in its entirety. The age preferences in choosing processes to swap guard against thrashing, but paging does so more effectively. Ideally, processes will not be swapped out unless they are idle, because each process will need only a small working set of pages in main memory at any one time, and the *pagedaemon* will reclaim unused pages for use by other processes.

The amount of memory the process will need is some fraction of that process' total virtual size, up to one-half if that process has been swapped out for a long time.

The VAX 512-byte hardware pages are too small for I/O efficiency, so they are clustered in groups of two so that all paging I/O is actually done in 1024-byte chunks. In other words, the effective page size is not necessarily identical to the hardware page size of the machine, although it must be a multiple of the hardware page size.

File System

The UNIX file system supports two main objects: files and directories. Directories are just files with a special format, so the representation of a file is the basic UNIX concept.

Blocks and Fragments

Most of the file system is taken up by *data blocks*, which contains whatever the users have put in their files. Let us consider how these data blocks are stored on this disk.

The hardware disk sector is usually 512 bytes. A block size larger than 512 bytes is desirable for speed. However, because UNIX file systems usually contain a very large number of small files, much larger blocks would cause excessive internal fragmentation. This is why the earlier 4.1BSD file system was limited to a 1024-byte (1K) block.

The 4.2BSD solution is to use two block sizes for files which have no indirect blocks: all the blocks of a file are of a large block size (such as 8K), except the last. The last block is an appropriate multiple of a smaller *fragment size* (for example, 1024) to fill out the file. Thus, a file of size 18,000 bytes would have two 8K blocks and one 2K fragment (which would not be filled completely).

The *block* and *fragment* sizes are set during file-system creation according to the intended use of the file system: If many small files are expected, the fragment size should be small; if repeated transfers of large files are expected the basic block size should be large. Implementation details force a maximum block-to-fragment ratio of 8:1, and a minimum block size of 4K, so typical choices are 4096:512 for the former case and 8192:1024 for the latter.

Suppose data are written to a file in transfer sizes of 1K bytes, and the block and fragment sizes of the file system are 4K and 512 bytes. The file system will allocate a 1K fragment to contain the data from the first transfer. The next transfer will cause a new 2K fragment to be allocated. The data from the original fragment must be copied into this new fragment, followed by the second 1K transfer. The allocation routines do attempt to find the required space on the disk immediately following the existing fragment so that no copying is necessary, but, if they cannot do so, up to seven copies may be required before the fragment becomes a block. Provisions have been made for programs to discover the block size for a file so that transfers of that size can be made, to avoid fragment recopying.

Inodes

A file is represented by an *inode*. An inode is a record that stores most of the information about a specific file on the disk. The name *inode* (pronounced *EYE node*) is derived from "index node" and was originally spelled "i-node"; the hyphen fell out of use over the years. The term is also sometimes spelled "I-node."

The inode contains the user and group identifiers to the file, the times of the last file modification and access, a count of the number of hard links (directory entries) to the file, and the type of the file (plain file, directory, symbolic, link, character device, block device, or socket). In addition, the inode contains 15 pointers to the disk blocks containing the data contents of the file. The first 12 of these pointers point to *direct blocks*; that is, they contain addresses of blocks that contain data of the file. Thus, the data for small files (no more than 12 blocks) can be referenced immediately, because a copy of the inode is kept in main memory while a file is open. If the block size is 4K, then up to 84K of data may be accessed directly from the inode.

The next three pointers in the inode point to *indirect blocks*. If the file is large enough to use indirect blocks, the indirect blocks are each of the major block size, the fragment size applies to only data blocks. The first indirect block pointer is the address of a *single indirect block*. The single indirect block is an index block, containing not data, but rather the addresses of blocks that do contain data. Then, there is a *double-indirect-block pointer*, the address of a block that contains the addresses of blocks that contain pointers to the actual data blocks. The last pointer would contain the address of a *triple indirect block*; however, there is no need for it. The minimum block size for a file system in 4.2BSD is 4K, so files with as many as 232 bytes will use only double, not triple, indirection. That is, as each block pointers takes 4 bytes, we have 49,152 bytes accessible in direct blocks, 4,194,304 bytes accessible by a single indirection, and 4,294,967,296 bytes reachable through double indirection, for a total of 4,299,210,752 bytes, which is larger than 232 bytes. The number 232 is significant because the file offset in the file structure in main memory is kept in a 32-bit word. Files therefore cannot be larger than 232 bytes. Since file pointers are signed integers (for seeking backward and forward in a file), the actual maximum file size is 232-1 bytes. Two gigabytes is large enough for most purposes.

Directories

There is no distinction between plain files and directories at this level of implementation; directory contents are kept in data blocks, and directories are represented by an inode in the same way as plain files. Only the inode type field distinguishes between plains files and directories. Plain files are not assumed to have a structure, however, whereas directories have a specific structure. In Version 7, file names were limited to 14 characters, so directories were a list of 16-byte entries: 2 bytes for an inode number and 14 bytes for a file name.

In 4.2BSD, file names are of variable length, up to 255 bytes, so directory entries are also of variable length. Each entry contains first the length of the entry, then the file name and the inode number. This variable-length entry makes the directory management and search routines more complex, but greatly improves the ability of users to choose meaningful names for their files and directories, with no practical limit on the length of the name.

The first two names in every directory are "." And "..". New directory entries are added to the directory in the first space available, generally after the existing files. A linear search is used.

The user refers to a file by a path name, whereas the file system uses the inode as its definition of a file. Thus, the kernel has to map the supplied user path name to an inode. The directories are used for this mapping.

First, a starting directory is determined. If the first character of the path name is "/", the starting directory is the root directory. If the path name starts with any character other than a slash, the starting directory is the current directory of the current process. The starting directory is checked for proper file type and access permissions, and an error is returned if necessary. The inode of the starting directory is always available.

The next element of the path name, up to the next "/", or to the end of the path name, is a file name. The starting directory is searched for this name, and an error is returned if the name is not found. If there is yet another element in the path name, the current inode must refer to a directory, and an error is returned if it does not, or if access is denied. This directory is searched, as was the previous one. This process continues until the end of the path name is reached and the desired inode is returned. This step-by-step process is needed because at any directory a mount point (or symbolic link, see below) may be encountered, causing the translation to move to a different directory structure for continuation.

Hard links are simply directory entries like any other. We handle symbolic links for the most part by starting the search over with the path name taken from the contents of the symbolic link. We prevent infinite loops by counting the number of symbolic links encountered during a path-name search and returning an error when a limit (eight) is exceeded.

Nondisk files (such as devices) do not have data blocks allocated on the disk. The kernel notices these file types (as indicated in the inode) and calls appropriate drivers to handle I/O for them.

Once the inode is found by, for instance, the **open** system call, a *file structure* is allocated to point to the inode. The file descriptor given to the user refers to this file structure. 4.3BSD added a *directory name cache* to hold recent directory-to-inode translations. This improvement greatly increased file system performance.

Mapping of a File Descriptor to an Inode

System calls that refer to open files indicate the file by passing a file descriptor as an argument. The file descriptor is used by the kernel to index a table of open files for the current process. Each entry of the table contains a pointer to a file structure. This file structure in turn points to the inode; see Figure CS4.7. The open file table has a fixed length which is only settable at boot time. Therefore, there is a fixed limit on the number of concurrently open files in a system.

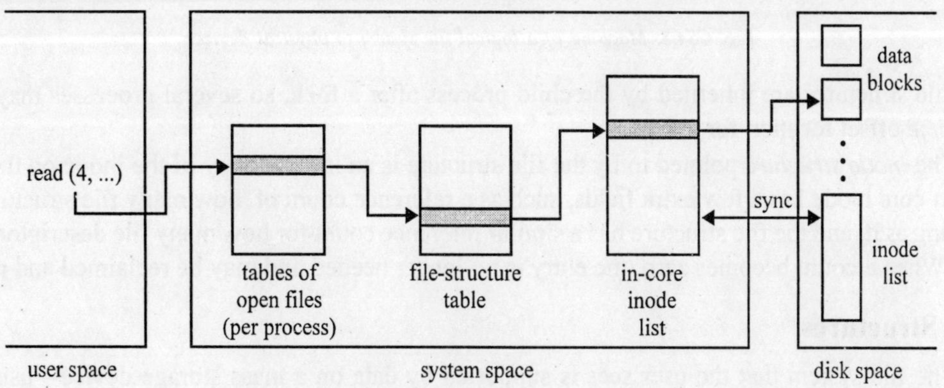

Fig. C.S4.7. File-system control blocks.

The **read** and **write** system calls do not take a position in the file as an argument. Rather, the kernel keeps a *file offset*, which is updated by an appropriate amount after each **read** or **write** according to the number of data actually transferred. The offset can be set directly by the **lseek** system call. If the file descriptor indexed an array of inode pointers instead of file pointers, this offset would have to be kept in the inode. Because more than one process may open the same file, and each such process needs its own offset for the file, keeping the offset in the inode is inappropriate. Thus, the file structure is used to contain the offset.

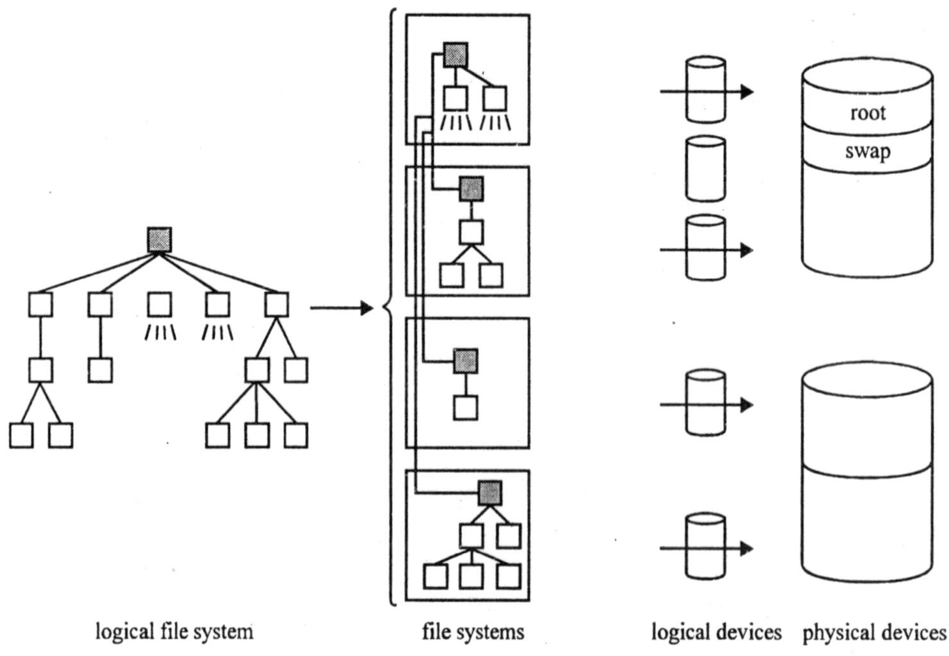

***Fig. CS4.8.** Mapping of a logical file system to physical devices.*

File structures are inherited by the child process after a **fork**, so several processes may share the *same* offset location for a file.

The *inode structure* pointed to by the file structure is an in-core copy of the inode on the disk. The in-core inode has a few extra fields, such as a reference count of how many file structures are pointing as it, and the file structure has a similar reference count for how many file descriptors refer to it. When a count becomes zero, the entry is no longer needed and may be reclaimed and reused.

Disk Structures

The file system that the user sees is supported by data on a mass storage device—usually, a disk. The user ordinarily knows of only one file system, but this one logical file system may actually consist of several *physical* file systems, each on a different device. Because device characteristics differ, each separate hardware device defines its own physical file system. In fact, it is generally desirable to partition large physical devices, such as disks, into multiple *logical* devices. Each logical device defines a physical file system. Figure CS4.8 illustrates how a directory structure is partitioned into file systems, which are mapped onto logical devices, which are partitions of physical devices. The sizes and locations of these partitions were coded into device drivers in earlier systems, but are maintained on the disk by 4.3BSD.

Partitioning a physical device into multiple file systems has several benefits. Different file systems can support different uses. Although most partitions would be used by the file system, at least one will be necessary for a swap area for the virtual-memory software. Reliability is improved, because software damage is generally limited to only one file system. We can improve efficiency by varying the file-system parameters (such as the block and fragment sizes) for each partition. Also, separate file systems prevent one program from using all available space for a large file, because files cannot be split across file systems. Finally, disk backups are done per partition, and it is faster to search a backup tape for a file if the partition is smaller. Restoring the full partition from tape is also faster.

The actual number of file systems on a drive varies according to the size of the disk and the purpose of the computer system as a whole. One file system, the *root file system*, is always available. Other file systems may be *mounted*—that is, integrated into the directory hierarchy of the root file system.

A bit in the inode structure indicates that the inode has a file system mounted on it. A reference to this file causes the *mount table* to be searched to find the device number of the mounted device. The device number is used to find the inode of the root directory of the mounted file system, and that inode is used. Conversely, if a path-name element is ".." and the directory being searched is the root directory of a file system that is mounted, the mount table is searched to find the inode it is mounted on, and that inode is used.

Each file system is a separate system resource and represents a set of files. The first sector on the logical device is the *boot block*, possibly containing a primary bootstrap program, which may be used to call a secondary bootstrap program residing in the next 7.5K A system needs only one partition containing boot-block data, but duplicates may be installed via privileged programs by the systems manager, to allow booting when the primary copy is damaged. The *superblock* contains static parameters of the file system. These parameters include the total size of the file system, the block and fragment sizes of the data blocks, and assorted parameters that affect allocation policies.

Implementations

The user interface to the file system is simple and well defined, allowing the implementation of the file system itself to be changed without significant effect on the user. The file system was changed between Version 6 and Version 7, and again between Version 7 and 4BSD. For Version 7, the size of inodes doubled, the maximum file and file-system sizes increased, and the details of free-list handling and superblock information changed. At that time also, *seek* (with a 16-bit offset) became *lseek* (with a 32-bit offset), to allow specification of offsets in larger files, but few other changes were visible outside the kernel.

In 4.0BSD, the size of blocks used in the file system was increased from 512 bytes to 1024 bytes. Although this increased size produced increased internal fragmentation on the disk, it doubled throughput, due mainly to the greater number of data accessed on each disk transfer.

This idea was later adopted by System V, along with a number of other ideas, device drivers, and programs.

4.2BSD added the Berkeley Fast File System, which increased speed, and was accomplished by new features. Symbolic links required new system calls. Long file names necessitated the new directory system calls to traverse the now-complex internal directory structure. Finally, the **truncate** calls were added. The Fast File System was a success, and is now found in most implementations of UNIX. Its performance is made possible by its layout and allocation policies, which we discuss next. In section 11.2.4, we discussed changes made in SunOS to further increase disk throughput.

Layout and Allocation Policies

The kernel uses a <*logical device number, inode number*> pair to identify a file. The logical device number defines the file system involved. The inodes in the file system are numbered in sequence. In the Version 7 file system, all inodes are in an array immediately following a single superblock at the beginning of the logical device, with the data blocks following the inodes. The *inode number* is effectively just an index into this array.

With the Version 7 file system, a block of a file can be anywhere on the disk between the end of the inode array and the end of the file system. Free blocks are kept in a linked list in the superblock. Blocks are pushed onto the front of the free list, and are removed from the front as needed to serve new files or to extend existing files. Thus, the blocks of a file may be arbitrarily far from both the inode and one another. Furthermore, the more a file system of this kind is used, the more disorganized the blocks in a file become. We can reserve this process only by reinitializing and restoring the entire file system, which is not a convenient task to perform.

Another difficulty is that the reliability of the file system is suspect. For speed, the super-block of each mounted file system is kept in memory. Keeping the superblock in memory allows the kernel to access a superblock quickly, especially for using the free list. Every 30 seconds, the superblock is written to the disk, to keep the in-core and disk copies synchronized (by the update program, using the **sync** system call). However, it is not uncommon for system bugs or hardware failures to cause a system crash, which destroys the in-core superblock between updates to the disk. Then, the free list on disk does not reflect accurately the state of the disk; to reconstruct it, we must perform a lengthy examination of all blocks in the file system. Note that this problem still remains in the new file system.

The 4.2BSD file-system implementation is radically different from that of Version 7. This reimplementation was done primarily to improve efficiency and robustness, and most such changes are invisible outside the kernel. There were other changes introduced at the same time, such as symbolic links and long file names (up to 255 characters), that are visible at both the system-call and the user levels. Most of the changes required for these features were not in the kernel, however, but rather were in the programs that use them.

Space allocation is especially different. The major new concept in 4.3BSD is the *cylinder group.* The cylinder group was introduced to allow localization of the blocks in a file. Each cylinder group occupies one or more consecutive cylinders of the disk, so that disk accesses within the cylinder group require minimal disk head movement. Every cylinder group has a superblock, a cylinder block, an array of inodes, and some data blocks (Figure CS4.9).

The superblock is identical in each cylinders group, so that it can be recovered from any one of them in the event of disk corruption. The *cylinder block* contains dynamic parameters of the particular cylinder group. These include a bit map of free data blocks and fragments, and a bit map of free inodes. Statistics on recent progress of the allocation strategies are also kept here.

The header information in a cylinder group (the superblock, the cylinder block, and the inodes) is not always at the beginning of the cylinder group. If it were, the header information for every cylinder group might be on the same disk platter; a single disk head crash could wipe out all of them. Therefore; each cylinder group has its header information at a different offset from the beginning of the group.

It is common for the directory-listing command *ls* to read all the inodes of every file in a directory, making it desirable for all such inodes to be close together on the disk. For this reason, the inode for a file is usually allocated from the same cylinder group as is the inode of the file's parent directory. Not everything can be localized, however, so an inode for a new directory is put in a *different* cylinder group from that of its parent directory. The cylinder group chosen for such a new directory inode is that with the greatest number of unused inodes.

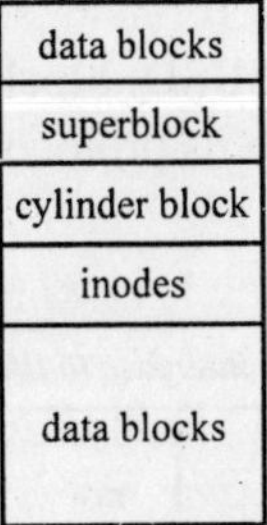

Fig. C.S4.9. *4.3BSD cylinder group.*

To reduce disk head seeks involved in accessing the data blocks of a file, we allocate blocks from the same cylinder group as often as possible. Because a single file cannot be allowed to take up all the blocks in a cylinder group, a file exceeding a certain size (such as 2 megabytes) has further block allocation redirected to a different cylinder group, the new group being chosen from among those having more than average free space. If the file continues to grow, allocation is again redirected (at each megabyte) to yet another cylinder group. Thus, all the blocks of a small file are likely to be in the same cylinder group, and the number of long head seeks involved in accessing a large file is kept small.

There are two levels of disk-block-allocation routines. The global policy routines select a desired disk block according to the considerations already discussed. The local policy routines use the specific information recorded in the cylinder blocks to choose a block near the one requested. If the requested block is not in use, it is returned. Otherwise, the block rationally closest to the one requested in the same cylinder, or a block in a different cylinder but in the same cylinder group, is returned. If there are no more blocks in the cylinder group, a quadratic rehash is done among all the other cylinder groups to find a block; if that fails, an exhaustive search is done. If enough free space (typically 10 percent) is left in the file system, blocks usually are found where desired, the quadratic rehash and exhaustive search are not used, and performance of the file system does not degrade with use.

Because of the increased efficiency of the Fast File System, typical disks are now utilized at 30 percent of their raw transfer capacity. This percentage is a marked improvement over that realized with the Version 7 file system, which used about 3 percent of the bandwidth.

4.3BSD Tahoe introduced the Fat Fast File System, which allows the number of inodes per cylinder group, the number of cylinders per cylinder group, and the number of distinguished rotational positions to be set when the file system is created. 4.3BSD used to set these parameters according to the disk hardware type.

I/O System

One of the purposes of an operating system is to hide the peculiarities of specific hardware devices from the user. For example, the file system presents a simple consistent storage facility (the file) independent of the underlying disk hardware. In UNIX, the peculiarities of I/O devices are also hidden from the bulk of the kernel itself by the *I/O system*. The I/O system consists of a buffer caching system, general device driver code, and drivers for specific hardware devices. Only the device driver knows the peculiarities of a specific device. The major parts of the I/O system are diagrammed in Figure CS4.10.

There are three main kinds of I/O in 4.3BSD: block devices, character devices, and the *socket* interface. The socket interface, together with its protocols and network interfaces, will be treated in previous paragraph.

<table>
<tr><td colspan="6">system-call interface to the kernel</td></tr>
<tr><td>socket</td><td>plain file</td><td rowspan="2">cooked block interface</td><td rowspan="2">raw block interface</td><td rowspan="2">raw tty interface</td><td>cooked TTY</td></tr>
<tr><td>protocols</td><td>file system</td><td>line discipline</td></tr>
<tr><td>network interface</td><td colspan="3">block-device driver</td><td colspan="2">character-device driver</td></tr>
<tr><td colspan="6">the hardware</td></tr>
</table>

Fig. CS4.10. *4.3BSD Kernel I/O structure.*

Block devices include disks and tapes. Their distinguishing characteristic is that they are directly addressable in a fixed block size—usually, 512 bytes. A block-device driver is required to isolate details of tracks, cylinders, and so on, from the rest of the kernel. Block devices are accessible directly through appropriate device special files (such as */dev/rp0*), but are more commonly accessed indirectly through the file system. In either case, transfers are buffered through the *block buffer cache*, which has a profound effect on efficiency.

Character devices include terminals and line printers, but also almost everything else (except network interfaces) that does not use the block buffer cache. For instance, */dev/mem* is an interface to physical main memory, and */dev/null* is a bottomless sink for data and an endless source of end-of-file markers. Some devices, such as high-speed graphics interfaces, may have their own buffers or may always do I/O directly into the user's data space; because they do not use the block buffer cache, they are classed as character devices.

Terminals and terminal-like devices use *C-lists*, which are buffers smaller than those of the block buffer cache.

Block devices and *character* devices are the two main device classes. Device drivers are accessed by one of two arrays of entry points. One array is for block devices; the other is for character devices. A device is distinguished by a class (block or character) and a *device number*. The device number consists of two parts. The *major device number* is used to index the array for character or block devices to find entries into the appropriate device driver. The *minor device number* is interpreted by the device driver as, for example, a logical disk partition or a terminal line.

A device driver is connected to the rest of the kernel only by the entry points recorded in the array for its class, and by its use of common buffering systems. This segregation is important for portability, and also for system configuration.

Block Buffer Cache

The block devices use a block buffer cache. The buffer cache consists of a number of buffer headers, each of which can point to a piece of physical memory, as well as to a device number and a block number on the device. The buffer headers for blocks not currently in use are kept in several linked lists, one each for

- Buffers recently used. Linked in LRU order (the LRU list)
- Buffers not recently used, or without valid contents (the AGE list)
- EMPTY buffers with no physical memory associated with them

The buffers in these lists are also hashed by device and block number for search efficiency.

When a block is wanted from a device (a read), the cache is searched. If the block is found, it is used, and no I/O transfer is necessary. If it is not found, a buffer is chosen from the AGE list, or the LRU list if AGE is empty. Then the device number and block number associated with it are updated, memory is found for it if necessary, and the new data are transferred into it from the device. If there are no empty buffers, the LRU buffer is written to its device (if it is modified) and the buffer is reused.

On a write, if the block in question is already in the buffer cache, the new data are put in the buffer (overwriting any previous data), the buffer header is marked to indicate the buffer has been modified, and no I/O is immediately necessary. The data will be written when the buffer is needed for other data. If the block is not found in the buffer cache, an empty buffer is chosen (as with a read) and a transfer is done to this buffer.

Writes are periodically forced for dirty buffer blocks to minimize potential file-system inconsistencies after a crash.

The number of data in a buffer in 4.3BSD is variable, up to a maximum over all file systems, usually 8K. The minimum size is the paging-cluster size, usually 1024 bytes. Buffers are page-cluster aligned, and any page cluster may be mapped into only one buffer at a time, just as any disk block may be mapped into only one buffer at a time. The EMPTY list holds buffer headers which are used if a physical memory block of 8K is split to hold multiple, smaller blocks. Headers are needed for these blocks and are retrieved from EMPTY.

The number of data in a buffer may grow as a user process writes more data following those already in the buffer. When this increase in the data occurs, a new buffer large enough to hold all the data is allocated, and the original data are copied into it, followed by the new data. If a buffer shrinks, a buffer is taken off the empty queue, excess pages are put in it, and that buffer is released to be written to disk.

Some devices, such as magnetic tapes, require blocks to be written in a certain order, so facilities are provided to force a synchronous write of buffers to these devices, in the correct order. Directory blocks are also written synchronously, to forestall crash inconsistencies. Consider the chaos that could occur if many changes were made to a directory, but the directory entries themselves were not updated.

The size of the buffer cache can have a profound effect on the performance of a system, because, if it is large enough, the percentage of cache hits can be high and the number of actual I/O transfers low.

There are some interesting interactions among the buffer cache, the file system, and the disk drivers. When data are written to a disk file, they are buffered in the cache, and the disk driver sorts its output queue according to disk address. These two actions allow the disk driver to minimized disk head seeks and to write data at times optimized for disk rotation. Unless synchronous writes are required, a process writing to disk simply writes into the buffer cache, and the system asynchronously writes the data to disk when convenient. The user process sees very fast writes. When data are read from a disk file, the block I/O system does read-ahead; however, writes are much nearer to asynchronous than are reads. Thus, output to the disk through the file system is often faster than is input for large transfers, counter to intuition.

Raw Device Interfaces

Almost every block device also has a character interface, and these are called *raw device interface*. Such an interface differs from the *block interface* in that the block buffer cache is bypassed.

Each disk driver maintains a queue of pending transfers. Each record in the queue specifies whether it is a read or a write, a main memory address for the transfer (usually in 512-byte increments), a device address for the transfer (usually the address of a disk sector), and a transfer size (in sectors). It is simple to map the information from a block buffer to what is required for this queue.

It is almost as simple to map a piece of main memory corresponding to part of a user process' virtual address space. This mapping is what a raw disk interface, for instance, does. Unbuffered transfers directly to or from a user's virtual address space are thus allowed. The size of the transfer is limited by the physical devices, some of which require an even number of bytes.

The kernel accomplishes transfers for swapping and paging simply by putting the appropriate request on the queue for the appropriate device. No special swapping or paging device driver is needed.

The 4.2BSD file-system implementation was actually written and largely tested as a user process that used a raw disk interface, before the code was moved into the kernel. In an interesting about-face, the Mach operating system has no file system per se. File systems can be implemented as user-level tasks.

C-Lists

Terminal drivers use a character buffering system, which keeps small blocks of characters (usually 28 bytes) in linked lists. There are routines to enqueue and dequeue characters for such lists. Although all free character buffers are kept in a single free list, most device drivers that use them limit the number of characters that may be queued at one time for any given terminal line.

A **write** system calls to a terminal enqueues characters on a list for the device. An initial transfer is started, and interrupts cause dequeuing of characters and further transfers.

Input is similarly interrupt driven. Terminal drivers typically support *two* input queues, however, and conversion from the first (raw queue) to the other (canonical queue) is triggered by the interrupt routine putting an end-of-line character on the raw queue. The process doing a read on the device is then awakened, and its system phase does the conversion; the character thus put on the canonical queue are then available to be returned to the user process by the read.

It is also possible to have the device driver bypass the canonical queue and return characters directly from the raw queue. This mode of operation is known as *raw mode*. Full-screen editors, and other programs that need to react to every keystroke, use this mode.

Interprocess Communication

Many tasks can be accomplished in isolated processes, but many others require interprocess communication. Isolated computing systems have long served for many applications, but networking in increasingly important. With the increasing use of personal workstations, resources sharing is becoming more common. Interprocess communication has not traditionally been one of UNIX's strong points.

Most UNIX systems have not permitted *shared memory* because the PDP-11 hardware did not encourage it. System V does not support a shared-memory facility, and one was planned for 4.2BSD, but was not implemented due to time constraints. Solaris 2 support shared memory, as do many other current versions of UNIX. In any case, shared memory presents a problem in a networked environment, because network accesses can never be as fast as memory accesses on the local machine. Although we could, of course, pretend that memory was shared between two separate machines by copying data across a network transparently; the major benefit of shared memory (speed) would be lost.

Sockets

The *pipe* is the IPC mechanism most characteristics of UNIX. A pipe permits a reliable unidirectional byte stream between two processes. It is traditionally implemented as an ordinary file, with a few exceptions. It has no name in the file system, being created instead by the pipe system call. Its size is fixed, and when a process attempts to write to a full pipe, the process is suspended. Once call data previously written into the pipe have been read out, writing continues at the beginning of the file (pipes are not true circular buffers). One benefit of the small size (usually 4096 bytes) of pipes is that pipe data are seldom actually written to disk; they usually are kept in memory by the normal block buffer cache.

In 4.3BSD, pipes are implemented as a special case of the *socket* mechanism. The socket mechanism provides a general interface not only to facilities such as pipes, which are local to one machine, but also to networking facilities. Even on the same machine, a pipe can be used only by two processes related through use of the **fork** system call. The socket mechanism can be used by unrelated processes.

A socket is an endpoint of communication. A socket in use usually has an *address* bound to it. The nature of the address depends on the *communication domain* of the socket. A characteristic property of a domain is that processes communicating in the same domain use the same *address format*. A single socket can communicate in only one domain.

The three domain currently implemented in 4.3BSD are the UNIX domain (AF_UNIX), the Internet domain (AF_INET), and the XEROX Network Services (NS) domain (AF_NS). The address format of the UNIX domain is ordinary file-system path names, such as */alpha/beta/gamma*. Processes communicating in the Internet domain use DARPA Internet Communications protocols (such as TCP/IP) and Internet addresses, which consists of a 32-bit host number and a 32-bit port number (representing a rendezvous point on the host).

There are several *socket types*, which represent classes of service. Each type may or may not be implemented in any communication domain. If a type is implemented in a given domain, it may be implemented by one or more protocols, which may be selected by the user:

- **Stream sockets:** These sockets provide reliable, duplex, sequenced data streams. No data are lost of duplicated in delivery, and there are no record boundaries. This type is supported in the Internet domain by the TCP protocol. In the UNIX domain, pipes are implemented as a pair of communicating stream sockets.
- **Sequenced packet sockets:** These sockets provide data stream like those of stream sockets, except that record boundaries are provided. This type is used in the XEROX AF_NS protocol.
- **Datagram sockets:** These sockets transfer messages of variable size in either direction. There is no guarantee that such message will arrive in the same order they were sent, or that they will be unduplicated, or that they will arrive at all, but the original message (record) size is preserved in any datagram that does arrive. This type is supported in the Internet domain by the UDP protocol.
- **Reliably delivered message sockets:** These sockets transfer messages that are guaranteed to arrive, and that otherwise are like the messages transferred using datagram sockets. This type is currently unsupported.
- **Raw sockets:** These sockets allow direct access by processes to the protocols that support the other socket types. The protocols accessible include not only the uppermost one, but also lower-level protocols. For example, in the Internet domain, it is possible to reach TCP, IP beneath that, or an Ethernet protocol beneath that. This capability is useful for developing new protocols.

The socket facility has a set of system calls specific to it. The **socket** system call creates a socket. It takes as arguments specifications of the communication domain, the socket type, and the protocol to be used to support that type. The value returned by the call is a small integer called a *socket descriptor*, which is in the same name space as file descriptors. The socket descriptor indexes the array of open "files" in the *u* structure in the kernel, and has a file structure allocated for it. The 4.3BSD file structure may point to a *socket* structure instead of to an inode. In this case, certain socket information (such as the socket's type, message count, and the data in its input and output queues) is kept directly in the socket structure.

For another process to address a socket, the socket must have a name. A name is bound to a socket by the **bind** system call, which takes the socket descriptor, a pointer to the name, and the length of the name as a byte string. The contents and length of the byte string depend on the address format. The **connect** system call is used to initiate a connection. The arguments are syntactically the same as those for **bind**; the socket descriptor represents the local socket and the address is that of the foreign socket to which the attempt to connect is made.

Many processes that communicate using the socket IPC follow the *client-server model.* In this model, the server process provides a *service* to the *client* process. When the service is available, the server process listen on a well-known address, and the client process uses **connect**, as described previously, to reach the server.

A server process uses **socket** to create a socket and **bind** to bind the well-known address of its service to that socket. Then, it uses the **listen** system call to tell the kernel that it is ready to accept connections from clients, and to specify how many pending connections the kernel should queue until the server can service them. Finally, the server uses the **accept** system call to accept individual connections. Both **listen** and **accept** take as an argument the socket descriptor of the original socket. **Accept** returns a new socket descriptor corresponding to the new connection; the original socket descriptor is still open for further connections. The server usually uses **fork** to produce a new process after the **accept** to service the client while the original server process continues to listen for more connections.

There are also system calls for setting parameters of a connection and for returning the address of the foreign socket after an **accept**.

When a connection for a socket type such as a stream socket is established, the addresses of both endpoints are known and no further addressing information is needed to transfer data. The ordinary **read** and **write** system calls may then be used to transfer data.

The simplest way to terminate a connection and to destroy the associated socket is to use the **close** system call on its socket descriptor. We may also wish to terminate only one direction of communication of a duplex connection; the **shutdown** systems call can be used for this purpose.

Some socket types, such as datagram sockets, do not support connections; instead, their sockets exchange datagrams that must be addressed individually. The system calls **sendto** and **recvfrom** are used for such connections. Both take as arguments a socket descriptor, a buffer pointer and the length, and an address-buffer pointer and length. The address buffer contains the address to send to for **sendto** and is filled in with the address of the datagram just received by **recvfrom**. The number of data actually transferred is returned by both system calls.

The **select** system call can be used to multiplex data transfers on several file descriptors and/or socket descriptors. It can even be used to allow one server process to listen for client connections for many services and to **fork** a process for each connection as the connection is made. The server does a **socket**, **bind** and **listen** for each service, and then does a **select** on all the socket descriptors. When **select** indicates activity on a descriptor, the server does an **accept** on it and forks a process on the new descriptor returned by **accept**, leaving the parent process to do a **select** again.

Network Support

Almost all current UNIX systems support the UUCP network facilities, which are mostly used over dial-up telephone lines to support the UUCP mail network and the USENET news network. These are, however, rudimentary networking facilities, as they do not support even remote login, mush less remoter procedure call or distributed file systems. These facilities are also almost completely implemented as user processes, and are not part of the operating system proper.

4.3BSD supports the DARPA Internet protocols UDP, TCP, IP, and ICMP on a wide range of Ethernet, token-ring, and ARPANET interfaces. The framework in the kernel to support this is intended to facilitate the implementation of further protocols, and all protocols are accessible via the socket interface. The first version of the code was written by Rob Gurwitz of BBM as an add-on package for 4.1BSD.

The International Standards Organization's (ISO) Open System Interconnection (OSI) Reference Model for networking prescribes seven layers of network protocols and strict methods of communication between them. An implementation of a protocol may communicate only with a peer entity speaking the same protocol at the same layer, or with the protocol-protocol interface of a protocol in the layer immediately above or below in the same system. The ISO networking model is implemented in 4.3BSD Reno and 4.4BSD.

The 4.3BSD networking implementation, and to certain, extent the *socket* facility, is more oriented toward the ARPANET Reference Model (ARM). The ARPANET in its original form served as a proof of concept for many networking concepts, such as packet switching and protocol layering. The ARPANET was retired in 1988 because the hardware that supported it was no longer state of the art. Its successors, such as the NSFNET and the Internet, are even larger, and serve as a communications utility for researchers and as a testbed for Internet gateway research. The ARM predates the ISO model; the ISO model was in large part inspired by the ARPANET research.

Although the ISO model is often interpreted as requiring a limit of the one protocol communicating per layer, the ARM allows several protocols in the same layer. There are only four protocol layers in the ARM, plus

- **Process/Applications:** This layer subsumes the application, presentation, and session layers of the ISO model. Such user-level programs as the File Transfer Protocol (FTP) and Telnet (remote login) exist at this level.
- **Host-Host:** This layer corresponds to ISO's transport and the top part of its network layers. Both the Transmission Control Protocol (TCP) and the Internet Protocol (IP) are in the layer, with TCP on top of IP. TCP corresponds to an ISO transport protocol, and IP performs the addressing functions of the ISO network layer.
- **Network Interface:** This layer spans the lower part of the ISO network layer and all of the data-link layer. The protocols involved here depend on the physical network type. The ARPANET uses the IMP-Host protocols, whereas an Ethernet uses Ethernet protocols.
- **Network Hardware:** The ARM is primarily concerned with software, so there is no explicit network hardware layer; however, any actual network will have hardware corresponding to the ISO hardware layer.

The networking framework in 4.3BSD is more generalized than is either the ISO model or the ARM, although it is most closely related to the ARM.

User processes communicate with network protocols (and thus with other processes on other machines) via the *socket* facility, which corresponds to the ISO Session layer, as it is responsible for setting up and controlling communications.

Sockets are supported by *protocols*—possibly by several, layered one on another. A protocol may provide services such as reliable delivery, suppression of duplicate transmissions, flow control, or addressing, depending on the socket type being supported and the services required by any higher protocols.

A protocol may communicate with another protocol or with the network interface that is appropriate for the network hardware. There is little restriction in the general framework on what protocols may communicate with what other protocols, or on how many protocols may be layered on top of one another. The user process may, by means of the raw socket type, directly access any layer of protocols from the uppermost used to support one of the other socket types, such as streams, down to a raw network interface. This capability is used by routing processes and also for new protocols development.

There tends to be one *network-interface* driver per network controller type. The network interface is responsible for handling characteristics specific to the local network being addressed. This arrangement ensures that the protocols using the interface do not need to be concerned with these characteristics.

ISO reference model	**ARPANET reference model**	**4.2BSD layers**	**Example layering**
application presentation	process application	user programs and libraries	telnet
session		sockets	sock_stream
transport	host–host	protocol	TCP
network data link			IP
hardware	network interface	network interface	Ethernet driver
	network hardware	network hardware	Interian controller

Fig. CS4.11. Network reference models and layering.

The functions of the network interface depend largely on the *network hardware*, which is whatever is necessary for the network to which it is connected. Some networks may support reliable transmission at this level, but most do not. Some networks provide broadcast addressing, but many do not.

The socket facility and the networking framework use a common set of memory buffers, or *mbufs*. These are intermediate in size between the large buffers used by the block I/O system and the C-lists used by character devices. An *mbuf* is 128 bytes long, 12 bytes of which may be used for data; the rest is used for pointers to link the *mbuf* into queues and for indicators of how much of the data area is actually in use.

Data are ordinarily passed between layers (socket-protocol, protocol-protocol, or protocol-network interface) in *mbufs*. This ability to pass the buffers containing the data eliminates some data copying, but there is still frequently a need to remove or add protocol headers. It is also convenient and efficient for many purposes to be able to hold data that occupy an area the size of the memory-management page. Thus, it is possible for the data of an *mbuf* to reside not in the *mbuf* itself, but rather elsewhere in memory. There is an *mbuf* page table for this purpose, as well as a pool of pages dedicated to *mbuf* use.

Summary

The early advantages of UNIX were that this system was written in a high-level language, was distributed in source form, and had provided powerful operating-system primitives on an inexpensive platform. These advantages led to UNIX's popularity at educational, research, and government institutions and eventually in the commercial world. This popularity first produced many strains of UNIX with variant and improved facilities. Market pressures are currently leading to the consolidation of these versions. One of the most influential versions is 4.3BSD, developed at Berkeley for the VAX, and later ported to many other platforms.

UNIX provides a file system with tree-structured directories. Files are supported by the kernel as unstructured sequences of bytes. Direct access and sequential access are supported through system calls and library routines.

Files are stored as an array of fixed-size data blocks with perhaps a trailing fragment. The data blocks are found by pointers in the inode. Directory entries point to inodes. Disk space is allocated from cylinder groups to minimize head movement and to improve performance.

UNIX is a multiprogrammed system. Processes can easily create new processes with the **fork** system call. Processes can communicate with pipes or, more generally, sockets. They may be grouped into jobs that may be controlled with signals.

Processes are represented by two structures: the process structure and the user structure. CPU scheduling is a priority algorithm with dynamically computed priorities that reduces to round-robin scheduling in the extreme case.

4.3BSD memory management is swapping supported by paging. A *pagedaemon* process uses a modified second-change page-replacement algorithm to keep enough free frames to support the executing processes.

Page and file I/O uses a block buffer cache to minimize the amount of actual I/O. Terminal devices use a separate character buffering system.

Networking support is one of the most important features in 4.3BSD. The socket concept provides the programming mechanism to access other processes, even across a network. Sockets provide an interface to several sets of protocols.

Select Bibliography

Time-sharing systems were proposed first by Strachey [1959]. The earliest time-sharing systems were the Compatible Time-Sharing System (CTSS) developed at MIT (Corbato et al.) [1962] and the SDC Q-32 system, built by the System Development Corporation (Schwartz et al. [1964], Schwartz and Weissman [1967]). Other early, but more sophisticated, systems include the MULTIplexed Information and Computing Services (MULTICS) system development at MIT (Corbato and Vyssotsky [1965]), the XDS-940 system developed at the University of California at Berkeley (Lichtenberger and Pirtle [1965]), and the IBM TSS/360 system (Lett and Konigsford [1968]).

MS DOS and PCs are described by Norton [1986] and by Norton and Wilton [1988]. An overview of the Apple Macintosh hardware and software is presented in Apple [1987]. The OS/2 operating system is covered in Microsoft [1989]. More OS/2 information can be found in Letwin [1988] and in Deitel and Kogan [1992]. Solomon and Russinovich [2000] discuss the structure of Microsoft Windows 2000 operating system.

A good coverage of cluster computing is presented by Buyya [1999]. Recent advances in cluster computing is offered by Ahmed [2000].

Discussions concerning hand-held devices are offered by Murray[1988] and Rhodes and McKeehan [1999].

Many general textbooks cover operating systems, including Milenkovic [1987], Finkel [1988], Deitel [1990], Stallings [2000b], Nutt [1999] and Tanenbaum [2001].

Hennessy amd Patterson [1996] provide coverage of I/O systems and buses, and of system architecture in general. Tanenbaum [1990] describes the architecture of microcomputers, starting at a detailed hardware level.

Discussions concerning magnetic-disk technology are presented by Freedman [1983] and by Harker et al. [1981]. Optical disks are covered by Kenville [1982], Fujitani [1984], O'Leary and Kitts [1985], Gait [1988], and Olsen and Kenley [1989]. Discussions of floppy disks are offered by Pechura and Schoeffler [1983] and by Sarisky [1983].

Cache memories, including associative memory, are described and analyzed by Smith [1982]. That paper also includes an extensive bibliography on the subject.

General discussions concerning mass-storage technology are offered by Chi [1982] and by Hoagland [1985].

Tanenbaum [1996] and Halsall [1992] provide general overviews of computer networks. Fortier [1989] presents a detailed discussion of networking hardware and software.

The mutual-exclusion algorithms 1 and 2 for two processes were first discussed in the classic paper by Dijkstra [1965a]. Dekker's algorithm (Exercise 6.3)—the first correct software solution to the two-process mutual-exclusion problem—was developed by the Dutch mathematician T. Dekker. This algorithm also was discussed by Dijkstra [1965a]. A simpler solution to the two-process mutual-exclusion problem has since been presented by Peterson [1981] (algorithm 3).

Dijkstra [1965b] presented the first solution to the mutual-exclusion problem for n processes. This solution, however does not have an upper bound on the amount of time a process must wait before it is allowed to enter the critical section. Knuth [1966] presented the first algorithm with a bound; his bound was 2^n turns. A refine ment of Knuth's algorithm by deBruijn [1967] reduced the waiting time to n^2 turns, after which Eisenberg and McGuire [1972] (Exercise 6.4) succeeded in reducing the time to the lower bound of n–1 turns. The bakery algorithm (algorithm 5) was developed by Lamport [1974]; it also requires n–1 turns, but it is easier to program and to understand. Burns [1978] developed the hardware-solution algorithm that satisfies the bounded waiting requirement.

General discussions concerning the mutual-exclusion problem were offered by Lamport [1986] and Lamport [1991]. A collection of algorithms for mutual exclusion was given by Raynal [1986].

The semaphore concept was suggested by Dijkstra [1965a]. Patil [1971] examined the question of whether semaphores can solve all possible synchronization problems. Parnas [1975] discussed some of the flaws in Patil's arguments. Kosaraju [1973] followed up on Patil's work to produce a problem that cannot be solved by wait and signal operations. Lipton [1974] discussed the limitations of various synchronization primitives.

The classic process-coordination problems that we have described are paradigms for a large class of concurrency-control problems. The bounded buffer problem, the dining-philosophers problem, and the sleeping-barber problem (Exercise 6.7) were suggested by Dijkstra [1965a] and Dijkstra [1971]. The cigarette-smokers problem (Exercise 6.8) was developed by Patil [1971]. The readers–writers problem was suggested by Courtois et al. [1971]. The issue of concurrent reading and writing was discussed by Lamport [1977]. The problem of synchronization of independent processes was discussed by Lamport [1976].

The critical-region concept was suggested by Hoare [1972] and by Brinch-Hansen [1972]. The monitor concept was developed by Brinch-Hansen [1973]. A complete description of the monitor was given by Hoare [1974]. Kessels [1977] proposed an extension to the monitor to allow automatic signaling. General discussions concerning concurrent programming were offered by Ben-Ari [1990].

Some details of the locking mechanisms used in Solaris 2 are presented in Mauro and McDougall [2001]. Note that the locking mechanisms used by the kernel are implemented for user-level threads as well, so the same types of locks are available inside and outside of the kernel. Details of the Windows 2000 synchronization can be found in Solomon and Russinovich [2000].

The write-ahead log scheme was first introduced in System R by Gray et al. [1981]. The concept of serializability was formulated by Eswaran et al. [1976] in connection with their work on concurrency control for System R. The two-phase locking protocol was introduced by Eswaran et al. [1976]. The timestamp-based concurrency-control scheme was provided by Reed [1983]. An exposition of various timestamp-based concurrency-control algorithms was presented by Bernstein and Goodman [1980].

(Ba80) Baer, J. L., *Computer Systems Architecture*, Rockville, Md: Computer Science Press, 1980.

(Bk70) Baskett, F.;J. C. Broune; and W. M. Raike, "The Management of a Multi-level Non paged Memory System," *Proc. Spring Joint Computer Conference*, 1970, pp. 459-465.

(By77) Bays, C., "A Comparison of Next-Fit, First-Fit, and Best-Fit," *Communications of the ACM*, Vol. 20, No. 3, March 1977, pp. 191-192.

(Be82) Beck, L., "A Dynamic Storage Allocation Technique based on Memory Residence Time," *CACM*, Vol. 25, No. 10, October 1982, pp. 714-724.

(Be81) Belady, L. A.; R. P. Parmelee; and C. A. Scalzi, "The IBM History of Memory Management Technology," *IBM Journal of Research and Development*, Vol. 25, No. 5, September 1981, pp. 491-503.

(Bo84) Bozman, G.; W. Buco; T. P. Daly; and W. H. Tetzlaff, "Analysis of Free-Storage Algorithms—Revisited," *IBM Systems Journal*, Vol. 23, No. 1, 1984, pp. 44-66.

(Cd59) Codd, E. F.; E. S. Lowry; E. McDonough; and C. A. Scalzi, "Multiprogramming STRETCH: Feasibility Considerations," *Communications of the ACM*, Vol. 2, 1959, pp. 13-17.

(Co72) Coffman, E. G., and T. A. Ryan, "A study of Storage Partitioning Using a Mathematical Model of Locality, "*Communications of the ACM*, Vol. 15, No. 3, March 1972, pp. 185-190.

(Da84) Davies, D. J. M., "Memory Occupancy Patterns in Garbage Collection Systems," *Communications of the ACM*, Vol. 27, No. 8, August 1984, pp. 819-825.

(De71) Denning, P. J., "Third Generation Computer Systems," *ACM Computing Surveys*, Vol. 3, No. 4, December 1971, pp. 175-216.

(Ha78) Hayes, J. P., *Computer Architecture and Organization*, New York, McGraw-Hill, 1978.

(Kn68) Knight, D. C., "An Algorithm for Scheduling Storage on a Non-Paged Computer," *Computer Journal*, Vol. 11, No. 1, February 1968, pp. 17-21.

(Kh73) Knuth, D. E., *The Art of Computer Programming: Fundamental Algorithms*, Vol. 1, 2nd Ed., Reading, MA: Addison-Wesley, 1973.

(Li72) Lin, Y. S., and R. L. Mattson, "Cost-Performance Evaluation of Memory Hierarchies," *IEEE Trans. Magn.*, MAG-8, No. 3, September 1972, p. 390.

(Mr71) Margolin, B. H.; R. P. Parmelee; and M. Schatzoff, "Analysis of Free-Storage Algorithms," *IBM Systems Journal*, Vol. 10, No. 4, 1971, pp. 283-304.

(Ma77) Matick, R. E., *Computer Storage Systems and Technology*, New York, John Wiley & Sons, 1977.

(Mi74) Mitra, D., "Some Aspects of Hierarchical Memory Systems," *JACM*, Vol. 21, No. 1, January 1974, p. 54.

(O185) Oldehoeft, R. R., and S. J. Allan, "Adaptive Exact-Fit Storage Management," *Communications of the ACM*, Vol. 28, No. 5, May 1985, pp. 506-511.

(Po81) Pohm, A. V., and T. A. Smay, "Computer Memory Systems," *IEEE Computer*, October 1981, pp. 93-110.

(Ra69) Randell, B., "A Note on Storage Fragmentation and Program Segmentation," *Communications of the ACM*, Vol. 12, No. 7, July 1969, pp. 365-372.

(Rc81) Ricart, G., and A. K. Agrawala, "An Optimal Algorithm for Mutual Exclusion in Computer Networks," *Communications of the ACM,* Vol. 24, No. 1, January 1981, pp. 9-17.

(Ri74) Ritchie, D. M., and K. T. Thompson, "The UNIX Time-sharing System," *Communications of the ACM,* Vol. 17, No. 7, July 1974, pp. 365-375.

(Ro69) Rosen, S., "Electronic Computers: A Historical Survey," *ACM Computing Surveys*, Vol. 1, No. 1, March 1969, pp. 7-36.

(Rn69) Rosin, R. F., "Supervisory and Monitor Systems," *ACM Computing Surveys*, Vol. 1, No. 1, March 1969, pp. 37-54.

(Sh75) Shore, J. E., "On The External Storage Fragmentation Produced by First-Fit and Best-Fit Allocation Strategies," *Communications of the ACM*, Vol. 18, No. 8, August 1975, pp. 403-410.

(Sh77) Shore, J. E., "Anomalous Behavior of the Fifty-Percent Rule," *Communications of the ACM*, Vol. 20, No. 11, November 1977, pp. 812-820.

(Sm82) Smith, A. J., "Cache Memories," *ACM Computing Surveys*, Vol. 14, No. 3, September 1982, pp. 473-530.

(St83) Stephenson, C. J., "Fast: New Methods for Dynamic Storage Allocation," *Proceedings of the 9th Symposium on Operating Systems Principles,* ACM, Vol. 17, No. 5, October 1983, pp. 30-32.

(Th86) Thakkar, S. S., and A. E. Knowles, "A High-Performance Memory Management Scheme," *Computer*, Vol. 19, No. 5, May 1986, pp. 8-22.

(Ye86) Yeh, D. Y.; and T. Munakata, "Dynamic Allocation and Lssocal Reallocation Procedures for Multiple Stacks," *Communications of the ACM*, Vol. 29, No. 2, February 1986, pp. 134-141.

Dijkstra [1965a] was one of the first and most influential contributors in the deadlock area. Holt [1972] was the first person to formalize the notion of deadlocks in terms of a graph-theoretical model similar to the one presented in this chapter. Starvation was covered by Holt [1972]. Hyman [1985] provided the deadlock example for the Kansas legislature.

The various prevention algorithms were suggested by Havender [1968], who has devised the resources-ordering scheme for the IBM OS/360 system.

The banker's algorithm for avoiding deadlocks was developed for a single resource type by Dijkstra [1965a], and was extended to multiple resource types by Habermannn [1969]. Exercises 8.8 and 8.9 are form Holt [1971].

The deadlock-detection algorithm for multiple instances of a resource type, which was described in Section 8.6.2, was presented by Coffman et al. [1971].

Bach [1987] describes how many of the algorithms in the traditional UNIX kernel handle deadlock.

Demand paging was first used in the Atlas system, implemented on the Manchester University MUSE computer around 1960 (Kilburn et al. [1961]). Another early demand-paging system was MULTICS, implemented on the GE 645 system (Organick [1972]).

Belady et al. [1969] were the first researchers to observe that the FIFO replacement strategy may have the anomaly that bears Belady's name. Mattson et al. [1970] demonstrated that stack algorithms are not subject to Belady's anomaly.

The optimal replacement algorithm was presented by Belady [1966]. It was proved to be optimal by Mattson et al. [1970]. Belady's optimal algorithm is for a fixed allocation; Prieve and Fabry [1976] have an optimal algorithm for situations where the allocation can vary.

The enhanced clock algorithm was discussed by Carr and Hennessy [1981]; it is used in the Macintosh virtual memory-management scheme, and was described by Goldman [1989].

The working-set model was developed by Denning [1968]. Discussions concerning the working-set model were presented by Denning [1980].

The scheme for monitoring the page-fault rate was developed by Wulf [1969], who successfully applied this technique to the Burroughs B5500 computer system. Gupta and Franklin [1978] provided a performance comparison between the working-set scheme and the page-fault frequency replacement scheme.

(Bb81) Babaoglu, O., and W. Joy, "Converting a Swap-Based System to do Paging in an Architecture Lacking Page-Referenced Bits," *Proceedings of the 8th Symposium on Operating System Principles*, ACM, Vol. 15, No. 5, December 1981, pp. 78-86.

(Ba80) Baer, J., *Computer Systems Architecture*, Rockville, Md.: Computer Science Press, 1980.

(B181) Belady, L. A.; R. P. Parmelee; and C. A. Scalzi, "The IBM History of Memory Management Technology," *IBM Journal of Research and Development*, Vol. 25, No. 5, September 1981, pp. 491-503.

(Be72) Bensoussan, A.; C. T. Clingen; and R. C. Daley, "The Multics Virtual Memory: Concept and Design," *Communications of the ACM*, Vol. 15, No. 5, May 1972, pp. 308-318.

(Bo72) Bobrow, D. G.; J. D. Burchfiel; D. L. Murphy; and R. S. Tomlinson, "TENEX, a Paged Time Sharing System for the PDP-10," *Communications of the ACM*, Vol. 15, No. 3, March 1972, pp. 135-143.

(Ca81) Carr, R., and J. Hennessy, "WSCLOCK—A Simple and Effective Algorithm for Virtus Memory Management," *Proceedings of the Eighth Symposium on Operating Systems Principles*, December 1981, pp. 87-95.

(Cr81) Creasy, R. J., "The Origin of the VM/370 Time-sharing System," *IBM Journal of Research and Development,* Vol. 25, No. 5, September 1981, pp. 483-490.

(Da68) Daley, R. C., and J. B. Dennis, "Virtual Memory, Processes and Sharing in Multics, *CACM*, Vol. 11, No. 5, May 1968, pp. 306-312.

(De70) Denning, P. J., "Virtual Memory," *ACM Computing Surveys*, Vol. 2, No. 3, September 1970, pp. 153-189.

(De71) Denning, P. J., "Third Generation Computing Systems," *ACM Computing Surveys*, Vol. 3, No. 4, December 1971, pp. 175-216.

(De80) Denning, P., "Working Sets Past and Present," *IEEE Transactions on Software Engineering*, Vol. SE-6, No. 1, January 1980, pp. 64-84.

(Ds65) Dennis, J. B., "Segmentation and the Design of Multiprogrammed Computer Systems," *Journal of the ACM*, Vol. 12, No. 4, October 1965, pp. 589-602.

(Do76) Doran, R. W., "Virtual Memory," *Computer*, Vol. 9, No. 10, October 1976, pp. 27-37.

(Ea79) Easton, M., and P. Franaszek, "Use Bit Scanning in Replacement Decisions," *IEEE Transactions on Software Engineering*, Vol. C-28, No. 2, February 1979, pp. 133-141.

(Fo85) Foster, C. C., and P. T. Iberall, *Computer Architecture* (3rd ed.), New York, NY: Van Nostrand Reinhold, 1985.

(Ft61) Fotheringham, J., "Dynamic Storage Allocation in the Atlas Computer, Including an Automatic Use of a Backing Store," *Communications of the ACM*, Vol. 4, 1961, pp. 435-436.

(Fu87) Furht, B., and V. Milutinovic, "A Survey of Microprocessor Architectures for Memory Management," *Computer*, Vol. 20, No. 3, March 1987, pp. 48-58.

(Ha66) Hanlon, A. G., "Content-Addressible and Associative Memory Systems— A Survey," *IEEE Transactions on Electronic Computers*, August 1966.

(Hr85) Harmon, T. L., and B. Lawson, *The Motorola MC 68000 Microprocessor Family*, Engle wood Cliffs, NJ: Prentice Hall, 1985.

(Ht71) Hatfield, D. J., and J. Gerald, "Program Restructuring for Virtual Memory," *IBM Systems Journal*, Vol. 10, 1971, pp. 168-192.

(Je85) Jefferson, D., "Virtual Time," *ACM Transactions on Programming Languages and Systems*, Vol. 7, No. 3, July 1985.

(Ke88) Kenah, L. J., R. E. Goldenberg; and S. F. Bate, *VAX/VMS Internals and Data Structures*, Bedford, MA: Digital Press, 1988.

(Ki61) Kilburn, T.; D. J. Howarth; R. B. Payne; and F. H. Summer, "The Manchester University Atlas Operating System, Part I: Internal Organization," *Computer Journal*, Vol. 4, No. 3, October 1961, pp. 222-225.

(Ki61a) Kilburn, T.; R. B. Payne; and D. J. Howarth, "The Atlas Supervisor," *Proceedings of the Eastern Joint Computer Conference*, AFIPS, Vol. 20, 1961.

(La78) Lavington, S. H., "The Manchester Mark I and Atlas: A Historical Perspective," *Communications of the ACM*, Vol. 21, No. 1, January 1978, pp. 4-12.

(Le87) Leonard, T. E. (ed.), *VAX Architecture Reference Manual*, Bedford, MA: Digital Press, 1987.

(Ln66) Lindquist, A. B.; R. R. Seeder; and L. W. Comeau, "A Time-Sharing System Using an Associative Memory," *Proceedings of the IEEE*, Vol. 54, 1966, pp. 1774-1779.

(Li68) Liptay, J. S., "Structured Aspects of System 360/85: The Cache," *IBM Systems Journal*, Vol. 7, No. 1, 1968, pp. 15-21.

(Mc83) MacGregor, D., and D. S. Mothersole, "Virtual Memory and the MC68010," *IEEE Micro*, Vol. 3, No. 3, June 1983, pp. 24-39.

(Ma77) Matick, R., *Computer Storage Systems and Technology*, New York, Wiley-Interscience, 1977.

(Mo86) Morse, S. P., and D. J. Albert, *The 80286 Architecture*, New York, NY: Wiley Press, 1986.

(Or72) Organick, E. I., *The Multics System: An Examination of its Structure*, Cambridge, Mass: M.I.T. Press, 1972.

(Pa72) Parmelee, R. P.; T. I. Peterson; C. C. Tillman; and D. J. Hatfield, "Virtual Storage and Virtual Machine Concepts," *IBM Systems Journal*, Vol. 11, 1972, pp. 99-130.

(Ra68) Randell, B., and C. J. Kuehner, "Dynamic Storage Allocation Systems," *Communications of the ACM*, Vol. 11, No. 5, May 1968, pp. 297-304.

(Sa75) Saltzer, J. H., and M. D. Schroeder, "The Protection of Information in Computer Systems," *Proceedings of the IEEE*, Vol. 63, No. 9, 1975, pp. 1278-1308.

(Se73) Scherr, A. L., "Functional Structure of IBM Virtual Storage Operating Systems Part II: OS/VS2-2 Concepts and Philosophies," *IBM Systems Journal*, Vol. 12, 1973, pp. 382-400.

(Sh86) Shiell, J., "Virtual Memory, Virtual Machines," *Byte*, Vol. 11, No. 11, 1986, pp. 110-121.

(Sc83) Schmitt, S., "Virtual Memory for Microcomputers," *Byte*, April 1983, pp. 210-238.

(Sh72) Schroeder, M. D., and J. H. Saltzer, "A Hardware Architecture for Implementing Protection Rings," *Communications of the ACM*, March 1972, pp. 157-170.

(Sm78) Smith, A. J., "A Comparative Study of Set Associative Memory Mapping Algorithms and Their Use for Cache and Main Memory," *IEEE Transactions on Software Engineering*, Vol. 4, No. 2, 1978, pp. 121-130.

(Sm82) Smith, A. J., "Cache Memories," *ACM Computing Surveys*, Vol. 14, No. 3, September 1982, pp. 473-530.

(St75) Stone, H. S. (ed.), *Introduction to Computer Architecture*, Chicago, SRA, 1975.

(Su87) Strauss, E., *80386 Technical Reference*, New York, NY: Brady, 1987.

(Th86) Thakkar, S. S., and A. E. Knowles, "A High-Performance Memory Management Scheme," *Computer*, Vol. 19, No. 5, May 1986, pp. 8-22.

(Tu88) Turley, J. L., *Advanced 80386 Programming Techniques*, Berkeley, CA: Osborne McGraw-Hill, 1988.

(Wa84) Wada, B. T., "A Virtual Memory System for Picture Processing," *Communications of the ACM*, Vol. 27, No. 5, May 1984, pp. 444-454.

(Wt70) Watson, R. W., *Timesharing System Design Concepts*, New York, NY: McGraw-Hill, 1970.

(Ah87) Ahituv, N.; Y. Lapid; and S. Neumann, "Processing Encrypted Data," *Communications of the ACM*, Vol. 30, No. 9, September 1987, pp. 777–780.

(Ak83) Akl, S. G., "Digital Signatures: A Tutorial Survey," *Computer*, Vol. 16, No. 2, February 1983, pp. 15-24.

(Am83) Ames, S. R., Jr., and M. Gasser, "Security Kernel Design and Implementation: An Introduction," *Computer*, Vol. 16, No. 7, July 1983, pp. 14-22.

(Aw86) Anyanwu, J. A., and L. F. Marshall, "A Crash Resistant UNIX File System," *Software–Practice and Experience*, Vol. 16, February 1986, pp. 107-118.

(At86) Athanasiou, T., "Encryption Technology, Privacy, and National Security," *Technology Review*, Vol. 89, No. 6, August/September 1986, pp. 57-66.

(At76) Attanasio, C. R.; P. W. Markstein; and R.J. Phillips, "Penetrating an Operating System: A Study of VM/370 Integrity," *IBM Systems Journal*, Vol. 11, No. 1, 1976, pp. 102-118.

(Ba88) Bauer, D. S., and M. E. Koblentz, "NIDX—A Real-Time Intrusion Detection Expert System," *USENIX Conference Proceedings*, San Francisco, June 20-24, 1988, pp. 261-274.

(Bl83) Blum, M., "How to Exchange (Secret) Keys," *ACM Transactions on Computer Systems*, Vol. 1, No. 2, May 1983, pp. 175-193.

(Bo87) Borg, A., "Fault Tolerance by Design," *UNIX Review,*, April 1987, pp. 46-53.

(Bo87a) Borning, A., "Computer System Reliability and Nuclear War," *Communication of the ACM*, Vol. 30, No. 2, February 1987, pp. 112-131.

(Bu87) Bruke, F., *UNIX System Administration*, San Diego, CA: Harcourt Brace Jovanovich, 1987.

(By86) *Byte Magazine*, Special Issue on Object-Oriented Languages, August 1986, McGraw-Hill.

(Ck88) Clarke, R. A., "Information Technology and Dataveillance," *Communications of the ACM*, Vol. 31, No. 5, May 1988, pp. 498-513.

(Co88) Coffin, S., *UNIX: The Complete Reference*, Berkeley, CA: Osborne McGraw-Hill, 1988.

(Co86) Cox, B., *Object-Oriented Programming*, Reading, MA: Addison-Wesley, 1986.

(Da88) Danforth, S., and C. Tomlison, "Type Theories and Object-Oriented Programming," *ACM Computing Surveys*, Vol. 20, No. 1, March 1988, pp. 29-72.

(Dv83) Davies, D. W., "Applying the RSA Digital Signature to Electronic Mail," *Computer*, Vol. 16, No. 2, February, 1983, pp. 55-62.

(Dv84) Davies, D. W., and W. L. Price, *Security for Computer Networks*, New York, NY: John Wiley, 1984.

(De81) Denning, D. E., "Secure Personal Computing in an Insecure Network," *Communications of the ACM*, Vol. 22, No. 8, August 1981, pp. 476-482.

(De83a) Denning, D. E., "Protecting Public Keys and Signature Keys," *IEEE Computer*, Vol. 16, No. 2, February 1983, pp. 27-35.

(De84) Denning, D. E., "Digital Signatures with RSA and Other Public-Key Cryptosystems," *Communications of the ACM*, Vol. 27, No. 4, April 1984, pp. 388-392.

(De81a) Denning, D. E., and G. M. Sacco, "Timestamps in Key Distribution Protocols," *Communications of the ACM*, Vol. 24, No. 8, August 1981, pp. 533-536.

(Dn66) Dennis, J. B., and E. C. Van Horn, "Programming Semantics for Multiprogrammed Computations," *Communications of the ACM*, Vol. 9, No. 3, March 1966, pp. 143-155.

(Ev85) Even, S.; O. Goldreich; and A. Lempel, "A Randomized Protocol for Signing Contracts," *Communications of the ACM*, Vol. 28, No. 6, June 1985, pp. 637-647.

(Fa74) Fabry, R. S., "Capability-Based Addressing," *Communications of the ACM*, Vol. 17, No. 7, July 1974, pp. 403-411.

(Fa86) Farrow, R., "Security Issues and Strategies for Users," *UNIX World*, April 1986, pp. 65-71.

(Fa86a) Farrow, R., "Security for Superusers, or How to Break the UNIX System," *UNIX World*, May 1986, pp. 65-70.

(Fe88) Fernandez, G., and L. Allen, "Extending the UNIX Protection Model with Access Control Lists," *USENIX Conference Proceedings*, San Francisco, June 20-24, 1988, pp. 119-132.

(Fi86) Filipski, A., and J. Hanko, "Making UNIX Secure," *Byte*, April 1986, pp. 113-128.

(Fi89) Fisher, S., "UNIX Security and Government Secrets," *UNIX World*, Vol. 6, No. 4, April 1989, pp. 36-42.

(Fr83) Fraim, L. J., "Scomp: A Solution to the Multilevel Security Problem," *Computer*, Vol. 16, No. 7, July 1983, pp. 26-34.

(Gt78) Gait, J., "Easy Entry: The Password Encryption Problem," *Operating Systems Review*, Vol. 12, No. 3, July 1978, pp. 54-59.

(Gr84) Grampp, F. T., and R. H. Morris, "UNIX Operating System Security," *AT&T Bell Laboratories Technical Journal*, Vol. 63, No. 8, October 1984, pp. 1649-1672.

(Ha88) Hafner, K. M.; G. Lewis; K. Kelly; M. Shao; C. Hawkins; and P. Angiolillo, "Is Your Computer Secure?" *Business Week*, August 1, 1988, pp. 64-72.

(He80) Hebbard, B., et. al., "A Penetration Analysis of the Michigan Terminal System," *Operating Systems Review*, Vol. 14, No. 1, June 1980, pp. 7-20.

(He88) Hecht, M. S.; A. Johri; R. Aditham; and T. J. Wei, "Experience Adding C2 Security Features to UNIX," *USENIX Conference Proceedings*, San Francisco, June 20-24, 1988, pp. 133-146.

(Ho80) Hoch, C., and J. C. Browne, "An Implementation of Capabilities on the PDP-11/45," *Operating Systems Review*, Vol. 13, No. 3, July 1980, pp. 22-32.

(IB80) *IBM System/38 Technical Developments*, IBM Corporation, General System Division, Atlanta, GA.: G580, July 1980.

(Jo85) Johnson, R. E., "Choosing Encryption: DES or Private Key?" *Infosystems*, July 1985, p. 36.

(Jo80) Jones, A. K., "Capability Architecture Revisited," *Operating Systems Review*, Vol. 14, No. 3, July 1980, pp. 33-35.

(Jp86) Joseph, T., and K. Birman, "Low Cost Management of Replicated Data in Fault-Tolerant Distributed Systems," *ACM Transactions on Computing Systems*, Vol. 4, No. 1, February 1986, pp. 54-70.

(Ka88) Kahane, Y.; S. Neumann; and C. S. Tapiero, "Computer Backup Pools, Disaster Recovery, and Default Risk," *Communications of the ACM*, Vol. 31, No. 1, January 1988, pp. 78-83.

(Ka83) Kak, S. C., "Data Security in Computer Networks," *Computer*, Vol. 16, No. 2, February 1983, pp. 8-10.

(Kr88) Kramer, S. M., "Retaining SUID Programs in a Secure UNIX," *USENIX Conference Proceedings*, San Francisco, June 20-24, 1988, pp. 107-118.

(Ku86) Kuhl, J. G., and S. M. Reddy, "Fault-Tolerance Considerations in Large, Multiple-Processor Systems," *Computer*, Vol. 19, No. 3, March 1986, pp. 56-67.

(La88) Lai, N., and T. E. Gray, "Strengthening Discretionary Access Controls to Inhibit Trojan Horse and Computer Viruses," *USENIX Conference Proceedings*, San Francisco, June 20-24, 1988, pp. 275-286.

(Lm81) Lamport, L., "Password Authentication with Insecure Communication," *Communications of the ACM*, Vol. 24, No. 11, November 1981, pp. 770-772.

(Lm84) Lamport, L., "Using Time Instead of Timeout for Fault-Tolerance in Distributed Systems," *ACM Transactions on Programming Languages and Systems*, Vol. 6, No. 2, April 1984, pp. 254-280.

(Le86) Lee, J. A. N.; G. Segal; and R. Steier, "Positive Alternatives: A Report on an ACM Panel on Hacking," *Communications of the ACM*, Vol. 29, No. 4, April 1986, pp. 297-299.

(Le87) Lehmann, F., "Computer Break-Ins," *Communications of the ACM*, Vol. 30, No. 7, July 1987, pp. 584-585.

(Lv84) Levy, H. M., *Capability-based Computer Systems*, Bedford, MA: Digital Press, 1984.

(Li75) Linde, R. R., "Operating System Penetration," *AFIPS Conference Proceedings*, Vol. 44, 1975.

(Lo86) Lobel, J., *Foiling the System Breakers: Computer Security and Access Control*, New York, NY: McGraw-Hill, 1986.

(Mc89) McAfee, J., "The Virus Cure," *Datamation*, February 15, 1989, pp. 29-40.

(Mc79) McCauley, E. J., "KSOS: The Design of a Secure Operating System," *AFIPS Conference Proceedings*, Vol. 48, 1979, pp. 345-353.

(Mi76) Millen, J., "Security Kernel Validation in Practice," *Communications of the ACM*, Vol. 19, No. 5, May 1976.

(Mi86) Minoli, D., "Protecting Communications from Disaster," *Infosystems*, Vol. 33, No. 2, February 1986, pp. 38-40.

(Md86) Morshedian, D., "How to Fight Password Pirates," *Computer*, Vol. 19, No. 1, January 1986.

(Mu86) Mullender, S. J., and A. S. Tanenbaum, "The Design of a Capability-Based Distributed Operating System," *Computer Journal*, Vol. 29, No. 4, 1986, pp. 289-299.

(Mu86a) Murray, W. H., "Security Considerations for Personal Computers," *IBM Systems Journal*, Vol. 23, No. 3, 1984, pp. 297-304.

(My86) Myers, W., "Can Software for the Strategic Defense Initiative Ever be Error-Free?" *Computer*, Vol. 19, No. 11, November 1986, pp. 61-68.

(Na77) National Bureau of Standards, "Data Encryption Standard," January 1977, NTIS *NBSFIPS PUB 46*.

(Pa86) Pascoe, G. A., "Elements of Object-Oriented Programming," *Byte*, Vol. 11, No. 8, August 1986, pp. 139-144.

(Pi80) Pinnow, K. W.; J. G. Ranweiler; and J. F. Miller, "System/38 Object-Oriented Architecture," *IBM System/38 Technical Developments*, IBM Corporation, General Systems Division, Atlanta, Ga.: G580, July 1980, pp. 55-58.

(Po78) Popek, G. J., and C. S. Kline, "Issues in Kernel Design," *AFIPS Conference Proceedings, 1978 NCC*, Vol. 47, pp. 1079-1086.

(Co75) "Computer Security Guidelines for Implementing the Privacy Act of 1974," *NBS FIPS Pub. 41*, May 1975.

(Re87) Reid, B., "Reflections on Some Recent Widespread Computer Break-Ins," *Communications of the ACM*, Vol. 30, No. 2, February 1987, pp. 103-105.

(Ri78) Rivest, R., and; A. Shamir; and L. Adleman, "On Digital Signatures and Public Key Cryptosystems," *Communications of the ACM*, Vol. 21, No. 2, February 1978, pp. 120-126.

(Ri84) Rivest, R.; A. Shamir, "How to Expose an Eavesdropper," *Communications of the ACM*, Vol. 27, No. 4, April 1984, pp. 393-394.

(Ru81) Rushby, J. M., "Design and Verification of Secure Systems," *Proceedings of the 8th Symposium on Operating Systems Principles*, Vol. 15, No. 5, December 1981, pp. 12-21.

(Ru83) Rushby, J., and B. Randell, "A Distributed Secure System," *Computer*, Vol. 16, No. 7, July 1983, pp. 55-67.

(Sc83) Schell, R. R., "A Security Kernel for a Multiprocessor Microcomputer," *Computer*, Vol. 16, No. 7, July 1983, pp. 47-53.

(Sc77) Schiller, W. L., "The Design and Abstract Specification of a Multics Security Kernel," Bedford, MA: The Mitre Corp., November 1977, *MTR-3 294*, Vol I; *EST-TR-77-259*, Vol I; (NTIS *AD A04876*).

(Sc86) Schmucker, K. J., *Object-Oriented Programming for the Macintosh*, Hayden Book Company, 1986.

(Sc77) Schroeder, M. D.; D. D. Clark; and J. H. Saltzer, "The Multics Kernel Design Project," Proceedings of the Sixth ACM Symposium on Operating Systems Principles, in *Operating Systems Review*, Vol. 11, No. 5, 1977, pp. 43-56.

(Sc77a) Schroeder, M. D.; D. D. Clark; J. H. Saltzer; and D. H. Wells, *Final Report of the Kernel Design Project*, MIT-LCS-TR-96, 1977.

(Sm79) Shamir, A., "How to Share a Secret," *Communications of the ACM*, Vol. 22, No. 8, November 1979, pp. 612-613.

(Sv83) Silverman, J. M., "Reflections on the Verification of the Security of an Operating System Kernel," *Proceedings of the 9th Symposium on Operating Systems Principles*, ACM, Vol. 17, No. 5, October 1983, pp. 143-154.

(Si79) Simmons, G. J., "Symmetric and Asymmetric Encryption," *ACM Computing Survey*, Vol. 11, No. 4, December 1979, pp. 305-330.

(Sp88) Spafford, E. H., "The Internet Worm Program: An Analysis," *Purdue Technical Report CSD-TR-823*, November 28, 1988.

(St88) Stoll, C., "Stalking the Wiley Hacker," *Communications of the ACM*, Vol. 31, No. 5, May 1988, pp. 484-497.

(St86) Stroustrup, B., *The C++ Programming Language*, Reading, MA: Addison-Wesley.

(St87a) Stroustrup, B., "The Evolution of C++: 1985 to 1987," *USENIX Proceeding a Additional Papers C++ Workshop, Santa Fe, NM*, 1987, pp. 1-21.

(St87b) Stroustrup, B., "Possible Directions of C++," *USENIX Proceeding a Additional Papers C++ Workshop, Santa Fe, NM*, 1987, pp. 399-416.

(St87c) Stroustrup, B., "What is Object-Oriented Programming," *USENIX Proceeding a Additional Papers C++ Workshop, Santa Fe, NM*, 1987, pp. 159-180.

(Su84) Summers, R. C., "An Overview of Computer Security," *IBM Systems Journal*, Vol. 2, No. 4, 1984, pp. 309-325.

(Vo83) Voydock, V. L., and S. T. Kent, "Security Mechanisms in High-Level Network Protocols," *Computing Surveys*, Vol. 15, No. 2, June 1983, pp. 135-171.

(Wa80) Walker, B.; R. A. Klemmerer; and G. J. Popek, "Specification and Verification of an UCLA Unix Security Kernel," *Communications of the ACM*, Vol. 23, No. 2, February 1980.

(Wh86) White, E., and R. Malloy, "Object-Oriented Programming," *Byte*, Vol. 11, No. 8, August 1986, p. 137.

(Wi88a) Wiener, R. S., and L. J. Pinson, *An Introduction to Object-Oriented Programming in C++, Reading*, MA: Addison-Wesley, 1988.

(Wi81) Wilkinson, A. L., et. al., "A Penetration Analysis of a Burroughs Large System," *Operating Systems Review*, Vol. 15, No. 1, January 1981, pp. 14-25.

(Wo85) Wood, P., and S. Kochan, *UNIX System Security*, NJ: Hayden Book Co., 1985.

(Zi86) Zimmermann, P., "A Proposed Standard Format for RSA Cryptosystems," *Computer*, Vol. 19, No. 9, September 1986, pp. 21-34.

Textbook coverage of distributed system is provided by Sloman and Kramer (1987) and by Couloris and Dolimar (1988). A detailed earlier treatment of the fundamental design issues may be found in the collection of lecture notes edited by Lampson et al. (1983).

Tanenbaum (1988) is a thorough reference on computer networks and protocols structured along the lines of the OSI model. Detailed technical specification of the local-area networks and architectures is provided in IEEE standards originally published in 1985 (802.3, 802.4, and 802.5).

Raynal (1988) provides a detailed coverage of distributed algorithms and protocols. Ordering of events and a time-stamp-based algorithm for mutual exclusion are presented in Lamport's paper (1978). Ricart and Agrawala's algorithm was published in 1981. Maekawa (1985) presents an efficient squareroot algorithm for mutual exclusion.

Kohler (1981) provides a survey of techniques for synchronization and recovery in decentralized computer systems. The concepts and theory of concurrency and recovery in centralized and distributed database systems is covered in a book by Bernstein et al. (1987). Two-phase transactions and the related theory are introduced in a paper by Eswaran et al. (1976).

Wait-die and wound-wait algorithms are due to Rozenkrantz et al. (1978). Singhal (1989) surveys deadlock detection in distributed systems.

The successor-election algorithm presented in this chapter is due to Chang and Roberts (1979). Garcia-Molina (1982) describes the bully algorithm. The token-regeneration algorithm is due to Misra (1983). The *OM* algorithm for reaching agreement is due to Lamport et at. (1982). Dolev and Strong (1983) discuss the ramifications of message authentication in solutions to the Byzantine Generals problem.

Since implementations of distributed operating systems are relatively recent and not very numerous, the field is only beginning to stabilize sufficiently for text coverage. Therefore, primary references should be sought in journals and in conference proceedings.

An early thorough treatment of the design issues in distributed operating systems is provided in the form of lecture notes edited by Bayer et al. (1979) and Lampson et al. (1983). A more recent set of lecture notes is edited by Paker et al. (1986).

Textbook treatment of some implementation issues may be found in Sloman and Kramer (1987) and in Couloris and Dollimore (1988). Popek and Walker (1985) describe the design of an integrated system called Locus.

A detailed survey of distributed operating systems is provided in an article by Tanenbaum and van Renesse (1985). Process migration is discussed by Power and Miller (1983) and by Artsy and Finkel (1989). Zayas (1987) discusses the virtual-memory-related performance improvements.

Naming based on prefix tables is described by Welch and Ousterhout (1986).

Remote procedure calls are presented in papers by Birrell and Nelson (1984) and by Birrell (1985). Lightweight procedure calls are analyzed by Bershad et al. (1990).

Distributed shared memory algorithms are surveyed and compared by Stumm and Zhou (1990). An early original implementation is described by Li and Hudak (1989).

Design and fault tolerance aspects of file servers are surveyed by Svobodova (1984). Practical implementations of workstation/server systems are discussed by Cheritone (1988), Balkovich et al. (1985), Howard et al. (1988), and Nelson et al. (1988). Distributed file systems are surveyed by Levy and Silberschatz (1990).

The access-matrix model of protection between domains and objects was developed by Lampson [1969] and Lampson [1979]. Popek [1974] and Saltzer and Schroeder [1975] provided excellent surveys on the subject of protection. Harrison et al. [1976] used formal version of this model to enable them to prove mathematically properties of a protection system.

The concept of a capability evolved from Iliffe's and Jodeit's *codewords*, which were implemented in the Rice University computer (Iliffe and Jodeit [1962]). The term *capability* was introduced by Dennis and Horn [1996].

The Hydra system was described by Wulf et. al. [1981]. The CAP system was described by Needham and Walker [1977]. Organick [1972] discussed the MULTICS ring protection system.

Revocation was discussed by Redell and Fabry [1974], Cohen and Jefferson [1975], and Ekanadham and Bernstein [1979]. The principle of separation of policy and mechanism as advocated by the designer or Hydra (Levin et al. [1975]). The confinement problem was first discussed by Lampson [1973] and was further by Lipner [1975].

The use of higher-level languages for specifying access control was suggested first by Morris [1973], who proposed the use of the seal and unseal operations discussed in Section 18.7 Kieburtz and Silberschatz [1978], Kieburtz and Silberschatz [1983], and McGraw and Andrews [1979] proposed various language constructs for dealing with general dynamic resource-management schemes. Jones and Liskov [1978] considered how a static access-control scheme can be incorporated in a programming language that supports abstract data types.

A more detailed analysis of stack inspection, including comparisons to other approaches to Java security, can be found in Wallach et al. [1987] and Gong et al. [1997].

General discussions concerning security are given by Hsiao et al. [1979], Landwehr [1981], Denning [1982], Pfleeger [1989], and Russell et al. [1991]. Also of general interest is the text by Lobel [1986].

Issues concerning the design and verification of secure systems are discussed by Rushby [1981] and by Silverman [1983]. A security kernel for a multiprocessor microcomputer is described by Schell [1993]. A distributed secure system is described by Rushby and Randell [1983].

Morris and Thompson [1979] discuss password security. Morshedian [1986] presents methods to fight password pirates. Password authentication with insecure communications is considered by Lamport [1981]. The issue of password cracking is discussed by Seely [1989]. Computer break-ins are discussed by Lehmann [1987] and by Reid [1987].

Discussions concerning UNIX security are offered by Grampp and Morris [1984], Wood and Kochan [1985], Farrow [1986b], Farrow [1986a], Filipski and Hanko [1986], Hecht et al. [1988], Kramer [1988], and Garfinkel and Spafford [1991]. Bershad and Pinkerton [1988] present the watchdogs extension to BSDUNIX. The COPS security-scanning package for UNIX was written by Farmer at Purdue University. It is available to users on the Internet via the ftp program from host ftp.uu.net in directory/pub/security/cops.

Spafford [1989] presents a detailed technical discussion of the Internet worm. The Spafford article appears with three others in a special section on the Internet worm in *Communications of the ACM* (Volume 32, Number 6, June 1989).

Input/output ports and elements of I/O programming are described in many books on microcomputer interfacing and architecture and on assembly-language programming. Among them are books by Leventhal (1978) and Wakerly (1981), which provide an excellent foundation for the material presented in this chapter. More general treatment of I/O systems, including mainframes and I/O channels, can be found in Stone (1980) and in Baer (1980). Examples of interrupt and channel I/O programming are provided by Madnick and Donovan (1974). A discussion of processor and I/O overlap can be found in Hsiao (1975). Hunt (1980) discusses some architectural and design issues related to interrupts.

The best source for actual device descriptions is the literature provided by hardware manufacturers, such as Intel (1984a) and Motorola (1984a). The wealth of useful practical information for implementation of communication links may be found in the manufacturer application notes, such as Smith (1976). Readers with access to a personal computer should by all means study the actual examples of low-level input/output programming provided in BIOS (Basic Input/Output System), whose source code is available for many CP/M and MS-DOS (PC-DOS) machines. One of the best-documented may be found in *Technical Reference for the IBM Personal Computer* (IBM 1983).

Issues in kernel design are discussed by Popek and Kline (1979). The duality of operating-system designs based on message exchange and on other interprocess synchronization and communication mechanisms is discussed by Lauer and Needham (1978). A conceptual description of operating-system kernel design is provided by Lister (1979) and Denning (1983).

Since our concern in this chapter was the detailed implementation of an operating system, in this section we list several books that provide detailed descriptions of concepts and designs of kernels and, in some cases, of other parts of operating systems.

The design of the operating system Solo and a report on the programming language Concurrent Pascal, in which Solo is written, are provided by Brinch Hansen (1977). A more recent book by the same author (1982) describes systems implementation language Edison and a design of a kernel written in Edison.

Holt (1983) describes the programming language Concurrent Euclid and Tunis, a Unix-like multitasking kernel written in Concurrent Euclid. A design of Xinu, another Unix-inspired operating system, is described by Comer (1984). Xinu is written in C, and it supports network configurations on Xinu machines.

Wulf et al. (1981) describe the ideas, concepts, and implementation aspects of the Hydra operating system running on the C.mmp multiprocessor.

Thorough textbook treatments of multiprocessors and parallel programming are provided by Stone (1980, 1987). A broad survey of parallel processing can be found in Hwang and Briggs (1984). Highly parallel computing is the subject of a book by Almasi and Gottlieb (1988).

Shared-bus implementations of commercial multiprocessors are described in Thakkar et al. (1988) and in Bernstein (1988). Seitz (1985) describes an early hypercube design. Siegel and Hsu provide a detailed discussion of interconnection networks in Chapter 6 of Milutinović (1988).

Beck and Olien (1989) discuss implementation of a Unix-based commercial multiprocessor operating system. Rashid (1986) provides a survey of the Mach operating system. Black (1990) discusses scheduling support for concurrency and parallelism in the Mach operating system. Wittie and van Tilborg (1980) describe wave scheduling. Ousterhout (1982) discusses concurrent scheduling and coscheduling. The duality of memory and communication in Accent is presented by Fitzgerald and Rashid (1986).

Multiprocessor synchronization is covered in detail in Stone (1987). Sites (1980) discusses implementation of enqueue and dequeue operations using compare-and-swap. The use of compare-double-and-swap is presented in Stone (1987) and in IBM's *System/370 Principles of Operation* (1987). Gottlieb et al. (1983) presents fetch-and-add and its uses.

Diffie and Hellman [1976] and Diffie and Hellman [1979] were the first researchers to propose the use of the public key-encryption scheme. The algorithm presented in Section 23.7.2 is based on the public key-encryption scheme; it was developed by Rivest et al. [1978]. Lempel [1979], Simmons [1979], Gifford [1982], Denning [1982], and Ahituv et al. [1987] explore the use of cryptography in computer systems. Discussions concerning protection of digital signatures are offered by Akl [1983], Davies [1983], Denning [1983], and Denning [1984].

The U.S. federal government is, of course, concerned about security. The *Department of Defense Trusted Computer System Evaluation Criteria* DoD [1985], known also as the *Orange Book*, describes a set of security levels and the features that an operating system must have to qualify for each security rating. Reading it is a good starting point for understanding security concerns. The *Microsoft Windows NT Workstation Resource Kit* (Microsoft [1996] described the security model of NT and how to use that model.

The RSA algorithm is presented in Rivest et al. [1978]. Information about NIST's AES activities can be found at http:// www.nist.gov/ aes/; information about other cryptographic standards for the U.S. can also be found at that site. More complete coverage of SSL 3.0 can be found at http:// home.netscape.com /eng/ssl3/. In 1999, SSL 3.0 was modified slightly and presented in an IETF Request for Comments (RFC) under the name TLS.

The example in Section 19.6 illustrating the impact of false-alarm rate on the effectiveness of IDSs is based on Axelsson [1999]. A more complete description of the swatch program and its use with syslog can be found in Hansen and Atkins [1993]. The description of Tripwire in Section 19.6.3 is based on Kim and Spafford [1993]. The description and example in Section 19.6.4 are taken from Forrest et al. [1996].

(An84) Anderson, J., "Irresistible DOS 3.0," *PC Tech Journal*, Vol. 2, No. 6, December 1984, pp. 74-87.

(Ar83) Archer, R., "The IBM PC XT and DOS 2.00," *Byte*, November 1983, pp. 294-304.

(Be87) Bender, E., "The Blue Sky's the Limit," *PC World*, June 1987, pp. 166-174.

(B187) Blackford, J., "IBM's New Systems: What Do You Do Now?" *Personal Computing*, June 1987, pp. 94-115.

(Br87) Brown, E.; E. Knorr; and C. Bermant, "Personal Systems Revealed," *PC World*, August 1987, pp. 212-223.

(Bu83) Burton, K., "Anatomy of a Colossus, Part II," *PC Magazine*, Vol. 1, No. 10, Feb. 1983, pp. 317-330.

(Ch89) Christopher, K. W.; B. A. Feigenbaum; and S. O. Saliga, *The New DOS 4.0*, New York, NY: John Wiley & Sons, Inc., 1989.

(C185) Claff, W. J., "Moving from the 8088 to the 80286," *Byte*, Vol. 10, No. 11, 1985.

(C184) Clune, T.; R. Malloy; and G. M. Vose, "The IBM PC AT," *Byte*, October 1984, pp. 107-111.

(Cu83) Curren, L., and R. S. Shuford, "IBM's Estridge," *Byte*, November 1983.

(De86) Derfler, F. J., Jr., and W. Stallings, "The IBM Token Ring LAN," *PC Magazine*, March 11, 1986, pp. 197-206.

(De84) DeVoney, C., *PC DOS User's Guide*, Indianapolis, Indiana: Que Corporation, 1984.

(Du88) Duncan, R. (General Editor), *The MS-DOS Encyclopedia*, Redmond, Washington: Microsoft Press, 1988.

(Du89) Duncan, R., "Taking a Realistic Look at DOS 4.0," *PC Magazine*, Vol. 8, No. I, January 17, 1989, pp. 329-334.

(Du83) Dunford, C., "Interrupts and the IBM PC, Part 1," *PC Tech Journal*, Vol. 1, No. 3, November/December 1983, pp. 173-199.

(Fa86) Fawcette, J. E., "80386: The Megabyte Manager," *PC World*, February 1986, pp. 238-243.

(Fi83) Field, T., "Installable Device Drivers for PC-DOS 2.0," *Byte*, November 1983, pp. 188-196.

(Fi85) Finger, A., "IBM PCT AT," *Byte*, May 1985, pp. 270-277.

(Fl87) Fleig, C. P., "The Well-Connected PC," *PC World*, August 1987, pp. 192-199.

(Fo86) Foard, R. M., "Multitasking Methods," *PC Tech Journal*, Vol. 4, No. 3, March 1986, pp. 49-60.

(Ge87) Getts, J., "A PC Geneology," *PC World*, August 1987, pp. 200-205.

(Gl85) Glecker, A. A., "File Search Help for PC-DOS," *PC Tech Journal*, Vol. 3, No. 4, April 1985, pp. 139-145.

(Gr86) Greenberg, K., "A Candid Conversation with William Lowe," *PC World*, March 1986, pp. 137-143.

(Gr84) Greenberg, K., and K. Koessel, "AT: The PC's Powerful Partner," *PC World*, December 1984, pp. 234-250.

(Gr84a) Greene, B., "The Evolution of the IAPX 286," *PC Tech Journal*, Vol. 2, No. 6, 1984, pp. 118-136.

(Ho84) Hoffman, T. V., "Analyzing the Advanced Technology," *PC Tech Journal*, Vol. 2, No. 6, December 1984, pp. 40-56.

(Ho87) Hoskins, J., *IBM Personal System/2: A Business Perspective*, New York, N.Y: John Wiley and Sons, Inc., 1987.

(IB84) IBM Corporation, *DOS Version 3.00 Technical Reference*, May 1984.

(IB85) IBM Corporation, *Disk Operating System Version 3.10 User's Guide*, 1985.

(IB86) IBM Corporation, *Disk Operating System Version 3.20 Reference*, Feb. 1986.

(IB87) International Business Machines Corporation, *IBM Personal System/2 Customer Reference Guide*, April 1987.

(IB88) International Business Machines Corporation, *Systems Applications Architecture An Overview*, Third Edition, File Number GC26-4341, February 1988.

(Ki88) Killen, M., IBM: *The Making of The Common View*, Orlando, FL: Harcourt Brace Jovanovich, 1988.

(Ko85) Kolod, M., "IBM PC Disk Performance and the Interleave Factor," *Byte*, 1985, pp. 283-290.

(La83) Larson, C., "MS-DOS 2.0: A Enhanced 16-bit Operating System," *Byte*, November 1983, pp. 285-290.

(Le82) Lemmons, P., and T. Roger, "Upward Migration: a Comparison of CP/M-86 and MS-DOS," *Byte*, July 1982, pp. 330-356.

(Le87) LePage, R., "The Road to MS-DOS," *Macworld*, August 1987, pp. 108-113.

(Lu84) Luhn, R., and R. Cook, "80286: Intel's Multitask Master," *PC World*, Vol. 2, No. 12, 1984. pp. 248-254.

(Ma84) Machrone, B., "IBM Nurtures a Network," *PC Magazine*, Vol. 3, No. 22, November 1984, pp. 135-141.

(Ma88) Malloy, R., "DOS 4.0," *Byte*, (IBM Special Edition), Fall 1988, pp. 75-78.

(Ma85) Marrin, K., "Realtime and Multiuser Operating Systems Target IBM PC AT," *Computer Design*, December 1985, pp. 135-143.

(Mc87) McKie, P. E., "Seeing Beyond PC Boundaries," *Personal Computing*, June 1987, pp. 110-115.

(Mc84) McManigal, D., "The First Heartbeat," *PC Magazine*, Vol. 3, No. 6, April 3, 1984, pp. 203-206.

(Mi84) Miller, H., "3.00 and Counting," *PC World*, Vol. 2, No. 11, 1984.

(Mt84) Millert, M. J., "IBM Compatibility," *Popular Computing*, April 1984, p. 108.

(Mi85) Mirecki, T., "Dipping into Directories," *PC Tech Journal*, Vol. 3, No. 2, February 1985, pp. 67-73.

(Mi86) Mirecki, T., "Expandable Memory," *PC Tech Journal*, February 1986, pp. 66-82.

(Ni85) Nisley, E., "Spinning Your Own VDISK," *PC Tech Journal*, Vol. 3, No. 3, March 1985, pp. 100-107.

(No83) Norton, P., *Inside the IBM PC*, Bowie, Maryland: Robert J. Brady Co., 1983.

(No84) Norton, P., *MS-DOS and PC DOS: User's Guide*, Bowie, Marryland: Robert J. Brady Co., 1984.

(No84a) Norton, P., "The Parts of DOS," *PC Magazine*, March 20, 1984.

(No84b) Norton, P., "When DOS is not Enough," *PC Magazine*, Vol. 3, No. 14, July 24, 1984, pp. 103-107.

(No84c) Norton, P., "Missing Pieces of the PC-DOS," *PC Magazine*, August 21, 1984, pp. 107-111.

(No84d) Norton, P., "The Dissection of DOS 3.0," *PC Magazine*, Vol. 3, No. 21, October 30, 1984, pp. 105-107.

(Om85) O'Malley, C., "What You Should Know About MS-DOS," *Personal Computing*, August 1985, pp. 43-51.

(Om86) O'Malley, C., "Getting More out of DOS," *Personal Computing*, June 1986, pp. 64-75.

(Pa83) Paterson, T., "An Inside Look at MS-DOS," *Byte*, June 1983, pp. 230-252.

(Pe86) Petzold, C., "Enlarging the Dimensions of Memory," *PC Magazine*, January 14, 1986, pp. 120-136.

(Pe87) Petzold, C., "Smooth Operator," *PC Magazine*, July 1987, pp. 157-170.

(Ph84) Phraner, R., "The Future of UNIX on the IBM PC," *Byte*, 1984, pp. 59-63.

(Re84) Redmond, W.J., "Managing Memory: A Guided Tour of DCS 2.0 Memory Management," *PC Tech Journal*, August 1984, pp. 42-62.

(Re87) Reed, S. R., "Welcome to the New Age of DOS," *Personal Computing*, May 1987, pp. 72-81.

(Ro84) Roskos, E., "Writing Device Drivers for MS-DOS 2.0," *Byte*, February 1984.

(Ro84b) Roskos, E., "Multitalented," *PC Tech Journal*, Vol. 2, No. 4, October 1984, pp. 64-72.

(Ru84) Rubin, C., and K. Strehlo, "Why So Many Computer Look Like the IBM Standard," *Personal Computing*, March 1984, pp. 52-65, 182-189.

(Sc72) Schroeder, M. D., and J. H. Saltzer, "A Hardware Architecture for Implementing Protection Rings," *Communications of the ACM*, Vol. 15, No. 3, March 1972, pp. 157-170.

(Sh85) Shiell, J., and J. Markoff, "IBM PC Family BIOS Comparison," *Byte*, November 1985.

(So87a) Somerson, P., "Personal System/2 Gives Life to a Smarter, More Agile DOS," *PC Magazine*, May 26, 1987, pp. 48-51.

(So87b) Somerson, P., "DOS Lives," *PC Magazine*, July 1987, pp. 175-182.

(Sp88) Spanbauer, S., and R. Luhn, "DOS Lives," *PC World*, Vol. 6, No. 10, October 1988, pp. 194-195.

(Ta82) Taylor, R., and P. Lemmons, "Upward Migration Part 2: A Comparison of CP/M-86 and MS-DOS," *Byte*, July 1982.

(Tu84) Tucker, D.M., "Understanding Operating Systems," *PC World*, May 1984, pp. 192-199.

(Ut86) Uttal, B., "Inside the Deal That Made Bill Gates $350,000,000," *Fortune*, July 21, 1986, pp. 23-33.

(Wa84) Waite, M.; J. Angermeyer; and M. Noble, "Climbing Around in the DOS Directory Tree," *PC Magazine*, Vol. 3, No. 11, June 12, 1984, pp. 275-288.

(We86) Weinreich, M., "A First Look at the 80386," *Micro/Systems Journal*, September/October 1986, pp. 34-37.

(We84) Wells, P., "The 80286 Microprocessor," *Byte*, Nov. 1984, pp. 231-242.

(Wh87) White, E., and R. Grehan, "Microsoft's New DOS," *BYTE*, June 1987, pp. 116-126.

(An87) Anderson, J., "Twilight of DOS." PC *Tech Journal*, Vol. 5, No. 8. August 1987, pp. 180-193.

(Ar87) Armbrust, S., and T. Forgeron, "Multiple Tasks," *PC Tech Journal*, Vol. 5, No. 11, November 1987, pp. 90-106.

(Ar87a) Armbrust, S., "Porting to OS/2," *PC Tech Journal,* Vol. 5, No 11, November 1987, pp. 140-148.

(Be87) Bender, E., "Why Buy a PS/2?" *PC World*, December 1987, pp. 278-283.

(Ca88) Campbell, J. L., *Inside OS/2: The Complete Programmer's Reference*, Blue Ridge Summit, PA: TAB BOOKS, Inc., 1988.

(Ch88) Chang, P. Y., and W. W. Myre, "OS/2 EE Database Manager Overview and Technical Highlights," *IBM Systems Journal*, Vol, 27, No. 2, 1988, pp. 105-118.

(Ch87) Chester, J. A., "*IBM* and OS/2 Take on the Clones," *Infosystems*, Vol. 34, No. 8, August 1987, pp. 34-36.

(Co88) Conklin, D., *OS/2: A Business Perspective*, New York, NY: John Wiley & Sons, Inc, 1988.

(Co88a) Cook, R. L.; F. L. Rawson III; J. A. Tunkel; and R. L. Williams, "Writing an Operating System/2 Application," *IBM Systems Journal*, Vol. 27, No. 2, 1988, pp. 134-157.

(Cr87) Crosswy, C., and M. Perez, "Upward to the 80386," *PC Tech Journal*, Vol. 5, No. 2, February 1987, pp. 51-66.

(Da89) Davis, S. R., and W. L. Rosch, "368 Multitasking Environments," *PC Magazine,* Vol. 8, No. 4, February 28, 1989, pp. 94-140.

(Du87b) Duncan, R., "OS/2 Multitasking: Exploiting the Protected Mode of the 80286," *Microsoft Systems Journal*, Vol. 2, No. 2, May 1987, pp. 27-36.

(Du87c) Duncan, R., "OS/2 Inter-Process Communication: Semaphores, Pipes, and Queues," *Microsoft Systems Journal,* Vol. 2, May 1987, pp. 37-50.

(Du87a) Duncan, R., "Porting MS-DOS Assembly Language Programs to the OS/2 Environment," *Microsoft Systems Journal*, Vol. 2, No. 3, July 1987, pp. 9-17.

(Du87) Duncan, R., "Character-Oriented Display Services Using OS/2's VIO Subsystem," *Microsoft Systems Journal*, Vol. 2, No. 4, September 1987, pp. 23-33.

(Du88) Duncan, R., "An Examination of the DevHlp API," *Microsoft System Journal*, Vol. 3, No. 2, March 1988, pp. 39-55.

(Du89a) Duncan, R., *Advanced OS/2 Programming*, Redmond, WA: Microsoft Press, 1989.

(Du89) Duncan, R., "Comparing DOS and OS/2 File System," *PC Magazine*, Vol. 8, No. 3, February 14, 1989, pp. 321-332.

(Ed89) Edelstein, H. A., "OS/2 Meets SQL," *PC Tech Journal*, Vol. 7, No. 2, February 1989, pp. 62-75.

(Fa87) Fastie, W., "The OS/2 Debate," *PC Tech Journal*, November 1987, pp. 21-27.

(Ge88) Geary, M., "Converting Windows Applications for Microsoft OS/2 Presentation Manager," *Microsoft Systems Journal*, Vol. 3, No. 1, January 1988, pp. 9-30.

(Gi87) Gillman, J., "Compatibility and Transition for MS-DOS Programs," *Microsoft Systems Journal*, Vol. 2, No. 2, May 1987, pp. 19-26.

(Gr88) Greenberg, R., M.,"Design Concepts and Considerations in Building an OS/2 Dynamic Link Library," *Microsoft System Journal*, Vol. 3, No. 3, May 1988, pp. 27-48.

(Gu88) Guttman, M., "Building a Foundation for Presentation Manager," *Computerworld Focus*, June 1988, pp. 31-33.

(Ha87) Hansen, M., and L. Sargent, "Increase the Performance of Your Programs with a Math Coprocessor," *Microsoft Systems Journal*, Vol. 2, No. 3, July 1987, pp. 59-69.

(He87) Heller, M., "An Architecture for the Future," *PC Tech Journal*, Vol. 5, No. 11, November 1987, pp. 67-83.

(He88) Heller, V., "OS/2 Virtual Memory Management," *Byte*, Vol. 13, No. 4, April 1988, pp. 227-233.

(Ia88) Iacobucci, E., *OS/2 Programmers Guide*, Berkeley, CA: Osborne McGraw-Hill, 1988.

(IB87a) IBM Corporation, *Operating System/2 Technical Reference (First Edition), Volume 1*, Copyright International Business Machines Corporation, 1986, 1987.

(IB87b) IBM Corporation, *Operating System/2 Technical Reference (First Edition), Volume 2*, Copyright International Business Machines Corporation, 1986, 1987.

(IB87) IBM Corporation, *Operating System/2 Standard Edition Users Reference,* Copyright International Business Machines Corporation, 1987.

(Ja88) Jamsa, K., *Using OS/2*, Berkeley, CA: Osborne McGraw-Hill, 1988.

(Je87) Jeffrey, B., "OS/2: Have We Seen the Future?" *Computerworld Focus*, July 8, 1987, pp. 25-26.

(Ke88) Kessler, A., "OS/2 LAN Manager Provides a Platform for Server-Based Network Applications," *Microsoft Systems Journal*, Vol. 3, No. 2, March 1988, pp. 29-38.

(Kn87) Knorr, E., "A Model for the 80's," *PC World*, December 1987, pp. 151-159.

(Kn88) Knorr, E., "Getting the Feel of OS/2," *PC World*, Vol. 6, No. 4, April 1988, pp. 188-193.

(Ko88) Kogan, M. S., and F. L. Rawson III, "The Design of Operating System/2," *IBM Systems Journal,* Vol. 27, No. 2, 1988, pp. 90-104.

(Kr88) Krantz, J. I.; A. M. Mizell; and R. L. Williams, *OS/2 Features, Functions, and Applications*, New York, N. Y.: John Wiley & Sons, Inc., 1988.

(La88) Lammers, S., (Editor-in-Chief), *The MS-DOS Encyclopedia*, Redmond, WA: Microsoft Press, 1988.

(Le88) Letwin, G., *Inside OS/2*, Redmond, WA: Microsoft Press, 1988.

(Le88a) Letwin, G., "Dynamic Linking in OS/2," *Byte*, Vol. 13, No. 4, April 1988, pp. 273-280.

(Li88) Linnell, D., "SAA: IBM's Road Map to the Future," *PC Tech Journal,* Vol. 6, No. 4, April 1988, pp. 86-105.

(Li89) Linnell, D., "The OS/2 Puzzle Takes Shape," *PC Tech Journal*, Vol. 7, No. 2, February 1989, pp. 45-48.

(Li89a) Linnell, D., "Cooperative Communications," *PC Tech Journal*, Vol. 7, No. 2, February 1989, pp. 52-61.

(Ma87) Machrone, B., and P. Somerson, "IBM Builds New Plateau With Personal System/2," *PC Magazine*, Vol. 6, No. 10, May 26, 1987, pp. 33-54.

(Mc87) McManus, R., "In Pursuit of Tomorrow's PC," *PC, World May*, 1987, pp. 260-271.

(Mc88) McNierney, E., "386 Operating Environments," *PC Tech Journal*, Vol. 6, No.1, January 1988, pp. 60-73.

(Mi87) Mirecki, T., "Enter OS/2," *PC Tech Journal*, November 1987, pp. 52-63.

(Mi88) Mizell, A. M., "Understanding Device Drivers in Operating System/2," *IBM Systems Journal*, Vol. 27, No. 2, 1988, pp. 170-184.

(Mo89) Morris, R. R., and W. E. Brooks, "UNIX Versus OS/2: A Graphic Comparison," *PC Tech Journal*, Vol. 7, No. 2, February 1989, pp. 106-118.

(Mo88) Morrow, G., "The IBM Micro Channel I/O Bus," *Micro/Systems Journal*, Vol. 4, No. 2, February 1988, pp. 18-26.

(Ne88) Newcom, K., "The Micro Channel Versus the AT Bus," *Byte* (IBM Special Issue), Vol. 13, No. 11, Fall 1988, pp. 91-98.

(Pr88) Perrone, G., OS/2 Developers Kit Offers Unusual Power," *IEEE Software*, July 1988, pp. 97-101.

(Pe87) Petzold, C., "A Complete Guide to Writing Your First OS/2 Program," *Microsoft Systems Journal*, Vol. 2, No. 2, May 1987, pp. 51-60.

(Pe88a) Petzold, C., "Utilizing OS/2 Multithread Techniques in Presentation Manager Applications," *Microsoft Systems Journal*, Vol. 3, No. 3, March 1988, pp. 11-27.

(Pe88) Petzold, C., "The Graphics Programming Interface: A Guide to OS/2 Presentation Spaces," *Microsoft Systems Journal*, Vol. 3, No. 3, May 1988, pp. 9-18.

(Pe88c) Petzold, C., Exploring The OS/2, EXE File," *PC Magazine*, Vol. 7, No. 9, May 17, 1988, pp. 329-341.

(Pe88b) Petzold, C., "Multiple Threads Make Better OS/2 Programs," *PC Magazine*, Vol. 7, No. 12, July 28, 1988, pp. 289-307.

(Pe88d) Petzold, C., "Introducing the OS/2 Presentation Manager," *PC Magazine*, Vol. 7, No. 13, July 1988, pp. 379-394.

(Pe89) Petzold, C., *Programming the OS/2 Presentation Manager*, Readmond, WA: Microsoft Press, 1989.

(Qu88) Quirk, K., "Model 80 Flagship," *PC Tech Journal*, Vol. 6, No. 4, April 1988, pp. 62-73.

(Ri87) Rizzo, T., "A Foundation for the Next Generation," *Microsoft Systems Journal*, Vol. 2, No. 2, May 1987, pp. 1-12.

(Ro88) Robbins, J., *Essential OS/2*, Alameda: CA SYBEX, 1988.

(Ro87) Rosch, W. L., "Heavy Metal 386s Weigh In," *PC Magazine*, Vol. 6, No. 16, September 29, 1987, pp. 91-150.

(Ro88) Rosch, W. L., "IBM's PS/2 Model 80-111: A //Dream Deferred," *PC Magazine*, Vol. 7, No. 8, April 26, 1988, pp. 93-100.

(Ru88) Ruddell, K., "Using OS/2 Semaphores to Coordinate Concurrent Threads of Execution, *Microsoft Systems Journal*, Vol. 3, No. 3, May 1988, pp. 19-26.

(Sc87) Schmitt, D. A., "The Flexible Interface," *PC Tech Journal*, Vol. 5, No. 11, November 1987, pp. 111-128.

(Sc88a) Schmitt, D. A., "Converting DOS Programs to OS/2 Protected Mode," *Micro/ Systems Journal*, Vol. 4, No. 3, March 1988, pp. 24-34.

(Sc88) Schmitt, D. A., "Family Ties," *PC Tech Journal*, Vol. 6, No. 6, June 1988, pp. 124-132.

(Se88) Seybold, A., "OS/2 Represents Future of Micro Operating Systems," *High Technology Business*, July 1988, pp. 58-59.

(St88) Stinson, C., "Preparing for Presentation Manager: Paradox® Steps up to Windows 2.0," *Microsoft Systems Journal*, Vol. 3, No. 1, Janurary1988, pp. 1-7.

(Ta88) Tallman, D., "PS/2 Turns 1," *PC Tech Journal* Vol. 6, No. 4, April 1988, pp. 48-57.

(Tr88) Tropp. W., and S. Wright, "The DOS-UNIX Union," *PC Tech Journal*, Vol. 6, No. 1, January 1988, pp. 78-91.

(Va87) Valigra, L., "OS/2: Turning off the Car to Change Gears," *Microsoft Systems Journal*, Vol. 2, No. 2, May 1987, pp. 61-66.

(Ve87) Vellon, M., "The OS/2 Windows Presentation Manager: Microsoft Windows on the Future," *Microsoft Systems Journal*, Vol. 2, No. 2, May 1987, pp. 13-18.

(Vi87) Vigorita, H., "Memory Addressing on the Intel 80386, "*Micro/ Systems Journal*, Vol. 3, No. 6, November/December1987, pp. 18-21.

(Wa88) Watson, S. L., "OS/2 Query Manager Overview and Prompted Interface," *IBM Systems Journal*, Vol. 27, No. 2, 1988, pp. 119-133.

(Wh88) White, E. M., "IBM OS/2 Standard Edition," *Byte*, Vol. 13, No. 6. June 1988, pp. 145-154.

Index

N

O

P

S

T

U

W

X

❑❑❑